List of Activities

Acknowledgments

The Guide to First-Year Writing, 5th edition, is the product of hard work by faculty, staff, and teachers in the Lower Division Studies program of the Department of English at Georgia State University. Feedback from instructors and students was instrumental in creating this edition of the *Guide to First-Year Writing.*

Editors

General Editor
Elizabeth Sanders Lopez

Managing and Contributing Editor
Angela M. Christie

Production and Contributing Editor
Kristen A. Ruccio

Editorial Staff

Art Committee Christine Anlicker, Randall Harrell, and Sara Harwood

Chapter Committee Kristeen Cherney, Patricia Godsave, Ben Kolenda, Lelania Ottoboni Watkins, and Donna Wroble

Essay Committee Jennifer Carter, Helen M. Cauley, Joshua Privett, and David St. John

Editorial Committee Anna Barattin, Charles Grimm, Mostafa Jalal, Shana Latimer, Xiaobo Wang, and Allison Wright

Survey Committee Kristen A. Ruccio and Yunye Yu

Special thanks to Jamie Bernhardt, Charles Grimm, Samantha Jakobeit, Emily Kimbell, Margaret Vath, and Nathan Wagner for additional editorial feedback.

Website Contributors
Stephanie Devine and Sara Harwood

Student Art Contributors
Rachel Cheek, Moira Catherine Clark, Jeffery Cordry, Betsy Cruz, Nadia Deljou, Michael Foster, Megan Glasscock, Melissa Graziano, The GSU Digital Asset Library, Sarah N. Kegley, Noe Martinez, Alexander Thomas Mitchell, Steve Osborne, Lesly Rodriguez, Joshua Sheridan, Toniah Smittick, James Supreme, Blake Vasquez, William Walsh, Taneisha White, Eun Kyoung Yang, and Hae Sung Yang

Student Writing Contributors
Joe Beard, Jessie Giles, Angell Green, Tammy Huynh, Monjima Kabir, Jessica Martinez, Olivia Sellers, and Amanda Tice

Cover Design
Deana Mounajjed, winner of the Design Contest for the 5th edition of *The Guide to First-Year Writing* at Georgia State University

GSU Digital Asset Library, *June Fountain*

Introduction to Lower Division Studies and First-Year Writing Classes

What is Lower Division Studies?

By now you have attended several orientation programs introducing you to university life. As a first-year student, you are probably excited to start on this path toward your degree. The Lower Division Studies program for the Department of English welcomes you to Georgia State University. Our program comprises all first- and second-year composition (English 1101, English 1102, and English 1103) and literature survey courses (English 2110, 2120, and 2130). Our directors and staff oversee the pedagogical design and curriculum for all Lower Division courses. In addition to this work, our program trains and supports all instructors who teach 1000 and 2000 level English courses. Since every student must complete first-year writing courses (part of the University's CORE classes), our program seeks to provide assistance and direction to over three thousand students a semester. One way we manage contact with so many students is by creating a centralized location for Lower Division information—the Lower Division Office, which is housed in the English Department (22nd floor of 25 Park Place). Another way we communicate information about our programs and monitor the progress of our first-year students is through the creation of this textbook and companion website for use in all composition courses. The material you learn in these introductory courses will serve as the foundation of your academic pursuits. No matter what your major, you will need to become an effective communicator. These CORE courses prepare you for academic and professional discourse. We encourage you to become familiar with Lower Division Studies (LDS).

Lower Division Studies Administration

Dr. Elizabeth Sanders Lopez, Director, Lower Division Studies
eslopez@gsu.edu

Dr. Angela M. Christie, Associate Director, Lower Division Studies
achristie@gsu.edu

Kristen Ruccio, Assistant Director, Lower Division Studies
kruccio1@gsu.edu

Web Resources

Lower Division Studies maintains its own webpage, which houses valuable administrative information. To visit this site, go to https://lds.gsu.edu/

The *Guide to First-Year Writing* also hosts a companion site, which is a good place to find supplemental learning resources. Please visit this site to search for information on the *Guide*, writing tutorials, links to educational resources, grammar tutorials, and sample student essays. You can find Lower Division Policy information pertinent to GSU students on this site. To visit this site, go to http://guidetowriting.gsu.edu

Why Do I Have To Take a Writing Class?

Regardless of major and intended career path, all students and professionals must know how to write well. Mastering course content and conducting research isn't enough—you will need to know how to appropriately and effectively articulate your findings and demonstrate mastery of the subject matter. Most college classes require writing as one of the ways instructors assess what you know. So, English courses are not the *only* courses that require writing. More pointedly, writing involves critical thinking. Those who learn how to write well must also learn valuable skills in reading comprehension, synthesizing, argumentation, rhetorical analysis, and organization. As you learn how to write better, you will also learn how to articulate your point of view, develop clear and ethically-driven arguments, and how to use research materials to support your ideas. Writing helps people become stronger *thinkers*. In addition, your participation in a university community and your ability to articulate your experiences can benefit your outside and personal interests.

What kind of writing do you imagine you will do as a professional in the work force? You may be surprised by the amount of writing required in most professions. The College Board's National Commission on Writing compiled a report representing responses from over 100 corporate leaders of American companies. This report, "Writing A Ticket to Work ... Or a Ticket Out: A Survey of Business Leaders," outlines the expectations those in the corporate world have regarding employee writing competencies. The research found that writing is not only a "threshold skill of employment and promotion, particularly among salaried employees," but that two-thirds of all salaried employees

Sheridan, Joshua. *Lord of the Arts.*

in industry has some writing responsibility" (3). Of course, a published report shouldn't be the only evidence to convince you of the benefit of effective writing skills. Have you ever sent an email to a coworker, teacher, or family member that didn't "say" what you meant? In every job, regardless of the industry, you will be required to communicate in writing: including, memos, emails, proposals, reports, formal findings analyses, and summaries of company materials. Research suggests that effective writers are hirable, marketable, and promotable.

What Happens in a Writing Class?

Georgia State University's composition courses are capped at 25 students per class, which allows more direct and individual classroom instruction. Instead of sitting in a lecture hall taking notes with one hundred other students, you will engage with the writing process through what's known as active and student-centered learning. What are these modes of learning? Well, your class may involve in-class writing assignments, oral presentations, classroom debates, community-driven assignments, peer editing, blog post discussion forums, and group projects. The classroom becomes a community of writers, who are all interested in developing modes of written expression. As a first-year composition student, you will be expected to engage in classroom discussions, to complete reading and writing assignments outside of class, and to participate in the peer editing process with your peers.

Think of the writing classroom as a space where you can both *learn* how to write and *write* in order to learn. The writing class invites inquiry and offers instruction for developing your initial questions and research plan, then articulating your findings. In addition to learning how to write better, your instructor will help you improve become an authority on a subject, express yourself, and refine your abilities to research, reflect, read actively, organize findings, and engage in critique.

Yes, mastering grammar conventions and mechanics are fundamental to developing clear writing and to illustrating credibility for your audience. However, effective composing involves logic, organization, research support, and consideration of the rhetorical situation in addition to correct grammar usage. In composition classes, we ask you to assess your writing weaknesses (as well as your strengths) and work on demonstrating scholarly writing skills. Your

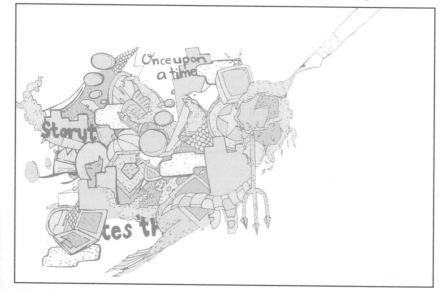

White, Taneisha. *Inside My Mind*

instructors are trained to help you through this process. So, be sure to become familiar with the classroom rules, the course expectations, and ways in which you can improve your writing by visiting your instructor during office hours and making appointments with a Writing Studio tutor: http://www.writingstudio.gsu.edu/.

How Do I Use This Book?

Your 1101 or 1102 instructor has assigned this book (and possibly others) in order to facilitate your understanding of the writing and critical thinking process. The first section of the *Guide to First-Year Writing* provides a rhetorical basis for learning. Chapters one through four come from *Praxis: A Brief Rhetoric* (Fountainhead Press) and aim to introduce fundamental elements of collegiate-level writing—principles and advice about invention, writing, and revising. The *Praxis* chapters also include writing activities.

The second part of the *Guide to First-Year Writing* is Georgia State specific. This fifth edition reflects the feedback we received from students in previous semesters as well as feedback from instructors who used the book in class. These thoughtfully revised chapters address civil engagement, public literacy, media literacy, writing and editing in public spaces, and visual analysis. If you are familiar with an earlier edition of this text, you may notice some changes. The fifth edition has updated materials, assignments, examples, art, and a new chapter, "Writing in the Englishes: The Complexities of Language Use". The authors of the Georgia State specific chapters incorporate student writing (from students just like you), campus-based assignments, and discussion prompts related to GSU and the surrounding Atlanta community. The *Guide to First-Year Writing* combines traditional information about research and composing with localized instructional materials that invite you to write and reflect about the GSU community and your experiences as a Georgia State student/scholar. We have also expanded content on our companion website for the textbook, *Guide to Writing* (http://guidetowriting.gsu.edu/). You will find companion readings for each chapter, important links, sample essays and assignments, and many other valuable resources on the website.

Lower Division Studies welcomes you to GSU. Since the *Guide to First-Year Writing* represents the ideas and work of our student body, we hope that you will add your voice to the 6th edition of the *Guide to First-Year Writing*. Be on the lookout for email invitations to submit your art work and writing for inclusion in the next edition.

Georgia State University's First-Year Book Program

All first-year students at Georgia State will read a common book, which is selected by the University's First Year Book Committee. By the time you find your classroom and meet your composition instructor, you should already be familiar with Sonia Nazario's *Enrique's Journey*.

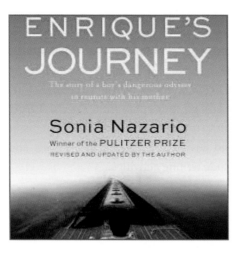

Georgia State, like many other research institutions, participates in a common reader program. According to the program's homepage,

> The First-Year Book Program at Georgia State University aims to provide all incoming freshmen with a common intellectual experience to stimulate discussion, to promote critical thinking, and to develop a sense of community among first-year students, faculty, and staff. (http://success.students.gsu.edu/first-year-programs/first-year-book/)

Previous selections have asked students to consider their role as academics within the context of citizenship. Other selections have focused on an event (Hurricane Katrina, 9/11) and how the event effected change. *Enrique's Journey* asks readers to consider our nation's current immigration policies, our stereotypical views of immigrants, and themes of identity loss. Now that you have read the novel, what parts of Enrique's journey to American had the greatest impact on you? Imagine his journey as a young boy—look at the map below and think of the miles of quiet, fear, danger, and kindness he encountered on the way.

To prepare you for class discussion, use Googlemaps/Google Earth to take a close look at the terrain: the mountains, and rivers, and deserts. What did Enrique see on his way to find his mother?

What is the current U.S. immigration policy? How many undocumented immigrants live in the United States? Do you know of any undocumented people in your neighborhood, family, or work community? How are the stories of immigrants from Honduras, Mexico, and other Parts of Central America different to immigrants we see fleeing from Syria, Central African Republic, or South Sudan? Use maps and other digital media to compare the journey undertaken by those from Central America to the journey undertaken by those leaving Syria.

Finally, take a look at Sonia Nazario's most recent article "Refugees at our Door" published on October 11, 2015 in the *New York Times* where she compares the Mexican policies on punishment and deportation for those fleeing violent areas in Central America to the refugee crisis in Europe. Do you think the two are comparable? If so, how? What is the American and global responsibility to those who risk it all to embark on a dangerous and often fatal journey in order to secure a better life for themselves and their families?

Our program works to weave the content of the First-Year book into the 1101 and 1102 curriculum. In addition to what you will find here, our companion site houses writing and discussion activities related to *Enrique's Journey*.

Foster, Michael. *Atlanta*.

Chapter 1

Defining Rhetoric

Why Rhetoric Is Important in My Writing

Meaghan Elliott
Ph.D. student in
Composition & Rhetoric
University of New Hampshire

Here is a partial list of the things I needed to write today:

- An email to someone in my field asking her questions for a seminar paper I'm writing
- A lesson plan I intend to use for my students in this week's class
- An email to a family member
- Text messages to a friend in the hospital
- A reading response for a doctoral course I'm taking
- A grocery list for my boyfriend
- This short essay about rhetoric

All of these are rhetoric. Rhetoric is inescapable because we use it every time we use words to address an audience. Rhetoric gives us tools for deciding how to be successful in any given situation, and it acknowledges that words and languages were designed for people to communicate with each other. People think, we feel, we judge others. In each of these actions, we have *logos*, *pathos*, and *ethos*. Rhetoric is what makes us human.

In the list I provided, I have seven different scenarios with seven different audiences. In each one, I judge (sometimes consciously, sometimes unconsciously) how effectively to present myself and my message. This means no two pieces of writing will look or sound the same. We make rhetorical judgments based on to whom we are speaking and what we know about our audience, and these judgments affect the way we write each document.

Rhetoric is important because it helps us get work done in the world, and it helps us organize how we interact with the places and people around us. This is a field older than Aristotle but still as relevant as it has ever been. Without my careful use of rhetoric, my lesson plans would fall flat, my family member may be insulted, and my boyfriend might bring home Brussels sprouts instead of broccoli. I hate Brussels sprouts. We use rhetoric all the time, whether we know it or not. But knowing about rhetoric and knowing how to use it effectively and creatively makes us better at it. I couldn't get through my day without it.

What Is Rhetoric?

You have probably heard someone say of a politician's speech, "Oh, that's just rhetoric," meaning the politician's words are empty verbiage or hot air. The politician is attempting to sound impressive while saying nothing that has real meaning. Or perhaps the politician is making promises listeners believe he or she has no intention of keeping. The use of rhetoric in speeches—both bad speeches and good ones—is only the most visible use of rhetoric.

Rhetoric happens all around us, every day. Rhetoric is a persuasive language act—whether accomplished by speech, written texts, or images. It is the video footage of a demonstration on YouTube. It is the headlines on blog articles. It is the *Declaration of Independence.* Sam Leith explains,

> Rhetoric is language at play—language plus. It is what persuades and cajoles, inspires and bamboozles, thrills and misdirects. It causes criminals to be convicted, and then frees those criminals on appeal. It causes governments to rise and fall, best men to be ever after shunned by their friends' brides, and perfectly sensible adults to march with steady purpose toward machine guns [. . .]
>
> It is made of ringing truths and vital declarations. It is a way in which our shared assumptions and understandings are applied to new situations, and the language of history is channeled, revitalized, and given fresh power in each successive age.[1]

Your parents and teachers have used rhetoric on you since you first understood the words "yes" and "no." And you've been using it right back to them, whenever you want to persuade them to let you do something that is contrary to their stance on a topic.

The word *praxis* (the title of this book) can be translated as "process" or "practice." Aristotle, the great Greek rhetorician, employed the term in a special way to mean practical reasoning for which the goal was action. To be practical in the Aristotelian sense is a little different from what being practical means today. It indicates the ability to apply abstract theory to concrete situations and, thus, to move from theory to action. Moreover, praxis embodies a creative element that raises it above the mundane or merely pragmatic. Therefore, "practicing rhetoric" is not practice in the sense of rehearsal. Rather, it is performing, or applying, or acting out rhetoric—taking theory and turning it into action.

Rhetoric has been studied in an organized manner since the days of the ancient Greeks and Romans. The elites of both countries studied persuasive argument out of necessity. Their democratic systems of government required that citizens

---

1. Leith, Sam. *Words Like Loaded Pistols: Rhetoric from Aristotle to Obama.* Basic, 2012, p. 6.

be able to argue persuasively in public, since there were no attorneys or professional politicians.

Today, rhetoric is still used in courts of law and political forums, but it is also studied in academia because it causes us to examine critically our own as well as others' ideas. Persuasive argument compels us to consider conflicting claims, to evaluate evidence, and to clarify our thoughts. We know that even wise, well-intentioned people don't always agree, so we consider others' ideas respectfully. After one person presents a persuasive argument, either orally or in writing, others respond to that argument with support, modification, or contradiction. Then, in turn, more individuals counter with their own versions, and thus, the interchange becomes a conversation.

Rhetoric and Power

Aristotle defined rhetoric as "the faculty of discovering, in a given instance, the available means of persuasion," which we might paraphrase as the power to see the means of persuasion available in any given situation. Each part of this definition is important. Rhetoric is power. The person who is able to speak eloquently, choosing the most suitable arguments about a topic for a specific audience in a particular situation, is the person most likely to persuade. In both Greece and Rome, the primary use of rhetoric was oratory—persuasion through public speaking. However, the texts of many famous speeches were studied as models by students, and prominent rhetoricians wrote treatises and handbooks for teaching rhetoric. To Greeks and Romans, a person who could use rhetoric effectively was a person of influence and power because he could persuade his audience to action. The effective orator could win court cases; the effective orator could influence the passage or failure of laws; the effective orator could send a nation to war or negotiate peace.

Skill with rhetoric has conveyed power through the ages, though in our contemporary world, rhetoric is often displayed in written text such as a book, newspaper or magazine article, or scientific report, rather than presented as a speech. Persuasive communication also can be expressed visually, as an illustration that accompanies a text or a cartoon that conveys its own message. Indeed, in our highly visual society, with television, movies, video games, and the Internet, images can often persuade more powerfully than words alone.

Using rhetoric effectively means being able to interpret the rhetoric we are presented with in our everyday lives. Knowledge of persuasive communication or rhetoric empowers us to present our views and persuade others to modify their ideas. By changing ideas, rhetoric leads to action. By influencing actions, rhetoric affects society.

Selected Definitions of Rhetoric

Aristotle, 350 BCE—Rhetoric is "the faculty of discovering, in a given instance, the available means of persuasion."

Cicero, 90 BCE—Rhetoric is "speech designed to persuade" and "eloquence based on the rules of art."

Quintilian, 95 CE—Rhetoric is "the science of speaking well."

Augustine of Hippo, ca. 426 CE—Rhetoric is "the art of persuading people to accept something, whether it is true or false."

Anonymous, ca. 1490–1495—Rhetoric is "the science which refreshes the hungry, renders the mute articulate, makes the blind see, and teaches one to avoid every lingual ineptitude."

Heinrich Cornelius Agrippa, 1531—Rhetoric is "nothing other than an art of flatter, adulation, and, as some say more audaciously, lying, in that, if it cannot persuade others through the truth of the case, it does so by means of deceitful speech."

Hoyt Hudson, 1923—Rhetoric is effective persuasion. "In this sense, plainly, the man who speaks most persuasively uses the most, or certainly the best, rhetoric; and the man whom we censure for inflation of style and strained effects is suffering not from too much rhetoric, but from a lack of it."

I. A. Richards, 1936—Rhetoric is "a study of misunderstanding and its remedies."

Sister Miriam Joseph, 1937—Rhetoric is "the art of communicating thought from one mind to another, the adaptation of language to circumstance."

Kenneth Burke, 1950—Rhetoric is, "the use of words by human agents to form attitudes or to induce actions in other human agents."

Gerard A. Hauser, 2002—"Rhetoric, as an area of study, is concerned with how humans use symbols, especially language, to reach agreement that permits coordinated effort of some sort."

Explore

Activity 1.1 • Historical Usage of the Word "Rhetoric"

Read through the list of historical definitions of the word "rhetoric," and choose one that you find interesting. In a discussion, compare your chosen definition with those of your classmates.

Are We All Greeks?

As Americans, we owe an immense debt to ancient Greek civilization. Our laws, our democratic form of government, our literature, and our art have their roots in ancient Athens. Earlier generations of Americans and Western Europeans who often studied Latin and Greek may have had a clearer understanding of the direct connections between our culture and Athens of the fourth and fifth centuries BCE. Indeed, the English poet Percy Bysshe Shelley famously said, "We are all Greeks" because of the essential influence of ancient Greek culture upon Western civilization. However, even translated into twenty-first-century American English, the linkage is still there.

Something quite amazing happened in Athens, around 500 BCE. Instead of being invaded by a foreign country who appointed a puppet ruler or experiencing a coup in which a strong man seized power, the people peaceably chose to put in place a direct democracy. Attica (with its capital Athens) was not the only city-state to have a democracy, but it was the most successful. During the golden age of Greece, from roughly 500 BCE to 300 BCE, art, architecture, and literature thrived.

Direct or radical democracy meant all male citizens of Attica over the age of 20 could vote in the Assembly, the policy-making body of the city-state. They did not elect senators or representatives as we do today. Each of these men *voted directly*. Moreover, they could settle differences with fellow citizens by suing in the law courts. Out of 250,000 to 300,000 residents in Attica, some 30,000 were citizens. Amazingly, it was not unusual for 10,000 of these eligible men to vote in the Assembly. The law courts had juries of 500 or more. Imagine trying to speak to an audience of 10,000 people without modern loudspeakers. Even with the wonderful acoustics in Greek theatres, it would have been a challenge.

Ordinary citizens were required to speak in the Assembly or the courts to promote laws or defend themselves from lawsuits, since there were no attorneys or professional politicians. Certainly, speaking before such large audiences necessitated special skills acquired only through extensive training and practice. Many sought out teachers to help them learn how to speak persuasively, and, indeed, training in rhetoric became the primary method of education for the elite young men (and even a few women).

The earliest teachers of the verbal persuasive skills we now call rhetoric were Sophists who migrated to Athens from Sicily and other Greek states. Some of their viewpoints were curiously modern—for example, some argued that knowledge is relative and that pure truth does not exist. However, they became known for teaching their pupils to persuade an audience to think whatever they wanted them to think. Sophists such as Gorgias often presented entertainment speeches during which they would argue, on the spur of the moment, any topic raised by the audience, just to show they were able to construct effective arguments for any subject.

Claiming the Sophists' rhetoric could be employed to manipulate the masses for good or ill, and that rhetoricians used it irresponsibly, Plato coined the term, *rhetorike*—from which we take the term, "rhetoric"—as a criticism of the Sophists. Ironically, Plato demonstrates excellent rhetorical techniques himself when he condemns rhetoric by arguing that only the elite who are educated in philosophy are suited to rule, not the rhetoricians. Aristotle, Plato's student, took a more moderate viewpoint toward rhetoric. Indeed, he was the first philosopher to classify rhetoric as a tool for practical debate with general audiences. His book *On Rhetoric* (though it was probably lecture notes possibly combined with student responses rather than a manuscript intended for publication) is the single most important text that establishes rhetoric as a system of persuasive communication.

Athens, even in its glory days, seethed with controversy and bickering over the many inefficiencies of democracy. Men trained in rhetoric executed two coups, the Tyranny of the Four Hundred in 411 BCE and the Tyranny of the Thirty in 404 BCE, neither of which was an improvement; after each coup, democracy returned. Moreover, Athenians fought wars with Persia (the Battle of Marathon in 490 BCE and the Battle of Thermopylae in 480 BCE) and Sparta (the Peloponnesian War in 431–404 BCE and the Corinthian War of 395–387 BCE). Finally, the armies of Philip II of Macedonia defeated Athens at the Battle of Chaeronea in 338 BCE, ending Athenian independence. Despite coups and wars, democracy remained in place in Athens for nearly 200 years.

If Americans might be called Greeks because our country is based on Greek traditions, this does not mean that rhetoric does not appear in all cultures. True, one might say that all civilizations have some sort of persuasive negotiation process; but profound differences exist between cultures in terms of what verbal strategies are considered persuasive. Indeed, disparity in expectations and the actions of individuals and groups from different traditions can be a cause of strife in any culture.

Explore

Activity 1.2 • Contemporary Usage of the Word "Rhetoric"

Find at least two recent but different examples involving uses of the word "rhetoric." For example, search your local newspaper for an example of how the word "rhetoric" is being used. A search of the *Dallas Morning News* for the word "rhetoric" led to a story about citizen efforts to clean up a neglected area of town: "He now hopes for help to finally fill the gap between rhetoric and reality." Or ask a friend, fellow employee, or a family member to tell you what the word "rhetoric" means, and write down what they say. Discuss your examples in your small group, and present the best ones to the class.

Visual Map of Meanings for the Word "Rhetoric"

The word map for the word "rhetoric" shown in Figure 1.1 on the next page has branches for different meanings of the word, with some branches splitting again to display subtle subsets of connotation. It was created by a website, *Visual Thesaurus* (www.visualthesaurus.com), which computes visual word maps for any word inputted in its search box. The idea is that words lead to branches that lead to more words, inspiring users to think of language in new ways.

If you recreate the rhetoric word map at the *Visual Thesaurus* site and place your cursor over any of the circles connecting the branches, a small box will pop up that defines that connection. One of these connection boxes is visible in Figure 1.1. Notice it says, "using language effectively to please or persuade." This is the branch of the visual map that is closest to the meaning of "rhetoric" as used in this book. The other branches illustrate other contemporary uses of the word.

Activity 1.3 • Explore the Visual Map of the Word "Rhetoric"

Explore

In your small group, choose one of the five branches of words in the visual map of the word "rhetoric." Go to one or more good dictionaries and explore the meanings of the words in that branch. A good place to start would be the *Oxford English Dictionary (OED)*, which your college library may offer online. The *OED* offers intricate analyses of the histories of word meanings. Report to the class what you find out about the words on your particular branch.

Figure 1.1 • Word Map for "Rhetoric"

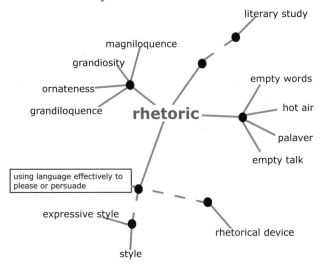

Reading 1.1

Have you bought hummus or coconut water at the grocery store? Worn a henna tattoo? Then you may have participated in Columbusing, the art of "discovering" something, usually from another culture, that is not new. The term echoes Columbus's "discovery" of the New World, which had long been inhabited by non-Europeans.

Brenda Salinas writes about Columbusing in this article published on NPR.com.

There isn't anything inherently wrong about eating hummus or getting a henna tattoo, argues Salinas. She attempts to persuade you that the problem is the stripping of cultural context from the item, in effect, engaging in cultural appropriation. To the Latinos who grew up eating empanadas, for example, it can feel like theft when Buzzfeed raves about "a hand pie, a little foldover pie that you can fit in your hand. They have flaky crusts and can be sweet or savory."

As you read Salinas's article, think about occasions when you may have engaged in Columbusing.

"Columbusing": The Art of Discovering Something that is Not New
by Brenda Salinas

If you've danced to an Afrobeat-heavy pop song, dipped hummus, sipped coconut water, participated in a Desi-inspired color run or sported a henna tattoo, then you've Columbused something.

Columbusing is when you "discover" something that's existed forever. Just that it's existed outside your own culture, nationality, race or even, say, your neighborhood. Bonus points if you tell all your friends about it.

Why not? In our immigrant-rich cities, the whole world is at our doorsteps.

Sometimes, though, Columbusing can feel icky. When is cultural appropriation a healthy byproduct of globalization and when is it a problem?

All the Rage

Buzzfeed Food published an article asking, "Have you heard about the new kind of pie that's *all the rage* lately?" It's a hand pie, a little foldover pie that you can fit in your hand. They have flaky crusts and can be sweet or savory. You know, exactly like an empanada, a Latin American culinary staple.

On face value, it seems stupid to get worked up over an empanada. I mean, it's just a pastry, right? But "discovering" empanadas on Pinterest and calling them "hand pies" strips empanadas of their cultural context. To all the people who grew up eating empanadas, it can feel like theft.

In this promotional photo shot, TV star Jennie Garth sprays the crowd with orange at the Shout Color Throw on June 21 at Dodger Stadium in Los Angeles. Events like this one are being held in Europe and the United States, but most organizers don't mention that these events are inspired by the Hindu festival of Holi—but stripped of religious meaning.

Photo Credit: Jeff Lewis/AP Images for SC Johnson

Feeling Overlooked

When it comes to our culinary traditions, Latinos are used to feeling robbed.

Latino activists spoke out in May when Chipotle announced plans to print original stories by famous writers on its paper goods and failed to include any Mexican-Americans or Latinos on the roster. The American-owned chain can profit from Mexican culture while overlooking the harsh reality of how Latinos have been treated in this country.

A man sprays colored dye on people dancing during Holi celebrations in India in 2012. Holi, the Hindu festival of colors, also heralds the coming of spring—a detail that partiers at the Shout Color Throw might miss.

Photo Credit: Rajesh Kumar Singh/AP

On Cinco de Mayo, chef Anthony Bourdain asked why Americans love Mexican food, drugs, alcohol and cheap labor but ignore the violence that happens across the border. "Despite our ridiculously hypocritical attitudes towards immigration," writes Bourdain, "we demand that Mexicans cook a large percentage of the food we eat, grow the ingredients we need to make that food, clean our houses, mow our lawns, wash our dishes, look after our children."

It's frustrating when even the staunchest anti-immigration activists regularly eat Mexican food. It seems like a paradox to relish your fajitas while believing the line cook should get deported.

Admittedly, cultural appropriation is an integral and vital part of American history. And one day, empanadas might become as American as pizza (yes, I appreciate the irony of that statement). But the day when Latinos are considered as American as Italian-Americans, well, that feels further away.

Why It Hurts

The condolence prize for being an outsider is that you can take solace in the cultural traditions that make you unique. When outsiders use tweezers to pick out the discrete parts of your culture that are worthy of their attention, it feels like a violation. Empanadas are trendy, cumbia is trendy, but Latinas are still not trendy.

Code Switch blogger Gene Demby writes, "It's much harder now to patrol the ramparts of our cultures, to distinguish between the appreciators and appropriators. Just who gets to play in which cultural sandboxes? Who gets to be the bouncer at the velvet rope?"

Playing Explorer

Of course, there is no bouncer, but we can be careful not to Columbus other culture's traditions. Before you make reservations at the hottest fusion restaurant or book an alternative healing therapy, ask yourself a few questions:

>   Who is providing this good or service for me?

>   Am I engaging with them in a thoughtful manner?

>   Am I learning about this culture?

Are people from this culture benefiting from my spending money here?

Are they being hurt by my spending money here?

It is best to enter a new, ethnic experience with consideration, curiosity and respect. That doesn't mean you have to act or look the part of a dour-faced anthropologist or an ultra-earnest tourist. You can go outside your comfort zone and learn about the completely different worlds that coexist within your city. If you're adventurous, you can explore the entire world without leaving the country and without needing a passport.

Just remember, it's great to love a different culture and its artifacts, as long as you love the people too.

Activity 1.4 • Analyzing Columbusing as an Argument

Collaborate

" 'Columbusing': The Art of Discovering Something that Is Not New" is a rhetorical document because the author is attempting to persuade her audience to believe something. In a group, use these review questions to discuss what Salinas is arguing.

1. What does Salinas want her audience to do differently? How does she define Columbusing? What does it have to do with Columbus?

2. Make a list of the examples Salinas gives of Columbusing. Then, make a list of other Columbusing items or activities you have bought or engaged in. Share your group's list with the class.

3. What does Salinas say we can do to avoid Columbusing other cultures' traditions? Do you agree that these are good suggestions? Why or why not? Discuss these questions in your group, and share your thoughts with the class.

Rhetorical Argument

Often, in our culture, the word *argument* is taken to mean a disagreement or even a fight, with raised voices, rash words, and hurt feelings. We have the perception of an argument as something that leads to victory or defeat, winners or losers. A *rhetorical argument,* however, is the carefully crafted presentation of a viewpoint or position on a topic and the giving of thoughts, ideas, and opinions along with reasons for their support. The persuasive strength of an argument rests upon the rhetorical skills of the rhetor (the speaker or the writer) in utilizing the tools of language to persuade a particular audience.

Types of Argument

Academic arguments can be divided into several different categories, depending upon the extent of the writer's desire to persuade and the scope of the conversational exchange.

1. **Makes a point.** One type of argument simply makes a point about a topic. The article in this chapter, " 'Columbusing': The Art of Discovering Something that Is Not New," argues, for example, that buying hummus or getting a henna tattoo is Columbusing, which labels as new something ancient from another culture. To do so strips the cultural context from things or activities. The subtext of the article suggests Columbusing is a bad thing and should be avoided. If the author of this type of argument offers sufficient evidence to back up the thesis, no one is likely to disagree, except to say, perhaps, the author is overreacting or the point the author makes is not important.

2. **Aims to persuade.** A second type of argument involves a controversial issue, and the writer's aim is to persuade the audience to change its stance on the matter. For the writer, the ideal result would be that members of the audience alter their positions to coincide with the writer's viewpoint. In this second type of argument, it is essential that the writer offer the complete structure of thesis, evidence, possible opposing viewpoints which are discussed and countered, and a conclusion. "The Sleepover Question," another reading in this chapter, presents this kind of argument. The author, who has conducted research in both America and Holland, argues the controversial position that if American parents would adopt more liberal attitudes toward their children's sexuality, like the parents in Holland, "the transition into adulthood need not be so painful for parents or children." A reading in Chapter 3, "Executions Should Be Televised," offers a more extreme version of this type of argument. Either executions are televised or they aren't, and the writer advocates that they should be.

3. **Tries to find common ground.** A third type of argument emphasizes multiple perspectives and viewpoints and tries to find common ground participants can agree upon. In Chapter 4, several readings are collected

in a casebook called "The $300 House." The *Harvard Business Review* initiated a design competition called The $300 House, which was intended to spark inclusive argument with the aim of gathering ideas about how to build inexpensive but adequate homes for the poor in the world's slums. One of the readings, "Hands Off Our Houses," opposes the design competition, saying that bringing $300 houses into the slums of Mumbai is not the answer to the housing problem. However, the author of "The $300 House: A Hands-On Approach to a Wicked Problem," attempts to find common ground with the authors of "Hands Off Our Houses" by saying he agrees housing for the poor is a complex problem "that can't be fixed with a clever shack alone."

In Chapter 5, Rogerian (or common ground) argument, named after psychologist Carl Rogers, is discussed and outlined. Rogerian argument has four elements: introduction, common ground and common arguments, a position or argument, and a positive statement of how the position could, at least in some instances, benefit the opposition.

These three types of arguments represent points in a spectrum, and all persuasive texts may not neatly fit into one of the three categories. A crucial thing to remember, though, is that all arguments involve the presentation of a line of reasoning about a topic or an issue—a thesis, hypothesis, or claim—and the support of that reasoning with evidence.

Aristotle's Three Appeals

Aristotle identified three appeals (see Figure 1.2 on the following page) or three ways to persuade an audience, and we are still using these today, though often without using the Greek terms to identify the means of persuasion.

Ethos—The rhetor persuades by means of his or her character or credibility. In oratory, the speaker projects an air of confidence and authority. In writing, *ethos* is conveyed by the writer's qualifications or the authorities cited and also by the quality of the writing.

Pathos—The rhetor persuades by playing upon the listener's (or reader's) emotions. He or she may refer to children, death, disaster, injustice, or other topics that arouse pity, fear, or other emotions.

Logos—The rhetor persuades by using reasoning and evidence. Arguments based on *logos* employ deductive or inductive reasoning.

Figure 1.2 • Aristotle's Three Appeals

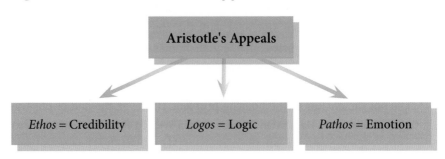

Although a good argument will contain at least traces of all three appeals, skilled rhetors analyze their audiences to determine which of the three will be most persuasive for that particular audience. Then, they construct arguments that emphasize that particular appeal.

In addition, a knowledgeable rhetor considers the time, place, audience, topic, and other aspects of the occasion for writing or speaking to determine the *kairos*, or opportune moment for the argument (see Figure 1.3). This factor or critical moment both provides and limits opportunities for appeals suitable to that moment. For example, someone giving a commencement address has certain opportunities and constraints. Likewise, an attorney writing a last-minute appeal for someone on death row has a very different set of options.

Figure 1.3 • *Kairos*

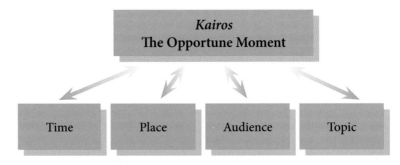

Microsoft Just Laid Off Thousands of Employees With a Hilariously Bad Memo

by Kevin Roose

Typically, when you're a top executive at a major corporation that is laying off more than 10 percent of your workforce, you say a few things to the newly jobless. Like "sorry." Or "thank you for your many years of service." Or even "we hate doing this, but it's necessary to help the company survive."

What you don't do is bury the news of the layoffs in the 11th paragraph of a long, rambling corporate strategy memo.

And yet, this was Microsoft honcho Stephen Elop's preferred method for announcing to his employees today that 12,500 of them were being laid off. (18,000 are being laid off companywide; Elop, the former head of Nokia, oversees the company's devices unit, which was hardest hit by the layoffs.)

How bad was Elop's job-axing memo? Really, really bad. It's so bad that I can't even really convey its badness. I just have to show you.

Here's how it starts:

> Hello there,

Hello there? *Hello there?* Out of all the possible "you're losing your job" greetings, you chose the one that sounds like the start to a bad OKCupid message? "Hello there" isn't how you announce layoffs; it's what you

Kevin Roose's essay, "Microsoft Just Laid Off Thousands of Employees With a Hilariously Bad Memo" illustrates the dangers of not considering kairos. When Stephen Elop needed to lay off more than 10 percent of Microsoft workers under his supervision, Elop did not say anything one might expect—like "sorry," or "I regret," or "thank you for your service." In a memo to the affected employees, he did not even get around to the news of layoff until the eleventh paragraph.

If Elop had considered the kairos of the situation, then he would have realized his audience would not be interested in all the planning information he crowded into the memo. They would want to know the bad news, if it had to be told, near the beginning of the memo. Elop, as Roose reveals in his analysis of the memo, was more interested in his corporate strategy than in what his audience at that time and place needed or wanted to hear.

The essay was published in New York Magazine.

Stephen Elop, lead-burier.

Photo Credit: Josh Edelson/AFP/Getty Images

say right before you ask, "What's a girl like you doing on a site like this? ;)" It's the fedora of greetings.

Anyway, carry on. Let's hear the bad news:

> Microsoft's strategy is focused on productivity and our desire to help people "do more." As the Microsoft Devices Group, our role is to light up this strategy for people. We are the team creating the hardware that showcases the finest of Microsoft's digital work and digital life experiences, and we will be the confluence of the best of Microsoft's applications, operating systems and cloud services.

Wait, what does this have to do with layoffs?

> To align with Microsoft's strategy, we plan to focus our efforts. Given the wide range of device experiences, we must concentrate on the areas where we can add the most value. The roots of this company and our future are in productivity and helping people get things done. Our fundamental focus—for phones, Surface, for meetings with devices like PPI, Xbox hardware and new areas of innovation—is to build on that strength. While our direction in the majority of our teams is largely unchanging, we have had an opportunity to plan carefully about the alignment of phones within Microsoft as the transferring Nokia team continues with its integration process.

Oh, I get it. This is the warm-up. You're giving me a few minutes to sit down, compose myself, grab the Kleenex. Now you're going to drop the hammer.

> **It is particularly important to recognize that the role of phones within Microsoft is different than it was within Nokia. Whereas the hardware business of phones within Nokia was an end unto itself, within Microsoft all our devices are intended to embody the finest of Microsoft's digital work and digital life experiences, while accruing value to Microsoft's overall strategy. Our device strategy must reflect Microsoft's strategy and must be accomplished within an appropriate financial envelope. Therefore, we plan to make some changes.**

"Financial envelope"? You don't literally keep all of Microsoft's cash in a big envelope, do you? Anyway, "changes." I know what that's supposed to mean. Now, please, give it to me straight: tell me I'm fired.

We will be particularly focused on making the market for Windows Phone. In the near term, we plan to drive Windows Phone volume by targeting the more affordable smartphone segments, which are the fastest growing segments of the market, with Lumia. In addition to the portfolio already planned, we plan to deliver additional lower-cost Lumia devices by shifting select future Nokia X designs and products to Windows Phone devices. We expect to make this shift immediately while continuing to sell and support existing Nokia X products.

To win in the higher price segments, we will focus on delivering great breakthrough products in alignment with major milestones ahead from both the Windows team and the Applications and Services Group. We will ensure that the very best experiences and scenarios from across the company will be showcased on our products. We plan to take advantage of innovation from the Windows team, like Universal Windows Apps, to continue to enrich the Windows application ecosystem. And in the very lowest price ranges, we plan to run our first phones business for maximum efficiency with a smaller team.

WTF. Is this some kind of joke? DO I HAVE A JOB OR NOT?

We expect these changes to have an impact to our team structure. With our focus, we plan to consolidate the former Smart Devices and Mobile Phones business units into one phone business unit that is responsible for all of our phone efforts. Under the plan, the phone business unit will be led by Jo Harlow with key members from both the Smart Devices and Mobile Phones teams in the management team. This team will be responsible for the success of our Lumia products, the transition of select future Nokia X products to Lumia and for the ongoing operation of the first phone business.

I AM GNAWING ON MY MOUSE PAD IN ANGER. ALL I WANT TO KNOW IS WHETHER I NEED TO START SELLING MY PLASMA TO MAKE RENT NEXT MONTH. PLEASE TELL ME THIS BIT OF INFORMATION.

As part of the effort, we plan to select the appropriate business model approach for our sales markets while continuing to offer our products in all markets with a strong focus on maintaining business continuity. We will determine each market approach based on local market dynamics, our ability to profitably deliver local variants, current Lumia momentum and the strategic importance of the market to Microsoft. This will all be balanced with our overall capability to invest.

Our phone engineering efforts are expected to be concentrated in Salo, Finland (for future, high-end Lumia products) and Tampere, Finland (for more affordable devices). We plan to develop the supporting technologies in both locations. We plan to ramp down engineering work in Oulu. While we plan to reduce the engineering in Beijing and San Diego, both sites will continue to have supporting roles, including affordable devices in Beijing and supporting specific US requirements in San Diego. Espoo and Lund are planned to continue to be focused on application software development.

Blah blah blah I don't even care anymore. You have numbed me to the afflictions of mankind with phrases like "business continuity" and "market dynamics." And now you're probably going to use some crazy euphemism, like "streamline," to tell me I'm fired. Go ahead.

We plan to right-size our manufacturing operations to align to the new strategy and take advantage of integration opportunities. We expect to focus phone production mainly in Hanoi, with some production to continue in Beijing and Dongguan. We plan to shift other Microsoft manufacturing and repair operations to Manaus and Reynosa respectively, and start a phased exit from Komaron, Hungary.

"Right-size"! "Phased exit"! Oh, you are so killing this. You get an extra snack ration at CEO summer camp.

In short, we will focus on driving Lumia volume in the areas where we are already successful today in order to make the market for Windows Phone. With more speed, we will build on our success in the affordable smartphone space with new products offering more differentiation. We'll focus on acquiring new customers in the markets where Microsoft's services and products are most concentrated. And, we'll continue building momentum around applications.

Life is empty. All that remains is dust.

We plan that this would result in an estimated reduction of 12,500 factory direct and professional employees over the next year.

> **These decisions are difficult for the team, and we plan to support departing team members' with severance benefits.**

There it is, finally. In paragraph 11. I would react more strongly to the news that I'm laid off, but my synapses are no longer firing properly. The badness of this email has rewired my brain's circuitry. All I understand now is business-school jargon. And death. Sweet death.

> **More broadly across the Devices team, we will continue our efforts to bring iconic tablets to market in ways that complement our OEM partners, power the next generation of meetings & collaboration devices and thoughtfully expand Windows with new interaction models. With a set of changes already implemented earlier this year in these teams, this means there will be limited change for the Surface, Xbox hardware, PPI/meetings or next generation teams.**

> **We recognize these planned changes are broad and have very difficult implications for many of our team members. We will work to provide as much clarity and information as possible. Today and over the coming weeks leaders across the organization will hold town halls, host information sharing sessions and provide more details on the intranet.**

Oh, good. Because if it's one thing I need right now, it's more details.

> **The team transferring from Nokia and the teams that have been part of Microsoft have each experienced a number of remarkable changes these last few years. We operate in a competitive industry that moves rapidly, and change is necessary. As difficult as some of our changes are today, this direction deliberately aligns our work with the cross company efforts that Satya has described in his recent emails. Collectively, the clarity, focus and alignment across the company, and the opportunity to deliver the results of that work into the hands of people, will allow us to increase our success in the future.**

> **Regards,**

"Regards?" Really? We started at OKCupid stalker, and you're ending at "over-eager candidate for summer internship?" Well, okay. Sure. Whatever. Not like it matters.

> **Stephen**

Collaborate

Activity 1.5 • Discuss Microsoft's Memo Laying Off Employees

In a small group, discuss Stephen Elop's memo to employees who were being laid off and Roose's colorful commentary.

1. What would you think if you received such a memo? How is Elop ignoring *kairos* in his memo? Reread the section earlier in the chapter in which *kairos* is discussed, and then decide with your group how Elop fails to take *kairos* into consideration in writing his memo. Report to the class.

2. Discuss what employees would have preferred to hear from Elop, assuming they must be laid off. Share your conclusions with the class.

Reading 1.3

This selection by Amy Schalet was first published in The New York Times. *"The Sleepover Question" hazards an argument that many Americans—or at least American parents—may find controversial. Backed by her credentials as a professor of sociology, Schalet cites research from 130 interviews, both in the United States and the Netherlands, and tackles the issue of whether or not American parents should allow their adolescent children to have sex in the family home. Pay particular attention, for she shows how to argue a subject that is not only controversial but often ignored.*

The Sleepover Question
by Amy Schalet

NOT under my roof. That's the attitude most American parents have toward teenagers and their sex lives. Squeamishness and concern describe most parents' approach to their offspring's carnality. We don't want them doing it—whatever "it" is!—in our homes. Not surprisingly, teenage sex is a source of conflict in many American families.

Would Americans increase peace in family life and strengthen family bonds if they adopted more accepting attitudes about sex and what's allowable under the family roof? I've interviewed 130 people, all white, middle class and not particularly religious, as part of a study of teenage sex and family life here and in the Netherlands. My look into cultural differences suggests family life might be much improved, for all, if Americans had more open ideas about teenage sex. The question of who sleeps where when a teenager brings a boyfriend or girlfriend home for the night fits within the larger world of culturally divergent ideas about teenage sex, lust and capacity for love.

Kimberly and Natalie dramatize the cultural differences in the way young women experience their sexuality. (I have changed their names to protect confidentiality.) Kimberly, a 16-year-old American, never received sex education at home. "God, no! No, no! That's not going to happen," she told me. She'd like to tell her parents that she and her boyfriend are having sex, but she believes it is easier for her parents not to know because the truth would "shatter" their image of her as their "little princess."

Natalie, who is also 16 but Dutch, didn't tell her parents immediately when she first had intercourse with her boyfriend of three months. But, soon after, she says, she was so happy, she wanted to share the good news. Initially her father was upset and worried about his daughter and his honor. "Talk to him," his wife advised Natalie; after she did, her father made peace with the change. Essentially Natalie and her family negotiated a life change together and figured out, as a family, how to adjust to changed circumstance.

Respecting what she understood as her family's "don't ask, don't tell" policy, Kimberly only slept with her boyfriend at his house, when no one was home. She enjoyed being close to her boyfriend but did not like having to keep an important part of her life secret from her parents. In contrast, Natalie and her boyfriend enjoyed time and a new closeness with her family; the fact that her parents knew and approved of her boyfriend seemed a source of pleasure.

The difference in their experiences stems from divergent cultural ideas about sex and what responsible parents ought to do about it. Here, we see teenagers as helpless victims beset by raging hormones and believe parents should protect them from urges they cannot control. Matters aren't helped by the stereotype that all boys want the same thing, and all girls want love and cuddling. This compounds the burden on parents to steer teenage children away from relationships that will do more harm than good.

The Dutch parents I interviewed regard teenagers, girls and boys, as capable of falling in love, and of reasonably assessing their own readiness for sex. Dutch parents like Natalie's talk to their children about sex and its unintended consequences and urge them to use contraceptives and practice safe sex.

Cultural differences about teenage sex are more complicated than clichéd images of puritanical Americans and permissive Europeans. Normalizing ideas about teenage sex in fact allows the Dutch to exert *more* control over their children. Most of the parents I interviewed actively discouraged promiscuous behavior. And Dutch teenagers often reinforced what we see as 1950s-style mores: eager to win approval, they bring up their partners in conversation, introduce them to their parents and help them make favorable impressions.

Some Dutch teenagers went so far as to express their ideas about sex and love in self-consciously traditional terms; one Dutch boy said the advantage of spending the night with a partner was that it was "Like Mom and Dad, like when you're married, you also wake up next to the person you love."

Normalizing teenage sex under the family roof opens the way for more responsible sex education. In a national survey, 7 of 10 Dutch girls reported that by the time they were 16, their parents had talked to them about pregnancy and contraception. It seems these conversations helped teenagers prepare, responsibly, for active sex lives: 6 of 10 Dutch girls said they were on the pill when they first had intercourse. Widespread use of oral contraceptives contributes to low teenage pregnancy rates—more than 4 times lower in the Netherlands than in the United States.

Obviously sleepovers aren't a direct route to family happiness. But even the most traditional parents can appreciate the virtue of having their children be comfortable bringing a girlfriend or boyfriend home, rather than have them sneak around.

Unlike the American teenagers I interviewed, who said they felt they had to split their burgeoning sexual selves from their family roles, the Dutch teens had a chance to integrate different parts of themselves into their family life. When children feel safe enough to tell parents what they are doing and feeling, presumably it's that much easier for them to ask for help. This allows parents to have more influence, to control through connection.

Sexual maturation is awkward and difficult. The Dutch experience suggests that it is possible for families to stay connected when teenagers start having sex, and that if they do, the transition into adulthood need not be so painful for parents or children.

Activity 1.6 • Analyze "The Sleepover Question"

In a group, discuss these review questions about the emphasis of *logos* in "The Sleepover Question."

Collaborate

1. Can you paraphrase the logic of the argument? How does emotion (*pathos*) play a role in resistance to this argument?

2. What do you think about the "not under my roof" approach to a parent controlling a teen's sexuality versus the Dutch approach of allowing a teen's partner to sleep over?

3. How do stereotypes play against the argument for a more open approach to teen sex in America? How much of parents' discomfort with their teen potentially having sex is guided by how their parents treated the subject when they were teens?

4. In the article, the writer discusses the link between the use of oral contraceptives and lower teen pregnancy rates but does not mention the risk of STDs or condom use. Is it irresponsible of the author not to discuss the risk of STDs and sex, especially when she is willing to discuss teen pregnancy? Does it feel like an incomplete argument without discussing STDs?

After you've discussed these questions as a group, individually reflect on what you would say in a letter to the editor about this article.

Become Part of the Academic Conversation

As a student, you are asked to comment on or analyze texts others have written. In effect, you are expected to join academic conversations that are already in progress. How do you do that? How do you know what kind of response is appropriate? Have you ever entered a party where everyone is talking excitedly? Most likely, you paused near the doorway to get a sense of who was there and what they were discussing before you decided who to talk to and what to say. Or, have you become part of a Facebook group or a listserv discussion group? If so, you know it is a good idea to "lurk" for a while before asking questions or contributing a remark. Writing an academic paper involves a similar process. You read about a subject until you have a good grasp of the points authorities are debating. Then you find a way to integrate your own ideas about that subject with the ideas of others and create an informed contribution to the conversation.

For example, the following students' introductions to movie reviews demonstrate they not only understand the films and have interesting things to say about them;

their writing also displays knowledge of what others have written about the films, whether the students agree with those evaluations or not.

▪   Roger Ebert claims that audience members who haven't seen the first two *Lord of the Rings* films (Peter Jackson, 2001, 2002) will likely "be adrift during the early passages of [the third] film's 200 minutes." But then again, Ebert continues, "to be adrift occasionally during this nine-hour saga comes with the territory" (par. 3). Ebert, though, misses one crucial fact regarding *Lord of the Rings: The Return of the King* (2003). This third installment opens with a flashback intended to familiarize new spectators about what happened in the previous two films. Within these five minutes, the audience discovers how Gollum (Andy Serkis) came to be corrupt through the destructive power of the Ring. The viewer, therefore, will not necessarily be "adrift," as Ebert claims, since the lighting, setting, and sound in the opening of *The Return of the King* show the lighter, more peaceful world before Gollum finds the ring, compared to the darker, more sinister world thereafter.

▪   "It's hard to resist a satire, even when it wobbles, that insists the most unbelievable parts are the most true" (*Rolling Stone* par. 1). This is Peter Travers's overarching view of Grant Heslov's satire, *The Men Who Stare at Goats* (2009). Travers is correct here; after all, Goats's opening title card, which reads, "More of this is real than you would believe," humorously teases the viewer that some of the film's most "unbelievable parts" will, in fact, offer the most truth. We experience this via Bill Wilson's (Ewan McGregor) interview of an ex "psy-ops" soldier, when Wilson's life spirals out of control, and all the other far-fetched actions presenting "reality." But again, it is the film's opening—specifically, its setting, camera movements and angles, dialogue, effects, and ambient noise—that sets the foundation for an unbelievably realistic satire.[2]

In both of these introductions, the students quote reviews by professional film critics and respond to the critics' opinions. Moreover, the students continue their arguments by using the critics' ideas as springboards for their own arguments. These two short examples indicate these students have learned how to counter positions advocated by authorities without losing their own voices. If the rest of their essays continue as they have begun, the students will have written essays

---

2. Marshall, Kelli. "Entering a Conversation, Teaching the Academic Essay." *Unmuzzled Thoughts about Teaching and Pop Culture,* Tumblr, 23 Oct. 2010, kellirmarshall.tumblr.com/post/1391060136/entering-a-conversation-teaching-the-academic.

to which others can reply, thus continuing the conversation. Later in this text-book, you will have your own chance to enter the conversation of film reviews by reviewing a favorite movie of your own.

The Burkean Parlor

Kenneth Burke, philosopher and rhetorician, described the "unending con-versation" that surrounds each of us. To do academic research, we must en-ter the conversation of people who already know the topic and have dis-cussed part or all of it before we are even aware the topic exists. Burke wrote,

> Imagine that you enter a parlor. You come late. When you arrive, others have long preceded you, and they are engaged in a heated discussion, a discussion too heated for them to pause and tell you exactly what it is about. In fact, the discussion had already be-gun long before any of them got there, so that no one present is qualified to retrace for you all the steps that had gone before. You listen for a while, until you decide that you have caught the tenor of the argument; then you put in your oar. Someone answers; you answer him; another comes to your defense; another aligns him-self against you, to either the embarrassment or gratification of your opponent, depending upon the quality of your ally's assis-tance. However, the discussion is interminable. The hour grows late, you must depart. And you do depart, with the discussion still vigorously in progress.[3]

Activity 1.7 • Joining the Conversation

Collaborate

Divide into groups of five or six members. Have one member of each group leave the room for five to ten minutes. Meanwhile, each group selects a topic and begins con-versing about it. When the excluded member of the group returns, the group simply continues their conversation. When the excluded member figures out what the con-versation is, he or she can join it by making a comment or asking a question.

After a few minutes, have each of the excluded group members tell the class what it was like to enter a conversation after it had already started. As a class, discuss how this is similar to what you experience when you research an academic topic and write about it.

---

3. Burke, Kenneth. *The Philosophy of Literary Form: Studies in Symbolic Action.* U of California, 1967, pp. 110-11.

Collaborative Groups Help Students Enter the Academic Conversation

Likely, your writing class will include collaborative group work as part of the mix of activities, along with lecture, class discussion, and in-class writing. You may wonder why there is so much talk in a writing class, which is a good question. Use of collaborative groups is based on extensive research, which shows that students who work in small groups as part of their courses tend to learn more and retain the knowledge longer than students who are not asked to work in groups. Also, research shows students who participate in collaborative group work generally are more satisfied with the course. Groups give students a chance to apply knowledge they have learned and provide a change of pace from lectures or other class activities. There are several types of groups, and your class may include one or all of them.

- **Informal, one-time pairs or groups.** After presenting some material, your instructor may ask you to turn to the person next to you and discuss the topic or answer a question.

- **Ongoing small classroom groups.** Usually, these groups work together for a significant part of the semester, and your instructor may assign roles to members of the group such as recorder, facilitator, editor, and spokesperson. Often, the roles will rotate, so everyone has a chance to try out each job. Your instructor may give you a job description for each role or train the class in the tasks for each role.

- **Task groups.** These groups are formed to write a report, complete a project, or do some other task together. These groups meet several times, often outside of class. The products of these groups are usually graded, and your instructor will often require members to rate each other on their performance.

- **Peer editing groups.** When you have completed a draft of an essay or other text, your instructor may ask you to exchange papers in pairs or within small groups. You will be asked to read your classmate's paper carefully and make comments, either on a peer editing form or on the paper itself. Likewise, your classmate will read and make comments on your paper. Then, when your paper is returned, you can make revisions based on your classmate's comments.

An added benefit to the use of collaborative groups in writing classes is that students can help each other figure out what the ongoing conversation is for a particular topic or issue before writing about it. Also, groups provide a forum where students can practice making comments that are part of that conversation.

Why Study Rhetoric?

Rhetoric, or persuasive communication, happens all around us every day, in conversation at the grocery store, in blogs, on television, and in the classroom. We Americans constantly air our opinions about almost everything. Sometimes it is to convince others to share our opinions, and sometimes the reason is to engage in a dialogue that will help us understand the world around us, and sometimes it is to persuade others to action.

Argument is essential to human interaction and to society, for it is through the interplay of ideas in argument that we discover answers to problems, try out new ideas, shape scientific experiments, communicate with family members, recruit others to join a team, and work out any of the multitude of human interactions essential for society to function. When issues are complex, arguments do not result in immediate persuasion of the audience; rather, argument is part of an ongoing conversation between concerned parties who seek resolution, rather than speedy answers.

Rhetoric provides a useful framework for looking at the world, as well as for evaluating and initiating communications. In the modern world, writing and communicating persuasively is a necessary skill. Those who can present effective arguments in writing are, in the business world, often the ones who are promoted. In addition, those who are able to evaluate the arguments presented to them, whether by politicians, advertisers, or even family members, are less likely to be swayed by logical fallacies or ill-supported research.

Also, writing rhetorically is a tool with sometimes surprising uses. Research shows that we are more likely to remember material we have written about rather than simply memorized. Also, through the process of writing, writers often find that they initiate ideas and connections between ideas that they might not otherwise have found. Thus, writing may lead to new discoveries.

Rhetoric is a part of our everyday lives. When we're in a conversation with someone, we use rhetoric on a conscious or subconscious level. If you go to class wearing the T-shirt of your favorite musician or band, you're ultimately sending a rhetorical message identifying yourself as a fan of that artist or group.

If you've ever written a profile on a dating site, you've used rhetorical principles to convince an audience of potential partners to contact you or to write you back if you have chosen to make the first contact. You build *ethos* by talking about yourself in order to build credibility among potential partners, and you establish *pathos* when you talk about an interest that is shared by a potential mate.

Being able to use the tools of rhetoric effectively gives you the power to control your communication—both incoming and outgoing—and to affect your environment in a positive way.

Collaborate

Activity 1.8 • How Do You Use Rhetoric?

In your small group, make a list of five ways that you use rhetoric in your everyday lives. Then, create a list of five ways studying rhetoric could make a difference in your lives. As a class, compare the lists.

Rhetorical Arguments Stand the Test of Time

Abraham Lincoln's Gettysburg Address is the short speech that the president delivered at the site of the Battle of Gettysburg where, four months previously, the Union Army defeated Confederate forces. His was not the only talk that day at the dedication of the Soldiers' National Cemetery, but it is the only one remembered. In just over two minutes, he was able to reframe the Civil War not just as a victory for the North but as a "new birth of freedom" for all Americans. Now, during the 150th anniversary of the Civil War, is a good time to remember Lincoln's rhetoric—in terms of both the content and the style of his speech.

Reading 1.4

Though no actual recording exists of Abraham Lincoln giving the speech, you can listen to others reading it aloud if you search on the Internet for "recording of Gettysburg Address." Listen to the speech, noting the phrase "Four score and seven years ago," which is so famous that Americans know instantly, when it is quoted by orators or writers, that it is a reference to Lincoln. Consider what arguments the president makes in his speech. Think about their relevance today.

Text of the Gettysburg Address
by Abraham Lincoln

Four score and seven years ago, our fathers brought forth on this continent, a new nation, conceived in Liberty and dedicated to the proposition that all men are created equal.

Now we are engaged in a great civil war, testing whether that nation, or any nation so conceived and so dedicated, can long endure. We are met on a great battlefield of that war. We have come to dedicate a portion of that field, as a final resting place for those who here gave their lives that that nation might live. It is altogether fitting and proper that we should do this.

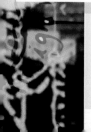

But, in a larger sense, we cannot dedicate—we cannot consecrate—we cannot hallow—this ground. The brave men, living and dead, who struggled here, have consecrated it, far above our poor power to add or detract. The world will little note, nor long remember what we say here, but it can never forget what they did here. It is for us the living, rather, to be dedicated here to the unfinished work which they who fought here have thus far so nobly advanced. It is rather for us to be here dedicated to the great task remaining before us—that from these honored dead we take increased devotion to that cause for which they gave the last full measure of devotion—that we here highly resolve that these dead shall not have died in vain—that this nation, under God, shall have a new birth of freedom—and that government of the people, by the people, for the people, shall not perish from the earth.

Activity 1.9 • Paraphrase the Gettysburg Address

Compose

Rephrase each sentence of the Gettysburg Address in your own words, putting it in twenty-first century wording rather than Lincoln's ceremonial, nineteenth-century phrasing. In a paraphrase, the text does not become shorter; it is recreated in different words. This is a useful technique in helping you understand a text. It is also helpful when you are writing an analysis of a text because you can use your paraphrase rather than long, block quotes. Remember, though, when you are writing an essay, you must cite a paraphrase in the text and also include it in your list of references.

Activity 1.10 • Comment on Your Classmate's Paraphrase of the Gettysburg Address

Compose

In your small group, trade your paraphrase of the Gettysburg Address with the paraphrase of the person next to you. Read through the document carefully, looking for how well your partner paraphrased, rather than commented on, Lincoln's words. Mark each place where a comment or analysis appears. Give the paper back to the author for revision, if needed.

Why might it be useful to paraphrase a document rather than analyze or comment on it?

Respond to Visual Rhetoric

To the ancient Greeks and Romans, rhetoric largely involved verbal skills—the use of words to persuade an audience. But rhetoricians were also aware that

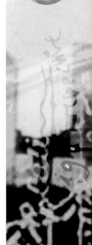

how something was said was sometimes as important as what was said, so they also studied the use of visual cues such as gestures and tone of voice to deliver oral arguments. Today, concern with gestures and other visual cues used to persuade an audience is encompassed in visual rhetoric, which could be defined as the use of images or other visual elements as argument.

Supreme Court Justice Ruth Bader Ginsburg, for example, wears different jabots, or collars, with her black robe to visually communicate her opinion of different court decisions. In this, she differs from the other justices who tend to wear similar collars, no matter their stance on a court ruling.

In an interview with Katie Couric, Justice Ginsberg decoded her jabots. She wears a studded black velvet collar when she issues a dissenting opinion about a court ruling. She wears her favorite, a white beaded jabot from South Africa, when she is not trying to send a message. When she wants to signal her agreement with the majority court opinion, she wears a beaded gold lace jabot.

As a student, you can train yourself to be aware of visual clues expressed in clothing choices such as messages on T-shirts, colors of men's ties, or women's preferences of jeans or dresses.

Ruth Bader Ginsberg's dissent jabot.

The favorite jabot from Cape Town, South Africa.

The majority opinion collar.

Activity 1.11 • Decoding Clothing Choices as Visual Rhetoric

In a small group, review these discussion questions in consideration of Supreme Court Justice Ruth Bader Ginsberg's choice of jabots or collars.

1.   Search the internet using the keywords "Ruth Bader Ginsberg jabot." What other jabots do you find? What do you think of her choices to indicate her agreement or dissent with the court decision on a case?

2.   Discuss your own clothing choices in your small group. Are you making a rhetorical statement when you choose your clothes for work, class, or leisure time? How so?

3.   Find an example of a rhetorical clothing choice on the Internet or in a magazine or newspaper. Bring it to class and explain to your group what the person is conveying with his or her clothing. Choose your group's most interesting example and present it to the class.

Activity 1.12 • Keep a Commonplace Book

Ancient rhetoricians performed speeches with little warning, often to advertise their services as teachers of rhetoric. Thus, they frequently memorized arguments about specific topics that could be adapted to the audience and situation on a moment's notice. They called these memorized arguments "commonplaces." Commonplace books are an outgrowth of the Greek concept of commonplaces, but they are a little different. They became popular in the Middle Ages as notebooks in which individuals would write down quotes or ideas about a particular topic. These notations might later be used to generate an idea for a composition. In more modern times, people have created commonplace books in the form of scrapbooks in which they collect quotes as well as drawings and clippings. Thus, they become a record of a person's intellectual life and can be saved for later reference.

For this class, take a notebook, perhaps one with a colorful or interesting cover, and keep notes, quotes, vocabulary words, and clippings related to the topics discussed in class. As your instructor directs, this commonplace book may be graded as evidence of class participation, or it may be a private journal. Take a look at the commonplace books shown here for ideas. Be creative and enjoy adapting this ancient journal form to record ideas that interest you.

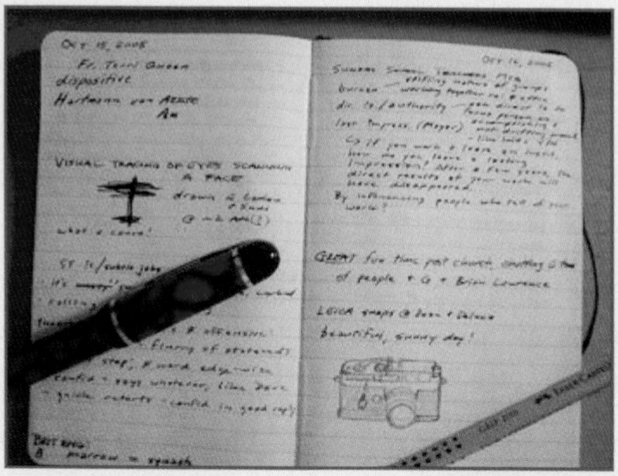

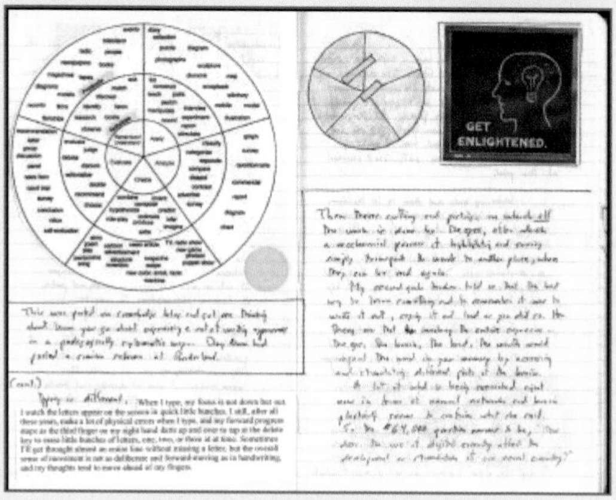

For thousands of years, people have been keeping commonplace books, a kind of journal or diary in which the author includes quotes, drawings, and images.

Activity 1.13 • Create Your Own Blog

Compose

Create your own blog by using a blog platform site such as *Tumblr*, *Blogger*, *WordPress*, or *LiveJournal* to create and publish it. Read the help screens for instructions on how to create your blog. Your design choices should reflect your personality. Keep in mind, though, that you are building an "academic self," so all the topics you write about should be of an academic nature and in an academic tone. Some students decide to have two blogs, one for their friends and one for professional networking, so you may want to do this, especially if you already have a blog.

During this class, you'll use the blog to explore different aspects of each chapter in the textbook (and other topics that your instructor directs). You can also blog about other topics related to your writing this semester, and you can link to other blogs that you think your readers would find interesting.

After you have created the look of your blog, write a first entry in which you introduce yourself to your readers. You might include your major, your college, and something interesting that might attract readers to your blog.

End of the Year... My Favorite Memory

May 15, 2011

Exactly one week ago, I was at my graduation ceremony receiving my college degree. Normally, graduating would be the last thing a student would do before summer vacation however I am still at CMC working away. You see, me and my RA crew had to stay in the residence halls for a few days after graduation to close down the building. Although they left 2 days ago, I am still here working on a special project. Sitting in an empty 250 bedroom mansion has given me a lot of time to think about my year. With all this reminiscing, I tried to think of my favorite memory of 2nd semester. It was difficult to choose but my 2nd semester Sky Club trip was my favorite memory of all.

For our 2nd semester Sky Club trip, we went to the McDonald Observatory in Fort David Texas. This was the 2nd trip we took and it was my favorite. We embarked out on April Fools Day (no joke) and headed south towards Texas. It was nice because we took two 11 man vans and only had 14 people on the trip so the drive was very comfortable.

We stopped in several spots throughout the day and finally 15 hours later we arrived in the famous town of Fort Davis! We were all shocked to actually be in Texas because our amusement for the entire ski season in Steamboat was making fun of Texan tourists. Since we were now tourists in Texas, we began acting like tourists. Immediately we busted out cameras and took pictures of anything and everything we could see.

This student's blog incorporates some pictures in her entry about her favorite memory. She also designed the blog with a personal title and category tabs.

Vasquez, Blake. *Pounce.*

Chapter 2
Responding Rhetorically

Praxis in Action

Why I Annotate Readings

Isidro Zepeda
M.A. in English Composition and
Applied Linguistics & TESL
California State University, San
Bernardino

Annotations are maps that detail our journeys through texts. My annotations are not random; instead, they show my responses to a text. As I engage the words of a text with my own words, complex ideas become more accessible to me. My words leave my footprints on the text.

When I annotate, I converse with voices that have traveled similar paths before me, and this activity allows my own ideas to flourish. These ideas are possessed with more than pleasure; they have a purpose that completes a specific task I have set forth to accomplish. For me, annotations are not simply notes on a text—they are marks demonstrating how my ideas interact with other authors' ideas to produce

something new, even if it is just another idea. Our annotations also describe our uniqueness, since they represent how we view and interpret the world.

To annotate means to experience, at a more intimate level, the relationship between text and reader. The annotation process allows the reader to merge with the text—to become an active voice within the margins. In its most simplistic function, annotations help us keep track of all the ideas, connections, and realizations we have during our conversations with texts.

Later, when I am composing my own essay or article, and I wish to utilize quotes or paraphrases from a text I have annotated, the footprints of my words immediately draw me to the portions of the other text I previously found important. Then my annotations can lead to more than a voice in the margins. The words of my new text can engage the annotated text in a conversation of ideas.

Thinking Critically, Reading Rhetorically

Today we study texts to encourage students to develop the critical thinking skills essential for understanding the scientific method and for making effective judgments in the workplace and in civil life. This student-centered emphasis would have seemed strange to ancient Greek and Roman rhetoricians and their students. They believed that a rhetor's skill was best developed by honoring the skills of those who excelled in the past. Therefore, a large part of the educational process involved having students study the texts of well-regarded speeches, memorize and recite them, and model new compositions based on those speeches' approaches to topics and language style. As Isocrates explained,

> Since language is of such a nature that it is possible to discourse on the same subject matter in many different ways—to represent the great as lowly or invest the little with grandeur, to recount the things of old in a new manner or set forth events of recent date in an old fashion—it follows that one must not shun the subjects upon which others have composed before, but must try to compose better than they. ("Panegyricus")

Thus, students in ancient Greece or Rome would have been presented with a text, often read aloud by a teacher, and they would be asked to transcribe or copy it down with the idea that they would internalize the skills of the master rhetor who had originally given the speech. Then, they would be asked to write about the same subject in a way that built upon what they had learned from the master text but incorporated their own personal attitudes or perspectives.

Today, rather than being asked to model new compositions based upon the techniques of classic texts, students are asked to read texts carefully and then to engage in critical thinking and discussion about those texts.

Critical thinking involves considering issues thoughtfully and independently. Critical thinkers do not believe facts or opinions just because they are published—whether in newspapers, textbooks, on television, or on the Internet. Nor do they focus upon just understanding or memorizing information, as in facts and figures. Critical thinkers examine the reasoning behind the information in front of them, looking for premises and considering the inferences drawn from those premises. They are able to think for themselves, making logical connections between ideas, seeing cause and effect relationships, and using information to solve problems.

Activity 2.1 • Think about Critical Reading

Compose

Freewrite for five minutes about a controversial issue about which you have a strong opinion. Consider why you believe what you do about this issue. What outside influences or sources have influenced your position? In what ways has the opposing side also influenced what you believe about the issue?

After you finish freewriting, look back at what you have written and consider the social (other people, articles, videos, etc.) nature of the sources that have influenced you. In your group or as a class, discuss the influences—not the particular issues themselves—that have affected your opinion. How have you decided what to believe?

Reading rhetorically makes use of critical thinking skills, but it also involves looking at texts as arguments and evaluating them for validity, adequacy of evidence, and presence of bias. Moreover, reading rhetorically involves having a knowledge of rhetoric and specialized Greek terms such as *logos, pathos, ethos,* and *kairos*—words that were defined briefly in Chapter 1 and will be discussed more extensively in Chapter 3. Practice reading rhetorically as you read the following article.

Reading 2.1

Do You Know How Your Mascara is Made?

by Arna Cohen

Customers grabbing a late-morning cup of coffee in downtown Brussels caught a strange sight two years ago. Suddenly, across the street, on the grounds of the European Commission, there were rabbits everywhere.

Some seemed to emerge from nearby bushes. Others slipped out from behind city walls as pedestrians stopped to watch and curious faces peered down from of-

Worldwide, activists protest the use of laboratory animals to test cosmetics, according to "Do You Know How Your Mascara is Made?" The article has a tag line that reads, "Across the globe, countless animals continue to suffer in painful tests simply to bring new skin creams, hair dyes, and other nonessential cosmetics to market. But the cruelty-free campaign is leading the charge to ban cosmetic animal testing worldwide by engaging consumers and companies, rewriting laws, and advancing the science of safety testing."

The article was printed in All Animals, *a publication of the Humane Society. The magazine aims to bring to the public stories about the Humane Society and the humane movement.*

Arna Cohen, the author, is online editor and producer for the Companion Animals Division, Humane Society of the U.S.

fice windows. And then, right there on an open stretch of sidewalk, on a Wednesday in June, those rabbits began to dance.

As a happy burst of music piped out over a nearby sound system—"Saturday night, I feel the air is getting hot"—27 advocates in white rabbit costumes stepped, hopped, clapped, and spun in unison. Reporters snapped photos. A few onlookers began to move with the song. And atop a stone wall, two women unfurled a large white banner: "350,000 Petition for EU Cosmetics to be Cruelty-Free in 2013."

The flash mob gathered to shine a spotlight on the issue of cosmetics animal testing in the European Union—one white rabbit representing each member country. "It attracted quite a lot of attention, as you might imagine," says Wendy Higgins, remembering a round of applause as the dancing concluded. The local media even asked for an encore, to capture more footage.

Immediately afterward, Humane Society International and Lush cosmetics company delivered stack upon stack of signatures to the European health commissioner, calling on him to support a March 2013 ban on the sale of animal-tested cosmetics.

"It was quite an emotional event, I have to say. I had a tear in my eye," says Higgins, HSI European communications director." This had a real sense of meaning, and it was such a joyful event. But all of us knew, for animals in laboratories being tested on for cosmetics, there is no joy. There is no happy moment. And we were there, speaking up for them."

The eventually successful petition was one in a series of rapid-fire victories achieved recently by HSI and The HSUS's Be Cruelty-Free Campaign. Last year alone, Israel banned the sale of all newly animal-tested cosmetics, India prohibited animal tests of cosmetics within its borders, and China announced that it will no longer require animal testing for domestically manufactured nonmedicated cosmetics. In South Korea, the government invested more than $150 million to establish the country's first nonanimal testing center, further committing to accept alternative methods for safety assurance of medicated cosmetics such as sunscreens and anti-wrinkle creams.

Progress has been most striking in the European Union: Five months after those white rabbits danced their jig in Belgium, the health commissioner stated he would fully implement the March 2013 ban on the import and sale of cosmetics newly tested on animals or containing ingredients tested on animals, regardless of where such tests are conducted. With an EU testing ban already in place since 2009, the 2013 sales ban marked the final piece in a 20-year struggle by advocates to remove cruelty from the beauty equation there, and the domino that is knocking down barriers worldwide, says Troy Seidle, HSI director of research and toxicology.

"With the EU closing its doors to animal-tested cosmetics, the beginning of the end of global cosmetics cruelty is within our grasp. It is a major moral milestone in the history of ending cosmetics animal testing."

Pascaline Clerc, HSUS senior director of animal research issues, adds that the EU decision has wider implications for animal testing of noncosmetic products such as paint, coffee sweeteners, and household cleaners. "This is the first step in replacing animals used for toxicity testing in general. People can see that it can be done."

An animated bunny is taken from the wild and imprisoned in a research laboratory. He is locked in a full-body restraint system and a chemical is applied to his eyes, which blister and turn red.

A rabbit-costumed flash mob marches toward EU headquarters in Brussels in June 2012, bearing 350,000 signatures against cosmetics animal testing. Exposing the cruelty behind the beauty industry has been the focus of intense efforts by the animal protection movement for decades, marked by boycotts, protests, petitions, and extraordinary levels of consumer participation.

Photo Credit: Virginia Mayo/Associated Press

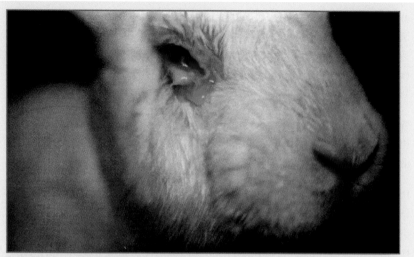

Pain-filled lives and deaths are the fate of rabbits and other animals used for cosmetics testing. Alternative methods are gaining traction thanks to a growing recognition that animal tests are poor predictors of how substances will affect people.

Photo Credit: PETA

Bright Eyes, a video created by HSI partner Choose Cruelty Free Australia, is based on a true story (with creative license: Unlike the animated specimen, laboratory rabbits are not obtained from the wild; they're purpose-bred for research). For 70 years, rabbits have been the go-to animal for the Draize eye irritation test the video depicts. They spend their short lives undergoing the procedure without anesthetic before being killed when no longer "useful."

The Draize test is only one in a litany of toxicity tests performed on animals, each more horrifying than the last. In the acute oral toxicity test, the needle of a syringe is forced down the throat of a rat and a massive dose of the test substance injected into her stomach to determine the amount that causes death. The animal can experience diarrhea, convulsions, bleeding from the mouth, seizures, and paralysis. The same procedure is used to assess smaller amounts in repeated dose toxicity tests, which last daily for one to three months or longer.

In carcinogenicity tests, rats and mice are exposed to substances daily for up to two years to see if they develop tumors; reproductive toxicity tests involve daily exposure of pregnant rats and up to two generation of pups, often by force-feeding (a method that seems doubly unnecessary given that most personal care products are applied to the skin). Even tests that aren't measuring fatal doses ultimately end in death, notes Catherine Willett, HSUS director of regulatory toxicology, risk assessment, and alternatives:

"Oftentimes you need to kill the animal to see what has actually happened at the microscopic level." Typical killing methods include asphyxiation, neck-breaking, and decapitation.

A dubious science underpins the physical and psychological suffering endured by animals in laboratories, as results of tests done on rodents and rabbits are poor predictors of a substance's effect on humans. Spurred by widening acknowledgment of these limitations, scientists are increasingly focused on developing state-of-the-art, human-relevant, animal-free alternatives.

The days of the Draize test, for one, look to be numbered. Many governments approve the use of cow or chicken corneas left over from the meat industry for certain types of eye irritancy tests. The next generation of tests will use human cells, such as a new artificial cornea under development by Japanese researchers that could ultimately replace rabbits entirely. Preliminary evaluations of the tissue have obtained results that more closely predict effects on human eyes than animal tests have.

Meanwhile, the number of rabbits used in skin irritation and corrosion tests is being reduced thanks to computer modeling analyses and other techniques. Skin cells can be grown in petri dishes, says Willett: "You add two or three different kinds of cells to an artificial scaffold, and they start to form tissues that look and behave just like living tissues"—imitating skin on body parts as varied as the nose, trachea, and lungs. And Procter & Gamble scientists recently developed the first nonanimal method for skin allergy testing; chemicals are assessed in test tubes for their allergic reactivity according to the amount of depletion they cause in proteins known as peptides.

As critical as these developments are, an emerging body of research is seeking to transcend such one-on-one test replacements with a more exhaustive approach that focuses on predicting chemical pathways in the human body. "Where does the chemical enter the body? How does it enter the body?" says Willett: "Does it bind to a receptor and cause a cascade of things to happen in the cell? Does it chemically modify a protein?

"And you can actually map this out from many different kinds of chemicals that cause different kinds of reactions," she continues. "You can actually get a pretty decent idea of what a chemical is going to do based on the biological pathway it affects. It's a completely different way of thinking about testing than has ever been done before. People who know about this are very excited about it."

Governments have embraced the changes, with agencies such as the FDA, EPA, and Department of Defense investing in complex computer models, "organs on a chip," and other technologies, says Willett. "Similar investment is being made around the world, in the European Union, Japan, Brazil, Korea, and elsewhere."

Where alternative testing methods are not available, companies can create new cosmetics by choosing among thousands of ingredients that have been tested in the past and proven to be safe.

Taken together, these options provide a counter argument to industry claims that animal testing is the only possible way to assess safety. "Now that we've had the technical progress, the politicians have become—well, they've lost sympathy," says Seidle.

The EU import and sales ban was the initial focus of the Be-Cruelty Free Campaign, a global push to rewrite laws, train technicians in alternative testing methods, and engage consumers and corporations. Stalled for years, an EU testing ban was originally passed in 1993, with a five-year phase-in period, but the cosmetics industry managed to secure delay after delay, claiming that it needed more time to replace animals in testing. Finally, in 2009, all animal testing of finished cosmetics and their ingredients was prohibited within EU borders; a ban on sales of products animal-tested elsewhere was slated to go into effect in 2013.

But in 2012, it again appeared that the cosmetics industry might impede progress. So HSI delivered the European health commissioner a large Valentine's Day card from singer Leona Lewis, asking him to have a heart for animals. They held meetings with policymakers. They asked European citizens to send postcards in support. And then, immediately following the purposely upbeat, positive white rabbit event, they brought 350,000 signatures to that pivotal June meeting, including ones from celebrities such as Ricky Gervais, Kesha, Sir Roger Moore, and Chrissie Hynde.

"Even though only two HSI lobbyists were allowed into the meeting, they weren't in that room alone," Higgins says. "They said that when they stepped into that room, they felt the hands of those 350,000 people on their shoulders, spurring them on. And that's what it's all about. That's what all of the petition-collecting was all about, was that moment where we could say: We're watching. Europe is waiting for you to do this."

Nine months later, they had their ban. "We probably would have been look-ing at more delays if our campaign hadn't been there to really hold the EU's feet to the flame," says Seidle.

With the mission accomplished in Europe, the Be Cruelty-Free Campaign is working to achieve similar progress in other lucrative sales markets: Brazil, South Korea, Russia. In India, dedicated personnel hired with funds from a Lush grant recruited Bollywood stars and thousands of consumers to help HSI pressure officials to replace animal tests with alternative methods in the country's regulations of cosmetics manufacturing. "We went as far as we could with the Bureau of Indian Standards," says Seidle, "and from there we engaged some lead members of parliament and really just ratcheted up the heat with a very high-impact public campaign, which got the drug control-ler's attention, and he personally went in with our letter in hand and said, 'Yes, we're just going to do this; get it done.'"

In June, HSI launched Be Cruelty-Free China, turning its focus to a criti-cal battleground where the government has required all cosmetics for sale, both domestically produced and imported, to be safety-tested on animals in government laboratories, and where in recent years the lure of huge prof-its—$24 billion spent on cosmetics and personal care items in 2012—has proven irresistible to Mary Kay and other companies that had been cruelty-free for decades.

Decisions by these companies to surrender their principles have outraged their customers. When Urban Decay, a popular cruelty-free company, an-nounced that it would sell in China, thousands expressed anger through email, social media, and online petitions, prompting company executives to reverse course.

Seeking to bring this element of popular pressure to bear on the govern-ment, HSI partnered with three Chinese organizations, "one that's very con-nected politically, one that's very media-wise, and one that's a youth social media organization," says Seidle. Advocates began spreading the cruelty-free message on the Chinese social media platform Weibo, with more than 500 million users, while press releases began naming companies that refuse to sell in China because of the testing policy.

"We've been actively disseminating information to the Chinese consumers for the first time ever," says Seidle. "No one has ever done that before, to explain this is how your cosmetics are being tested; this is what's involved;

this is what the idea of cruelty-free means." The European Union health commissioner applied additional leverage, meeting with Chinese officials to discuss animal testing as a barrier to trade.

A significant breakthrough came in November, when the China Food and Drug Administration announced that it would allow domestic cosmetics manufacturers to opt out of mandatory animal testing in favor of using previously collected ingredient safety data and possibly alternative test methods accepted by EU regulators—allowing Chinese goods to be sold in the world's largest cosmetics market. The Institute for In Vitro Sciences is now training Chinese scientists in alternative methods, thanks to an $80,000 grant from HSI, The HSUS, and the Human Toxicology Project Consortium.

The change comes into force in June and doesn't yet apply to imported cosmetics or to "special-use" products like hair dyes, sunscreens, and antiperspirants. But in meetings with HSI, the CFDA has indicated that, after the change has been implemented and assessed, it may be extended to the other categories. Companies are still free to continue animal testing if they so choose, so HSI's next focus will be to persuade regulators to ban the tests altogether.

In small ways, consumers have shown their approval of the government's change of heart. In Dalian, a port city in northeast China, animal advocates adorned with rabbit ears held several events that attracted 2,700 people, hundreds of whom signed HSI's Be Cruelty-Free China pledge and a petition supporting the government's plans. A tiny percentage of a huge populace, but notable in a nation not known for freedom of expression.

In the U.S., the state of cosmetics testing is somewhat of a different story. Even with the availability of cutting-edge technology, even with years of safety data on thousands of chemicals, even with no legal requirements that cosmetics be tested on animals, many American companies continue the practice in part because it's what they've always done.

Fear of lawsuits is a factor in their conservatism, says The HSUS's Willett. In our litigious society," people will sue the company and they will sue the FDA. Not only do you have to convince the regulators that the method you used to evaluate your chemical was sound, but you have to make it legally defensible. Because animal tests are the historical measure that we've used, people feel that they're on safer ground."

And profit sings its siren song. The bulk of animal testing these days is done in the lucrative field of anti-aging products that claim to reduce wrinkles, lighten brown spots, or lift sagging skin. The chemical ingredients in these treatments affect the body's structure, thus pushing them into the category of over-the-counter drugs and, if an ingredient has never been used before, making it subject to mandatory animal testing (see "What's in a Name," p. 20).

"It's so sad that these animals are dying for . . . the myth that we can hold back the march of time," says Lush ethics director Hilary Jones." Companies sell that myth and sell us these miracle ingredients that disappear two or three months later, to be replaced by a new miracle ingredient, all of them tested on animals."

With a strong industry lobby keeping a legislative ban on animal testing a nonstarter, the Be Cruelty-Free Campaign's focus in the U.S. has been on public education. According to a 2013 poll, a majority of Americans oppose animal testing of cosmetics, and they actually feel safer if alternatives are used instead. But even so, consumers here simply aren't as engaged, or informed, as they have been in the EU, says The HSUS's Clerc. "When we started this campaign, people were surprised that animal testing was still around. They thought we had moved beyond that."

Reaching out especially to a new generation concerned about what they put in and on their bodies, the campaign engages music, television, and film stars to spread the message through Twitter and public service announcements. It recently teamed with Miss DC 2013 Bindhu Pamarthi, who announced she was willing to compete barefaced in the Miss America 2014 pageant if it would draw attention to her platform of ending cosmetics animal testing. Although Pamarthi didn't ultimately compete barefaced and didn't ultimately win the crown, she did get a Facebook shout-out from R.E.I.G.N., the pageant's makeup partner, which honored her "thought provoking platform" and called her "a beyond beauty inspiration to us all."

The campaign also partners with bloggers who search out cruelty-free cosmetics and personal care products, doing intensive detective work on manufacturers before making recommendations. On Jen Mathews's My Beauty Bunny blog, every item is tested on staff members before being recommended to readers. Today, the blog receives 100,000 views a month, while 140,000 people follow along on Facebook. But Mathews's reach extends beyond the known numbers, with the blog winning multiple awards and featured in magazines and on television, radio, and websites.

Mathews began supporting animal welfare in college. "I was one of those college students who was posting things on billboards all over campus and the faculty were constantly taking them down." She would put animal rights fliers in her bill payment envelopes, "doing everything I could, grass roots, to get the message out. [. . .] Now I'm able to take that to the Web."

While Mathews's mission is to show consumers that cruelty-free beauty products are high quality, affordable, and widely available, Clerc focuses within the industry, seeking examples to share with companies that want to adopt humane business models. The strategy, she says, "is to find those companies that have done the right thing from the beginning and prove they can still be profitable; they can innovate without animal testing."

One such company is Biao, whose laboratory evaluates skin care compounds for safety using technology such as gene chips that allow mass in vitro cell testing. Founder Nicole Baldwin's entrepreneurial journey began as a little girl, when she suffered serious burns on her face, neck, and chest after upsetting a pot of boiling water on herself. Her grandmother, who was a nurse at the time, created a treatment from botanicals and other natural products, using formulas that had been passed down to her from her own mother.

Years later, when Baldwin was stationed with the U.S. Army in Afghanistan, her skin suffered again, this time from stress, dust, and the extreme temperatures of the arid desert climate. When none of the commercial products she tried provided relief, Baldwin decided to develop her own skincare line. Returning home to Houston after her tour, she became a licensed aesthetician.

A second tour of duty took Baldwin back to Afghanistan, where, using her grandmother's remedies and her own experience as inspiration, she began to create face and body treatments formulated with sustainable organic plant oils and extracts. She named the line Biao—an acronym for "beautiful inside and out"—as a tribute to her grandmother, whose care healed not just Baldwin's skin but her self-esteem and confidence. "I am following in her footsteps," Baldwin said in an interview with ABC News, "and I'm very glad that at 81 years old she's able to see me do this."

Baldwin attributes her cruelty-free philosophy to her relationship with her childhood pet, a German shepherd abandoned by his previous owners. After she saved Spicy from choking on a chicken bone, Baldwin says he "followed behind me everywhere. When I would awake for school, he would be in . . . my bedroom door. . . . When I would ask him to get me a newspaper, he would go get it. . . . I discovered that animals were so similar to humans. Spicy knew that I had saved his life." Experiencing this kind of bond, Baldwin couldn't fathom subjecting an animal to the cruelty of testing.

Prai Beauty, a skincare company founded in 1999 by HSUS board member Cathy Kangas, shares its cruelty-free status as a key component of its sales pitch on the home shopping networks where it sells in the U.S. and six countries. Kangas says a survey following the product launch found that "the most overwhelming thing that excited [customers] . . . was it being cruelty-free. It really mattered to 72 percent of all of our customers."

The financial success of Prai, with $30 million in annual sales, and other companies founded on humane principles, such as Paul Mitchell, Aubrey Organics, and Burt's Bees, clearly demonstrates that cruelty-free can be good business—business that the cosmetics industry can no longer profitably ignore. "Companies that are still testing on animals will soon lose money and market shares," notes Clerc. And now, the stakes are even higher for those selling in countries that have taken a stand against animal testing. "Those companies will see those markets slipping away from them if they don't move away from animal testing rapidly."

Activity 2.2 • Analyze "Do You Know How Your Mascara is Made?"

Collaborate

In your small group, discuss the following questions, and then report your group's opinion(s) to the class.

1. After reading "Do You Know How Your Mascara is Made?" identify the problem the author is concerned with.

2. What is the author arguing in the article?

3. What evidence of animal testing does the author offer? Is it sufficient to support the argument?

4. What laws or changed laws does the author mention that lend credibility to the argument?

5. Does the argument appeal primarily to *ethos, pathos,* or *logos*? How so?

6. Who published the article? Does the organization have a particular bias?

Compose

Activity 2.3 • Why Is Activity 2.2 Critical Reading?

After your group completes Activity 2.2, freewrite for five minutes about the questions you answered in your group in response to Activity 2.2. What do those questions ask you to do that is reading critically?

Ways of Reading Rhetorically

Reading theorist Louise Rosenblatt suggests a technique for analyzing written texts—particularly those with few visual cues other than words on paper or a computer screen. She says that we take the pattern of verbal signs left by the author and use them to recreate the text, not in the exact way the author perceived the text, but guided by it.

So, as we read, there is a constant stream of response to the text. However, Rosenblatt says that even as the reader is recreating the text, he or she is also reacting to it. Thus, there are two interacting streams of response involved as the person moves through the text. The reader, rather than being a passive receptor for the author's text, actually participates in the creative process during reading.

However, we read differently depending on the text and the occasion. For example, if you take a paperback novel on an airplane trip, you probably read simply for entertainment and to pass the time in the air. If you read *King Lear* for a literature class, you read for the plot, characterization, and other elements that you know will be discussed in class. If you read a chapter in your chemistry textbook before an exam, you are focusing on remembering concepts and details that might be on the test. Reading as a writer is another type of reading. You examine the text with an eye for the choices the writer made when crafting the text, such as whether the writer begins with a narrative introduction, a quote from a noted authority, or a startling statement. You notice, for example, what people are mentioned in the text, either as authorities or participants in activities.

Rosenblatt also makes a useful distinction between two main kinds of reading—aesthetic reading and efferent reading.[1] In **aesthetic reading**, the reader is most interested in what happens "during the reading event, as he fixes his attention on the actual experience he is living through," according to Rosen-

---

1. Rosenblatt, Louise Michelle. "Efferent and Aesthetic Reading." *The Reader, the Text, the Poem: The Transactional Theory of the Literary Work*, Southern Illinois UP, 1994, pp. 22-47.

blatt. Readers focus upon the ideas, images, and story of the text that evoke an aesthetic experience in the moment of reading. **Efferent readers**, in contrast, read to learn from the text, and, thus, according to Rosenblatt, "concentrate on the information, the concepts, the guides to action, that will be left with him when the reading is over."

Reading rhetorically is efferent reading, focusing not on the experience of reading but on the information the text conveys and upon the way an argument is established and supported in a text. Some arguments are written in an engaging style that is a pleasure to read, while others are written in a highly emotional tone that arouses a visceral response in the reader. A text that inspires aesthetic reading must sometimes be read several times in order for the reader to focus on the structure of the argument beneath the creative language.

Some theorists say that critical thinking is "thinking about thinking" or "reasoning about reasoning," and that is exactly what reading rhetorically involves— reasoning about whether or not a text presents a reasoned argument. A good way to begin reading rhetorically is to be aware of the essential elements of an argument and identify these elements in the text you are evaluating.

The elements of an argument include a debatable issue, clearly stated, for which an audience is to be persuaded. Without an issue, a text may be simply informative, rather than persuasive. Those individuals or groups holding a position may be considered biased toward that position. For example, the reading in this chapter, "Do You Know How Your Mascara is Made?" was published by the Humane Society and expresses a clear argument against the use of animals for testing cosmetics. Because the Humane Society has a stated agenda about animal rights, the article should not, then, be the only source cited in an academic essay about the issue of animal testing in the production of cosmetics. An argument about this issue, put forward in academic writing, should be backed by additional reliable evidence from sources that are unbiased— independent articles not written by the Humane Society. The use of biased sources for support evidence can lead to a biased argument. Moreover, to be fair and complete, an argument must contain an acknowledgment of opposing argument(s). Otherwise, the reader may be left with unanswered questions about why alternatives are not considered. And finally, a well-written argument features a conclusion, which may include a call to action.

See the Checklist of Essential Elements in an Argument on the next page.

Checklist of Essential Elements in an Argument

☑ **A debatable issue.** By definition, for a text to be an argument, there must be at least two sides that can be asserted and supported.

☑ **A clearly stated position, claim statement, or thesis.** Arguments assert different kinds of claims, such as taking a position on an issue of fact, asserting a cause and effect relationship, declaring the value of some entity, or advocating for a solution to a problem; but, in each case, after you read the argument, you should be able to restate or summarize the position, claim, or thesis in one or two sentences.

☑ **An audience.** To evaluate an argument, you need to know the original intended audience or place of publication, so that you can decide if the argument takes into account the audience's attitudes, background, and other factors. Ask yourself, for example, if the writer is assuming too much or too little background knowledge on the part of the audience or if the writer is using language that assumes the reader's agreement on the issue when that assumption is not warranted.

☑ **Evidence from reliable sources.** Quotes, statistics, and other evidence should be credited to reputable sources, even if your text is not a document that offers academic-style citations. The evidence should be sufficient to support the author's position or thesis.

☑ **Acknowledgment of the opposing argument.** A good rhetorician does not ignore any potential weaknesses in the argument. It is better to acknowledge points in favor of the opposing argument and then, if possible, refute the opposition's strong points than it is to allow an audience to poke holes in an argument.

☑ **A conclusion and/or call to action.** An argument can be concluded in a variety of effective ways, but it is important to note that it does, indeed, conclude. The conclusion can be a call to action on the part of the audience, but it should not be the beginning of an additional argument that is not supported by the evidence presented.

The Web Means the End of Forgetting

by Jeffrey Rosen

Several years ago, Stacy Snyder was a fairly typical 25-year-old college student training to be a teacher. That all changed forever when she did something that she probably thought was harmless fun—she posted a photo of herself on a social network site. In this article published in The New York Times, *Jeffrey Rosen uses Snyder's case to illustrate how notions of privacy are changing because of the ever-growing presence and popularity of social networking sites. What is even more alarming, according to Rosen, is that photos and information, once posted on the web, are there forever. The web does not forget, and this lack of forgetting is changing society's ability to forgive and forget.*

You may enjoy posting status updates about your life on a Facebook or Twitter account; however, with employers increasingly conducting background checks on such sites, it's very important to be careful about what you choose to post. This includes status updates, photographs, and videos. If you read the following article carefully, you may never look at social networking sites quite the same again.

Four years ago, Stacy Snyder, then a 25-year-old teacher in training at Conestoga Valley High School in Lancaster, Pa., posted a photo on her MySpace page that showed her at a party wearing a pirate hat and drinking from a plastic cup, with the caption "Drunken Pirate." After discovering the page, her supervisor at the high school told her the photo was "unprofessional," and the dean of Millersville University School of Education, where Snyder was enrolled, said she was promoting drinking in virtual view of her underage students. As a result, days before Snyder's scheduled graduation, the university denied her a teaching degree. Snyder sued, arguing that the university had violated her First Amendment rights by penalizing her for her (perfectly legal) after-hours behavior. But in 2008, a federal district judge rejected the claim, saying that because Snyder was a public employee whose photo didn't relate to matters of public concern, her "Drunken Pirate" post was not protected speech.

When historians of the future look back on the perils of the early digital age, Stacy Snyder may well be an icon. The problem she faced is only one example of a challenge that, in big and small ways, is confronting millions of people around the globe: how best to live our lives in a world where the Internet records everything and forgets nothing—where every online photo, status update, Twitter post and blog entry by and about us can be stored forever. With websites like LOL Facebook Moments, which collects and shares embarrassing personal revelations from Facebook users, ill-advised photos and online chatter are coming back to haunt people months or years after the fact.

Examples are proliferating daily: there was the 16-year-old British girl who was fired from her office job for complaining on Facebook, "I'm so totally bored!!"; there was the 66-year-old Canadian psychotherapist who tried to enter the United States but was turned away at the border—and barred permanently from visiting the country—after a border guard's Internet search found that the therapist had written an article in a philosophy journal describing his experiments 30 years ago with LSD. According to a recent survey by Microsoft, 75 percent of U.S. recruiters and human-resource professionals report that their companies require them to do online research about candidates, and many use a range of sites when scrutinizing applicants—including search engines, social networking sites, photo- and video-sharing sites, personal websites and blogs, Twitter and online gaming sites. Seventy percent of U.S. recruiters report that they have rejected candidates because of information found online, like photos and discussion-board conversations and membership in controversial groups.

Technological advances, of course, have often presented new threats to privacy. In 1890, in perhaps the most famous article on privacy ever written, Samuel Warren and Louis Brandeis complained that because of new technology—like the Kodak camera and the tabloid press—"gossip is no longer the resource of the idle and of the vicious but has become a trade." But the mild society gossip of the Gilded Age pales before the volume of revelations contained in the photos, video and chatter on social media sites and elsewhere across the Internet. Facebook, which surpassed MySpace in 2008 as the largest social-networking site, now has nearly 500 million members, or 22 percent of all Internet users, who spend more than 500 billion minutes a month on the site. Facebook users share more than 25 billion pieces of content each month (including news stories, blog posts and photos), and the average user creates 70 pieces of content a month. There are more than 100 million registered Twitter users, and the Library of Congress recently announced that it will be acquiring—and permanently storing—the entire archive of public Twitter posts since 2006.

In Brandeis's day—and until recently, in ours—you had to be a celebrity to be gossiped about in public: today all of us are learning to expect the scrutiny that used to be reserved for the famous and the infamous. A 26-year-old Manhattan woman told *The New York Times* that she was afraid of being tagged in online photos because it might reveal that she wears only two outfits when out on the town—a Lynyrd Skynyrd T-shirt or a basic black dress. "You have movie-star issues," she said, "and you're just a person."

We've known for years that the web allows for unprecedented voyeurism, exhibitionism and inadvertent indiscretion, but we are only beginning to understand the costs of an age in which so much of what we say, and of what others say about us, goes into our permanent—and public—digital files. The fact that the Internet never seems to forget is threatening, at an almost existential level, our ability to control our identities; to preserve the option of reinventing ourselves and starting anew; to overcome our checkered pasts.

In a recent book, "Delete: The Virtue of Forgetting in the Digital Age," the cyberscholar Viktor Mayer-Schönberger cites Stacy Snyder's case as a reminder of the importance of "societal forgetting." By "erasing external memories," he says in the book, "our society accepts that human beings evolve over time, that we have the capacity to learn from past experiences and adjust our behavior." In traditional societies, where missteps are observed but not necessarily recorded, the limits of human memory ensure that people's sins are eventually forgotten. By contrast, Mayer-Schönberger notes, a society in which everything is recorded "will forever tether us to all our past actions, making it impossible, in practice, to escape them." He concludes that "without some form of forgetting, forgiving becomes a difficult undertaking."

It's often said that we live in a permissive era, one with infinite second chances. But the truth is that for a great many people, the permanent memory bank of the web increasingly means there are no second chances—no opportunities to escape a scarlet letter in your digital past. Now the worst thing you've done is often the first thing everyone knows about you.

The Crisis—and the Solution?

Concern about these developments has intensified this year, as Facebook took steps to make the digital profiles of its users generally more public than private. Last December, the company announced that parts of user profiles that had previously been private—including every user's friends, relationship status and family relations—would become public and accessible to other users. Then in April, Facebook introduced an interactive system called Open Graph that can share your profile information and friends with the Facebook partner sites you visit.

What followed was an avalanche of criticism from users, privacy regulators and advocates around the world. Four Democratic senators—Charles Schumer of New York, Michael Bennet of Colorado, Mark Begich of Alaska and Al Franken of Minnesota—wrote to the chief executive of Facebook,

Mark Zuckerberg, expressing concern about the "instant personalization" feature and the new privacy settings. In May, Facebook responded to all the criticism by introducing a new set of privacy controls that the company said would make it easier for users to understand what kind of information they were sharing in various contexts.

Facebook's partial retreat has not quieted the desire to do something about an urgent problem. All around the world, political leaders, scholars and citizens are searching for responses to the challenge of preserving control of our identities in a digital world that never forgets. Are the most promising solutions going to be technological? Legislative? Judicial? Ethical? A result of shifting social norms and cultural expectations? Or some mix of the above? Alex Türk, the French data protection commissioner, has called for a "constitutional right to oblivion" that would allow citizens to maintain a greater degree of anonymity online and in public places. In Argentina, the writers Alejandro Tortolini and Enrique Quagliano have started a campaign to "reinvent forgetting on the Internet," exploring a range of political and technological ways of making data disappear. In February, the European Union helped finance a campaign called "Think B4 U post!" that urges young people to consider the "potential consequences" of publishing photos of themselves or their friends without "thinking carefully" and asking permission. And in the United States, a group of technologists, legal scholars and cyberthinkers are exploring ways of recreating the possibility of digital forgetting. These approaches share the common goal of reconstructing a form of control over our identities: the ability to reinvent ourselves, to escape our pasts and to improve the selves that we present to the world. [. . .]

In the near future, Internet searches for images are likely to be combined with social-network aggregator search engines, like today's Spokeo and Pipl, which combine data from online sources—including political contributions, blog posts, YouTube videos, web comments, real estate listings and photo albums. Increasingly these aggregator sites will rank people's public and private reputations. In the Web 3.0 world, Michael Fertik, a Harvard Law School graduate, predicts people will be rated, assessed and scored based not on their creditworthiness but on their trustworthiness as good parents, good dates, good employees, good baby sitters or good insurance risks.

One legal option for responding to online setbacks to your reputation is to sue under current law. There's already a sharp rise in lawsuits known as Twittergation—that is, suits to force websites to remove slanderous or false posts. Last year, Courtney Love was sued for libel by the fashion designer Boudoir Queen for supposedly slanderous comments posted on Twitter, on Love's MySpace page and on the designer's online market-place-feedback page. But even if you win a U.S. libel lawsuit, the website doesn't have to take the offending material down any more than a newspaper that has lost a libel suit has to remove the offending content from its archive.

Some scholars, therefore, have proposed creating new legal rights to force websites to remove false or slanderous statements. Cass Sunstein, the Obama administration's regulatory czar, suggests in his new book, "On Rumors," that there might be "a general right to demand retraction after a clear demonstration that a statement is both false and damaging." (If a newspaper or blogger refuses to post a retraction, they might be liable for damages.) Sunstein adds that websites might be required to take down false postings after receiving notice that they are false—an approach modeled on the Digital Millennium Copyright Act, which requires websites to remove content that supposedly infringes intellectual property rights after receiving a complaint.

As Stacy Snyder's "Drunken Pirate" photo suggests, however, many people aren't worried about false information posted by others—they're worried about true information they've posted about themselves when it is taken out of context or given undue weight. And defamation law doesn't apply to true information or statements of opinion. Some legal scholars want to expand the ability to sue over true but embarrassing violations of privacy—although it appears to be a quixotic goal.

Daniel Solove, a George Washington University law professor and author of the book, *The Future of Reputation*, says that laws forbidding people to breach confidences could be expanded to allow you to sue your Facebook friends if they share your embarrassing photos or posts in violation of your privacy settings. Expanding legal rights in this way, however, would run up against the First Amendment rights of others. Invoking the right to free speech, the U.S. Supreme Court has already held that the media can't be prohibited from publishing the name of a rape victim that they obtained from public records. Generally, American judges hold that if you disclose something to a few people, you can't stop them from sharing the information with the rest of the world.

That's one reason that the most promising solutions to the problem of embarrassing but true information online may be not legal but technological ones. Instead of suing after the damage is done (or hiring a firm to clean up our messes), we need to explore ways of preemptively making the offending words or pictures disappear.

Zuckerberg said in January to the founder of the publication TechCrunch that Facebook had an obligation to reflect "current social norms" that favored exposure over privacy. "People have really gotten comfortable not only sharing more information and different kinds but more openly and with more people, and that social norm is just something that has evolved over time," he said.

However, norms are already developing to recreate off-the-record spaces in public, with no photos, Twitter posts or blogging allowed. Milk and Honey, an exclusive bar on Manhattan's Lower East Side, requires potential members to sign an agreement promising not to blog about the bar's goings on or to post photos on social-networking sites, and other bars and nightclubs are adopting similar policies. I've been at dinners recently where someone has requested, in all seriousness, "Please don't tweet this"—a custom that is likely to spread.

But what happens when people transgress those norms, using Twitter or tagging photos in ways that cause us serious embarrassment? Can we imagine a world in which new norms develop that make it easier for people to forgive and forget one another's digital sins? [. . .]

Perhaps society will become more forgiving of drunken Facebook pictures in the way Samuel Gosling, the University of Texas, Austin, psychology professor says he expects it might. And some may welcome the end of the segmented self, on the grounds that it will discourage bad behavior and hypocrisy: it's harder to have clandestine affairs when you're broadcasting your every move on Facebook, Twitter and Foursquare. But a humane society values privacy, because it allows people to cultivate different aspects of their personalities in different contexts; and at the moment, the enforced merging of identities that used to be separate is leaving many casualties in its wake. Stacy Snyder couldn't reconcile her "aspiring-teacher self" with her "having-a-few-drinks self": even the impression, correct or not, that she had a drink in a pirate hat at an off-campus party was enough to derail her teaching career.

That doesn't mean, however, that it had to derail her life. After taking down her MySpace profile, Snyder is understandably trying to maintain her privacy: her lawyer told me in a recent interview that she is now working in human resources; she did not respond to a request for comment. But her success as a human being who can change and evolve, learning from her mistakes and growing in wisdom, has nothing to do with the digital file she can never entirely escape. Our character, ultimately, can't be judged by strangers on the basis of our Facebook or Google profiles; it can be judged by only those who know us and have time to evaluate our strengths and weaknesses, face to face and in context, with insight and understanding. In the meantime, as all of us stumble over the challenges of living in a world without forgetting, we need to learn new forms of empathy, new ways of defining ourselves without reference to what others say about us and new ways of forgiving one another for the digital trails that will follow us forever.

Activity 2.4 • Discuss "The Web Means the End of Forgetting"

Explore

In your small group, discuss the following questions, and then report your group's opinion(s) to the class.

1. What is the significance of the article's title?

2. What does Rosen mean when he suggests that in the future Stacy Snyder may be an icon?

3. What is the main point in Rosen's essay? What is he arguing?

4. Does Rosen offer sufficient evidence to make you take his argument seriously? Why or why not?

5. Are you a member of any social networking sites? What can you do in order to protect your reputation?

6. A woman interviewed in the article said, in regard to being tagged in online photos, "you have movie-star issues—and you're just a person." If you are a member of any social networking sites, do you tag friends in photos? Is it important to be careful about this? Why or why not?

Collaborate

Activity 2.5 • Apply the Checklist of Essential Elements in an Argument

Apply the Checklist of Essential Elements in an Argument (discussed on p. 50) to "The Web Means the End of Forgetting" or another text that your instructor specifies. In your group or individually, check off the following elements and be prepared to explain your selections.

- A debatable issue

- A clearly stated position, claim statement or thesis

- An audience

- Evidence from reliable sources

- Acknowledgment of the opposing argument

- A conclusion and/or call to action

Explore

Activity 2.6 • What Is the Current State of Identity Protection in Social Networking Sites?

In your group, explore news, watchdog, and government sites to see if any new laws or other protections have been implemented to safeguard individuals posting personal information on the web. Report what you learn to the class.

Close Reading of a Text

Rhetorical reading involves careful and patient attention to the text, even reading the text several times. Following are several strategies for close reading rhetorically. You do not need to use all of the reading strategies suggested for each essay you read, but as you begin to read rhetorically, you should try all of the strategies at least once to see which ones supplement your natural reading and learning style.

1. **Learn about the author.** Knowing whether an author is a biologist, a professional writer, or a politician can guide your expectations of the essay. If you are reading in a magazine or journal, you can often discover information in the contributor's notes at the beginning or end of the essay or at the beginning or end of the magazine. Many books have a dust jacket or a page giving a short biography of the author. As you learn about the author, jot down any impressions you may have about the author's purpose in writing the essay. Does the author have an obvious agenda in promoting a certain viewpoint on the topic?

2. **Skim the text.** Once you've gotten to know the author a little, it is helpful to read the essay quickly and superficially by reading the introduction, the first sentence in every paragraph, and the conclusion. Read quickly. When you skim a text, you are not trying to understand it. You are preparing for the more careful read that will follow. If the essay tells a story, skimming will give you a good sense of the chronology of the story. When is the story taking place? How much time seems to pass? If the essay is argumentative, skimming will provide knowledge of the basic structure of the argument and will introduce you to the main points of support. If the essay is primarily informative, you will learn some of the important distinctions and classifications the author uses to organize the information.

    It may be interesting to note whether you can get the gist of the reading by skimming. Has the writer provided topic sentences for paragraphs or sections? If so, the writer is trying to make his or her message easily accessible.

3. **Explore your own knowledge and beliefs on the subject.** Make a list of what you already know about the topic of the text. Then, make a list of what you believe about this topic. Finally, make a note beside each entry that marks where that information or belief came from.

4. **Reflect on the topic.** The final step before reading is reflecting on what you expect from the essay before you begin a careful reading. What does the title lead you to expect from the essay? Does your quick glance at the essay seem to support the title? How do you feel about the essay so far? Does it anger you, interest you, bore you? Do you think you have any experience that relates to the essay? Will your experience and the author's experience lead you to the same conclusions? One effective way to reflect is to freewrite on the topic of the essay. Exploring what you know before you embark on a careful reading of the essay can deepen your responses.

5. **Annotate.** Read the essay slowly, thinking about what meaning the author is trying to convey. It is a good idea to annotate as you read, particularly points that seem important and/or raise questions in your mind. If you don't want to write in your text, try photocopying assigned essays so you can annotate them. You'll probably develop your own system of annotation as you begin to use this technique more often, but here are some basic guidelines to help you begin your annotations.

▌ Underline sentences, phrases, and words that seem important to the essay.

▌ Circle words you don't know but think you understand from the context. You can look them up later to see if the dictionary definition matches the definition you assumed from the context.

▌ Write questions in the margins. If the margins aren't large enough to write a complete question, a couple of words to remind you of what you were thinking and a question mark will do. You can also write brief comments in the margins, again just a few words to remind you of your thoughts.

▌ Number or put check marks in the margin by major points. Careful annotation of each point in the margin will help you later if you choose to outline.

▌ Use arrows, lines, and symbols in the margins to connect ideas in the essay that seem related or depend on each other.

▌ Note transitions, sentence structures, examples, topic sentences, and other rhetorical moves that seem particularly effective in the essay by writing a brief comment or an exclamation mark in the margin next to the underlined text.

See Figure 2.1 on page 65 for an example of an annotated article.

6. **Outline.** An excellent way to distill the meaning of a text is to create an informal outline of the argument. If, as part of annotating the essay, you jot down the main subject of each paragraph in the margin, this will allow you to see the organization of the essay and outline it easily. An outline should list the focus of the essay and track how that focus unfolds paragraph by paragraph. If you are outlining a narrative essay, the outline will probably follow the chronology of the events. Outlining an informative essay, you might find that the outline tracks the steps of a process or reveals divisions and classifications. Outlining an argumentative essay, you'll probably find your outline works to prove a thesis by making statements which support that thesis, raising objections and refuting them, or, perhaps, proposing solutions to solve a problem.

7. **Freewrite about the text.** Another way to distill the meaning of a text after you have read it carefully is to lay the essay aside and freewrite for a few minutes about the content and purpose of the essay. If you have not tried freewriting before, it is easy. You simply put your pen to

the paper, focus the topic in your mind, and write whatever comes to mind about the topic for a set period of time, perhaps five minutes. If you cannot think of anything to write, you write, "I can't think of anything to write," and then you continue writing what is in your mind. You may find it helpful to begin your freewriting by writing, "This essay is about . . ." and continue writing, explaining to yourself what you think the essay is about.

8. **Summarize the text.** Write a summary of what you consider to be the primary meaning of the text. Your summary should answer certain questions about claims, support, purpose, and audience.

    ▌ What is the author of the essay trying to show or prove (claim)?

    ▌ What does the writer use to convince me that he or she is well in-formed or right (support)?

    ▌ Why did the writer choose to write this essay (purpose)?

    ▌ Who is the author addressing or writing for (audience)?

    To write a clear summary, you have to understand the essay. You might test your understanding by reading the essay again and deciding whether your summary is accurate. Writing summaries helps you understand your assignments and prepares you for the numerous summaries you will complete.

Checklist for Close Reading of a Text

☑ Learn about the author.

☑ Skim the text.

☑ Explore your knowledge and beliefs on the subject.

☑ Reflect on the topic.

☑ Annotate the text.

☑ Outline the text.

☑ Freewrite about the text

☑ Summarize the text.

Reading 2.3

Have you read health-scare articles like "If You've Ever Eaten Pizza, You'll Want to Read About the Toxin That Is Pretty Certainly Ravaging Us From the Bowels Outward" or "This Common House-hold Item Is Definitely Killing You, Says a New Study"? Can you trust the information presented by such sensationalized articles? Maybe not. According to the Atlantic *article, "The Point When Science Becomes Publicity," the actual studies that are the basis of such articles may blur the distinction between a possible association and a definite connection. Moreover, psychology professor Petroc Sumner traced the source of numerous extreme articles to press releases written by public relations departments of the researchers' own universities rather than to the news media or the researchers themselves.*

James Hamblin, M.D., the article's author, is a senior editor at the Atlantic, *where he writes a health column.*

The Point When Science Becomes Publicity
by James Hamblin, M.D.

One of the sources of academic disdain for popular health media is its reputation for sensationalism and exaggeration. "If You've Ever Eaten Pizza, You'll Want to Read About the Toxin That Is Pretty Certainly Ravaging Us From the Bowels Outward" or "This Common Household Item Is Definitely Killing You, Says a New Study"—when the actual study only posited that a "possible association may potentially exist" between, say, exposure to antibacterial soap and liver disease in a handful of mice who were exposed to more antibacterial soap than any human could ever dream of using, even if they washed their hands literally every time they went to the bathroom.

Petroc Sumner, a professor of psychology at Cardiff University in Wales, has been trying to pinpoint exactly where exaggeration in science reporting comes from. At what level, in the ladder from lab data to news headline, are most inaccuracies introduced?

Yesterday Sumner and colleagues published some important research in the journal BMJ that found that a majority of exaggeration in health stories was traced not to the news outlet, but to the press release—the statement issued by the university's publicity department.

"The framing of health-related information in the national and international media has complex and potentially powerful impacts on healthcare utilization and other health-related behavior," Sumner and colleagues write. "Although it is common to blame media outlets and their journalists for news perceived as exaggerated, sensationalized, or alarmist, most of the inflation detected in our study did not occur de novo in the media but was already present in the text of the press releases."

The goal of a press release around a scientific study is to draw attention from the media, and that attention is supposed to be good for the university, and for the scientists who did the work. Ideally the endpoint of that press release would be the simple spread of seeds of knowledge and wisdom; but it's about attention and prestige and, thereby, money. Major universities employ publicists who work full time to make scientific studies sound engaging and amazing. Those publicists email the press releases to people like me, asking me to cover the story because "my readers" will "love it." And I want to write about health research and help people experience "love" for things. I do!

Across 668 news stories about health science, the Cardiff researchers compared the original academic papers to their news reports. They counted exaggeration and distortion as any instance of implying causation when there was only correlation, implying meaning to humans when the study was only in animals, or giving direct advice about health behavior that was not present in the study. They found evidence of exaggeration in 58 to 86 percent of stories when the press release contained similar exaggeration. When the press release was staid and made no such errors, the rates of exaggeration in the news stories dropped to between 10 and 18 percent.

Even the degree of exaggeration between press releases and news stories was broadly similar.

Sumner and colleagues say they would not shift liability to press officers, but rather to academics. "Most press releases issued by universities are drafted in dialogue between scientists and press officers and are not released without the approval of scientists," the researchers write, "and thus most of the responsibility for exaggeration must lie with the scientific authors."

In an accompanying editorial in the journal, Ben Goldacre, author of the book *Bad Science,* noted that bad news tends to generate more coverage than good and that less rigorous observational studies tend to generate more coverage than robust clinical trials, probably due to the applicability of the subject matter to lay readers.

Guidelines for best practices already exist among academic journals and institutional press officers, he notes, "but these are routinely ignored." So Goldacre corroborates Sumner's argument for accountability: that academics should be held responsible for what's said in the universities' press releases that publicize said academics' research. The press releases will often be read much more widely than the actual journal article, yet many academics take little to no interest in them. Instead, writing an accurate press release should be considered part of the scientific publication process.

"This is not a peripheral matter," writes Goldacre, citing research that has found that media coverage has important effects on people's health behaviors and healthcare utilization, and even on subsequent academic research.

He notes that Sumner was "generous" to avoid naming particular offenders in this study. But Sumner did share with me some of the less egregious examples by email. In one case, a journal article read[,] "This observational study found significant associations between use of antidepressant drugs and adverse outcomes in people aged 65 and older with depression." The press release went on to read[,] "New antidepressants increase risks for elderly." There are of course many reasons why taking antidepressants would be associated with worse outcomes. For example, people with worse symptoms to begin with are more likely to take antidepressants.

"It is very common for this type of thing to happen," said Sumner, "probably partly because the causal phrases are shorter and just sound better. There may be no intention to change the meaning."

There is also, almost always, an implied causal relationship when reporting on a correlation. Every time we note a correlation in anything we publish on this site, at least one of our fair commenters will jump to point out that correlation is not causation. That comment may as well just auto-populate on any article that involves science. Which is fine—even though we're deliberate in not mistaking the relationships for causal—because why even report on a correlation if you don't mean to imply in some way that there is a chance there could be causation?

I asked Sumner how he felt about the press release for his study, because I thought that would be kind of funny.

"We were happy with our press release," he said. "It seemed to stick closely to the article and not claim causal relationships, for example, where we had not."

Appropriately reported scientific claims are a necessary but not sufficient condition in cultivating informed health consumers, but misleading claims are sufficient to do harm. Since many such claims originate within universities, Sumner writes, the scientific community has the ability to improve this situation. But the problem is bigger than a lack of communication between publicists and scientists. The blame for all of this exaggeration is most accurately traced back, according to the researchers, to an "increasing culture of university competition and self-promotion, interacting with the increasing pressures on journalists to do more with less time."

In his ivory tower, in his ivory cap and gown, the academic removes his ivory spectacles just long enough to shake his head at the journalists who are trying to understand his research. The headlines and tweets are wretched misappropriations. Wretched! The ink-stained journalists shake their ink-stained heads in time at the detached academics, at the irrelevance of work written in jargon behind giant paywalls where it will be read by not more than five to seven people, including the nuclear families of the researchers. The families members who, when the subject of the latest journal article comes up at dinner, politely excuse themselves.

But the divide is narrowing every day.

"Our findings may seem like bad news, but we prefer to view them positively," Sumner and colleagues conclude. "If the majority of exaggeration occurs within academic establishments, then the academic community has the opportunity to make an important difference to the quality of biomedical and health-related news."

Figure 2.1 • Example of Close Reading Annotation

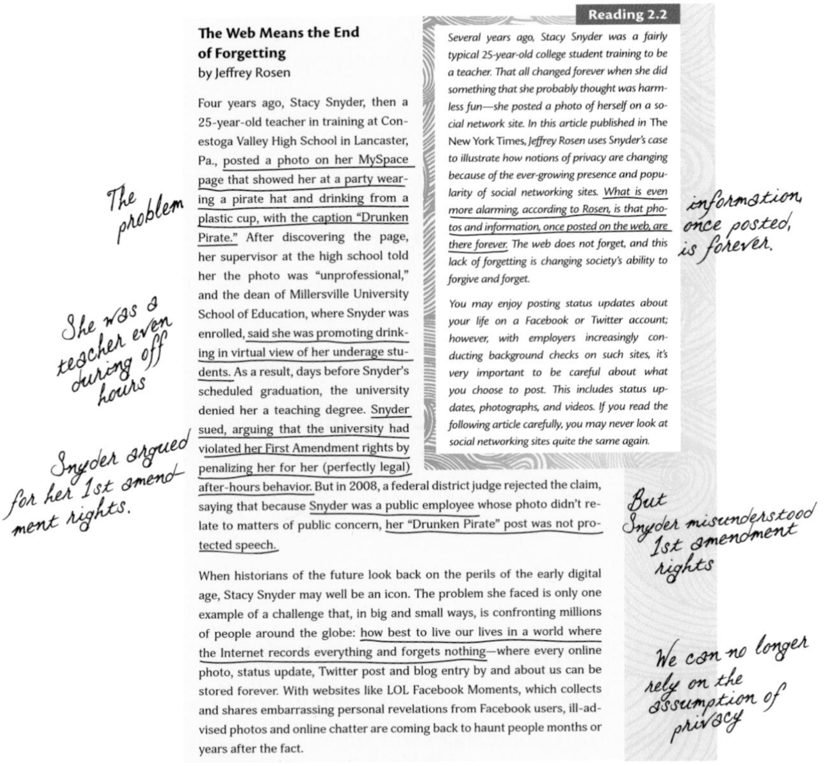

The Web Means the End of Forgetting
by Jeffrey Rosen

Four years ago, Stacy Snyder, then a 25-year-old teacher in training at Conestoga Valley High School in Lancaster, Pa., posted a photo on her MySpace page that showed her at a party wearing a pirate hat and drinking from a plastic cup, with the caption "Drunken Pirate." After discovering the page, her supervisor at the high school told her the photo was "unprofessional," and the dean of Millersville University School of Education, where Snyder was enrolled, said she was promoting drinking in virtual view of her underage students. As a result, days before Snyder's scheduled graduation, the university denied her a teaching degree. Snyder sued, arguing that the university had violated her First Amendment rights by penalizing her for her (perfectly legal) after-hours behavior. But in 2008, a federal district judge rejected the claim, saying that because Snyder was a public employee whose photo didn't relate to matters of public concern, her "Drunken Pirate" post was not protected speech.

When historians of the future look back on the perils of the early digital age, Stacy Snyder may well be an icon. The problem she faced is only one example of a challenge that, in big and small ways, is confronting millions of people around the globe: how best to live our lives in a world where the Internet records everything and forgets nothing—where every online photo, status update, Twitter post and blog entry by and about us can be stored forever. With websites like LOL Facebook Moments, which collects and shares embarrassing personal revelations from Facebook users, ill-advised photos and online chatter are coming back to haunt people months or years after the fact.

Reading 2.2

Several years ago, Stacy Snyder was a fairly typical 25-year-old college student training to be a teacher. That all changed forever when she did something that she probably thought was harmless fun—she posted a photo of herself on a social network site. In this article published in The New York Times, Jeffrey Rosen uses Snyder's case to illustrate how notions of privacy are changing because of the ever-growing presence and popularity of social networking sites. What is even more alarming, according to Rosen, is that photos and information, once posted on the web, are there forever. The web does not forget, and this lack of forgetting is changing society's ability to forgive and forget.

You may enjoy posting status updates about your life on a Facebook or Twitter account; however, with employers increasingly conducting background checks on such sites, it's very important to be careful about what you choose to post. This includes status updates, photographs, and videos. If you read the following article carefully, you may never look at social networking sites quite the same again.

Handwritten annotations:
- The problem
- She was a teacher even during off hours
- Snyder argued for her 1st amendment rights.
- information, once posted, is forever.
- But Snyder misunderstood 1st amendment rights
- We can no longer rely on the assumption of privacy

Compose

Activity 2.7 • Apply Close Reading to a Text

Apply the eight steps of close reading to "The Point When Science Becomes Publicity" or another reading that your instructor specifies. Review the annotation example in Figure 2.1 to begin. Next, make a copy of the text, so that you can annotate it. Then answer these questions in a small group or individually.

1. What can you learn about the author by reading a headnote or doing a search on Google or Wikipedia? Explain briefly.

2. Skim the text of the reading. What did you learn about the purpose of the text?

3. Briefly explain your own knowledge or beliefs about the subject.

4. Reflect on the topic before you read it thoroughly. What does the title lead you to expect? How do you feel about the text so far? Freewrite for five minutes, and then summarize your freewriting in a few coherent sentences.

5. Annotate then outline the essay, then freewrite for five minutes before summarizing the text. Follow the instructions on pp. 59–61 for each step.

Explore

Activity 2.8 • Discuss "The Point When Science Becomes Publicity"

According to James Hamblin, articles published in popular health media often sensationalize scientific findings. Use these questions to inform your discussion of "The Point When Science Becomes Publicity" in a small group.

1. What do you think is the source of the sensationalism in this article?

2. In effect, university publicity departments misuse rhetoric to attract reporters' attention. According to Hamblin's argument, why do they do this? Why is it a misuse of rhetoric?

3. Identify one of the examples Hamblin gives of sensationalized health news.

4. In your group, brainstorm other articles you may have read that sensationalize health news. Alternatively, find examples on the Internet. Report the most interesting ones to the class.

The Rhetorical Triangle

When reading a text or listening to a speech, keep in mind the three parts of the rhetorical triangle—writer, audience, and subject (see Figure 2.2). Each of these can be framed as a question.

Figure 2.2 • The Rhetorical Triangle

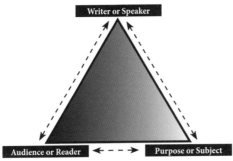

Writer or Speaker

Audience or Reader ← – – → Purpose or Subject

▌ Who is the **writer**? What is the impression the writer wants to make on the audience? What does the writer do to establish credibility (*ethos*)? How does the writer create common ground with the audience?

▌ Who is the **intended audience**? How would a logical appeal influence the audience? An ethical appeal? An emotional appeal? What does the audience anticipate in terms of organization and format of the presentation or paper? What is the extent of their knowledge about the subject, and do they have prejudices or preferences?

▌ What is the **purpose** of the communication? In the case of an argument, the purpose is to persuade. Is that the case with this reading? Is it clear what the writer wants to persuade the audience to believe or to do? Is the request phrased in a logical manner?

Activity 2.9 • Apply the Rhetorical Triangle

Explore

For each of the readings presented thus far in the textbook, identify the speaker, the audience, and the purpose. Then, analyze how each of those elements affects the content of the reading.

▌ "'Columbusing': The Art of Discovering Something that Is Not New," Chapter 1, p. 8.

▌ "Microsoft Just Laid Off Thousands of Employees with a Hilariously Bad Memo," Chapter 1, p. 15.

▌ "The Sleepover Question," Chapter 1, p. 20.

▌ "The Gettysburg Address," Chapter 1, p. 28.

▌ "Do You Know How Your Mascara is Made?" Chapter 2, p. 37.

▌ "The Web Means the End of Forgetting," Chapter 2, p. 51.

▌ "The Point When Science Becomes Publicity," Chapter 2, p. 62.

Compose

Activity 2.10 • Write a Summary

Summarizing is an excellent technique to use when preparing for an exam or researching for an essay. It allows you to discern the main points of a text to see what is beneficial for you to know for the exam or paper.

With a classmate, search for an article from a newspaper or magazine that presents a strong argument. Read the article, and list the main points individually. After you've listed the main points, put them into paragraph form.

Beware of the temptation to add your own analysis of what the text is saying. For example, if you are summarizing a scientist's article on global warming, you need to be careful not to reveal your personal opinion about whether or not global warming is occurring or whether or not human actions are to blame. In this assignment, you summarize only. You do not argue or analyze.

When you're finished, compare your summary with that of your partner.

Respond to Multimedia

Increasingly, young "politically minded viewers" are plugging into YouTube, Facebook, and comedy shows like *The Daily Show* and other alternative media instead of traditional news outlets. According to a *New York Times* article, surveys and interviews during the 2008 presidential election indicate that "younger voters tend to be not just consumers of news and current events but conduits as well—sending out emailed links and videos to friends and their social networks. And in turn, they rely on friends and online connections for news to come to them." **Word of mouth** (via email) is replacing traditional media as the major news filter, at least for young viewers. Moreover, in this new process, "viewers" or "writers of email" move seamlessly back and forth between email, text-messaging, television viewing, and Internet surfing, appreciating and sharing the choicest rhetorical pieces with others. "We're talking about a generation that doesn't just like seeing the video in addition to the story—they expect it," said Danny Shea, 23, the associate media editor for *The Huffington Post* (huffingtonpost.com). "And they'll find it elsewhere if you don't give it to them, and then that's the link that's going to be passed around over email and instant message." This multistream, cross-platform method of communication among younger viewers/readers is a fertile forum for rhetorical analysis.

Actually, the lines between oral, written, and visual "texts" have always been somewhat blurred. Speeches delivered orally in person or on television have a visual component, as the audience sees the speaker present the text. A written text is also, in a sense, visual because the audience's mind must process the little squiggles of ink on paper or on the computer screen into words. A visual text such as an advertisement or cartoon often includes written text, and, even if it does not, the image will inspire thoughts that are often distilled into language for expression. Reasonably, many of the same techniques used to analyze written and oral texts also can be applied to visual media (cartoons, advertisements, television, etc.).

Reading 2.4

Excerpt from "Flawless"
by Beyoncé and Chimamanda Ngozi Adichie

We teach girls to shrink themselves

To make themselves smaller

We say to girls,

"You can have ambition

But not too much

You should aim to be successful

But not too successful

Otherwise you will threaten the man."

Because I am female

I am expected to aspire to marriage

I am expected to make my life choices

Always keeping in mind that

Marriage is the most important

Now marriage can be a source of

Joy and love and mutual support

But why do we teach girls to aspire to marriage

And we don't teach boys the same?

We raise girls to see each other as competitors

Not for jobs or for accomplishments

Which I think can be a good thing

But for the attention of men

We teach girls that they cannot be sexual beings

In the way that boys are

Feminist: the person who believes in the social

Political, and economic equality of the sexes

"Flawless," the hit song from Beyoncé's fifth studio album, includes the voice of Nigerian novelist Chimamanda Ngozi Adichie delivering an excerpt from her 2012 TEDx Talk, "We Should All be Feminists." Beyoncé Giselle Knowles-Carter is a Grammy-award-winning singer, songwriter, and actress.

Adichie is the author of the acclaimed 2013 novel Americanah, *that Carolyn Kellogg of the* Los Angeles Times *calls "a smart and surprisingly funny take on race and gender in contemporary society." Adichie was awarded a MacArthur "Genius" Fellowship in 2008 after the publication of her novel,* Half a Yellow Sun, *which is set during Nigeria's Biafran War. Kellogg praises the inclusion of Adichie's excerpt in the middle of Beyoncé's song.*

Explore

Activity 2.11 • Respond to Song Lyrics

In a small group or on your own, explore these discussion questions in response to the excerpt from "Flawless" by Beyoncé and Chimamanda Ngozi Adichie.

1. What does Chimamanda Ngozi Adichie's excerpt (from her *TEDx Talk* "We Should All be Feminists") say about what society teaches girls? What does the message in the excerpt have to do with being a feminist?

2. On the Internet, locate the complete lyrics for Beyoncé's song "Flawless" and/or listen to the complete song. How do Beyonce's own lyrics compliment Adichie's excerpt?

3. What argument is Beyoncé making in her song "Flawless"?

4. What do you think of including a non-singing element such as this excerpt in the middle of a popular song? Does it add to or detract from the song's effect?

Collaborate

Activity 2.12 • Consider a Song as an Argument

In your small group, explore the Internet for a song that seems to make an argument, and answer the following questions. Share your findings with the class.

1. What message is the artist/group trying to transmit with the song?

2. What are some lyrics that help to support this message?

3. How would you describe the musical style of the song? In what ways does the style of singing and instrumentation help convey the rhetorical argument?

Respond to Visual Rhetoric

Methods of analyzing visual rhetoric draw upon several theoretical traditions. In art criticism, viewers may look for symbolism in an image or consider what meaning the artist was trying to convey. Semiotics views images as having intertextuality, as similar images come to have similar meanings, and those meanings may create similar emotions in the viewer. Rhetoricians, as you might expect, consider the argument that an image may present to a viewer. They think about how the subject of the image is presented in relation to other elements in the visual, how the image is cropped, and what types of lighting and colors are present. Rhetoricians also pay particular attention to the interplay between the visual image and any text that may appear with the image and how the two together construct an argument.

Courtesy BMW premium advertising

In the BMW advertisement shown above, for example, a beautiful blonde-haired young woman is presented without clothes and lying down with her hair artfully arranged in waves. *Salon* magazine reprinted a copy of the BMW advertisement, pointing out that, "in small print scrawled across her bare shoulder, it reads: 'You know you're not the first.' As your eyes drift to the bottom of the advertisement—and the top of her chest—you learn that it's an advertisement for BMW's premium selection of used cars."

Of course, sexual appeal has been used for decades to sell a whole range of products. However, what do you think is BMW's argument here? *Salon* thinks the ad is implying, "Used cars, used women" and that the ad gives a "whole new meaning" to BMW's slogan, printed in the ad: "Sheer Driving Pleasure."

The image that appears on the next page, surprisingly, isn't advertising a car. No, it is selling a community college, West Hills College, capitalizing on the idea that with all the money you would save by going to a community college, you could buy a nice car.

Courtesy West Hills College

Activity 2.13 • Interpret Advertisements

On your own, explore the rhetorical implications of the two advertisements referenced in this section using these discussion questions.

1. What is the symbolism of the beautiful young woman (presumably naked) posed as she is in the BMW advertisement?

2. What meaning do you think the tag line, "You know you're not the first," adds to the image? Then, when you realize that the image is an ad for BMW used cars, does your interpretation of this tag line's meaning change?

3. What are the creators of the West Hills College advertisement trying to say by showing the image of the student sitting on the car?

4. The use of fonts is another important element in transmitting a message in an advertisement. In the West Hills College ad, why are the words "and save" written in a different font and inserted with the caret?

5. As a college student, would you be convinced by the West Hills advertisement? Why or why not? What elements exist in the ad that would or would not convince you to attend the college mentioned?

6. Do you find the BMW advertisement amusing, objectionable, or appealing? Does it make you want to buy a used BMW?

Activity 2.14 • Find Advertisements with Effective Arguments

Bring to class an advertisement that you think makes an effective argument. It can be torn from a magazine or downloaded from the Internet. In your small group, evaluate each advertisement for its effectiveness in selling something, and choose the one with the most successful argument. Present your choice to the class along with an explanation of why you think it is effective.

Reading 2.5

Why Has Godzilla Grown?

by Lisa Wade

Recently, the Internet chuckled at the visual below. It shows that, since Godzilla made his first movie appearance in 1954, he has tripled in size.

Kris Holt, at PolicyMic, suggests that his enlargement is in response to growing skylines. She writes:

> As time has passed, buildings have grown ever taller too. If Godzilla had stayed the same height throughout its entire existence, it would be much less imposing on a modern cityscape.

This seems plausible. Buildings have gotten taller and so, to preserve the original feel, Godzilla would have to grow too.

Why has Godzilla grown over the years? One possible explanation is that buildings have grown taller, and Godzilla has grown to keep up. However, Godzilla has grown at a faster rate than skyscrapers, as you can see from the graphs "Godzilla Through the Years" and "History of the World's Tallest Skyscrapers." The most recent Godzilla is three times the size of the original, while today's tallest skyscraper is much less than three times the size of the Empire State Building, the tallest building at the time of the original Godzilla.

According to an article in Sociological Images by professor Lisa Wade, the best explanation is that the flood of advertising spawned by the Internet has resulted in advertisers resorting to shock value. The article quotes media guru Sut Jhally asking, "So overwhelming has the commercial takeover of culture become, that it has now become a problem for advertisers who now worry about clutter and noise. That is, how do you make your ads stand out from the commercial impressions that people are exposed to?"

You make Godzilla stand out by making her disproportionally large. Though the article doesn't use the term "visual rhetoric," that's what it is talking about. In today's media climate, for something, even Godzilla, to make a medial splash, it has to be bigger, weirder, more violent, or more gorgeous.

Godzilla through the Years

50 Meters	55 Meters	80 Meters	100 Meters	120-150 Meters
1954-1975, 2001	1999-2000, 2002-2003	1984-1989	1991-1995, 2004	2014

But rising buildings can't be the only explanation. According to this graphic, the tallest building at the time of Gozilla's debut was the Empire State Building, rising to 381 meters. The tallest building in the world today is (still) the Burj Khalifa. At 828 meters, it's more than twice as tall as the Empire State Building, but it's far from three times as tall, or 1,143 meters.

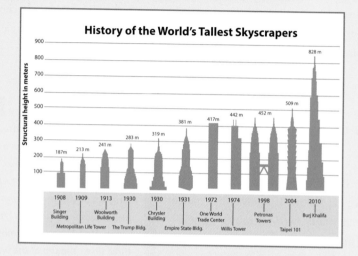

Is there an alternate explanation? Here's one hypothesis.

In 1971, the average American was exposed to about 500 advertisements per day. Today, because of the Internet, they are exposed to over 5,000. Every. Day.

Media critic Sut Jhally argues that the flood of advertising has forced marketers to shift strategies. Specifically, he says

So overwhelming has the commercial takeover of culture become, that it has now become a problem for advertisers who now worry about clutter and noise. That is, how do you make your ads stand out from the commercial impressions that people are exposed to.

One strategy has been to ratchet up shock value. "You need to get eyeballs. You need to be loud," said Kevin Kay, Spike's programming chief.

So, to increase shock value, everything is being made more extreme. Compared to the early '90s, before the Internet was a fixture in most homes and businesses, advertising—and I'm guessing media in general—has gotten more extreme in lots of ways. Things are sexier, more violent, more gorgeous, more satirical, and weirder.

So, Godzilla because, eyeballs.

Explore

Activity 2.15 • Consider Shock Value in Today's Cartoon Characters

After you read Wade's article, discuss the following in your group.

1. What argument does sociology professor Lisa Wade make about the growth of Godzilla's size in advertisements over the years?

2. If you accept Wade's argument, what does it have to do with visual rhetoric?

3. What other cartoon characters in advertisements or other media also have grown or otherwise changed because of a response to the pressure to stand out from the clutter and noise of today's media world?

4. How have other cartoon characters been altered for shock value?

Interaction between Texts and Images

Many of the texts we encounter in everyday life—in newspapers, magazines, and on the Internet—are not texts in isolation but texts combined with images. Indeed, when readers first glance at one of these media, likely their attention is caught first by photos, then by headlines. Only after being engaged by these attention-getting visual elements (for headlines are visual elements as well as written) are readers likely to focus on the written text. Student writers today, like professionals, have access to the use of visual elements in their compositions, and adding photos can not only catch the reader's attention but also emphasize particular points of an argument or create an overall mood.

Reading 2.6

Take a look at the images in this Rolling Stone *article by Andy Greene. Greene writes about a tribute record on Buddy Holly called* Rave *that several famous musical artists contributed to. Think about how Greene's choice of text and image pairings affect the rhetorical impact of the article.*

All-Star Rockers Salute Buddy Holly
by Andy Greene

All-Star Rockers Salute Buddy Holly

McCartney, Cee Lo, the Black Keys, Kid Rock and more cut killer covers disc

NOT FADE AWAY Holly in 1950. McCartney and Cee Lo recorded new songs commemorating Holly's 75th birthday.

When Buddy Holly died in a plane crash in 1959, he was just 22 years old and had been writing and recording songs for only about two years. But that music—including immortal hits like "Not Fade Away" and "Peggy Sue"—has had an incalculable impact on rock history. "He was a major influence on the Beatles," Paul McCartney told Rolling Stone recently. "John and I spent hours trying to work out how to play the opening riff to "That'll Be the Day," and we were truly blessed by the heavens the day we figured it out. It was the first song John, George and I ever recorded."

A half-century later, McCartney has returned to Holly's catalog, cutting a smoking rendition of "It's So Easy." It's one of 19 newly recorded Holly covers—by an all-star lineup including the Black Keys, My Morning Jacket, Kid Rock Fiona Apple, Patti Smith, and Lou Reed—for the tribute

disc *Rave on Buddy Holly*, spearheaded by Randall Poster, music supervisor of movies such as *The Royal Tenenbaums* and *I'm Not There*. "We wanted to commemorate Buddy's 75th birthday," Poster says. "I've used a lot of his songs in movies, and they're so powerful and so ripe for interpretation."

Florence and the Machine cut a New Orleans-flavored version of "Not Fade Away" while on tour in the Big Easy last year. "My grandmother took me to the musical *Buddy: The Buddy Holly Story* when I was a kid, and it changed my life," says singer Florence Welch. "When we were in New Orleans, we decided

it would be good to use the environment around us, so we brought in local Cajun musicians." Cee Lo Green tackled the relatively obscure "You're So Square (Baby, I Don't Care)." "We wanted to keep the rockabilly intact," he says. "But we broadened it and gave it a bit of something unique to me. There's something Americana about it, something country and something African."

Smith selected "Words of Love." "During the song she talks in Spanish and is sort of channeling [Holly's widow] Maria Elena Holly," says Poster. "It's so romantic and so novel. More times than not, we were just overwhelmed by the power of the renditions that we received." Despite Holly's extremely brief career, Poster thinks the set could have been even longer: "There's probably a half-dozen more songs we could have done. If I had more time and more of a budget, I would have kept on going."   ANDY GREENE

Explore

Activity 2.16 • Analyze Interaction between Texts and Images

Read the article, "All-Star Rockers Salute Buddy Holly," by Andy Greene, published in *Rolling Stone* magazine. Look at how the images and layout work together, and respond to these questions on your own.

1. What rhetorical purpose do the photos of these musicians achieve in relation to the article? Hint: think about the *ethos* (credibility, reputation, power) of these particular musicians, especially when they appear together on the page.

2. Consider the way the text is wrapped around the pictures. In particular, notice how this layout suggests a close relationship between Buddy Holly, Paul McCartney, and Cee Lo Green. What does this layout signify?

How to Make a Kindle Cover from a Hollowed Out Hardback Book

by Justin Meyers

Kindle users love reading. But let's face it—nothing compares to the feel of a book is in your hands.

Sure, Amazon's Kindle makes it possible to read more books, clears up a lot of shelf space, fits snugly in anyone's baggage and can actually be cheaper in the long run. But each reading feels the same. The only difference is the words you read and your reaction to them. You begin to miss that sometimes rough feel of a hardback book, along with the slick, almost slippery design of a paperback. Each book seems to have a smell of its own, something unique. And getting your hands dirty with ink from the finely written words was half the journey.

The Kindle erases that part of your reading experience. It feels the same, smells the same and even looks the same. Instead of turning pages, which is different sizes, thicknesses and colors from book to book, you're pressing the same button over and over again. In some ways, reading a classic on your Kindle actually devalues its adventure. But the eBook reader is convenient, practically weightless and serves up immediate literature consumption.

So where's the compromise?

Well, you can have the best of both worlds—sort of . . .

The author of the following article explains why you would want to make a Kindle cover out of an old book instead of buying a new Kindle cover. What does the article say are the drawbacks of the Kindle? Think about it. These instructions are an argument, saying in text and photos that as wonderful as the Kindle is, it does not satisfy the needs of a reader to touch and smell a book. The author attempts to rectify the Kindle's shortcomings through these instructions for making a cover out of a book.

Notice also how the author uses photos to illustrate his text. If you had just the text and no photos, following the instructions would be much more difficult.

[Twitter user] @ebonical has crafted the perfect Kindle case—out of a hard-cover book. Kindle cases can be expensive, so making a homemade Kindle cover is the perfect weekend project. And chances are you already have the perfect book for your Kindle collecting dust on your bookshelf. If not, you'll need to shop the local bookstores.

"I decided to carve out the pages of a printed book and thus complete the poetic circle of digital book readers destroying the printed word.

"Getting the right book turned out to be harder than I thought as most hard-cover books are designed to be a particular size and variance is slight. Too small and the edges would be brittle. Too large and it would just become a hassle and ruin the point of having the small digital reader in the first place. With some time spent scouring thrift shops and second hand book stalls I managed, with some luck, to find what seemed to be the right book."

So, then how do you actually make the Kindle book cover?

STEP 1 Gather the Materials

▌ Your perfectly-sized hardcover book

▌ Hobby PVA glue (polyvinyl acetate) or Elmer's white glue

▌ Paintbrush

▌ Scalpel, box cutter or other sharp utility knife

▌ Ruler

▌ Pencil

▌ More books (for use as weights)

STEP 2 Crafting Your Kindle Case

Getting your book ready for your Kindle is an easy process, though a lengthy one.

You begin by choosing where you want your hole to start. Once you have your spot picked, you use the paintbrush to spread the glue onto the edges of the pages where the hole will be cut. Use your extra books to weigh it down during the drying process.

When dry, open the book back up to your chosen starting point. Use the ruler and pencil to mark your hole the size of the Kindle. Once all marked, use your utility knife to start cutting on the outline. It's probably best to use your ruler as a straight edge to help guide the blade along, for a better, straighter cut. This is the longest step, because you have a lot to cut through. The time will vary depending on how deep your book is. I wouldn't recommend *War and Peace.*

Once you've gotten all the way to the back cover, the rest is easy. Just clean up the edges of your cuts as best you can, then use your paintbrush again to spread some glue along the cut edges.

TIP: When choosing your first page to cut, it's good to actually save it for later. Don't cut with the rest of them. When you have your hole fully cut open and have applied the glue, apply another thin line on the top border of your actual first page cut (essentially, the second page). Then close the book and add the weights to the top and let dry. Saving the first page helps reduce the chance of you accidentally gluing unwanted pages to cut ones, causing you to have to cut the pages you didn't want to cut to open the hole back up. Saving your first page makes it premeditated.

After fully dried, open it up and cut the final page (first page) to open the hole up. Then, you'll need to let it dry again, with the book open. After dried, that's it. You're done!

Activity 2.17 • Write and Illustrate Instructions

Write and illustrate your own set of instructions for an activity that includes an argument.

For example, during a lawn party at the White House, First Lady Michelle Obama served Carrot Lemonade to children who gave the drink rave reviews. Such a recipe could include an introduction explaining that creating healthy adaptations of popular foods and drinks for children only works if they taste good. Or, you might write instructions for how to remove geotags from photos before posting them on Facebook or other social networking sites.

In your instructions, you could explain that this process prevents people you don't know from learning where you took the picture—and possibly learning where you live if you took it at home. Your argument would be that it is important to protect your privacy when you post photos on the Internet.

Try out your instructions on a friend, so you are sure you have included all the necessary steps and illustrated them adequately. Don't forget to include a brief statement of your argument, as does the writer of the Kindle cover article.

Activity 2.18 • Summarize the Argument in Your Illustrations

Write one or more sentences summarizing your argument in the illustrations you wrote for Activity 2.17. For example, the author of "How to Make a Kindle Book Cover from a Hollowed Out Hardback Book" is arguing in his instructions that the Kindle is wonderful but does not completely satisfy the desire of a reader to touch and smell a book.

Activity 2.19 • Write on Your Blog

Read an article on the Internet related to a topic in which you're interested. Make sure the article has a substantial amount of text and related images. In your blog, discuss how the text and the images both contribute to the article's rhetorical message. Include the title of the article, the author, the name of the publication or web page, and a link to the article.

Activity 2.20 • Write in Your Commonplace Book

What do you read for fun? Magazines, blogs, books? Do you engage in what Louise Rosenblatt calls "aesthetic reading"? (See the section titled, "Ways of Reading Rhetorically") Write down a quote in your commonplace book from something that you have read for fun. First, reflect about what the quote means to you. Then, comment about why it is important to read things for fun and how that experience is different than reading to learn.

Compose

Glasscock, Megan. *I Don't Want to Die.*

Chapter 3

Persuading Rhetorically

Praxis in Action

If You Want to Write Well, Then Read

Amber Lea Clark, M.L.S. Student in Liberal Studies, Southern Methodist University

"Readers make the best writers." I can't tell you how many times my instructors have said those words. As I have become a reader, I have learned that this is true. Reading teaches me about the construction of stories and arguments. In a movie or TV show, I almost instantly know who did it or who not to trust based on previous movies or TV shows I've watched. The same goes for analyzing arguments. Through reading critically, I have learned to see when an author is trying to convince me by manipulating my feelings versus persuading me by providing all of the facts. I can distinguish between fair representation of an issue, embellishment of truth, and bitter sarcasm. Every text needs to be taken with a grain of salt, slowly simmered, and thought about before the final evaluation can be made.

This chapter provides sample essays that illustrate different types of rhetorical arguments or appeals—arguments from *ethos* (credibility), *pathos* (emotion), or *logos* (logic). I encourage you to read them carefully. What do you see? How has each writer used his or her credibility, your emotions, or logic to reach you—the audience? How would each essay be different if the author had chosen to emphasize a different appeal, or would that even be possible?

Sentence structure, word use, and argument construction—the ability to perform each of these writing tasks effectively comes from more than just the practice we get from completing an assignment. It comes from analyzing others' arguments—my classmates' and published authors'. It comes from thinking critically as I read. Does this convince me? What is the author using for sources? Is this logical or a logical fallacy? Had I not read how other writers construct their arguments, I would never have become a better writer. Start now; become a reader.

Discover the *Kairos*–The Opening for Argument

Kairos is a Greek word often translated as the right or opportune moment to do something, though it has no exact English translation. The first recorded use of the word *kairos* is in Homer's *Iliad*, where it appears as an adjective referring to an arrow striking the "deadliest spot" on the human body. When the word appears again later in Greek writing as a noun—a *kairos*—it retains this essential meaning as an opening or aperture. Twelve bronze axes with ring openings for wooden shanks are positioned in a line, so archers can practice by aiming at the *kairos* or ring opening, with the arrow passing down the line, through each ax. Clearly,

Ancient Greek archer

launching an arrow through the *kairos* of twelve axes placed a yard apart required strength, training, practice, and a precise visual and muscle awareness of place. When people today say, "I saw my opening, and I took it," they are conveying this meaning of *kairos* as an opening, combined with the idea of *kairos* as an opportunity.[1]

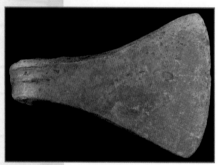

Ancient bronze ax with a ring hole for a wooden shank

Each time a rhetor (a speaker or writer) constructs an argument, he or she is working within the context of a certain moment, a particular time and place, that come together in a unique opportunity or opening for action—a *kairos*. A *kairos* both constrains and enables what a rhetor can say or write effectively in a particular situation. So, to compose the most effective text, a rhetor must do more than develop a thesis or statement of the main idea that takes a position about the subject—he or she must discover the *kairos* of the argument and its ramifications. What opportunities does the *kairos* present for making a persuasive argument, and what restrictions may be wise in consideration of the audience or occasion?

Use Kairos *to Make Your Own Argument*

Consider the following suggestions for determining the kairotic moment for your argument—the opening of sensitivity where you can shoot your metaphoric arrow.

▌ **Consider timeliness.** What is going on right now with the issue, and how can you emphasize that in an argument? For example, if you are writing

1. Rickert, Thomas. "Invention in the Wild: On Locating *Kairos* in Space-Time." *The Locations of Composition*, edited by Christopher J. Keller and Christian R. Weisser, SUNY, 2007, pp. 72-73.

about the death penalty, choose to write about the current cases on death row or the most recent person to be executed. Or, if your topic is about the unemployed exhausting their government benefits and you have, yourself, recently become unemployed, you can use your own experience as an illustration of the problem.

■ **Know your audience.** What are the characteristics of the audience? Do they agree with your position on the issue or not? What is their educational level and the extent of their knowledge about the subject? For example, if you are writing about immigration policy reform, does your audience believe there is a need for reform? Do they have personal experience with illegal or legal immigrants? You can judge the amount of background information you need to provide based upon the characteristics of your audience. Also, the most important members of the audience, so far as an argument is concerned, are not those who already agree with you but those who are neutral or even slightly opposed to your position but willing to listen. Be careful not to phrase your argument in ways that are insulting to people who do not agree with you, for if you do so, they will stop listening to you.

■ **Find a place to stand.** In the reading that follows, Dr. Martin Luther King, Jr. stood in front of the Lincoln Memorial as he gave his famous speech, "I Have a Dream." This location greatly impacts the speech and increases King's *ethos*, which we discuss in more detail below. You can make a similar rhetorical move, for example, if you live in a border community because you stand, metaphorically and physically, at an important juncture for issues such as immigration, free trade, and national security.

When Dr. Martin Luther King, Jr., gave his "I Have a Dream" speech, his words were carefully crafted to take into consideration the setting in front of the Lincoln Memorial. He said, "Five score years ago, a great American, in whose symbolic shadow we stand today, signed the Emancipation Proclamation." The words "five score" recall the "four score and seven years ago" of President Abraham Lincoln's words in the Gettysburg Address. And King also pointed out that he and his audience that day stood in the "symbolic shadow" of the president who signed the Emancipation Proclamation. In these ways, he made use of Lincoln's shadow to legitimize what he was saying about civil rights.

In other ways, however, the *kairos* of the moment limited what he could say. His audience included both the thousands of people in front of him who were dedicated to the cause of racial equality and also the audience of those millions watching on television who may or may not have agreed with his message.

Thus, the tone of his message needed to be subtly measured not to antagonize those among his audience, particularly the television audience, who may have opposed aspects of the civil rights movement such as school integration. However, he spoke to let both his supporters and his opponents know, "The whirlwinds of revolt will continue to shake the foundations of our nation until the bright day of justice emerges." Yes, King advocated nonviolent demonstrations, but they were demonstrations nonetheless; he was putting opponents on notice that the disruptions caused by demonstrations would continue "until justice emerges." King consistently took the high road while maintaining the power of the kairotic moment when he spoke. This is one reason why his words continue to be studied decades after his death.

Reading 3.1

Dr. Martin Luther King, Jr. delivered this speech on August 28, 1963, at the Lincoln Memorial in Washington, D.C., as part of the March on Washington for Jobs and Freedom. A Baptist minister, King received the Nobel Peace Prize in 1964 for his efforts to end racial discrimination through nonviolent means. He was assassinated in 1968.

I Have a Dream
by Dr. Martin Luther King, Jr.

I am happy to join with you today in what will go down in history as the greatest demonstration for freedom in the history of our nation.

Five score years ago, a great American, in whose symbolic shadow we stand today, signed the Emancipation Proclamation. This momentous decree came as a great beacon light of hope to millions of Negro slaves who had been seared in the flames of withering injustice. It came as a joyous daybreak to end the long night of their captivity.

But one hundred years later, the Negro still is not free. One hundred years later, the life of the Negro is still sadly crippled by the manacles of segregation and the chains of discrimination. One hundred years later, the Negro lives on a lonely island of poverty in the midst of a vast ocean of material prosperity. One hundred years later, the Negro is still languished in the corners of American society  and finds himself an exile in his own land. And so we've come here today to dramatize a shameful condition.

In a sense we've come to our nation's capital to cash a check. When the architects of our republic wrote the magnificent words of the Constitution and the Declaration of Independence, they were signing a promissory note to which every American was to fall heir. This note was a promise that all men, yes, black men as well as white men, would be guaranteed the "un-alienable Rights" of "Life, Liberty and the pursuit of Happiness." It is obvious today that America has defaulted on this promissory note, insofar as her citizens of color are concerned. Instead of honoring this sacred obligation, America has given the Negro people a bad check, a check which has come back marked "insufficient funds."

But we refuse to believe that the bank of justice is bankrupt. We refuse to believe that there are insufficient funds in the great vaults of opportunity of this nation. And so, we've come to cash this check, a check that will give us upon demand the riches of freedom and the security of justice.

We have also come to this hallowed spot to remind America of the fierce urgency of Now. This is no time to engage in the luxury of cooling off or to take the tranquilizing drug of gradualism. Now is the time to make real the promises of democracy. Now is the time to rise from the dark and desolate valley of segregation to the sunlit path of racial justice. Now is the time to lift our nation from the quicksands of racial injustice to the solid rock of brotherhood. Now is the time to make justice a reality for all of God's children.

It would be fatal for the nation to overlook the urgency of the moment. This sweltering summer of the Negro's legitimate discontent will not pass until there is an invigorating autumn of freedom and equality. Nineteen sixty-three is not an end, but a beginning. And those who hope that the Negro needed to blow off steam and will now be content will have a rude awakening if the nation returns to business as usual. And there will be neither rest nor tranquility in America until the Negro is granted his citizenship rights. The whirlwinds of revolt will continue to shake the foundations of our nation until the bright day of justice emerges.

But there is something that I must say to my people, who stand on the warm threshold which leads into the palace of justice: In the process of gaining our rightful place, we must not be guilty of wrongful deeds. Let us not seek to satisfy our thirst for freedom by drinking from the cup of bitterness and hatred. We must forever conduct our struggle on the high plane of dignity and discipline. We must not allow our creative protest to degenerate into physical violence. Again and again, we must rise to the majestic heights of meeting physical force with soul force.

The marvelous new militancy which has engulfed the Negro community must not lead us to a distrust of all white people, for many of our white brothers, as evidenced by their presence here today, have come to realize that their destiny is tied up with our destiny. And they have come to realize that their freedom is inextricably bound to our freedom.

> We cannot walk alone.
> And as we walk, we must make the pledge that we shall always march ahead.
> We cannot turn back.

There are those who are asking the devotees of civil rights, "When will you be satisfied?" We can never be satisfied as long as the Negro is the victim of the unspeakable horrors of police brutality. We can never be satisfied as long as our bodies, heavy with the fatigue of travel, cannot gain lodging in the motels of the highways and the hotels of the cities. We cannot be satisfied as long as the negro's basic mobility is from a smaller ghetto to a larger one. We can never be satisfied as long as our children are stripped of their selfhood and robbed of their dignity by a sign stating: "For Whites Only." We cannot be satisfied as long as a Negro in Mississippi cannot vote and a Negro in New York believes he has nothing for which to vote. No, no, we are not satisfied, and we will not be satisfied until "justice rolls down like waters, and righteousness like a mighty stream."[1]

I am not unmindful that some of you have come here out of great trials and tribulations. Some of you have come fresh from narrow jail cells. And some of you have come from areas where your quest—quest for freedom left you battered by the storms of persecution and staggered by the winds of police brutality. You have been the veterans of creative suffering. Continue to work with the faith that unearned suffering is redemptive. Go back to Mississippi, go back to Alabama, go back to South Carolina, go back to Georgia, go back to Louisiana, go back to the slums and ghettos of our northern cities, knowing that somehow this situation can and will be changed.

Let us not wallow in the valley of despair, I say to you today, my friends.

And so even though we face the difficulties of today and tomorrow, I still have a dream. It is a dream deeply rooted in the American dream.

I have a dream that one day this nation will rise up and live out the true meaning of its creed: "We hold these truths to be self-evident, that all men are created equal."

I have a dream that one day on the red hills of Georgia, the sons of former slaves and the sons of former slave owners will be able to sit down together at the table of brotherhood.

I have a dream that one day even the state of Mississippi, a state sweltering with the heat of injustice, sweltering with the heat of oppression, will be transformed into an oasis of freedom and justice.

I have a dream that my four little children will one day live in a nation where they will not be judged by the color of their skin but by the content of their character.

I have a dream today!

I have a dream that one day, down in Alabama, with its vicious racists, with its governor having his lips dripping with the words of "interposition" and "nullification"—one day right there in Alabama little black boys and black girls will be able to join hands with little white boys and white girls as sisters and brothers.

I have a dream today!

I have a dream that one day every valley shall be exalted, and every hill and mountain shall be made low, the rough places will be made plain, and the crooked places will be made straight; "and the glory of the Lord shall be revealed and all flesh shall see it together."[2]

This is our hope, and this is the faith that I go back to the South with.

With this faith, we will be able to hew out of the mountain of despair a stone of hope. With this faith, we will be able to transform the jangling discords of our nation into a beautiful symphony of brotherhood. With this faith, we will be able to work together, to pray together, to struggle together, to go to jail together, to stand up for freedom together, knowing that we will be free one day.

And this will be the day—this will be the day when all of God's children will be able to sing with new meaning:

> My country 'tis of thee, sweet land of liberty, of thee I sing.
> Land where my fathers died, land of the Pilgrim's pride,
> From every mountainside, let freedom ring!
> And if America is to be a great nation, this must become true.
> And so let freedom ring from the prodigious hilltops of New Hampshire.
> Let freedom ring from the mighty mountains of New York.
> Let freedom ring from the heightening Alleghenies of Pennsylvania.
> Let freedom ring from the snow-capped Rockies of Colorado.
> Let freedom ring from the curvaceous slopes of California.
> But not only that:
> Let freedom ring from Stone Mountain of Georgia.
> Let freedom ring from Lookout Mountain of Tennessee.
> Let freedom ring from every hill and molehill of Mississippi.
> From every mountainside, let freedom ring.

And when this happens, when we allow freedom to ring, when we let it ring from every village and every hamlet, from every state and every city, we will be able to speed up that day when all of God's children, black men and white men, Jews and Gentiles, Protestants and Catholics, will be able to join hands and sing in the words of the old Negro spiritual:

> Free at last! Free at last!
> Thank God Almighty, we are free at last![3]

[1] Amos 5:24 (rendered precisely in The American Standard Version of the Holy Bible)

[2] Isaiah 40:4–5 (King James Version of the Holy Bible). Quotation marks are excluded from part of this moment in the text because King's rendering of Isaiah 40:4 does not precisely follow the KJV version from which he quotes (e.g., "hill" and "mountain" are reversed in the KJV). King's rendering of Isaiah 40:5, however, is precisely quoted from the KJV.

[3] "Free at Last" from *American Negro Songs* by J. W. Work.

Activity 3.1 • Use Microsoft's Comment Feature to Annotate a Text

If you download Dr. Martin Luther King, Jr.'s speech from *American Rhetoric* (www.americanrhetoric.com), you can make use of Microsoft's Comment feature to annotate the speech with your comments, as is done in the example below. In Microsoft Word, highlight the text you want to annotate, go to the "Insert" pull-down menu, and select "Comment." A box will appear where you can enter your comment.

> I am happy to join with you today in what will go down in history as the greatest demonstration for freedom in the history of our nation.
>
> Five score years ago, a great American, in whose symbolic shadow we stand today, signed the Emancipation Proclamation, This momentous decree came as a great beacon light of hope to millions of Negro slaves who had been seared in the flames of withering injustice. It came as a joyous daybreak to end the long night of their captivity.
>
> But one hundred years later, the Negro still is not free. One hundred years later, the life of the Negro is still sadly crippled by the manacles of segregation and that chains of discrimination. One hundred years later, the Negro lives on a lonely island of poverty in the midst of a vast ocean of material prosperity. One hundred years later, the Negro is

Comment [1]: Reference to Lincoln's Gettysburg Address

Activity 3.2 • Discuss "I Have a Dream"

Read the "I Have a Dream" speech by Dr. Martin Luther King, Jr., and, if possible, watch the speech. It is archived at *AmericanRhetoric.com*, where it is listed as the most requested speech and is #1 in the website's list of the top 100 American speeches.

Discuss the *kairos* of Dr. King's speech. What was the occasion? Who was his audience, both present and absent? What were the issues he spoke about?

How did Dr. King take advantage of the *kairos* of the situation in the wording of his speech?

Why do you think the speech continues to be so popular and influential?

Collaborate

Activity 3.3 • Identify the *Kairos*

Identifying the *kairos* in Dr. Martin Luther King, Jr.'s speech in front of the Lincoln Memorial is easy. In some speeches, however, identifying the *kairos* is more difficult. Every speech and every text has a *kairos*, but some rhetors are better at identifying it and utilizing it than others. Identify the *kairos* in the following readings that have appeared thus far in the text. Then discuss in your group how the writer or speaker does or does not utilize *kairos* to maximum effect.

- " 'Columbusing': The Art of Discovering Something that is Not New," Chapter 1, p. 8.

- "Microsoft Just Laid Off Thousands of Employees with a Hilariously Bad Memo," Chapter 1, p. 15.

- "The Sleepover Question," Chapter 1, p. 20.

- "Do You Know How Your Mascara is Made?" Chapter 2, p. 37.

- "The Web Means the End of Forgetting," Chapter 2, p. 51.

- "The Point When Science Becomes Publicity," Chapter 2, p. 62.

- "Why Has Godzilla Grown?" Chapter 2, p. 73.

Compose

Activity 3.4 • Analyze an Audience

Select a group that you do not belong to, and analyze it as a potential audience. To begin your analysis, you might locate a blog on the Internet that advocates a point of view different from your own. For example, if you agree with theories about climate change, read a blog frequented by those who do not share your perspectives. If you are a Democrat, look for an Independent or Republican blog. Find a yoga blog if you are a football fan. Read a week's worth of blog entries, and write a one-page analysis, including the answers to these questions.

1. What are the two or three issues of primary interest to the group? What is the group's general position on each issue?

2. Who are these people? Where do they live? What is their educational level?

3. What is the extent of their knowledge about the issues of primary interest? Are they familiar with the evidence, or do they just repeat opinions?

Aristotle's Persuasive Appeals

Some theorists associate the rhetorical triangle directly with Aristotle's appeals (or proofs): *ethos*, *pathos*, and *logos*. *Ethos* refers to the writer's (or speaker's) credibility; *pathos* refers to emotion used to sway the audience; and, finally, *logos* refers to the writer's purpose (or subject), for an effective argument will include evidence and other supporting details to back up the author's claims.

Aristotle wrote:

> Of those proofs that are furnished through the speech there are three kinds. Some reside in the character [*ethos*] of the speaker, some in a certain disposition [*pathos*] of the audience and some in the speech itself, through its demonstrating or seeming to demonstrate [*logos*].

Contemporary theorist Wayne C. Booth said something similar:

> The common ingredient that I find in all writing that I admire—excluding for now novels, plays, and poems—is something that I shall reluctantly call the rhetorical stance, a stance which depends upon discovering and maintaining in any writing situation a proper balance among the three elements that are at work in any communicative effort: the available arguments about the subject itself [*logos*], the interests and peculiarities of the audience [*pathos*], and the voice, the implied character of the speaker [*ethos*].

Arguments from *Logos*

Logos, or reason, was Aristotle's favorite of the three persuasive appeals, and he bemoaned the fact that humans could not be persuaded through reason alone, indeed that they sometimes chose emotion over reason. Aristotle also used the term *logos* to mean rational discourse. To appeal to *logos* means to organize an argument with a clear claim or thesis, supported by logical reasons that are presented in a well-organized manner that is internally consistent. It can also mean the use of facts and statistics as evidence. However, *logos* without elements of *pathos* and *ethos* can be dry, hard to understand, and boring.

Consider the following logical argument that advocates televising executions.

Reading 3.2

In this opinion piece published in The New York Times, *Zachary B. Shemtob and David Lat argue what they know is going to be an unpopular position in the United States—that executions should be televised. Shemtob is an assistant professor of criminal justice at Connecticut State University, and Lat is a former federal prosecutor who also founded a legal blog,* Above the Law. *They reason, "democracy demands maximum accountability and transparency." Knowing that their position contradicts present policy, they carefully address possible objections to their position, such as the idea that executions are too gruesome to put on television.*

Executions Should Be Televised

by Zachary B. Shemtob and David Lat

[In July of 2011], Georgia conducted its third execution of the year. This would have passed relatively unnoticed if not for a controversy surrounding its video-taping. Lawyers for the condemned in-mate, Andrew Grant DeYoung, had per-suaded a judge to allow the recording of his last moments as part of an effort to obtain evidence on whether lethal injection caused unnecessary suffering.

Though he argued for videotaping, one of Mr. DeYoung's defense lawyers, Brian Kammer, spoke out against releasing the footage to the public. "It's a horrible thing that Andrew DeYoung had to go through," Mr. Kammer said, "and it's not for the public to see that."

We respectfully disagree. Executions in the United States ought to be made public.

Right now, executions are generally open only to the press and a few select witnesses. For the rest of us, the vague contours are provided in the morn-ing paper. Yet a functioning democracy demands maximum accountability and transparency. As long as executions remain behind closed doors, those are impossible. The people should have the right to see what is being done in their name and with their tax dollars.

This is particularly relevant given the current debate on whether specific methods of lethal injection constitute cruel and unusual punishment and therefore violate the Constitution.

There is a dramatic difference between reading or hearing of such an event and observing it through image and sound. (This is obvious to those who saw the footage of Saddam Hussein's hanging in 2006 or the death of Neda Agha-Soltan during the protests in Iran in 2009.) We are not calling for opening executions completely to the public—conducting them before a live crowd—but rather for broadcasting them live or recording them for fu-ture release, on the Web or TV.

When another Georgia inmate, Roy Blankenship, was executed in June, the prisoner jerked his head, grimaced, gasped and lurched, according to a medical expert's affidavit. The *Atlanta Journal-Constitution* reported that Mr. DeYoung, executed in the same manner, "showed no violent signs in death." Voters should not have to rely on media accounts to understand what takes place when a man is put to death.

Cameras record legislative sessions and presidential debates, and court-rooms are allowing greater television access. When he was an Illinois state senator, President Obama successfully pressed for the videotaping of homi-cide interrogations and confessions. The most serious penalty of all surely demands equal if not greater scrutiny.

Opponents of our proposal offer many objections. State lawyers argued that making Mr. DeYoung's execution public raised safety concerns. While riot-ing and pickpocketing occasionally marred executions in the public square in the 18th and 19th centuries, modern security and technology obviate this concern. Little would change in the death chamber; the faces of witnesses and executioners could be edited out, for privacy reasons, before a video was released.

Of greater concern is the possibility that broadcasting executions could have a numbing effect. Douglas A. Berman, a law professor, fears that people might come to equate human executions with putting pets to sleep. Yet this seems overstated. While public indifference might result over time, the initial broadcasts would undoubtedly get attention and stir debate.

Still others say that broadcasting an execution would offer an unbalanced picture—making the condemned seem helpless and sympathetic, while keeping the victims of the crime out of the picture. But this is beside the point: the defendant is being executed precisely because a jury found that his crimes were so heinous that he deserved to die.

Ultimately the main opposition to our idea seems to flow from an unthinking disgust—a sense that public executions are archaic, noxious, even barba-rous. Albert Camus related in his essay "Reflections on the Guillotine" that viewing executions turned him against capital punishment. The legal scholar John D. Bessler suggests that public executions might have the same effect on the public today; Sister Helen Prejean, the death penalty abolitionist, has urged just such a strategy.

That is not our view. We leave open the possibility that making executions public could strengthen support for them; undecided viewers might find them less disturbing than anticipated.

Like many of our fellow citizens, we are deeply conflicted about the death penalty and how it has been administered. Our focus is on accountability and openness. As Justice John Paul Stevens wrote in *Baze v. Rees*, a 2008 case involving a challenge to lethal injection, capital punishment is too often "the product of habit and inattention rather than an acceptable delibera-tive process that weighs the costs and risks of administering that penalty against its identifiable benefits."

A democracy demands a citizenry as informed as possible about the costs and benefits of society's ultimate punishment.

Collaborate

Activity 3.5 • Analyze an Argument from *Logos*

In your small group, discuss the following points, and prepare to present and defend your responses to the class.

1. Go over the Checklist of Essential Elements in an Argument (Chapter 2, p. 50), and decide if the authors of this article fulfill each one.

2. Shemtob and Lat present a logical argument about why executions should be televised. Ignoring your own reaction to their editorial, outline the main points.

3. Explain how the authors handle their audience's possible emotional objec-tions to their argument.

4. What is your reaction to the argument that executions should be televised? Did reading and evaluating the article cause you to see the issue differently? If so, in what way?

Explore

Activity 3.6 • Find an Argument from *Logos*

Find an essay or article in print or on the Internet that uses *logos* as its primary ap-peal. Make a copy, and bring it to class. In your small group, discuss the texts the group members brought in, and decide which one contains the strongest argument based on *logos*. Describe the argument for the class.

Deductive Reasoning

Aristotle was the first person in Western culture to write systematically about logic, and he is credited with developing and promoting syllogistic or **deductive reasoning** in which statements are combined to draw a **conclusion**. He wrote that "a statement is persuasive and credible either because it is directly self-evident or because it appears to be proved from other statements that are so." This logical structure is called a **syllogism**, in which premises lead to a conclusion. The following is perhaps the most famous syllogism:

Major premise: All humans are mortal.

Minor premise: Socrates is human.

Conclusion: Socrates is mortal.

The **major premise** is a general statement accepted by everyone that makes an observation about all people. The second statement of the syllogism is the **minor premise**, which makes a statement about a particular case within the class of all people. Comparison of the two premises, the general class of "all humans" and the particular case of "Socrates" within the class of "all humans" leads to the conclusion that Socrates also fits in the class "mortal," and therefore his death is unavoidable. Thus, the logic moves from the general to the particular.

Similarly, if you try the pumpkin bread at one Starbucks and like it, you may infer that you will like the pumpkin bread at another Starbucks. The argument would look like this:

Major premise: Food products at Starbucks are standardized from one Starbucks to another.

Minor premise: You like the pumpkin bread at one Starbucks.

Conclusion: You will like the pumpkin bread at another Starbucks.

Often in deductive reasoning, one of the premises is not stated, resulting in what is called a truncated syllogism or **enthymeme**.

For example, in the above syllogism about pumpkin bread, an enthymeme might leave out the major premise, "Food products at Starbucks are standardized from one Starbucks to another." In that case, the syllogism could be shortened to this:

Enthymeme: If you like the pumpkin bread at one Starbucks, you will like it at another Starbucks.

However, if your major premise is wrong (whether it is stated or not) because the owner of one Starbucks substitutes an inferior stock of pumpkin bread, then your conclusion is wrong.

An enthymeme also relies upon common experience between speaker and audience. If your audience has never tasted pumpkin bread at Starbucks, then they are less likely to believe your enthymeme.

Deductive reasoning is dependent upon the validity of each premise; otherwise the syllogism does not hold true. If the major premise that food products are standardized at all Starbucks franchises does not hold true, then the argument is not valid. A good deductive argument is known as a valid argument and is such that if all its premises are true, then its conclusion must be true. Indeed, for a deductive argument to be valid, it must be absolutely impossible for both its premises to be true and its conclusion to be false.

Collaborate

Activity 3.7 • Develop a Deductive Argument

In your small group, develop a deductive argument by creating a major premise, a minor premise, and a conclusion for a topic of your group's choice. Present the argument to the class.

Inductive Reasoning

Aristotle identified another way to move logically between premises, which he called "the progress from particulars to universals." Later logicians labeled this type of logic **inductive reasoning**. Inductive arguments are based on probability. Even if an inductive argument's premises are true, that doesn't establish with 100 percent certainty that its conclusions are true. Even the best inductive argument falls short of deductive validity.

Consider the following examples of inductive reasoning:

Particular statement: Milk does not spoil as quickly if kept cold.

General statement: All perishable foods do not spoil as quickly if kept cold.

Particular statement:	Microwaves cook popcorn more quickly than conventional heat.
General statement:	All foods cook more quickly in a microwave.

In the first example, inductive reasoning works well because cold tends to prolong the useable life of most perishable foods. The second example is more problematic. While it is true that popcorn cooks more quickly in a microwave oven, the peculiarities of microwave interaction with food molecules does not produce a uniform effect on all food stuffs. Rice, for example, does not cook much, if any, faster in a microwave than it does on a stovetop. Also, whole eggs may explode if cooked in their shells.

A good inductive argument is known as a strong (or "cogent") inductive argument. It is such that if the premises are true, the conclusion is likely to be true.

Collaborate

Activity 3.8 • Develop an Inductive Argument

In your small group, develop an inductive argument by creating a particular statement and a general statement for a topic of your group's choice. Present the argument to the class. Be sure that your inductive argument is strong or "cogent."

Logical Fallacies

Generally speaking, a **logical fallacy** is an error in reasoning, as opposed to a factual error, which is simply being wrong about the facts. A **deductive fallacy** (sometimes called a *formal fallacy*) is a deductive argument that has premises that are all true, but they lead to a false conclusion, making it an invalid argument. An **inductive fallacy** (sometimes called an *informal fallacy*) appears to be an inductive argument, but the premises do not provide enough support for the conclusion to be probable. Some logical fallacies are more common than others and, thus, have been labeled and defined. Following are a few of the most well-known types.

Ad hominem (Latin for "to the man") arguments attempt to discredit a point of view through personal attacks upon the person who has that point of view. These arguments are not relevant to the actual issue because the character of the person that holds a view says nothing about the truth of that viewpoint.

> *Example*: Noam Chomsky is a liberal activist who opposes American intervention in other countries. Noam Chomsky's theory of

transformational grammar, which suggests that humans have an innate ability to learn language, is ridiculous.

Non sequitur (Latin for "it does not follow") arguments have conclusions that do not follow from the premises. Usually, the author has left out a step in the logic, expecting the reader to make the leap over the gap.

> *Example*: Well, look at the size of this administration building; it is obvious this university does not need more funding.

Either/or or **false dichotomy** arguments force an either/or choice when, in reality, more options are available. Issues are presented as being either black or white.

> *Example*: With all the budget cuts, we either raise tuition or massively increase class size.

Red herring arguments avoid the issue and attempt to distract with a side issue.

> *Example*: Why do you question my private life issues when we have social problems with which to deal?

Ad populum (Latin for "appeal to the people") arguments appeal to popularity. If a lot of people believe it, it must be true.

> *Example*: Why shouldn't I cheat on this exam? Everyone else cheats.

Ad vericundiam (Latin for "argument from that which is improper") arguments appeal to an irrelevant authority.

> *Example*: If the President of Harvard says it is a good idea, then we should follow suit. Or, That is how we have always done it.

Begging the question arguments simply assume that a point of view is true because the truth of the premise is assumed. Simply assuming a premise is true does not amount to evidence that it *is* true.

> *Example*: A woman's place is in the home; therefore, women should not work.

Confusing cause and effect is a common problem with scientific studies in which the fact that two events are correlated implies that one causes the other.

> *Example*: Obese people drink a lot of diet soda; therefore, diet soda causes obesity.

Post hoc (from the Latin phrase *Post hoc, ergo proper hoc,* or "after this, therefore because of this") is a fallacy that concludes that one event caused another just because one occurred before the other.

> *Example*: The Great Depression caused World War II.

In a **straw man** fallacy, a position of an opponent is exaggerated or weakened, so that it is easier for the opponent to argue against it.

> *Example*: Pro-choice advocates believe in murdering unborn children.

A **slippery slope** argument asserts that one event will inevitably lead to another event.

> *Example*: This Dilbert cartoon:

DILBERT © 2008 Scott Adams. Used by permission of UNIVERSAL UCLICK. All rights reserved.

Table 3.1 • Descriptions and Examples of Logical Fallacies

Fallacy	The Error in Reasoning	Example
Ad populum	When we attempt to persuade people by arguing our position is reasonable because so many other people are doing it or agree with it.	"Why shouldn't I cheat on this exam? Everyone else cheats."

Ad vericundiam	An appeal to persuasion based on higher authority or tradition.	"If the president of Harvard says it is a good idea, then we should follow suit." Or, "That is how we have always done it."
Begging the question	When a speaker presumes certain things are facts when they have not yet been proven to be truthful.	"Oh, everyone knows that we are all Christians."
Confusing cause and effect	A common problem with scientific studies in which the fact that two events are correlated implies that one causes the other.	"Obese people drink a lot of diet soda; therefore, diet soda causes obesity."
Either/or	Presents two options and declares that one of them must be correct while the other must be incorrect.	"We either raise tuition or massively increase class size."
Non sequitur	When you make an unwarranted move from one idea to the next.	"Well, look at the size of this administration building; it is obvious this university does not need more funding."
Post hoc	Assumes that because one event happened after another, then the preceding event caused the event that followed.	"Every time Sheila goes to a game with us, our team loses. She is bad luck."
Red herring	When a speaker introduces an irrelevant issue or piece of evidence to divert attention from the subject of the speech.	"Why do you question my private life issues, when we have social problems with which to deal?"
Slippery slope	Assumes that once an action begins it will follow, undeterred, to an eventual and inevitable conclusion.	"If we let the government dictate where we can pray, soon the government will tell us we cannot pray."

Activity 3.9 • Identify Logical Fallacies

Match the following types of logical fallacies with the examples below.

Types:

Ad hominem

Begging the question

Confusing cause and effect

Post hoc

Straw man

Slippery slope

Examples:

1. Legalization of medical marijuana will lead to increased marijuana use by the general population.

2. Twenty-one is the best age limit for drinking because people do not mature until they are 21.

3. If you teach birth control methods, more teenage girls will get pregnant.

4. The culture wars of the 1960s were a result of parents being unable to control their children after the post–World War II baby boom.

5. Al Gore claims that climate change is a dangerous trend. Al Gore is a liberal. Therefore, there is no climate change.

6. Immigration reform advocates want to separate families and children.

Activity 3.10 • Create Examples of Logical Fallacies

In your small group, work through the chart of logical fallacies above and create a new example for each type of fallacy. Then report to the class, one fallacy at a time, with the instructor making a list of each group's examples on the chalk board. Discuss any examples that are not clear cases of a particular fallacy.

Arguments from *Pathos*

Pathos makes use of emotion to persuade an audience.

Aristotle wrote:

> Proofs from the disposition of the audience are produced whenever they are induced by the speech into an emotional state. We do not give judgment in the same way when aggrieved and when pleased, in sympathy and in revulsion.

Effective rhetors know their audiences, particularly what emotions they hold that are relevant to the issue under consideration. What motivates them? What are their fears, their hopes, their desires, and their doubts? If the audience has the same emotions as you do, fine. However, if they do not already hold those emotions, you need to bring them to share the hurt, the anger, or the joy that will persuade them to share your viewpoint—through the stories you tell, the statistics you cite, and the reasoning you offer.

For example, when Dr. Martin Luther King, Jr., in his "I Have a Dream" speech referred to the "hallowed spot" of the Lincoln Memorial, he was appealing to his audience's feelings of patriotism and reverence for the accomplishments of President Lincoln. Subtly, he was also garnering this emotion toward Lincoln in contemporary support of civil rights. Lincoln had issued the Emancipation Proclamation that declared all slaves to be free, yet, according to King, America had not lived up to Lincoln's promise.

Reading 3.3

E. Benjamin Skinner has written on a wide range of topics. His articles have appeared in News-week International, Travel and Leisure, *and other magazines. This essay was adapted from* A Crime So Monstrous: Face-to-Face with Modern-Day Slavery *and appeared in* Foreign Policy.

People for Sale
by E. Benjamin Skinner

Most people imagine that slavery died in the nineteenth century. Since 1810, more than a dozen international conventions banning the slave trade have been signed. Yet today there are more slaves than at any time in human history.

And if you're going to buy one in five hours, you'd better get a move on. First, hail a taxi to JFK International Airport and hop on a direct flight to Port-au-Prince, Haiti. The flight takes three hours. After landing, take a tap-tap, a flatbed pickup retrofitted with benches and a canopy, three-quarters of the way up Route de Delmas, the capital's main street. There, on a side street, you will find a group of men standing in front of Le Réseau (the Network) barbershop. As you approach, a man steps forward: "Are you looking to get a person?"

Meet Benavil Lebhom. He smiles easily. He has a trim mustache and wears a multicolored striped golf shirt, a gold chain, and Doc Martens knockoffs. Benavil is a courtier, or broker. He holds an official real estate license and calls himself an employment agent. Two-thirds of the employees he places are child slaves. The total number of Haitian children in bondage in their own country stands at 300,000. They are restavèks, the "stay-withs," as they are euphemistically known in Creole. Forced, unpaid, they work in captivity from before dawn until night. Benavil and thousands of other formal and informal traffickers lure these children from desperately impoverished rural parents with promises of free schooling and a better life.

The negotiation to buy a child slave might sound a bit like this:

"How quickly do you think it would be possible to bring a child in? Somebody who could clean and cook?" you ask. "I don't have a very big place; I have a small apartment. But I'm wondering how much that would cost? And how quickly?"

"Three days," Benavil responds.

"And you could bring the child here?" you inquire. "Or are there children here already?"

"I don't have any here in Port-au-Prince right now," says Benavil, his eyes widening at the thought of a foreign client. "I would go out to the countryside."

You ask about additional expenses. "Would I have to pay for transportation?"

"Bon," says Benavil. "A hundred U.S."

Smelling a rip-off, you press him, "And that's just for transportation?"

"Transportation would be about 100 Haitian," says Benavil, "because you'd have to get out there. Plus, [hotel and] food on the trip. Five hundred gourdes"—around $13.

"OK, 500 Haitian," you say.

Now you ask the big question: "And what would your fee be?" Benavil's eyes narrow as he determines how much he can take you for.

"A hundred. American."

"That seems like a lot," you say, with a smile so as not to kill the deal. "Could you bring down your fee to 50 U.S.?"

Benavil pauses. But only for effect. He knows he's still got you for much more than a Haitian would pay. "Oui," he says with a smile.

But the deal isn't done. Benavil leans in close. "This is a rather delicate question. Is this someone you want as just a worker? Or also someone who will be a 'partner'? You understand what I mean?"

You don't blink at being asked if you want the child for sex. "Is it possible to have someone who could be both?"

"Oui!" Benavil responds enthusiastically.

If you're interested in taking your purchase back to the United States, Benavil tells you that he can "arrange" the proper papers to make it look as though you've adopted the child.

He offers you a 13-year-old girl.

"That's a little bit old," you say.

"I know of another girl who's 12. Then ones that are 10, 11," he responds.

The negotiation is finished, and you tell Benavil not to make any moves without further word from you. You have successfully arranged to buy a human being for 50 bucks.

It would be nice if that conversation were fictional. It is not. I recorded it in October 2005 as part of four years of research into slavery on five continents. In the popular consciousness, "slavery" has come to be little more than just a metaphor for undue hardship. Investment bankers routinely refer to themselves as "high-paid wage slaves." Human rights activists may call $1-an-hour sweatshop laborers slaves, regardless of the fact that they are paid and can often walk away from the job.

The reality of slavery is far different. Slavery exists today on an unprecedented scale. In Africa, tens of thousands are chattel slaves, seized in war or tucked away for generations. Across Europe, Asia, and the Americas, traffickers have forced as many as 2 million into prostitution or labor. In South Asia, which has the highest concentration of slaves on the planet, nearly 10 million languish in bondage, unable to leave their captors until they pay off "debts," legal fictions that in many cases are generations old.

Few in the developed world have a grasp of the enormity of modern-day slavery. Fewer still are doing anything to combat it. . . . Between 2000 and 2006, the U.S. Justice Department increased human trafficking prosecutions from 3 to 32, and convictions from 10 to 98. By the end of 2006, 27 states had passed anti-trafficking laws. Yet, during the same period, the United States liberated only about 2 percent of its own modern-day slaves. As many as 17,500 new slaves continue to enter bondage in the United States every year . . . Many feel that sex slavery is particularly revolting—and it is. I saw it firsthand. In a Bucharest brothel, I was offered a mentally handicapped suicidal girl in exchange for a used car. But for every woman or child enslaved in commercial sex, there are some 15 men, women, and children enslaved in other fields, such as domestic work or agricultural labor.

Save for the fact that he is male, Gonoo Lal Kol typifies the average slave of our modern age. (At his request, I have changed his name.) Like a majority of the world's slaves, Gonoo is in debt bondage in South Asia. In his case, in an Indian quarry. Like most slaves, Gonoo is illiterate and unaware of the Indian laws that ban his bondage and provide for sanctions against his master. His story, told to me near his four-foot-high stone and grass hutch, represents the other side of the "Indian Miracle."

Gonoo lives in Lohagara Dhal, a forgotten corner of Uttar Pradesh, a north Indian state that contains 8 percent of the world's poor. I met him one evening in December 2005 as he walked with two dozen other laborers in tattered and filthy clothes. Behind them was the quarry. In that pit, Gonoo, a member of the historically outcast Kol tribe, worked with his family 14 hours a day. His tools were a hammer and a pike. His hands were covered in calluses, his fingertips worn away.

Gonoo's master is a tall, stout, surly contractor named Ramesh Garg. He makes his money by enslaving entire families forced to work for no pay beyond alcohol, grain, and subsistence expenses. Slavery scholar Kevin Bales estimates that a slave in the 19th-century American South had to work 20 years to recoup his or her purchase price. Gonoo and the other slaves earn a profit for Garg in two years.

Every single man, woman, and child in Lohagara Dhal is a slave. But, in theory at least, Garg neither bought nor owns them. The seed of Gonoo's slavery, for instance, was a loan of 62 cents. In 1958 his grandfather borrowed that amount from the owner of a farm where he worked. Three generations and three slave masters later, Gonoo's family remains in bondage.

Recently, many bold, underfunded groups have taken up the challenge of tearing out the roots of slavery. Some gained fame through dramatic slave rescues. Most learned that freeing slaves is impossible unless the slaves themselves choose to be free. Among the Kol of Uttar Pradesh, for instance, an organization called Pragati Gramodyog Sansthan (PGS)—the Progressive Institute for Village Enterprises—has helped hundreds of families break the grip of the quarry contractors.

The psychological, social, and economic bonds of slavery run deep, and for governments to be truly effective in eradicating slavery, they must partner with groups that can offer slaves a way to pull themselves up from bondage. One way to do that is to replicate the work of grassroots organizations such as the India-based MSEMVS (Society for Human Development and Women's Empowerment). In 1996 the group launched free transitional schools where children who had been enslaved learned skills and acquired enough literacy to move on to formal schooling. The group also targeted mothers, providing them with training and start-up materials for microenterprises. . . . In recent years, the United States has shown an increasing willingness to help fund these kinds of organizations, one encouraging sign that the message may be getting through.

For four years, I encountered dozens of enslaved people, several of whom traffickers like Benavil actually offered to sell to me. I did not pay for a human life anywhere. And, with one exception, I always withheld action to save any one person, in the hope that my research would later help to save many more. At times, that still feels like an excuse for cowardice. But the hard work of real emancipation can't be the burden of a select few. For thousands of slaves, grassroots groups like PGS and MSEMVS can help bring freedom. Until governments define slavery in appropriately concise terms, prosecute the crime aggressively in all its forms, and encourage groups that empower slaves to free themselves, however, millions more will remain in bondage. And our collective promise of abolition will continue to mean nothing at all.

Activity 3.11 • Write about an Argument from *Pathos*

After reading Skinner's essay on slavery, reread the passage in which he negotiated to buy a child slave. Then freewrite for five minutes about how that negotiation made you feel.

Compose

Activity 3.12 • Analyze an Argument from *Pathos*

Most people feel emotional when they read about a child in distress, and Skinner further highlights that emotional effect by putting this particular episode in dialogue, always a point of emphasis in an essay. Discuss these questions in your small group.

Collaborate

1. Do you think Skinner deliberately appealed to *pathos* in this part of his essay?

2. List other areas where the essay evokes an emotional response. Consider why, and freewrite on the feelings and beliefs that are brought into play on your own. Discuss with your group your responses and how you think the author knew you would probably react this way.

3. Although much of Skinner's argument relies on *pathos*, he also provides statistics and references to authorities to bolster his argument. Identify the paragraphs which provide statistics or other evidence that would qualify as *logos*.

Activity 3.13 • Find an Argument from *Pathos*

Find an essay or article in print or on the Internet that uses *pathos* or emotion as its primary appeal. Make a copy and bring it to class. In your small group, discuss the texts that the group members brought in, and decide which one contains the strongest argument based on *pathos*. Describe the argument for the class.

Explore

Arguments from *Ethos*

No exact translation exists in English for the word *ethos*, but it can be loosely translated as the credibility of the speaker. This credibility generates good will which colors all the arguments, examples, and quotes the rhetor utilizes in his or her text. Rhetors can enhance their credibility by providing evidence of intelligence, virtue, and goodwill and diminish it by seeming petty, dishonest, and mean-spirited. In addition, a speaker or writer can enhance his or her own credibility by incorporating references to quotes or the actions of authorities or leaders.

Aristotle wrote:

> Proofs from character [*ethos*] are produced, whenever the speech is given in such a way as to render the speaker worthy of

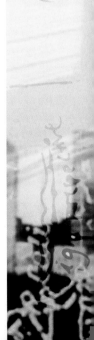

credence—we more readily and sooner believe reasonable men on all matters in general and absolutely on questions where precision is impossible and two views can be maintained.

For example, Dr. Martin Luther King, Jr., pointed out in his "I Have a Dream" speech, that, according to the framers of the Constitution and the Declaration of Independence, "unalienable Rights" of "Life, Liberty and the pursuit of Happiness" apply equally to black men and white men. He was, in effect, borrowing the *ethos* of Thomas Jefferson and the framers of the Constitution in support of the unalienable rights of black people.

Consider the following article and how the author's credibility or *ethos* enhances the appeal of his arguments.

Reading 3.4

Ray Jayawardhana, the author of "Alien Life Coming Slowly into View," which was originally published in The New York Times, *is a professor of astronomy and astrophysics at the University of Toronto. He is also the author of* Strange New Worlds: The Search for Alien Planets and Life Beyond Our Solar System.

Alien Life Coming Slowly into View
by Ray Jayawardhana

I remember the first time the concept of another world entered my mind. It was during a walk with my father in our garden in Sri Lanka. He pointed to the Moon and told me that people had walked on it. I was astonished: Suddenly that bright light became a place that one could visit.

Schoolchildren may feel a similar sense of wonder when they see pictures of a Martian landscape or Saturn's rings. And soon their views of alien worlds may not be confined to the planets in our own solar system.

After millenniums of musings and a century of failed attempts, astronomers first detected an exoplanet, a planet orbiting a normal star other than the Sun, in 1995. Now they are finding hundreds of such worlds each year. Last month, NASA announced that 1,235 new possible planets had been observed by Kepler, a telescope on a space satellite. Six of the planets that Kepler found circle one star, and the orbits of five of them would fit within that of Mercury, the closest planet to our Sun.

By timing the passages of these five planets across their sun's visage—which provides confirmation of their planetary nature—we can witness their graceful dance with one another, choreographed by gravity. These discoveries remind us that nature is often richer and more wondrous than our imagination. The diversity of alien worlds has surprised us and challenged our preconceptions many times over.

It is quite a change from merely 20 years ago, when we knew for sure of just one planetary system: ours. The pace of discovery, supported by new instruments and missions and innovative strategies by planet seekers, has been astounding.

What's more, from measurements of their masses and sizes, we can infer what some of these worlds are made of: gases, ice or rocks. Astronomers have been able to take the temperature of planets around other stars, first with telescopes in space but more recently with ground-based instruments, as my collaborators and I have done.

Two and a half years ago, we even managed to capture the first direct pictures of alien worlds. There is something about a photo of an alien planet—even if it only appears as a faint dot next to a bright, overexposed star—that makes it "real." Given that stars shine like floodlights next to the planetary embers huddled around them, success required painstaking efforts and clever innovations. One essential tool is adaptive optics technology, which, in effect, takes the twinkle out of the stars, thus providing sharper images from telescopes on the ground than would otherwise be possible.

At the crux of this grand pursuit is one basic question: Is our warm, wet, rocky world, teeming with life, the exception or the norm? It is an important question for every one of us, not just for scientists. It seems absurd, if not arrogant, to think that ours is the only life-bearing world in the galaxy, given hundreds of billions of other suns, the apparent ubiquity of planets, and the cosmic abundance of life's ingredients. It may be that life is fairly common, but that "intelligent" life is rare.

Of course, the vast majority of the extra-solar worlds discovered to date are quite unlike our own: many are gas giants, and some are boiling hot while others endure everlasting chills. Just a handful are close in size to our planet, and only a few of those may be rocky like the Earth, rather than gaseous like Jupiter or icy like Neptune.

But within the next few years, astronomers expect to find dozens of alien earths that are roughly the size of our planet. Some of them will likely be in the so-called habitable zone, where the temperatures are just right for liquid water. The discovery of "Earth twins," with conditions similar to what we find here, will inevitably bring questions about alien life to the forefront.

Detecting signs of life elsewhere will not be easy, but it may well occur in my lifetime, if not during the next decade. Given the daunting distances between the stars, the real-life version will almost certainly be a lot less sensational than the movies depicting alien invasions or crash-landing spaceships.

The evidence may be circumstantial at first—say, spectral bar codes of interesting molecules like oxygen, ozone, methane and water—and leave room for alternative interpretations. It may take years of additional data-gathering, and perhaps the construction of new telescopes, to satisfy our doubts. Besides, we won't know whether such "biosignatures" are an indication of slime or civilization. Most people will likely move on to other, more immediate concerns of life here on Earth while scientists get down to work.

If, on the other hand, an alien radio signal were to be detected, that would constitute a more clear-cut and exciting moment. Even if the contents of the message remained elusive for decades, we would know that there was someone "intelligent" at the other end. The search for extraterrestrial intelligence with radio telescopes has come of age recently, 50 years after the first feeble attempt. The construction of the Allen Telescope Array on an arid plateau in northern California greatly expands the number of star systems from which astronomers could detect signals.

However it arrives, the first definitive evidence of life elsewhere will mark a turning point in our intellectual history, perhaps only rivaled by Copernicus's heliocentric theory or Darwin's theory of evolution. If life can spring up on two planets independently, why not on a thousand or even a billion others? The ramifications of finding out for sure that ours isn't the only inhabited world are likely to be felt, over time, in many areas of human thought and endeavor—from biology and philosophy to religion and art.

Some people worry that discovering life elsewhere, especially if it turns out to be in possession of incredible technology, will make us feel small and insignificant. They seem concerned that it will constitute a horrific blow to our collective ego.

I happen to be an optimist. It may take decades after the initial indications of alien life for scientists to gather enough evidence to be certain or to decipher a signal of artificial origin. The full ramifications of the discovery may not be felt for generations, giving us plenty of time to get used to the presence of our galactic neighbors. Besides, knowing that we are not alone just might be the kick in the pants we need to grow up as a species.

Activity 3.14 • Analyzing an Argument from *Ethos*

Collaborate

Ray Jayawardhana draws upon the *ethos* of his position as a professor of astronomy and astrophysics to formulate a convincing argument for the strong possibility of the existence of alien life. In your group, discuss how Jayawardhana's profession increases the credibility of his argument.

1. How do you think this essay would compare to essays by people with greater credentials who argue that no alien life exists? What kinds of additional evidence could Jayawardhana have offered that would strengthen his argument?

2. Is Jayawardhana appealing to *pathos* with his opening narrative? What effect does he want to have on his audience by describing this childhood memory?

Activity 3.15 • Find an Argument from *Ethos*

Explore

Find an essay or article in print or on the Internet that uses *ethos* or the credibility of the author as its primary appeal. Make a copy and bring it to class. In your small group, discuss the texts that the group members brought in, and decide which contains the strongest argument based on *ethos*. Describe the argument for the class.

Combining *Ethos, Pathos,* and *Logos*

The *ethos*, *pathos*, and *logos* appeals are equally important and merit equal attention in the writing process. No text is purely based on one of the three appeals, though more of the argument in a particular text may be based on one appeal rather than another. In each writing situation, however, an effective rhetor will think about how each plays into the structure of the argument.

Today, for example, a public speaker's effectiveness is influenced by his or her ability to use a teleprompter, or, if one is not available, to memorize a speech well enough so he or she can speak without frequently referring to notes. If a speaker's eyes flit from left to right across the text of a teleprompter, it shows on television. This reduces the credibility, or *ethos*, of the speaker, no matter

how well the other appeals are executed in the speech. The equivalent of strong public speaking skills for a written text would be to produce a document that is essentially free from grammatical errors, spell-checked, and printed on good paper stock with the correct margins and type size. If the document does not look professional, it will lose credibility or *ethos* no matter what it says.

To give another example, E. Benjamin Skinner's essay, "People for Sale," relies on the highly emotional image of a child being sold into slavery for its major appeal. However, if you read back through the essay, you will see that it has a clear thesis, which could be stated as the following: Slavery exists in the present time, even in the United States, and it is not even that difficult to buy a slave. The essay is well organized and offers a variety of evidence, including statistics and first-person observation. *Logos* may not stand out as the primary appeal in Skinner's essay, but it is nevertheless strong in its appeal to *logos*.

If you want to develop your writing skills, it is essential that you pay attention to each of Aristotle's appeals—*ethos*, *pathos*, and *logos*.

Compose

Activity 3.16 • Identify *Ethos, Pathos,* and *Logos*

Choose one of the texts in Chapters 1, 2, or 3, and identify in your small group the *ethos, pathos,* and *logos* of the particular text. Then discuss how the three appeals together are used by the author to produce an effective essay. Alternatively, discuss which of the appeals is weak in the particular essay and how that affects the effectiveness of the essay.

Photos Heighten *Ethos*

Caitlyn Jenner, formerly Bruce Jenner, asserted her visual *ethos* as a transgender woman when she accepted the Arthur Ashe Courage Award at the ESPY Awards in Los Angeles in July 2015. News outlets worldwide carried videos or photos of Jenner wearing a stunning white Versace gown as she received a standing ovation from some of sport's greatest stars and celebrities. The same month, further enhancing Jenner's *ethos* as a transgender woman, *Vanity Fair* featured her on its cover in a traditionally female pose, wearing a glamorous white swimsuit. The

Caitlyn Jenner wore a feminine Versace evening gown at the ESPY Awards.
Photo Credit: Getty Images.

A transgender woman posted her own magazine "cover" on the Internet.
Photo Credit: Tumblr/ missinginanus

Vanity Fair cover received both praise and criticism, with some bloggers saying Jenner's photos perpetuated white female beauty stereotypes. However, other transgender women were inspired to create their own "covers" and post them on the Internet. Thus, having a "cover" photo became a new way for transgender women to establish their gender *ethos*.

Activity 3.17 • Locate a Photo that Presents an Argument from *Logos, Ethos,* or *Pathos*

Locate and print or photocopy a photo that presents an argument from *logos, ethos,* or *pathos*. In one sentence, state the photo's argument, identifying whether it is from *logos, ethos,* or *pathos*. Bring the photo and your sentence to class, and share them with your group. Then the group will select one photo and sentence to present to the class.

Activity 3.18 • *Logos* Activity: Write a Letter to the Editor

In the following letter to the editor of *The Baltimore Sun* (published in the Readers Respond section), the author takes exception to the new city policy of equipping police officers with body cameras. The cameras are not being deployed as a crime deterrent but rather to collect data to be used in lawsuits alleging police brutality and misconduct.

Be Prudent with Police Cameras

Though I understand the rush to hold police officers accountable for their behavior, I do not understand placing body cameras on all cops ("Police Body Cameras Will Yield Important Data, Baltimore Task Force Says," Feb. 21 [2015]). This would be like putting every citizen who commits a crime on supervised probation. It is not necessary for all folks, but some need the extra incentive to remain lawful.

I suggest we treat cops like society in general. If one's behavior merits extra scrutiny, then by all means place a camera on him or her. If, however, an officer is honoring the oath and not acting outside of legal authority, leave him or her alone. The cost to place a camera on thousands of police officers is not a great way to spend tax dollars.

I believe this rational response is more prudent than an overreaction. I also believe that facts, not emotion, should dictate how we react to issues that matter.

Mike Snyder, Havre de Grace

---

1. Choose one of your favorite newspapers or magazines and write a letter to the editor. Express your opinion about an issue profiled in a recent article published in the periodical, as the writer does in the above sample letter to the editor, or about a recent editorial or op-ed. Your letter does not need to be long, but you need to make your argument clear and support it with specific examples.

(continued on next page)

2. After you have written your letter to the editor, write a paragraph describing your target publication, what you have written in your letter, and why your letter is an illustration of *logos*. Turn in your paragraph with your letter to the editor.

Explore

Activity 3.19 • *Pathos* Activity: Portray an Emotion in a Collage

Think of an emotion that you've been feeling lately and that you are willing to explore. Create a collage to express that emotion. Use these criteria.

▌ You can create your collage with cut and paste paper or you can create it through a computer program.

▌ Have little white space. Use colors with emotional connotations (blue for calm, for example).

▌ Have at least three images. You can find these on the Internet or in magazines, or take your own photos.

▌ Before you begin your collage, write down the emotion you are trying to explore, and describe how you plan to represent it. In other words, make a plan, even though you will likely deviate from it.

▌ When you finish, write a paragraph describing the experience of creating the collage. Turn your paragraph in with your collage.

Compose

Activity 3.20 • *Ethos* Activity: Create a Professional LinkedIn Page

LinkedIn, the world's largest professional network, provides a unique opportunity for aspiring professionals. Using several basic steps, you can create a page on LinkedIn that projects your professional *ethos*—the "you" that you want others in your field to see—so you can find opportunities and make meaningful connections with other LinkedIn participants.

Stephanie Laszik, a M.A. student and instructor at the University of Texas at Tyler shares these tips for creating your own LinkedIn page.

* * *

(continued on next page)

Remember that LinkedIn is a social media network in which both employers and employees create user profiles and establish professional connections. LinkedIn provides users with the opportunity to present their educational and professional accolades, seek and post potential jobs, follow companies and employees of companies, maintain supportive professional relationships, and network with other users in similar professions.

For this assignment, create a professional-looking LinkedIn page similar to the one shown here. Discuss in your small group what information and photos you want to use on a page intended for networking with others in your professional field. In effect, you are creating an *ethos* for yourself by these choices.

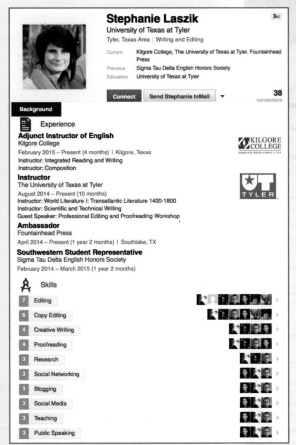

▌ Access LinkedIn at www.Linke-dIn.com and complete the free registration using a reliable email account and password.

▌ Be sure to include a professional head shot as your identity photo. This is often the first component potential employers and connections will see when they browse LinkedIn.

▌ The key to a strong LinkedIn profile and relevant connections is thoroughly documenting your education and job experiences. LinkedIn allows you to include current and previous positions, skills you possess in your field, your education, and volunteer experiences.

▌ When completing each section, be as thorough as possible. The more relevant information you include under each section of your profile the better the network will be able to match you with companies and connections.

(continued on next page)

▌ While LinkedIn communicates information in a similar manner as traditional employment documents, the site is also live and interactive. After you complete your profile, LinkedIn will recommend connections, often within the companies and fields of employment you have added to your profile. Your connections are able to endorse you and suggest skills to be added to your profile.

▌ As you build a database of connections on your LinkedIn profile, you will notice the site enables you to track your profile views, gauge your ranking among other profiles from your companies, and observe trends in member traffic to your profile.

▌ For up-to-date maintenance of your profile and connections, the LinkedIn app can be downloaded to your devices such as a smart phone or tablet computer.

After you have completed your LinkedIn page, write a paragraph that explains the *ethos* you wanted to project in your page and how your content projects that *ethos*.

Compose

Activity 3.21 • Write a Rhetorical Analysis

In this assignment, you will make use of rhetorical vocabulary to analyze a text or combined text and images. A sample student essay in Chapter 6 (see p. 238) analyzes a speech archived on the *American Rhetoric* website (www.americanrhetoric.com), which features many presidential and other prominent speeches. Alternatively, you can write a rhetorical analysis of a Facebook page, a newspaper or magazine article, or website of your choice.

In your analysis, apply several of the rhetorical concepts you have studied this semester.

▌ Speaker or writer—Does the speaker's identity affect the text?

▌ Purpose—What was the speaker or writer trying to achieve?

▌ Audience—Who was the speech/text directed to? Are there multiple audiences?

▌ Rhetorical appeals—How does the speaker or writer use *ethos*, *pathos*, and *logos*?

▌ *Kairos*—What is special about the rhetorical moment of the text/speech in terms of place and time?

Activity 3.22 • Reflect on Your Rhetorical Analysis

Freewrite for five minutes about the writing of a rhetorical analysis. You can answer one or more of these questions or comment about something else related to the writing of the essay. What made you choose this particular essay to analyze? Was it easy or difficult to identify the rhetorical concepts? Why or why not? How did you choose to organize your essay? Did the writing of this essay further your under-standing of rhetorical concepts?

If your instructor directs, revise your freewriting into a coherent paragraph with a topic sentence and points to support the thesis.

Activity 3.23 • Write on Your Blog

In your blog, do a freewrite exercise in which you argue for some type of policy change related to a topic you are interested in writing about. What is the *kairos* of your topic? Where can you use the three rhetorical appeals (*pathos*, *ethos*, and *logos*)?

Activity 3.24 • Write in Your Commonplace Book

Do a search on the Internet for *kairos*, *ethos*, *pathos*, and *logos*. Print out and paste a short section about each from the Internet. Then comment briefly about each section.

Cruz, Betsy. *Pencil Building.*

Chapter 4

Inventing Rhetorically

Praxis in Action

My Invention Strategies

Jenelle Clausen
M.F.A., Creative Writing
Bowling Green State University

The key to writing based on research is to begin with an open mind. When I start thinking about topic ideas for a paper, I try not to solidify my opinion on a topic until I've researched the subject widely. The impulse I feel is often the exact opposite—I know enough about my topic that I know what angle I want to take, so now I just need sources to confirm that, right? Wrong! That kind of thinking limits topic options and inhibits learning. I want my writing to benefit me as well as my readers. If I want my readers to listen to me, I should listen to others who have already been part of the conversation concerning my topic.

I like to take time to explore a broad topic. If I start early on an assignment, then I have time to meander the Internet, search library databases, read books and talk to friends,

librarians, and experts. I bookmark sources, physically and electronically, and keep a separate Word document with notes about sources, so I can later trace my way back to the information I need. Though I won't use all of my research as I narrow down my topic, it is helpful, since it immerses me in my subject and exposes me to diverse perspectives.

As I narrow down my topic, I also need to determine the audience for and purpose of my essay. When writing for class, the instructor is an audience, of course, because he or she wields the red grading pen. But it's important also to think outside the context of the classroom and consider whom I might want to reach in a larger or "real-world" context. What do I want to persuade this broader audience to think, feel, or do? How do I effectively communicate with this audience ("with" is important since a writer has to anticipate a reader's response(s), not just throw assertions at him or her)? And what is the answer to the looming question, "So what?" In other words, I need to clarify why others should also care about my topic. All of this will further guide my research and drafting.

Aristotle's Classification of Rhetoric

Aristotle, in *The Art of Rhetoric* (or *Rhetoric*), laid the groundwork for today's persuasive writing by being the first to write systemically about how to teach rhetoric. In contrast, his teacher, Plato, distrusted rhetoric. Plato deplored the way rhetoricians (or politicians) of his era skillfully manipulated the people of Athens, particularly the masses of up to 10,000 voters in the Assembly or 500 in the juries of the law courts. Aristotle, on the other hand, perceived great potential in rhetoric, when taught properly. Rhetoric, as he envisioned it, could be both persuasive and ethical, and in *The Art of Rhetoric* he laid out an organization and classification of rhetoric as he believed it should be taught.

Aristotle divided the process of writing and delivering a composition into five parts. The first of these was **invention**, during which the writer or speaker expanded a topic into ideas that were later arranged into a text or speech. According to the ancient Greeks, the rhetor *invented* these ideas, though they may have mirrored or adapted thoughts presented by previous rhetors. Today, we call this the **prewriting stage** of the writing process, an adaptation of Aristotle's invention stage.

The Five Canons of Rhetoric

Greek and Roman teachers of rhetoric divided rhetoric into five parts or canons. These canons corresponded to the order of activities in creating a speech, as they perceived the process: invention, arrangement, style, memory, and delivery. These five parts are described in many handbooks of rhetorical instruction, including the *Rhetorica ad Herennium*, which was composed by an unknown author between 86 and 82 CE:

> The speaker. . .should possess the faculties of Invention, Arrangement, Style, Memory, and Delivery. Invention is the devising of matter, true or plausible, that would make the case convincing. Arrangement is the ordering and distribution of the matter, making clear the place to which each thing is to be assigned. Style is the adaptation of suitable words and sentences to the matter devised. Memory is the firm retention in the mind of the matter, words, and arrangement. Delivery is the graceful regulation of voice, countenance, and gesture.

Today, classes in composition or writing studies still emphasize the necessity of **invention**, now interpreted as prewriting activities that enable writers to develop the logic and words needed for effective arguments. **Arrangement** involves organizing an argument into a logical format that leads the reader easily from the thesis to the conclusion. **Style** has to do with the author's voice and tone and the structure of sentences and paragraphs. **Memory** is used somewhat differently today, as students are no longer required to memorize compositions for oral presentation. Instead, memory is utilized in ways such as remembering how and where to retrieve information from the Internet, books, and other reference materials. Finally, **delivery**, which once involved gestures and tone of voice in an oral presentation, today has to do with document design, so that the final product is presented in a professional manner according to Modern Language Association (MLA) or American Psychological Association (APA) style. Delivery also involves grammatical accuracy because surface errors detract from the effective impact of a document. See Table 4.1 for a summary of the five parts of rhetoric.

Table 4.1 • The Five Parts (or Canons) of Rhetoric

English	Greek	Latin
invention	*heuresis*	*inventio*
arrangement	*taxis*	*dispositio*
style	*lexis*	*elocutio*
memory	*mneme*	*memoria*
delivery	*hypocrisis*	*actin*

The Modern Writing Process Overview

Prewriting (Inventing)

Writing is not only about putting the pen to paper. As did rhetors in ancient Greece and Rome, you have to think deeply and critically about a subject before you begin a composition. The "invention" step of the writer's process is designed to help you find a worthwhile topic and develop your ideas about that topic before you start to write a draft. It includes writing, discussion, and research, as well as informal writing to help you explore your thoughts and feelings about a subject. Whatever method you choose, keep a record of your thoughts and discoveries as you spend this time in close examination of your subject.

Drafting

It may seem odd that writing a draft should come in the middle of the writer's process. However, research has shown that students and professionals alike write more effective essays when they don't reach for the pen too quickly. If you have spent enough time in the invention stage, the actual drafting stage may go more quickly. After writing the first draft, in succeeding drafts you can add details, observations, illustrations, examples, expert testimony, and other support to help your essay entertain, illuminate, or convince your audience.

Revising

Today, we talk more about the revision stage of writing than did ancient rhetoricians. If you are a student who tends to write assigned essays at the last minute, you may have missed this step entirely, yet many writers claim this is the longest and most rewarding step in the writing process. To revise, you must, in a sense, learn to let go of your writing. Some students think their first drafts should stay exactly the way they are written because they are true to their feelings and experience. Many writers find, however, that first drafts assume too much about the reader's knowledge and reactions. Sometimes readers, reading a first draft essay, are left scratching their heads and wondering what it is the writer is trying to convey. Writers who revise try to read their writing as readers would, taking note of gaps in logic, the absence of clear examples, the need for reordering information, and so on. Then they can revise their content with the reader in mind.

Editing and Polishing

Once writers have clarified their messages and the methods by which they will present those messages, one more step must be taken. Particularly because their compositions are written, rather than presented orally, writers must go over their work again to check for correct spelling, grammar, and punctuation, as well as the use of Standard Written English. Some students finish with an essay, print it, and turn it in without ever examining the final copy. This is a critical mistake, because misspelled words and typographical and formatting errors can make an otherwise well-written essay lose its credibility. The five canons of rhetoric and the modern writing process are summarized in Table 4.2.

Table 4.2 • The Five Canons of Rhetoric and the Modern Writing Process

Five Canons of Rhetoric	Modern Writing Process
Invention—Devising the arguments that will make the case convincing, often basing them on models of famous speeches.	Prewriting—Determining the thesis, points of argument, counterargument, and rebuttal. Researching evidence to support the argument.
Arrangement—Ordering the argument into a logical format.	Drafting, revising, and editing—Putting ideas and prewriting into a useable form through a recursive process of drafting, revising, and editing.
Style—Finding suitable words and figures of speech. [Note: This may have been a recursive process, but the ancients did not consider that aspect important.]	
Memory—Retaining the argument in the mind, including its content and arrangement.	Knowing how and where to retrieve information from the Internet, books, and other reference materials.
Delivery—Effective use of voice and gestures to present argument.	Publication—Putting text, images, and other elements in a suitable format and releasing the document to an audience.

Activity 4.1 • Compare the Five Canons of Rhetoric and the Modern Writing Process

In your group, reread the discussions in this chapter on the five canons of rhetoric and the modern writing process and review the table above. What parts of the five canons correspond to the modern writing process? What step in the five canons is not included in the contemporary writing process? If the similarities and differences are not clear to you, consult the Internet. If you search for either "Five Canons of Rhetoric" or "Writing Process" you will find resources. What explanations can you offer for the differences? The similarities?

Collaborate

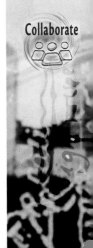

Stasis Theory

Stasis theory presents a series of four questions that were developed by Greek and Roman rhetoricians, primarily Aristotle, Quintilian, and Hermagoras. Answering these questions for an issue enabled rhetors to determine the critical (or stasis) point in a disagreement. This was a technique the ancients developed for the law courts to enable advocates to focus their arguments on the crux of the case. Quintilian, the great Roman teacher of rhetoric, explained in regard to a defendant:

> By far the strongest mode of defense is if the charge which is made can be denied; the next, if an act of the kind charged against the accused can be said not to have been done; the third, and most honorable, if what is done is proved to have been justly done. If we cannot command these methods, the last and only mode of defense is that of eluding an accusation, which can neither be denied nor combated, by the aid of some point of law, so as to make it appear that the action has not been brought in due legal form.

Marcus Fabius Quintilianus (Quintilian) was a Roman orator from Spain who taught stasis theory.

In other words, Quintilian is saying that in law cases, advocates have four choices in developing a focus for their arguments. You have probably watched a courtroom drama on television or film and can recall various defenses made on behalf of defendants. The strongest and most obvious defense is that the defendant is not guilty, that is, he or she did not do the deed in question. The same was true in Quintilian's day. However, sometimes an argument of innocence is not possible, perhaps because it seems obvious that the defendant did perform the deed in question. Thus, the advocate must develop a different strategy. For example, in defense of one accused of murder, the attorney may argue self-defense or mitigating circumstances (such as that the killing was an act of war). In rare cases, other defenses are offered; for example, if the supposed victim's body has not been found, the advocate can argue that the victim may still be alive. An attorney can discover these possible defenses by using stasis theory to analyze the situation.

Another great advantage of stasis theory is that, if pursued diligently, it prevents the rhetor from making the mistake of organizing an argument by simply forwarding reasons why he or she is correct and the opposition is wrong. That approach may please people who agree with the rhetor, but it will not likely gain any support from the opposition. Answering the stasis questions carefully forces the writer to consider aspects of the issue that may have been over-looked but are crucial to an effective argument.

The wording of the four questions has varied somewhat over time, but essentially they are questions of fact, definition, quality, and policy. The same questions can be applied to any issue, not only issues of law. The four stasis questions are as follows:

1. What are the facts? (conjecture)

2. What is the meaning or nature of the issue? (definition)

3. What is the seriousness of the issue? (quality)

4. What is the best plan of action or procedure? (policy)

Many writers prefer stasis theory to other prewriting techniques because answering the questions determines whether or not the different sides of an argument are at stasis. Being at stasis means that the opponents are in agreement about their disagreement—the stasis point—which can be identified by one of the four stasis questions. If the sides are at stasis, they have common ground to build upon, for they are arguing the same issue. There is, thus, a greater chance the sides can reach a workable consensus or compromise. If opponents are not at stasis, there is much more work to be done to reach consensus.

For example, in the argument about the teaching of evolution and/or intelligent design in schools, the two sides are not in agreement about how to discuss the issue. Those in favor of teaching evolution claim intelligent design should not be called science, which is an issue of definition. Those who propose teaching intelligent design along with (or instead of) evolution tend to focus on "prov-ing" evidence, an issue of fact. Until the two sides can agree upon what is the stasis point, or crux of the issue, they cannot debate effectively. They are not presenting arguments about the same question.

The four stasis questions can be broken into the subquestions listed in Table 4.3 on the following page. If you want to find the stasis point, work through the list for your issue, answering all of the subquestions. However, for each question, you must identify not only how *you* would answer the question but also how the opposing side or sides would answer. For example, if you are considering the issue of climate change, people with different positions will not agree on the facts. Thus, you must identify the basic facts of climate change represented by your side, and then identify the facts that might be presented by the opposing side.

Table 4.3 • Stasis Questions

Fact
<ul><li>Did something happen?</li><li>What are the facts?</li><li>Is there a problem/issue?</li><li>How did it begin, and what are its causes?</li><li>What changed to create the problem/issue?</li><li>Can it be changed?</li></ul>It also may be useful to ask the following critical questions of your own research and conclusions:<ul><li>Where did I obtain my data, and are these sources reliable?</li><li>How do I know they're reliable?</li></ul>

Definition
<ul><li>What is the nature of the problem/issue?</li><li>What exactly is the problem/issue?</li><li>What kind of a problem/issue is it?</li><li>To what larger class of things or events does it belong?</li><li>What are its parts, and how are they related?</li></ul>It also may be useful to ask the following critical questions of your own research and conclusions:<ul><li>Who/what is influencing my definition of this problem/issue?</li><li>How/why are these sources/beliefs influencing my definition of the issue?</li></ul>

Quality
<ul><li>Is it a good thing or a bad thing?</li><li>How serious is the problem/issue?</li><li>Who might be affected by this problem/issue (stakeholders)?</li><li>What happens if we don't do anything?</li><li>What are the costs of solving the problem/issue?</li></ul>It also may be useful to ask the following critical questions of your own research and conclusions:<ul><li>Who/what is influencing my determination of the seriousness of this problem/issue?</li><li>How/why are these sources/beliefs influencing my determination of the issue's seriousness?</li></ul>

Policy
• Should action be taken?
• Who should be involved in helping to solve the problem/address the issue?
• What should be done about this problem?
• What needs to happen to solve this problem/address this issue?
It also may be useful to ask the following critical questions of your own research and conclusions:
• Who/what is influencing my determination of what to do about this problem/issue?
• How/why are these sources/beliefs influencing my determination of what to do about this issue?
Adapted from Brizee, Allen. "Stasis Theory." *OWL Purdue Online Writing Lab,* Purdue University, 1 Mar. 2013, owl.english.purdue.edu/owl/resource/736/1/.

Using Stasis Questions

To illustrate the use of stasis questions, a team of writers working together to compose a report on racism in America might use the stasis questions to talk through information they will later use in their report. In the following sample dialogue, team members disagree about what actions are racist.

"Flying the Confederate battle flag is racist."

"Flying the Confederate battle flag is *not* racist."

"Yes, it is, because it represents the Confederate states that supported slavery, and it's generally accepted that slavery in America was racist."

"Flying the Confederate battle flag is not racist, because it's a part of American history and Southern heritage."

"After the June 2015 shooting in the Charleston church, more people have come to see flying the Confederate flag as a racist act."

"Yes, but flying the flag is still protected by the First Amendment as free speech."

These two team members disagree about whether or not flying the Confederate battle flag is a racist act. This sort of disagreement might lead to a complete breakdown of group work if common ground cannot be found.

In this example, the team members go on to agree that some people still exhibit the Confederate battle flag (*fact*) on their vehicles and on their clothes, and that the flag is also displayed in museums (*fact*).

The group members agree that the issue is still very important to many people, since a number of American states have recently debated the flag in legislatures and assemblies. For example, the South Carolina Legislature voted in 2015 to remove the Confederate battle flag from the state capitol grounds, while some opposed to the change said the removal disrespected the state's Confederate history (*quality*).

Moreover, a number of legal suits have been filed for and against the display of the flag in public places. For example, the Supreme Court in 2015 decided that Texas's refusal to allow specialty license plates to bear the Confederate flag did not violate the First Amendment. However, those selling and displaying the flag have suggested that the flag does not represent an endorsement of slavery but, rather, regional pride (*quality*).

In this sense, the team members have achieved stasis on two of the four stases—*fact* (people still display the flag) and *quality* (it's a very important issue). Where the team members disagree, however, is in the stases of *definition* (is the display of the flag "racist"?) and *policy* (what should we do about this?).

Thinking about this disagreement using stasis theory allows people to build common ground so that parties who disagree can move toward resolution and action even if they can't agree on all levels. For example, team members who disagree about whether or not flying the Confederate battle flag is racist might still be able to agree on what to do about it.

> "Okay, we disagree about whether flying the flag is racist, but we can agree that flying the flag is probably protected under the First Amendment to the United States Constitution—that flying the flag is protected by our freedom of speech."

> "Yeah."

> "So, people are free to display the flag on their vehicles, on their clothes, and on their property, as well as in museums. But, state legislatures and assemblies, like the one in South Carolina, will have to debate and vote on whether or not the flag can be displayed on publicly funded property or in public symbols, such as state flags and seals. And it may be that the courts may some-

Figure 4.1 • Disallowed Texas License Plate

License plate that Texas refused to allow because of its incorporation of the Confederate flag.

times need to be involved, like in the case of the Supreme Court decision about license plates in Texas.

"That sounds pretty democratic. Sure."

Not every team situation is going to end this amicably; however, by using the stasis questions to help keep the dialogue going—on a reasonable course— team members can find common ground and work toward action that is acceptable to most, if not all, of the group members.[1]

Stasis Theory and Kairos

As you will remember from Chapter 3, the *kairos* of an argument is the context, opportune moment, or point in time in which the rhetor, the audience, the issue, and the current situation provide opportunities and constraints for an argument. If you keep *kairos* in mind as you analyze an issue, you take advantage of timeliness. For example, if you want to write an argument about the death penalty, you might consider that United States courts are increasingly questioning the validity of eyewitness testimony, evidence which has been the deciding factor in many death penalty cases.

As part of your use of stasis theory, consider the four questions in relation to *kairos.*

1. How do recent developments (new facts) or the local situation affect the issue? Will it change your audience's perception of the facts?

2. Does the current situation affect your audience's definition of the issue? Is it defined differently by an audience in this location than elsewhere?

---

1. Adapted from Brizee, Allen. "Stasis Theory for Teamwork." *OWL Purdue Online Writing Lab,* Purdue University, 17 Apr. 2010, owl.english.purdue.edu/owl/resource/736/03/.

3. Have recent events made the issue more or less important to your audience? Is it more or less important in your location than elsewhere?

4. Do recent events, locally or widely, affect the need or lack of need for action in your audience's perception?

As a rhetorician, it is important for you to be aware of the history of a controversy. But it is equally important to have an awareness of the *kairos* of the argument. Such an awareness enables you to adopt a "ready stance" and adjust your argument, so that it reflects an awareness of your audience's position and interests, as well as contemporary developments in the issue. Such a flexible stance may afford you an opportunity to be persuasive that you might otherwise miss.

Explore

Activity 4.2 • Identify the Defense in a Television or Film Courtroom Drama

As your instructor directs, watch a courtroom drama on television or film and decide what defense the defendant's attorney is offering. Report your conclusion to your small group or the class. Then, after you have discussed the stasis questions, identify which of the four questions the attorney in the drama is focusing upon as the crux of the defense. Discuss with your group or the class.

Explore

Activity 4.3 • Use Stasis Theory to Explore Your Topic

Choose an issue that interests you and answer all the stasis questions in Table 4.3 on pp. 128–29, both for your position and for the opposing argument. Elaborate with three or four sentences for each subquestion that is particularly relevant to your topic. Is your issue at stasis for any of the questions? Report to your group or to the class.

Compose

Activity 4.4 • Evaluate a Public Debate

Locate a public debate that has been reported recently in newspaper editorials, television programs, or other media that can be analyzed by using stasis theory. In a paper of 350 to 500 words, address these points.

- ▮ Describe the context (*kairos*).
- ▮ Identify the sides of the argument and their main points.
- ▮ Decide which stasis question each side is primarily addressing.
- ▮ Determine whether or not the issue is at stasis and explain your answer.
- ▮ Include a citation in MLA or APA format for your source or sources.

The $300 House Casebook

Situation: Professors Vijay Govindarajan and Christian Sarkar launched a competition on the *Harvard Business Network* blog for designs to build $300 houses for people in developing countries. Word of the competition spread quickly, and a wide variety of people began to write about the competition in editorials in *The New York Times, The Economist,* and in a companion blog, www.300house.com/blog.

Read the four articles written about the $300 house competition that appear on the following pages. Discuss them in class and in small groups. In particular, note that Matias Echanove and Rahul Srivastava write in their *New York Times* op-ed essay, "Hands Off Our Houses," that the idea of a $300 house is impractical and will fail in places such as Mumbai, India. In contrast, "A $300 Idea that Is Priceless," the editorial from *The Economist*, praises the design competition for initiating an "explosion of creativity." Yet, both articles agree on the point that new approaches need to be tried to improve the housing situation for the world's poor.

If you visit the website for the $300 house, www.300house.com, you can see that many things are happening to move the concept forward, though there is still no consensus about the best way to build houses for the poor.

Casebook Reading 1

The $300 House: A Hands-On Lab for Reverse Innovation?
by Vijay Govindarajan and Christian Sakar

The $300 house is the concept of a one-room shed built around a slum family's ecosystem.

Published in the *Harvard Business Review Online.*

David A. Smith, the founder of the Affordable Housing Institute (AHI) tells us that "markets alone will never satisfactorily house a nation's poorest citizens . . . whether people buy or rent, housing is typically affordable to only half of the population."

The result? Smith points to a "spontaneous community of self-built or informally built homes—the shanty towns, settlements, and ever-expanding slums that sprout like mushrooms on the outskirts of cities in the developing world."

We started discussing the issue, examining the subject through the lens of reverse innovation.

Here are five questions Christian and I asked ourselves:

How can organic, self-built slums be turned into livable housing?

What might a house-for-the-poor look like?

How can world-class engineering and design capabilities be utilized to solve the problem?

What reverse-innovation lessons might be learned by the participants in such a project?

How could the poor afford to buy this house?

Livable Housing. Our first thought was that self-built houses are usually built from materials that are available—cardboard, plastic, mud or clay, metal scraps and whatever else is nearby. Built on dirt floors, these structures are prone to collapse and catching fire. Solution: replace these unsafe structures with a mass-produced, standard, affordable, and sustainable solution. We want to create the $300-House-for-the-Poor.

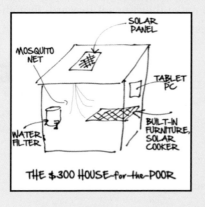

THE $300 HOUSE-for-the-POOR

Look and Feel. To designers, our sketch of this house might be a bit of a joke, but it's useful nonetheless to illustrate the concept, to get started. We wanted the house to be an eco-system of products and solutions designed around the real needs of the inhabitants. Of course it would have to be made out of sustainable, green materials, but more crucially, it would have to be durable enough to withstand torrential rains, earthquakes, and the stress of children playing. The house might be a single room structure with drop-down partitions for privacy. Furniture—sleeping hammocks and fold-down chairs would be built in. The roof would boast an inexpensive solar panel and battery to light the house and charge the mobile phone and tablet computer. An inexpensive water filter would be built in as well.

In effect, the house is really a one-room shed designed around the family ecosystem, a lego-like aggregation of useful products that "bring good things to life" for the poor.

World-Class Design. Our next question was: "Who will do this?" We decided that it would have to be a collaboration between global design and engineering companies and non-profits with experience solving problems for the poor. The usual suspects ran through our minds—IDEO, GE, TATA, Siemens, Habitat-for-Humanity, Partners In Health, the Solar Electric Light Fund, the Clinton Global Initiative, the Gates Foundation, Grameen. Governments may play an important part in setting the stage for these types of cross-country innovation projects.

The Reverse Innovation Payoff. Participating companies will reap two rewards. First, they will be able to serve the unserved, the 2.5 billion who make up the bottom of the pyramid. Second, they create new competencies which can help transform lives in rich countries by creating breakthrough innovations to solve several problems (scaled housing for hurricane victims, refugees, and even the armed forces).

A House of One's Own: Affordability. To move beyond charity, the poor must become owners of their homes, responsible for their care and upkeep. The model of social business introduced by Muhammad Yunus resonates strongly with us. Micro-finance must surely play a role in making the $300 House-for-the-Poor a viable and self-sustaining solution.

Of course, the idea we present here is an experiment. Nevertheless, we feel it deserves to be explored. From the one-room shacks in Haiti's Central Plateau to the jhuggi clusters in and around Delhi, to the favelas in São Paulo, the problem of housing-for-the-poor is truly global.

We ask CEOs, governments, NGOs, foundations: Are there any takers?

Govindarajan, Vijay, and Christian Sakar. "The $300 House: A Hands-On Lab for Reverse Innovation?" *Harvard Business Review Online,* Harvard Business Review, 26 Aug. 2010, hbr.org/2010/08/the-300-house-a-hands-on-lab-f.html.

Casebook Reading 2

Hands Off Our Houses
by Matias Echanove and Rahul Srivastava

Published in *The New York Times.*

Matias Echanove and Rahul Srivastava suggest that the $300 house will fail in places like Mumbai, India, because the concept ignores the reality of the slum's condition.

Mumbai, India

Last summer, a business professor and a marketing consultant wrote on *The Harvard Business Review*'s website about their idea for a $300 house. According to the writers, and the many people who have enthusiastically responded since, such a house could improve the lives of millions of urban poor around the world. And with a $424 billion market for cheap homes that is largely untapped, it could also make significant profits.

The writers created a competition, asking students, architects and businesses to compete to design the best prototype for a $300 house (their original sketch was of a one-room prefabricated shed, equipped with solar panels, water filters and a tablet computer). The winner will be announced this month. But one expert has been left out of the competition, even though her input would have saved much time and effort for those involved in conceiving the house: the person who is supposed to live in it.

We work in Dharavi, a neighborhood in Mumbai that has become a one-stop shop for anyone interested in "slums" (that catchall term for areas lived in by the urban poor). We recently showed around a group of Dartmouth students involved in the project who are hoping to get a better grasp of their market. They had imagined a ready-made constituency of slum-dwellers eager to buy a cheap house that would necessarily be better than the shacks they'd built themselves. But the students found that the reality here is far more complex than their business plan suggested.

To start with, space is scarce. There is almost no room for new construction or ready-made houses. Most residents are renters, paying $20 to $100 a month for small apartments.

Those who own houses have far more equity in them than $300—a typical home is worth at least $3,000. Many families have owned their houses for two or three generations, upgrading them as their incomes increase. With additions, these homes become what we call "tool houses," acting as workshops, manufacturing units, warehouses and shops. They facilitate trade and production, and allow homeowners to improve their living standards over time.

None of this would be possible with a $300 house, which would have to be as standardized as possible to keep costs low. No number of add-ons would be able to match the flexibility of need-based construction.

In addition, construction is an important industry in neighborhoods like Dharavi. Much of the economy consists of hardware shops, carpenters, plumbers, concrete makers, masons, even real-estate agents. Importing pre-fabricated homes would put many people out of business, undercutting the very population the $300 house is intended to help.

Worst of all, companies involved in producing the house may end up supporting the clearance and demolition of well-established neighborhoods to make room for it. The resulting resettlement colonies, which are multiplying at the edges of cities like Delhi and Bangalore, may at first glance look like ideal markets for the new houses, but the dislocation destroys businesses and communities.

The $300 house could potentially be a success story, if it was understood as a straightforward business proposal instead of a social solution. Places like refugee camps, where many people need shelter for short periods, could use such cheap, well-built units. A market for them could perhaps be created in rural-urban fringes that are less built up.

The $300 house responds to our misconceptions more than to real needs. Of course problems do exist in urban India. Many people live without toilets or running water. Hot and unhealthy asbestos-cement sheets cover millions of roofs. Makeshift homes often flood during monsoons. But replacing individual, incrementally built houses with a ready-made solution would do more harm than good.

A better approach would be to help residents build better, safer homes for themselves. The New Delhi–based Micro Homes Solutions, for example, provides architectural and engineering assistance to homeowners in low-income neighborhoods.

The $300 house will fail as a social initiative because the dynamic needs, interests and aspirations of the millions of people who live in places like Dharavi have been overlooked. This kind of mistake is all too common in the trendy field of social entrepreneurship. While businessmen and professors applaud the $300 house, the urban poor are silent, busy building a future for themselves.

Echanove, Matias, and Rahul Srivastava. "Hands Off Our Houses." *The New York Times,* 31 May 2011, www.nytimes.com/2011/06/01/opinion/01srivastava.html.

Sponsors of the $300 house competition respond to criticism.

The $300 House: A Hands-On Approach to a Wicked Problem

by Vijay Govindarajan with Christian Sarkar

Published in the *Harvard Business Review Online*.

When *The New York Times* printed "Hands Off Our Houses," an op-ed about our idea for a $300 House for the poor, we were both delighted and dismayed—delighted because the $300 House was being discussed, and dismayed because authors Matias Echanove and Rahul Srivastava, co-founders of the Institute of Urbanology, didn't seem to have read the series of blog posts about our idea.

Nearly every criticism the authors levy in their op-ed is answered in 12 blog posts, a magazine article from January/February 2011, a video interview, and a slideshow that integrated community and commentary, which were published between last October and this May.

In critiquing our vision, the authors cite Micro Homes Solutions as "a better approach." In fact, the leaders of that venture were invited several months ago to contribute a blog post to our series as a way of joining the discussion and helping us understand what they've seen on the ground there. They declined to be part of the conversation.

The authors also write that students who tried to write a business plan to serve the poor and who visited poor urban areas of India found "the reality here is far more complex than their business plan suggested."

Yet a fundamental tenet of our project and the blog series about it is that slums present complex challenges that can't be fixed with a clever shack alone. Rather than creating an echo chamber of rah-rah rhetoric, we told blog authors to focus on one of the many knotty issues that Echanove and Srivastava cite in their critique. From the start we asked: What are the complexities of financing these homes? How do you get energy and infrastructure into such dwellings? How do you get corporations to invest in a significant way? We acknowledged that we didn't have the answers. "Just because it is going to take longer than it should doesn't mean we should walk away," wrote Seth Godin in one of the posts. "It's going to take some time, but it's worth it."

The op-ed suggests that the $300 House doesn't acknowledge that "space is scarce" in urban poor areas. Yet, Sunil Suri wrote in a post on the urban challenge that "slums by their nature are located where land and space are limited." Suri proposed potential solutions, including innovative materials, new ways of thinking of the construction process, and building up.

The authors also say that "one expert has been left out of the challenge. . . the person who is supposed to live in it." But a post in the series on the co-creation challenge from Gaurav Bhalla addressed this squarely. "It will be unfortunate if the house were to be designed by those who will never live in it," wrote Bhalla. "Investments need to be made understanding the daily habits and practices of people for whom the house is being designed." Bhalla used the case study of the chulha stove, co-created by businesses, NGOs, and slum dwellers, to make his point. We are also bringing students to India and Haiti to do ethnographic research that will inform development of a $300 House, and when prototypes are developed, they will be deployed and tested with those who will live in them.

Echanove and Srivastava also state that a $300 House "would have to be as standardized as possible to keep costs low. No number of add-ons would be able to match the flexibility of need-based construction." While we agree that a one-size-fits-all approach will not work, we disagree that a $300 House would be inflexible. Core tenets from a blog post about the overall design challenge of creating a $300 House by Bill Gross include "give your customers options" and "make it aspirational." And David Smith's entry on the financial challenge shows that flexibility can be born out of financing options as well. A need-based approach alone also ignores the scale of the problem we are facing. "Triple the U.S. population by three. That's how many people around the world live on about a dollar a day," Godin writes. "Triple it again and now you have the number that lives on $2. About 40% of the world lives on $2 or less a day." In any situation where scale is required, so is some level of standardization.

The most puzzling critique in the op-ed was that "construction is an important industry in neighborhoods like Dharavi. Much of the economy consists of hardware shops, carpenters, plumbers, concrete makers, masons, even real-estate agents. Importing prefabricated homes would put many people out of business, undercutting the very population the $300 house is intended to help."

In fact, our contest's design briefing said these dwellings should be "self built and/or self-improvable." It also stated that the design should rely as much as possible on local materials, which of course would be harvested and crafted by local workers. Our goal is to increase demand for local trades, not drive them away. And the idea that jobs would disappear belies the fact that with progress comes new jobs; teachers for the kids who can now go to school; health care professionals for the families that can now afford check-ups; technology professionals who could service solar panels or internet access devices; farmers who could manage shared crop spaces in the neighborhoods. The $300 House project is a housing ecosystem project.

Finally, Echanove and Srivastava state that "The $300 house could potentially be a success story, if it was understood as a straightforward business proposal instead of a social solution."

We disagree completely. We do support other applications for low-cost housing—bringing these dwellings back to the industrialized world for hurricane relief, for example, would be a reverse innovation success story. However, trying to pigeonhole ideas as either "for good" or "for profit" is an outmoded way of thinking.

The authors have an implicit negative view on business. For them, profit seems to be a dirty word. For us, good business and social innovation are one and the same. The rising tide of New Capitalism, what Michael Porter calls "shared value" and what Umair Haque calls "thick value," is perhaps the most important reaction to the corruption and greed that spurred the most recent global economic crisis. The *Economist* was right when it suggested that this is a "can do" moment in history.

Our goal is neither to start yet another charity—one of our advisers, Paul Polak, tells us that "you can't donate your way out of poverty"—nor to start just another business. Rather we must encourage existing businesses to find ways to create new, scalable markets; to get NGOs to share their on-the-ground expertise; and to force governments to make it as simple as possible to work across the hybrid value chain in order to make such a project a reality and begin the process of instilling dignity in and creating options for individuals who now don't have either.

We are happy that Echanove and Srivastava share our passion for the problem of affordable housing, which is a wicked problem. We simply disagree with the idea that if it's a market, it can't also be a socially progressive solution. Trying to categorize the regeneration of slums as either a business problem or social problem is like trying to categorize a flame as either heat or light. It is both, always.

Govindarajan, Vijay, and Christian Sarkar. "The $300 House: A Hands-On Approach to a Wicked Problem." *Harvard Business Review Online,* Harvard Business Review, 7 June 2011, hbr.org/2011/06/when-the-new-york-times.html.

A $300 Idea that Is Priceless

from *Schumpeter*, a column in *The Economist*

Economist *editorial praises the $300 House competition for initiating an "explosion of creativity."*

Casebook Reading 4

Friedrich Engels said in "The Condition of the Working Class in England," in 1844, that the onward march of Manchester's slums meant that the city's Angel Meadow district might better be described as "Hell upon Earth." Today, similar earthly infernos can be found all over the emerging world: from Brazil's favelas to Africa's shanties. In 2010 the United Nations calculated that there were about 827m people living in slums—almost as many people as were living on the planet in Engels's time—and predicted that the number might double by 2030.

Last year Vijay Govindarajan, of Dartmouth College's Tuck School of Business, along with Christian Sarkar, a marketing expert, issued a challenge in a *Harvard Business Review* blog: why not apply the world's best business thinking to housing the poor? Why not replace the shacks that blight the lives of so many poor people, thrown together out of cardboard and mud, and prone to collapsing or catching fire, with more durable structures? They laid down a few simple guidelines. The houses should be built of mass-produced materials tough enough to protect their inhabitants from a hostile world. They should be equipped with the basics of civilized life, including water filters and solar panels. They should be "improvable," so that families can adapt them to their needs. And they should cost no more than $300.

Mr. Govindarajan admits that the $300 figure was partly an attention-grabbing device. But he also argues that it has a certain logic. Muhammad Yunus, the founder of Grameen Bank, has calculated that the average value of the houses of people who have just escaped from poverty is $370. Tata Motors has also demonstrated the value of having a fixed figure to aim at: the company would have found it more difficult to produce the Tata Nano if it had simply been trying to produce a "cheap" car rather than a "one lakh" car (about $2,200).

The attention-grabbing certainly worked. The blog was so inundated with positive responses that a dedicated website, 300house.com, was set up, which has attracted more than 900 enthusiasts and advisers from all over the world. On April 20th Mr. Govindarajan launched a competition inviting people to submit designs for a prototype of the house.

Why has a simple blog post led to such an explosion of creativity? The obvious reason is that "frugal innovation"—the art of radically reducing the cost of products while also delivering first-class value—is all the rage at the moment. General Electric has reduced the cost of an electrocardiogram machine from $2,000 to $400. Tata Chemicals has produced a $24 purifier that can provide a family with pure water for a year. Girish Bharadwaj, an engineer, has perfected a technique for producing cheap footbridges that are transforming life in rural India.

Another reason is that houses can be such effective anti-poverty tools. Poorly constructed ones contribute to a nexus of problems: the spread of disease (because they have no proper sanitation or ventilation), the perpetuation of poverty (because children have no proper lights to study by) and the general sense of insecurity (because they are so flimsy and flammable). Mr. Govindarajan's idea is so powerful because he treats houses as ecosystems that provide light, ventilation and sanitation.

Numerous innovators are also worrying away at this nexus of problems. Habitat for Humanity, an NGO, is building durable houses of bamboo in Nepal. Idealab, a consultancy, is on the verge of unveiling a $2,500 house that will be mass-produced in factories, sold in kits and feature breakthroughs in ventilation, lighting and sanitation. Philips has produced a cheap cooking stove, the Chulha, that cuts out the soot that kills 1.6m people a year worldwide. The Solar Electric Light Fund is demonstrating that you can provide poor families with solar power for roughly the same cost as old standbys such as kerosene and candles.

Profits and other problems

These thinkers, like the advocates of the $300 house, must solve three huge problems to succeed. They must persuade big companies that they can make money out of cheap homes, because only they can achieve the economies of scale needed to hit the target price. They need to ensure sufficient access to microloans: $300 is a huge investment for a family of squatters living on a couple of dollars a day. And they need to overcome the obstacle that most slum-dwellers have weak or non-existent property rights. There is no point in offering people the chance to buy a cleverly designed house if they have no title to the land they occupy. Solving these problems will in turn demand a high degree of co-operation between people who do not always get on: companies and NGOs, designers and emerging-world governments.

However, the exciting thing about the emerging world at the moment is a prevailing belief that even the toughest problems can be solved. And a similar can-do moment, in the late 1940s, offers a striking historical precedent for the application of mass-production techniques to housing: as American servicemen flooded home after the second world war to start families, Levitt & Sons built Levittowns at the rate of 30 houses a day by mass-producing the components in factories, delivering them on lorries and using teams of specialists to assemble them.

Some emerging-world governments are beginning to realize that providing security of tenure is the only way to deal with the problem of ever-proliferating slums. And big companies that face stagnant markets in the West are increasingly fascinated by the "fortune at the bottom of the pyramid." Bill Gross of Idealab reckons the market for cheap houses could be worth at least $424 billion. But in reality it is worth far more than that: preventing the Earth from becoming what Mike Davis, a particularly gloomy follower of Marx and Engels, has termed a "planet of slums."

"A $300 Idea That Is Priceless." *Schumpeter*, 28 Apr. 2011, *The Economist*, www.economist.com/node/18618271.

Activity 4.5 • Use Stasis Questions to Analyze the $300 House Casebook

Collaborate

In your small group, work through the stasis questions with one side of the controversy being those who support this design initiative. The other side will be those who foresee problems in applying this idealistic initiative in the real world; a viewpoint that is expressed in "Hands Off Our Houses." Identify a subquestion or subquestions in which the two sides are at stasis. Discuss why the two sides are at stasis on this point or points.

Use this analysis to help you write the essay specified in Activity 4.6.

Activity 4.6 • Persuasive Essay about the $300 House Casebook Utilizing Stasis Theory

Compose

After you have completed Activity 4.5, write a paper of approximately 750 words in which you:

  ▌ briefly present the idea of the design competition,

  ▌ summarize the arguments of those in favor of the initiative,

  ▌ explain the reservations expressed in "Hands Off Our Houses,"

  ▌ identify a stasis point, if one exists, and explain why you think the sides have common ground on that particular stasis question, and

  ▌ discuss whether the discovery of common ground might allow individuals involved in this debate to talk to one another and work toward solutions for the problem of substandard housing in slums worldwide.

As your instructor directs, cite your sources in APA or MLA style. After each of the three casebook readings is an MLA citation that you can import into your Works Cited. However, you will still need to write citations for your sources in the text.

Compose

Activity 4.7 • Comment on Your Essay about the $300 House

Freewrite for five minutes about your experience working through the stasis questions for the $300 House Casebook and writing an essay based on the information you collected by answering the stasis questions. Did you find the stasis questions useful in developing your argument for the essay? Why or why not? Is this a technique you would use again? Why or why not?

If your instructor directs, revise your freewriting into a paragraph to turn in.

Other Invention Strategies

Great myths have grown up around writers who can supposedly sit down, put pen to paper, and write a masterpiece. If these myths had developed about any other type of artist—a musician or a painter—we would scoff about them and ask about the years of study and practice those artists had spent before they created their masterpieces. Since all of us can write to some degree, perhaps it seems more feasible that great authors simply appear magically amongst us. Alas, it is not so; like all talented artists, good writers must learn their craft through consistent and continuous practice. Similar to how the ancient Greeks used **stasis questions** or *topoi* (a strategy or heuristic made up of questions about a topic which allows a rhetor to construe an argument) to generate raw material for their compositions, many writers today use the following invention strategies as prewriting activities.

Freewriting

One practice method developed in the 1970s and often attributed to Peter Elbow, author of *Writing without Teachers*, is called freewriting. This method is just what it sounds like—writing that is free of any content restrictions. You simply write what is on your mind. This method is freeform, but there is some structure—you must set a time limit before you begin, and once you begin, you must not stop. The time period is usually 10 to 20 minutes, and you must keep your pen or pencil moving on the page—no hesitations, no corrections, no rereading. Don't worry about spelling, or punctuation, or grammar—just download onto the paper whatever comes to mind. It will seem awkward at best; some have said it is downright painful. But after a few weeks of practice, you will realize it is effective and a wonderful individual method of getting at your thoughts on a subject.

Invisible Freewriting

If you just cannot stop paying attention to your spelling and grammar, or if you find yourself always stopping to read what you have written, you can freewrite invisibly. To do this, you will need carbon paper and a pen that is retracted or out of ink. You sandwich the carbon paper, carbon side down, between two sheets of paper and write on the top sheet with your empty pen. You cannot see what you are writing, but it will be recorded on the bottom sheet of paper. If you prefer to work on the computer, you can easily modify this technique by taping a blank sheet of paper over the monitor while you type.

Focused Freewriting

When freewriting, you are writing without sticking to any particular topic. You are exploring many ideas and your sentences may roam from your day at work, the letter you just got from your sister, or a story you read in the paper about a man who tracks the nighttime migrations of songbirds. With focused freewriting, you are trying to concentrate on one particular subject. You can write the name of that subject at the top of the page to remind you of your topic as you write. The rules are the same as the other types of freewriting, but you are focusing on one question or idea and exploring it in depth.

One drawback of focused freewriting is that students sometimes confuse it with a different step in the writing process: drafting. Remember that freewriting is "invention" work, intended only to help you explore ideas on paper. Drafting takes place only after you have explored, analyzed, and organized those ideas. Freewriting helps you think and write critically about a topic while drafting occurs once you have done the critical thinking necessary to come up with a unified, cohesive, and organized plan for an essay.

Listing/Brainstorming

This method of mapping is the least visual and the most straightforward. Unlike freewriting, where you write continuously, with listing you write down words and/or phrases that provide a shorthand for the ideas you might use in your essay, much as you would a grocery or "to-do" list. Brainstorming is a bit looser. Lists usually follow line after line on the page; brainstorming consists of words and phrases placed anywhere you want to write them on the page.

Example of Brainstorming about Climate Change

Global warming

Polar ice caps melting

Cities underwater as water rises

Natural process or human caused?

People will lose homes when in places where ocean will rise

UK built Thames barrier

How much will preventative measures cost, and who pays for them?

Clustering

When you think of a cluster, you think of several like things grouped together, often with something holding them together. Peanut clusters, a type of candy, are peanuts joined together with milk chocolate. Star clusters are groupings of stars, like the Pleiades or the Big Dipper, connected by their relative positions to each other in space. You can create clusters of like ideas by grouping your ideas around a central topic on a blank sheet of paper. Figure 4.2 shows a sample clustering exercise.

Figure 4.2 • Sample Clustering Exercise

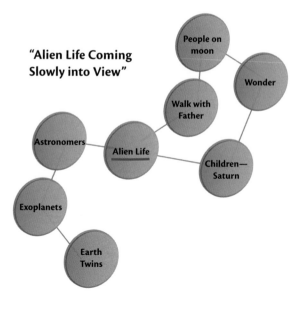

Activity 4.8 • Try Different Prewriting Techniques

Choose a topic, and try each of the prewriting techniques listed below. Save your work. Then, in your group, discuss which technique or techniques you prefer.

■ Freewriting

■ Invisible Freewriting

■ Focused Freewriting

■ Listing

■ Clustering

Activity 4.9 • Organize or Arrange Your Prewriting

The "invention" process is intended to get our ideas out of our heads and onto a piece of paper, but rarely do these ideas arrive in the most logical or effective order. Take some time to analyze the material that you produced when you completed the previous activity. Make a list, placing all the ideas in a logical order, and combine similar ideas.

Next, look for your most significant point, the most important thing you want to say about your subject. This may become your tentative thesis.

Then, identify which of the other items will help you communicate your thesis, and delete items that are irrelevant to it. Keep organizing and deleting until you are satisfied with your list of topics or main points.

Reading 4.1

Take a Leap into Writing
by Craig Wynne

When I was working at Berkeley's College Academic Support Center, I often tutored second-language learners who struggled with sentences that had awkward constructions. Sometimes, I would say to a student, "What is it you're trying to

Craig Wynne is an Assistant Professor of English and Modern Foreign Languages at Hampton University who also consults professionals on overcoming writing anxiety. In this article, Wynne uses skydiving as both a figurative and literal representation of "jumping" into the writing process. As you read, think about the times in your academic career when you have had hesitations about writing and how that affected your writing process.

say here?" The student inevitably could state the point orally with accuracy and clarity. I would then say to the student, "Write down what you just said." The student would write it down with pen and paper. Then I'd say, "Okay, pretend you're the professor. Which do you think is the easier sentence to understand: what you wrote or what you typed?" The student would say, "What I wrote. Whenever I type, I'm always afraid of what the professor will say."

Craig Wynne says, "When jumping out of an airplane, you don't have time to think about consequences. You just have to do it. [. . .] The same principle applies to writing."

Photo Credit: Craig Wynne

Around that time, I read an article in *Writer* magazine entitled "Forget the Rules and Take a Leap," by an author named Deanna Roy. In this article, Roy had been suffering from writer's block, and she found that skydiving was a way for her to release her thoughts without fear of saying the "wrong thing." So I decided to put this idea into practice myself for the purposes of teaching my students about overcoming their inhibitions when it came to writing.

When jumping out of an airplane, you don't have time to think about consequences. You just have to do it. You can see from the photo, jumping wasn't an easy thing for me to do, but afterwards I was glad I had gone through with taking that leap.

The same principle applies to writing. You need to find a way to write without thinking about whether your words are spelled correctly or whether the professor won't like the idea. Those thoughts get in the way with your writing process. Some students can write with that kind of freedom on a computer, but others find that with the computer comes an uninvited editor who looks over their shoulder and criticizes. Yet, they can escape that editor by talking out their thoughts and then writing with pen and paper. Whatever works. This doesn't mean that writing is ever going to be easy. It's just easier if you can get your thoughts down on a piece of paper before that internal editor starts looking for errors.

A professor named Peter Elbow developed a process called freewriting, which helps writers take that leap from thoughts into words. To freewrite, you put your pen to paper and just write. You don't want to think about whether something is spelled incorrectly or whether the professor will like an idea. Freewriting is the chance for you to get your ideas down on paper (or on the computer). When you freewrite, you don't stop. You just write. Even if you have an idea you think sounds completely stupid or off-the-wall, just write it down. You never know. Sometimes, those "silly" ideas could contain something you might be able to use for your assignment. When I start a project, I begin by letting all my ideas out in words in a row, even if they don't sound quite right. Professor Elbow remarked that freewriting results in a lot of words that are garbage. That's true. However, eventually, I come to words that express an idea I like. In order to get to the point of liking my words, I have to take that leap onto the page. Eventually, I have to worry about grammar, structure, and the end product, but not while I'm freewriting.

Activity 4.10 • Consider "Take a Leap into Writing"

In your small group or on your own, consider and answer the following questions.

1. How do you write most easily? On a computer? With pen and paper? Share your experience getting words onto a page.

2. What do you think of Wynne's comparison of writing to skydiving? What do the two things have in common?

3. Do you have an internal editor that keeps you from writing freely? Can you describe your editor? What does it do?

Collaborate

Compose

Activity 4.11 • Focused Freewriting

Practice doing some focused freewriting by following these steps.

1. Write your topic at the top of a blank sheet of paper.

2. Write a list of at least 10 aspects or characteristics of your topic.

3. Choose two or three items from your list, and do a focused freewriting on each item for five to eight minutes.

4. Add more items to your list if you have discovered new ideas during your freewriting.

Artistic and Inartistic Proofs

In the previous chapter, we discussed the three appeals or means that a rhetor can use to persuade an audience: *ethos, pathos,* and *logos.* In *The Art of Rhetoric,* Aristotle divides these appeals or means of persuasion into two types of proofs: artistic and inartistic. Today, these proofs are still part of the writing process though we call them by different names.

Artistic proofs are logical arguments constructed by rhetors from ideas plucked from their minds. An individual then develops these thoughts into a line of reasoning and, in the process, explores and narrows the topic, creates a thesis, and determines the ideas that need to be conveyed to the audience. These proofs are the ones that Aristotle and other ancient rhetoricians believed were critically important, for they are the ones developed from the *rhetor's own mind* and, thus, *invented.* These ideas can be shaped into two types of arguments—deductive and inductive—which we will discuss in the next few pages.

Inartistic proofs are direct evidence that the speaker might use to support the argument, such as testimony, documents, and anything else that rhetors do not invent through their own thinking. Today, we would call these proofs research. They, also, are essential to writing, but they should *support* the writer's ideas, rather than lead them.

For Aristotle's students, the use of artistic and inartistic proofs might not have been a two-step process—first one and then the other, though the proofs are arranged that way in *The Art of Rhetoric,* as they are in this book. Rather, they might have developed both proofs in an alternating or recursive process. After developing basic ideas for a composition through invention, these students would then collect information from authorities (testimony). Then they would return to inventing artistic proofs about the project, followed by more references to inartistic proofs. Today, we have more resources for research than did the ancient Greeks, but this does not make artistic proofs any less important. The differences between artistic and inartistic proofs are summarized in Table 4.4.

Table 4.4 • Aristotle's Artistic and Inartistic Proofs

Artistic	Inartistic
Ideas from the rhetor's own mind, thus *invented*	Information gained from external sources
Personal knowledge	Authorities
Observation	Testimony
Patterns of reasoning	Documents

Activity 4.12 • Begin with What You Know

Collaborate

In your small group, make a list of controversial topics that you already have some knowledge about because of personal experience or course work. For example, one of you may be among the millions of Americans without health insurance or you may know someone else in this position. If so, you probably know about some of the failings of the American health care system. Alternatively, you may have lost a job during the Great Recession or been unable to find a job when you needed one. If so, you probably have some thoughts about the efforts of the federal government to deal with the economic crisis. These personal experiences give you knowledge which you can use as artistic proofs in an essay. Share your group's list with the class.

Develop Artistic Proofs through Observation

Close observation for descriptive detail can enhance almost any topic. If you are writing a paper on the effectiveness of recycling in your community, you might take a trip to your community's processing area for recycled glass. There you could gather information through observing the glass recycling process. Good observations become personal knowledge which makes them artistic proofs.

You may need to call to get permission to visit certain places. You'll need to identify yourself and your topic. Usually you can get permission to visit and observe. However, if you cannot get permission to visit an area, you can ask your contact if there is a similar area nearby. Again, look at your research questions before you visit to decide which questions might be answered by your observations. For

example, if you have read about recycling centers in other communities, during your visit to the local center, you could observe the similarities and differences in their procedures. Good writers always gather more detail than they actually use so they have choices about what to include.

The key to successful observation is tuning the senses. Can you remember what your room smelled like when you woke up this morning, the first thing you saw when you opened your eyes, the way your sheets or blanket felt against your skin, the sounds in the room after you turned off your alarm, or the taste of the orange juice or coffee you had with breakfast? Our minds are trained to ignore seemingly unimportant information, so if you can't remember any sensory details from your morning, you're not alone. When conducting an observation, however, those sensory responses are an important part of your research. Sitting in the place you're observing, freewrite for at least five minutes on each of the senses: touch, taste, smell, sight, and sound. You might even freewrite on each of the senses from several different vantage points, depending on the size of the place or the event you're observing. Take notes on the responses given by those you speak with.

Within fifteen minutes of leaving the place you have been observing, take a few minutes to read over your notes and write a few overall impressions or add details you missed in your description. Look again at your research questions, and decide which ones have been answered by your visit.

Explore

Activity 4.13 • Observation Exercise to Develop Artistic Proofs

In this exercise, describe your classroom. Alternatively, go to another setting such as a museum, restaurant, or library and describe that space and the people in it.

- How large is the space, approximately? Describe the shape of the room, and the color and texture of the walls, the ceiling, and the floor.
- How is the space furnished? Describe the color, shape, and style of the furnishings.
- What about representing the other senses? Is the room silent or noisy? Does it have a characteristic smell? Describe.
- How many people are in the room? What are they doing? Describe their ages, general style of dress, and possessions such as computers, backpacks, or purses.
- Pick two or three people that stand out in some way from the other occupants and write a sentence or two about each, describing what it is about each person that caught your attention.

Porsche Macan S: Is This Compact Crossover Barbie's Dream Car?

By Dan Neil

You just knew when Porsche decided to build Barbie's Dream Car it was going to be awesome.

And it is. The 2015 Macan S ($49,900 MSRP) is Porsche's entry to the exploding luxury compact crossover segment, and it is a dram of excelsior, a proud, darling thing: quick off the line (5.0 seconds to 60 mph, with the optional launch control engaged) and nimble at the helm, with a steel-spring suspension (wishbone front and trapezoidal-link rear) that's as tight as a speed skater's buttocks. Actually, the Macan S drives shockingly well considering it weighs in around 4,500 pounds and is a foot taller than a 911. More on that later.

Curb appeal? Forget about it. Among the details to savor is the clamshell hood that extends to the front wheel arches, so that the hood shut lines go away. The Macan isn't dripping in aggression, design-wise, with soft,

Dan Neil, auto columnist for the Wall Street Journal, *reviewed the new Porsche Macan S in his weekly column "Rumble Seat." He calls the vehicle Barbie's dream car, meaning that Porsche has designed it with well-to-do, fashion-conscious women in mind. See if you think that stereotype fits the car.*

As you read the article, pay attention to how the author uses details from his personal knowledge of the auto world, as well as his close observation from driving and inspecting the Porsche, to enrich his writing. Notice, also, how some details—such as the $500 million Porsche spent to build an assembly line for the car in Leipzig, Germany—likely came from promotional materials or interviews with Porsche personnel.

Sexy Beast. The Porsche Macan S has a leg up in the luxury compact crossover market with soft contours and the best interior among its rivals.

Photo Credit: Porche Cars North America

rounded corners inherited from the 911 and an open, expressive face. It has nothing like the Range Rover Evoque's narrow, predatory stare. And yet the Macan is low, wide and stance-y, with staggered tires (a wider set in back) and heavy haunches. It's a Cayenne in short pants.

Porsche has made no secret of the desire to expand the brand to more women. Translating that desire into product design is a perilous business, especially for such a macho brand. But I think the Porsche design team, led by Michael Mauer, got exactly what it was looking for. The Macan hits a mall parking lot like a fishing lure hits the water, if smartly dressed women were largemouth bass.

The category, Alex, is premium/luxury compact crossovers and/or sport-utilities. The yard marks are wide, but you are going to shell out anywhere from about $40,000-$70,000—I recommend leasing such nonsense—and the competitive set includes the cream of the world auto-making crop: Acura RDX, Audi Q3, BMW X3, Land Rover Discovery Sport, Mercedes-Benz GLA, the Evoque and a few others.

In this category you are free to spend like you are on cocaine. There is such a thing as a Macan Turbo (with a 3.6-liter, 400-hp version of the V6) that starts at $72,300 and can top six figures when you start adding carbon-ceramic brakes ($8,150) and air suspension ($1,385).

Our Macan S test car—painted ermine-white with beige leather interior — came in at $72,620 and included 20-inch alloy wheels ($1,260), the active dampers ($1,360), the upgraded Bose stereo ($1,400) and infotainment package ($2,990) and the Premium Package Plus ($5,990). Oof!

The powertrain is a thing of beauty, starting with the all-aluminum, 90-degree, 3.0-liter direct-injection twin-turbo V6, producing a nicely focused 339 pound-feet, from 1,450 rpm all the way to 5,000 rpm, and peak horsepower from 5,500-6,500 rpm. Golly, what a sewing machine. When you switch to Sport + mode and add some throttle, the engine bawls, it purrs, it chuckles. Hot, guttural overrun sounds come courtesy of the active exhaust valve. But the symphony is turned way down in volume, a bit too far to seem threatening, just adorable. Growl, kitty, growl!

Downstream of the engine is Porsche's seven-speed dual-clutch PDK automatic transmission and the full-time all-wheel drive system, based around a digitally managed multi-plate center differential. The Macan's front diff is open and the rear is limited-slip, with the option of the Porsche Torque Vectoring Plus on the rear diff, slewing torque left or right as needed to help the car turn harder and accelerate sooner.

Romp it and all this actuates with greased flawlessness one might expect in a late-model Porsche, even to a fault. There isn't a sharp edge to be found is this car. Even in Sport + mode, the PDK acts like/drives like any other high-tech, torque-converter based automatic transmission, with upshift events that flutter among the ratios, never bang.

Honestly, Porsche. If the camera could zoom into the ghostly face of Ferdinand Porsche as he surveyed his legendary sports-car empire, now building glammy luxe crossovers for the recently divorced in West Palm Beach, would he have a single tear, like Iron Eyes Cody?

Oh, I've had it all explained to me: Porsche, now a holding of Volkswagen AG, has been fully entrained into the group's product slipstream. The Macan is a platform cousin to the Audi Q5, sharing VW's MLB platform, for light-duty vehicles with front-longitudinal engine orientation and all-wheel drive.

About a third of the Porsche's structure is common to the Audi, but Macan gets Porsche-proprietary engines and the PDK gearbox; exterior and interior; suspensions and dynamics software. Porsche AG also spent more than $550 million to construct the Macan assembly line in Leipzig, Germany—where car-building counts—with an annual capacity of 50,000 cars. So pedigree really isn't an issue.

And yet, I can't help thinking the Macan would have been a lot—what's the word?—lighter, had it not been born to share the girdle of the corporate platform.

If the Macan wins, it's to the credit of Porsche's interior-trim department. This is the best interior of any in the competitive set: clean and Nordic in design, wintry with polished alloy, rich with skins, with lots of very nice parts from the company's bins, including Porsche's new, three-spoke steering wheel, like the one in the 918 Spyder. The seats are terrific, and the fully upholstered rear cargo space large and useful (17.7 cubic feet). My kids had no problems riding in the back seat. The whole thing is surprisingly undiminished by the price point.

If the Macan stumbles, it might be because it feels a bit soft to enthusiasts. This truckette is well over two tons, and all the adaptive suspension, torque vectoring and sport tires only defray the costs of that mass. Yes, it has good road-holding in corners, considering, but the weight makes it feel antsy. Yes, the electric-assist steering is tactile and responsive, but it could be more of both. The short-stroke engine of the Macan S (69 mm stroke and 96 mm bore) spins like a bandit, but it's all so at a distance, so muted and isolated. The Macan's missing piece is driver involvement.

But maybe you don't feel like driving at the moment. In that case, switch on the Macan's optional Lane Keeping Assist, a ghost-in-the-machine system that will keep a car heading down a road with minimal input from the driver. Now you can smile. And don't forget to wave, Barbie.

Explore

Activity 4.14 • Find Artistic and Inartistic Proofs in a Reading

Much of the information for Dan Neil's column, "Porsche Macan S: Is This Compact Crossover Barbie's Dream Car?" comes from his own personal experience and observation. For example, his description of the car: "[I]t is a dram of excelsior, a proud, darling thing: quick off the line…with a steel-spring suspension (wishbone front and trapezoidal-link rear) that's as tight as a speed skater's buttocks," is his own evaluation or thought and, thus, an artistic proof. So is the sentence, "Porsche has made no secret of the desire to expand the brand to more women. Translating that desire into product design is a perilous business, especially for such a macho brand." That knowledge comes from his long experience with reviewing the automobile market.

However, the numbers Neil uses to describe the powertrain—"all-aluminum, 90-degree, 3.0-liter direct-injection twin-turbo V6, producing a nicely focused 339 pound-feet, from 1,450 rpm all the way to 5,000 rpm, and peak horsepower from 5,500-6,500 rpm"—may have come from the manufacturer's promotional literature or an interview, though the conclusion of "nicely focused" may be his own.

For this activity, go through the reading and highlight (or underline) the parts that you think come from Neil's own knowledge or observation. These are the artistic proofs. Information he has obtained from other sources (such as the car company) would be inartistic proofs.

If you aren't sure whether or not a sentence is Neil's own knowledge or observation, make a note of that in the margin. Discuss this as a class.

Activity 4.15 • Develop Criteria for Reviews

Explore

In your small group, discuss these questions in response to Neil's article about the Porsche Macan S.

1. What criteria did Dan Neil use in evaluating the Porsche Macan S? Share your answers with the class.

2. What reviews do you plan to write for Activity 4.16? Discuss in your group how each of you plans to develop criteria to evaluate your topics.

Individually, make a short list of criteria you will use to evaluate your topic for Activity 4.16.

Activity 4.16 • Write a Product Review

Compose

Choose a new product in a category you know well, such as a computer or a motorcycle, and write a review as if you were a columnist for a newspaper, magazine, or blog. Using the techniques explained in this chapter, such as freewriting or brainstorming, prewrite to elicit what you know about the product and the product category. Then, observe the product and try it out, so that you can review its positives and negatives. If you need specific information that you do not know, consult the product advertising, packaging, or instruction manual.

Like Dan Neil's auto product review, you can use vivid language and insider slang in order to provide an enjoyable experience for your reader. Remember, however, that this is an argument. You need to evaluate whether the product is a good or bad selection for its target audience and why.

Reading 4.3

Guardians of the Galaxy's **Happy Satire of the Sad Origin Story**

by Katie Kilkenny

Superhero origin stories, for the most part, aren't very original. They all to some extent involve a young child or particularly immature man falling prey to a terrible crime, accident, experiment, or, alternately, reluctantly getting chosen by higher powers. Then comes a period of shock swiftly followed by a period of combat training—for, as all comic lovers

Katie Kilkenny's film review, published on theatlantic.com, makes use of the superhero origin story plot format to review Guardians of the Galaxy. *Superhero origin stories, according to Kilkenny, are not generally very original. However,* Guardians *adds a satire twist to the plot pattern because the deep trauma's of the film's heroes has not endowed them with any nobility, as it usually does in an origin story; rather, they are misfit sell-outs who are, nevertheless, called upon to save the galaxy.*

understand, a true hero directs his mournful energies toward coordinating outfits, gadgets, and crime-fighting prowess around a theme. The takeaway: Superheroes are just like you and me until something genuinely terrible befalls them—then, an inhumanly noble hunger to fight crime takes over.

On the surface, *Guardians of the Galaxy,* Marvel's latest movie, is an origin story, too. Given the obscurity of the source comic, it has to be: Our heroes, a bunch of alien rogues, were introduced briefly in a 1969 issue of *Marvel Superheroes,* played benchwarmers to the likes of the Avengers for about 50 years, then were revived by writers Dan Abnett and Andy Lanning in 2008 to middling sales. To counteract the risk of the venture we follow recognizable white male Chris Pratt, newly buff and emotional, playing Peter Quill, a boy who was abducted by aliens and now calls himself "Star-Lord."

Sensibly, Peter's chosen alias is roundly mocked by his fellow Guardians in the film—as is his masculinity, wooing capabilities, general leadership, and other qualities that usually endorse newbie heroes in tights. Pratt is at the point in his career when critics would label him an "unlikely leading man"; here he actually plays one to his scrappy, squabbling intergalactic crew. As the title suggests, they're the real heroes of this kinda-sorta-superhero movie. If *Guardians of the Galaxy* is an origin story, it is also a satire of the origin story, one that emphasizes the power of the "We" over that of the "Chosen One."

Photo Credit: Everett Collection, Inc.

Every member of the Guardians has known deep trauma. Chris Pratt's lead Peter Quill lost his mom (cancer); Zoe Saldana's Gamora is practically dead to the last surviving member of her family Nebula (Karen Gillan); her previous colleague-in-crime Ronan (Lee Pace) slaughtered the family of Dave Bautista's Drax; and Rocket Raccoon (Bradley Cooper) doesn't even have a family since, as a human experiment in anthropomorphization gone wrong, he's basically a lab animal. As for his pet, the sentient tree Groot (Vin Diesel), who knows? He can only string together three words (the innocuous truth, "I am Groot"). Judging by the way he tortures his adversaries—pushing his roots into their nostrils, out other orifices—it's safe to assume the tree has issues, too.

But in contrast to the rest of the genre, these sob stories don't bestow nobility. No one's particular woes are more "super" than another's. In fact, any attempt at tragedy one-upmanship would counteract the movie's shaggy, communal comedy. The Guardians aren't superheroes so much as they are a heterogeneous mix of losers, bandits, and outlaws who know just how unexceptional they are. As Chris Pratt's character says to rally the troops, "I look around and I see losers. Like, people who have lost something."

The real reason they connect is because they're all lucky sellouts, not Chosen Ones. The point of their big entrée into superherodom is to scrape together some prize money by selling the mysterious Infinity Stone, this franchise's equivalent of the equally irrelevant MacGuffin in *The Avengers,* the Cosmic Cube. The film then becomes a series of encounters that all lead up to the faceoff with the slithery highest bidder. While *Guardians* welcomes comparisons to *Star Wars*, there's no Luke, paragon of high-minded heroic ideals—our heroes are all a bunch of opportunistic Hans, ineloquent Wookies, and cowardly C-3POs. Yes, they're a strong, sad bunch, but in total it's a managerial nightmare to corral a team around a single crime-fighting objective sans incessant arguments.

In fact, *Guardians of the Galaxy* makes the case that a hero's individual strength amounts to merely a culturally acceptable form of pigheadedness. Take the movie's portrayal of Drax, a conflicted vigilante with only one thing on his mind—avenging his murdered wife and child. It's a generic motivation, and another movie might try to use him to bring us to tears. But here he nearly dies in the attempt for revenge, thus endangering the greater mission, to make money. "We've all got dead people!" his compatriot Rocket Raccoon scoffs. And for one moment of wonderful lucidity a Marvel movie makes sport of Marvel's big, profitable trope: the prolonged mourning of buff guys in tights.

The lampooning is more playful than genuinely threatening to the Marvel universe, though. For however much Guardians critiques the usual fare, it's still bookended by Chris Pratt's tragic flashbacks, a technique reminiscent of Christopher Nolan's super-serious *Batman Begins*. The flashbacks are the movie's least convincing moments, either because they're too earnest for the self-conscious flick or the actor isn't as good at shedding tears as he is at acting a buffoon on *Parks and Recreation*.

The origin story isn't some morally fraught trope that needs toppling, either. In fact, psychologist Robin Rosenburg has noted that superhero origin stories teach us "how to be heroes, choosing altruism over the pursuit of wealth and power."

But if we're going to take them seriously as instructions for how to be altruistic super-individuals, origin stories could also teach teamwork. This is where *Guardians of the Galaxy,* at its most delightfully self-aware, has a new take. It doesn't pretend like its heroes are not all mortals with an interest in pursuing that plebeian concern, money. Even so, it does show that a group of flawed losers can take down a planetary dictator with an enchanted stone if, for one moment, they forget their own baggage and hack out a semblance of a plan first.

Collaborate

Activity 4.17 • Discuss Review of *Guardians of the Galaxy*

Katie Kilkenny describes *Guardians of the Galaxy* as a superhero origin story. In your small group, discuss the following points and share your responses with the class.

1. Make a list of other superhero origin movies. In what ways do they fit the pattern Kilkenny lays out in her first paragraph? In what ways do they deviate from Kilkenny's pattern?

2. How does Kilkenny say *Guardians* fits the pattern, and in what ways does it not? What is the main strength of the movie, and how is it a new take on the superhero origin story?

3. Is Kilkenny's review effective? Why or why not?

Activity 4.18 • Develop Criteria for Film Reviews

Explore

In your small group, discuss the following points.

1. How does Katie Kilkenny employ the use of the superhero origin story movie plot pattern to create her criteria for reviewing *Guardians of the Galaxy*?

2. What film reviews do you plan to write for your next assignments? Is there a plot pattern such as a love story or buddy film that you can apply to your chosen movies? Perhaps there is an outstanding performance by an actor or an excellent rendering of a book into film. What other criteria might you employ? How would you evaluate a film based on your chosen criteria?

Individually, search the Internet for reviews of your chosen film to use as resources to back up you evaluation. Be sure to cite any quotes or paraphrases from other reviews you incorporate into your review. Then, write down the criteria you plan to use to review your film. Discuss these criteria with your group, and, if requested, turn in your writing to your instructor.

Activity 4.19 • Write a Film Review

Compose

In this assignment, you are a film critic. Write a review that could appear in a newspaper, magazine, or blog. Your style and tone will be dictated by your audience, so identify the publication just under the title of your review by saying something like this: "Written for Undergroundfilms.com." Be sure to read several reviews published in your chosen media outlet.

▪ Select a film you would like to review. Films that are social commentaries are particularly good for reviewing. It does not have to be a serious movie, but it should be one that makes you think about some social trend or historical event.

▪ After you decide on a film, learn about its context. Who is the director, producer, and primary actors? What films have these individuals worked on before? Have they won awards? Are they known for a certain style? Read and annotate other reviews of the film, marking sections that you might paraphrase or quote to support your opinions.

▪ Employ the criteria you developed in the previous activity to write a working thesis that makes an argument about your chosen film.

▪ Create a working thesis that makes an argument about the film. You can modify this thesis later, but it helps to identify early on what you want to argue.

▪ Use some of the invention strategies from this chapter to help you articulate what proofs you can use to support your argument.

▪ Near the beginning of your draft, briefly summarize enough of the film that your review will be interesting to those who have not seen it. However, don't be a "spoiler." Don't ruin the film for potential viewers by giving away the ending.

▪ Organize your essay into three main points that support your thesis and at least one counterargument that complicates or disagrees with your argument.

▪ Write a compelling introduction that uses one of the approaches discussed in Chapter 5, pp. 196-197. You want your reader to be interested in what you have to say. For example, you might begin with a startling quote from the film or a vivid description of a pivotal scene.

▪ Be sure to include specific examples and colorful details. These are essential to make your review interesting to the reader.

Activity 4.20 • Reflect on Your Film Review

Freewrite for five minutes about the movie review you just wrote. Answer one or more of the questions in the previous activity, or write about something else related to your product review. Why did you choose that particular film? What was it like combining your personal knowledge, observation, and information you obtained from the movie website or another review?

If your instructor requests, turn your freewriting into a polished paragraph with a thesis and supporting sentences.

Activity 4.21 • Write on Your Blog

Choose a controversial topic, and speculate in your blog whether or not that topic is at a stasis point for any of the stasis questions.

Activity 4.22 • Write in Your Commonplace Book

In your commonplace book, freewrite about how you do invention. What methods do you use to extract from your mind what you already know about a subject (what Aristotle would call artistic proofs)?

Mitchell, Alexander Thomas. *Pretty.*

Chapter 5

Research and Documentation

Introduction to Research

In college writing, you will be expected to think critically; to offer strong, compelling, and appropriate research to advance your arguments; to discern between scholarly and non-scholarly sources in your research; and to write directly and clearly.

Academic writing has conventional practices, like any other endeavor. For example, scholars writing in their fields routinely include a "Literature Review" in academic papers, showing that they are familiar with the works of scholars who've gone before. Conventions of academic research can be easily learned, and your research skills will expand and improve with practice.

You engage in research every day. If you're in the market for a car, you may research online or talk to a knowledgeable family member about which model best fits your needs. If your car requires repair, you may consult online reviews to find a trustworthy mechanic near you. Perhaps you've read the nutritional information on a can or box to find the sugar content of your favorite foods or consulted an online medical article to learn more about artificial sweeteners. The information-gathering you will do for college research simply builds on these informal research skills.

By the end of ENGL 1101, and throughout ENGL 1102, you will be expected to write a *researched argument paper.* In this paper, you will make an argument—a *claim.* Your claim may be an opinion, an interpretation, a policy proposal, or a cause-and-effect statement. In your paper, you will be expected to:

1. Make a concise, compelling claim (your argument)

2. Support your argument with evidence gathered from your research

3. Avoid misuse of published works (see information on plagiarism, page 178)

MLA Documentation Style

In college writing, you must *document* all of the sources you use. Each discipline uses a particular style according to the priorities and nature of their written discourse. The American Psychological Association (APA) style, for example, is followed in business, social sciences, and education, and journalism usually follows the Chicago Style guidelines. In the humanities, including English Studies, scholars use the documentation style of the Modern Language Association (MLA).

The MLA Handbook for Writers of Research Papers, Eighth Edition provides guidelines for the MLA style of documentation. For detailed information on MLA citation, please visit the *Guide to First-Year Writing* companion Website at www.guidetowriting.gsu.edu.

Reviewing the *MLA Documentation* section of this chapter serves as a great introduction to the style guide, but the best way—by far—to get the hang of documentation is to read the model research essays included here and on our Website.

Note how authors:

1.   smoothly incorporate and synthesize research sources into their texts

2.   create in-text parenthetical citations

3.   format Works Cited pages (see page 231 for citation format information)

Influenced by Nietzsche and his idea that, "God and man have died a common death," Foucault examines how that death occurs and what the death means (Foucault 105).

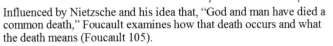

Works   Cited

Benn, Aphra. *The Rov-   er*. Ed. By Robyn Bolam. New York: A & C Pubs., 2007. Print.

Derrida, Jacques. *Writing and Difference*. Chicago: Chicago UP, 1978. Print.

Foucault, Michele. *The Foucalt Reader*. Ed. Paul Rabinow. New York: Vintage Books, 2010. Print.

If you are like many first-year writing students, you may be intimidated by the prospect of thorough scholarly documentation, not only because of the multiplicity of documentation styles that each have detailed rules to follow, but also because of the looming spectre of plagiarism. First-year students frequently, and rightfully, worry about using the undocument-ed words or ideas of others.

Your instructor is here to help you learn modes of documentation. So stop, ask questions, and be sure you understand the documentation rules so that you learn how to responsibly ac-knowledge the work of others while maintain-ing your credibility as an author.

Supreme, James. *Reach for More*

Evaluating Sources

In researching and writing rhetorically, you boost your **ethos,** or credibility as a writer, by synthesizing your personal knowledge with expert knowledge in a field. As you begin the research process, ask, "How will this source strength-en my argument? Is the source truly relevant and timely?" The goal is to find sources that are appropriate, compelling, complete, and expert. For any source, key factors to consider include *academic credibility, argument, accuracy,* and *currency.* Scholarly journals and books published by university presses usually carry the most credibility in academic writing. Some popular sources (popu-lar = written by journalists, not by experts in the field) are credible, depend-ing on context; a news item from *The New York Times,* for example, may be a source of accurate, up-to-the-minute data on a topic. Many popular sources that are meant for entertainment—glossy magazines like *Glamour*—are usu-ally not credible as sources in academic writing (depending upon your topic, of course). In addition, most instructors discourage citing Wikipedia as a source because entries are written by volunteers; readers cannot always evaluate the accuracy of entries. Wikipedia articles on your topic, however, can provide ex-cellent bibliographies and links as starting points for your research.

To succeed in academic writing, you must develop a practiced eye for the dif-ference between scholarly and popular sources, and commit to using scholarly sources.

Scholarly Journals

In general, scholarly journals

- Are peer reviewed (remember to use the delimiter function in Galileo to narrow your results to scholarly materials)
- Are written for an audience of professors and students in an academic field
- Are published usually by a university press
- Include few, if any, advertisements within the articles
- Make use of highly specialized vocabulary
- Include articles, graphics, tables, charts
- Append an extensive bibliography at the end of each journal article or book

Examples:

JAMA: The Journal of the American Medical Association (Written by experts in the field of medicine for others in the field.)

The Journal of Economic Theory (Writer/audience of economics PhDs, researchers, and students.)

American Literature (Published by Duke University Press for an academic audience.)

Popular Publications

Popular publications generally

- Are written by journalists or other contributing writers
- Are published by a news or popular press
- Include glossy or eye-catching color, many photos
- Rely upon non-technical vocabulary
- Do not include bibliographies

Examples:

The Wall Street Journal (Despite "journal" in the title, it is a popular source—a newspaper written by journalists for a wide audience)

The Economist (Written by journalists, full color, with many ads)

PCWorld (Full color, many ads. Written by journalists for a wide audience)

Primary and Secondary Sources

You also need to learn to distinguish between primary and secondary research tools.

Primary research involves first-hand interaction with your subject, including interviewing people and analyzing/working with original material like diaries, novels and films (rather than working with second-hand analyses of these primary sources). Primary sources stand alone in that they are not overtly analyzing other source materials. *The Diary of a Young Girl* by Anne Frank is a primary source.

Secondary research materials, on the other hand, interpret and analyze primary sources. Secondary sources include scholarly journal articles, analyses, and biographies, such as *Anne Frank: The Biography* by Melissa Müller.

The Value of a Library Search; Or, Why You Can't "Just Google It"

Google searching returns a world of information—but often not a world of credible sources. Suppose you are researching the history behind Dr. Martin Luther King's "Letter from Birmingham Jail." You google "Martin Luther King," and you click on the link for "www.martinlutherking.org."

As a ".org" the source seems credible. The site is visually pleasing, in terms of neatness and layout. At first glance, you think the site might be sponsored by the Martin Luther King Center or a memorial foundation, or serve as a reputable archive of King's speeches. You read the plausible website heading: "Martin Luther King Jr: A True Historical Examination. A Valuable Resource for Teachers and Students Alike."

Walsh, William. *Books.*

Unfortunately, this page is indeed the work of an organization—a supremacist hate group offering their take on King's life and on the accomplishments of African Americans in general. The site includes numerous hateful statements about African Americans and other groups.

A good rule of thumb:

To be used in an academic paper, a Web source:

1. must list an author (the above source does not);

2. must cite its sources; and

3. should not exist to advertise and sell products.

Of note, GoogleScholar—not just Google—provides an excellent search engine for finding online scholarly articles. What is the downside of GoogleScholar? Unlike a library database search, this site doesn't always give the full text of an article; often, you must pay for the article. The good news: most scholarly articles are available free of charge through a GSU Library search.

Quick-Start: Searching the GSU Library Website

You can search the Georgia State University Library website and numerous scholarly databases from your personal computer. Go to http://www.library.gsu.edu/ and click "Libraries" and then "University Library." Last year, the library's website was visited 1.7 million times. If you're searching for books, the library houses 1.5 million volumes. Whether you are accessing the library from home or from a library computer, use the following steps to complete a simple and quick search.

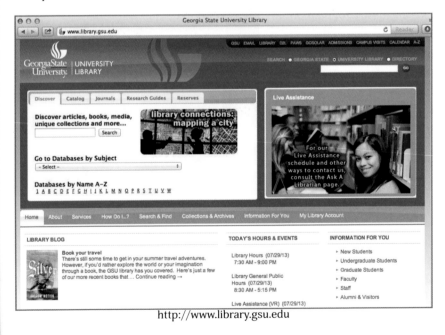

http://www.library.gsu.edu

For Academic Search Complete, click on "A" in Discover's "Databases A to Z" field. Then, click "Academic Search Complete."

Finding Articles in Scholarly Journals

To establish credibility in your academic writing, research and include peer-reviewed scholarly journal articles in your work. **Peer-reviewed** means that articles have been screened and vetted by experts in the field for reliability and relevance before being published and used by other scholars.

Go to the library webpage http://www.library.gsu.edu/ and view the Discover field.

You can use Discover for your search, as it searches many other databases. The results, however, are often cumbersome, and many will be irrelevant to your topic.

For a more efficient search, go to the bottom of the Discover search box and click "Databases By Name A-Z." Click "A," and then choose the database "EB-SCO Host/Academic Search Complete." You will then be asked for your campus ID and password.

Academic Search Complete is a comprehensive, multi-disciplinary source of more than 10,000 scholarly publications. Once you're in Academic Search Complete, conduct a basic search using keywords from your topic (for example, *water quality*), a title, or an author. Academic Search Complete also will limit the results to scholarly journals if you click "Search Options" and then "Scholarly Journals Only." You may choose to see only articles with full-texts available, and you also can earmark desired articles to an electronic folder.

Use Boolean operators to tailor your search. Use quotation marks to search for phrases, like "bipolar disorder" or "a midsummer night's dream." Use *AND, OR* and *NOT* in ALL CAPS, as in biomedical AND engineering NOT nuclear. Use an asterisk* for *wild card searches;* cinema* will return "cinematic" and "cinematography." Use multiple search terms to narrow the results; keep in mind that a search for a term like "environment" will yield millions of hits.

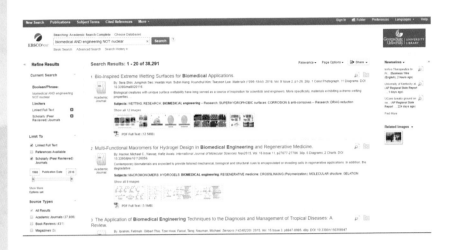

Note: EBSCO Host/Academic Search Complete is one of more than 100 databases available through the library, serving a wide range of disciplines. For discipline-specific databases, seek out the Subject Librarian for your field (art, for example), or browse "Databases A-Z" in Discover. You'll find everything from NASA's database to MedLine to ARTstor to Rock'N'Roll and Counterculture.

Here are some suggested databases for different disciplines:

- Humanities, including Languages and Literatures—EBSCO Host/ Academic Search Complete, JSTOR, MLA International Bibliography, Project Muse
- Social Sciences—ERIC, Government Document Catalog Services, PsychInfo
- Business—ProQuest, LexisNexis Academic
- Sciences—Academic Search Complete, Web of Science, General Science Index
- News, Legal Cases—LexisNexis Academic

Finding Library Books

Scholarly books usually treat academic topics with in-depth discussion and careful documentation of evidence. Scholarly books are often published by university presses, such as Oxford University Press or the University of California Press. However, keep in mind that a well-researched popular book with a thorough bibliography is also a good research find; the bibliography can point you toward scholarly books/articles on your topic. Remember: In academic writing, we build on the work of scholars who have come before us.

It is easy to search for library books. Go to the Discover window and click "Catalog"; under "All Fields," search by title, subject, or author. At the bottom of the catalog entry for each book, you will find the location of the book in the library:

"Library North 3"—and the call number by which you can find the book on the shelves: "RC516 .B526." Proceed to third floor north and find the RCs on the shelves.

Using Internet Sources Wisely

Earlier we cautioned you to not "just google it"; however, the World Wide Web is an extremely useful resource for legitimate research when following scholarly research practices. Through the Web, you can find full texts of pending legislation, searchable online editions of Shakespeare's plays, scholarly articles, environmental impact statements, stock quotes, and much more. Finding credible sites for research through a Google search, however, is not that easy. Sites range, in terms of credibility and usefulness, from the spectacularly good (like Google Books, with millions of searchable titles) to the spectacularly bad. When evaluating a website, your job as a scholar is to learn to recognize the difference between legitimate resources, and those that are not credible. Remember, you are trying to build ethos: Which is more credible, a paper citing nothing but unexamined Web sources or one that cites statistics from published studies, articles from peer-reviewed journals, and news reports providing historical and social context?

A rule of thumb—just like a scholarly journal, a reliable Internet source

1.   lists an author,

2.   lists its sources, and

3.   isn't selling a product or service.

Researchers, in general, evaluate websites for r*elevance, reliability, accuracy and currency.* In addition to asking *"How does this information fit my research purpose?"* they ask questions such as:

Who is the author of the site? Is he or she a legitimate expert? What organization or entity does the writer represent? Think of the credibility gap—and the gap between the writer's rhetorical stance and tone—between the American Medical Association website (ama-assn.org) and "The Anti-Liberal Page" (a .com site). Researchers view .com sites, short for "commercial," with a healthy dose of skepticism. The .edu suffix, indicating a college or university, indicates credibility, as does .gov, which indicates a government agency or search engine like www.searchusa.gov.

What is the purpose of the site? What is its agenda? Compare the purpose of a recognized informational website (like the United Nations website, at http://www.un.org/en/), to the purpose of the www.MartinLutherKing.org site mentioned earlier. One seeks to provide accurate information; one is a supremacist-group smear campaign that seeks to destroy reputations.

To help you in your Internet research, two specialized search engines yield only results that have been vetted by university librarians for accuracy and credibility. They are:

▯ Information You Can Trust, http://www.ipl.org, and
▯ Infomine: Scholarly Internet Resource Collections, http://infomine.ucr.edu.

The Thesis Statement and Research Proposal

To review, an *argumentative* paper makes a claim, which is supported with specific evidence gleaned from your research.

Early in the research process, your argument—the main claim of your research paper—will begin to take shape, and you will form ideas of how you will incorporate resources.

Before you work on the research proposal, stop to formulate a research question. The question should be guided by the following:

▯ Assignment
▯ Audience
▯ Purpose
▯ Scope

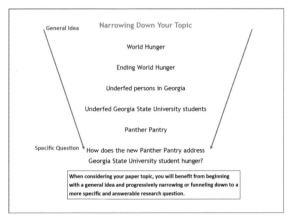

Narrowing Down Your Topic

General Idea

World Hunger

Ending World Hunger

Underfed persons in Georgia

Underfed Georgia State University students

Panther Pantry

Specific Question — How does the new Panther Pantry address Georgia State University student hunger?

When considering your paper topic, you will benefit from beginning with a general idea and progressively narrowing or funneling down to a more specific and answerable research question.

Dejou. Nadia. *Colored Bricks of Wisdom.*

Keep in mind, your research proposal should hone in on a specific and supportable question. For instance, you might like to write about "ending world hunger." Ask yourself if this topic meets the requirements of the assignment, is appropriate for your audience, if writing about "ending world hunger" meets the purpose of your assignment, and if it exceeds the assignment's scope. Suppose you are writing an argumentative research paper. You would quickly find that the topic "ending world hunger" likely does not meet your specific assignment requirements, that the topic is much too broad to be effectively written about, and that it exceeds the scope of your assignment. You will also notice, quickly, that you cannot develop a supportable claim from such a broad topic. Go back to the brainstorming techniques that you've learned (in Chapter 4), consider what it is about hunger that interests you, and rather than write about global hunger, perhaps generate a research question about underfed children in Georgia. Focusing your topic in this way is not only more manageable, but can lead to a solid, arguable claim. You are establishing the foundation of your paper, so if you aren't sure that you're on the right track, ask your instructor for assistance or meet with a tutor in the Writing Studio.

Rhetorical Précis Worksheet

(A)_____(Author)_____ in the _____(1)_____ , _____(Title)_____

(publication year), _____(2)_____ that _____

_____.

(B)_____(Author's Last Name)_____ supports his/her _____(2)_____ by ___(3)___

_____

_____.

(C) The author's purpose is to _____(4)_____

_____ in order to

_____. (D) The author writes

in a _____(5)_____ tone for _____(Audience)_____.

A = Who and What?   B = How is it done?   C = Why? What's the purpose?   D = Who's the audience?

1 – Genre	2 – Action Word	3 – Method	4 - Purpose	5 – Tone
Book	Explains	Describing, Illustrating,	Illuminate	Scholarly
Essay	Asserts	Comparing/Contrasting,	Persuade	Formal
Article	Claims	Showing, Demonstrat-	Inform	Informal
Book review	Suggests	ing,	Suggest	Humorous
	Argues	Explaining, Defining,	Show	Defensive
		Listing, Elaborating	Reveal	Scathing
				Reverent

In the research proposal, you specify the argument and sources for your research project. The proposal is not a contract, and you are not locked into the topic at this point. In fact, your proposal most likely will be refined, narrowed, or changed based on conversations with your instructor and peers, as part of the writing process. As your research proposal develops, think of it as a guide to help you keep your writing and research focused on your primary claims.

The art of crafting a research statement (or question) requires study and practice; consult your writing textbook for techniques and examples. As for the research proposal, requirements vary among instructors; your teacher may ask for a bare-bones outline (see example below) or a multiple-page written document.

Here is an outline-form proposal with some typical required elements, as assigned by one instructor:

SAMPLE RESEARCH PROPOSAL

My Classical Argument Proposal: Why Writing Teachers Should Study Depression and Bipolar Disorder in Student Writers

My Audience: Writing teachers, including my writing instructor, and my 1102 class members

My Thesis/Argument: Composition teachers should study how depression and bipolar disorder affect student writing.

Three Reasons Why:

1. Depression and bipolar illness have long been associated with writing creativity.

   I knew this, and will find more examples in research.

2. Seven percent of undergraduates nationwide currently take antidepressants; a full one in four say depression has hurt their academic performance.

   I knew this generally, but didn't know the numbers until I researched. Wow!

3. Depression can cause writer's block; perhaps not all late papers are due to laziness.

   I didn't know this; I found more data to illustrate it.

Possible Counter-Arguments

THEY SAY: Writing teachers don't need to study this. They're not therapists.

I SAY: True, but this affects the writing of many, many students. It's relevant for the study of composition.

Preliminary Research Sources:

At this point, I have found three main sources:

1. A website (The National College Health Association's major mental health study of 200 colleges nationwide). *I will use data from this study to illustrate the breadth of depression and bipolar illness in the student population.*

2. An article (from the academic journal *Comprehensive Psychiatry*). *I will use this article for Reason No. 3, that depression can cause writer's block, which may affect students' academic performance.*

3. A library book (published by Columbia University Press). *I will use this book for background on depression and mania in writers in English.*

Plagiarism

Before discussing how to quote, paraphrase, and summarize sources, we want to define and explain what constitutes plagiarism.

Graziano, Marissa. *Awakening*

Plagiarism means handing in some-one else's words, thoughts, or artifacts as your own. Intentional plagiarism is forbidden in academic writing, and the stigma of a plagiarism charge follows students throughout their academic ca-reers. The basic concepts of plagiarism are straightforward.

At Georgia State, *"The student is respon-sible for understanding the legitimate use of sources . . . and the consequences of violating this responsibility."* In other words, the burden rests upon you as the writer to give credit where credit is due.

Common types of plagiarism include

1. Turning in a paper that was written by someone else as your own, including papers obtained from online paper banks and papers that you purchase.

2. Copying from a source without acknowledging that source in the proper format (in English courses, you must follow MLA documentation guide-lines, which includes an in-text parenthetical citation and a source entry on the Works Cited page).

3. Paraphrasing materials from a source without attributing the information to that source.

4. Copying materials from a text but treating them as your own, leaving out quotation marks and acknowledgements.

All instances of plagiarism are reported to the College of Arts & Sciences. Please be sure you understand your instructor's policy for plagiarism as stated on the course syllabus.

To learn how to avoid plagiarism and properly cite sources, talk to your in-structor, closely read the MLA guidelines, and visit comprehensive websites like The Purdue Online Writing Lab (owl.english.purdue.edu/). If you are a student at GSU's downtown campus, be sure to visit the Writing Studio for further help with understanding plagiarism.

Internet searches, anti-plagiarism software like turnitin.com, and instructors' in-depth knowledge of students' writing make it easy to catch plagiarism among composition students. The "easy way," paradoxically, is simply to do the work.

From the GSU Policy on Academic Honesty (Section 409 of GSU Faculty Handbook)

"The University expects students and faculty to be academically honest, and it expects faculty members to communicate expectations to students in their syllabi. That said, it is the student's final responsibility to understand plagiarism and avoid it. See the definitions below.

GSU's Definitions of Academic Honesty

The examples and definitions given below are intended to clarify the standards by which academic honesty and academically honorable conduct are to be judged. The list is merely illustrative of the kinds of infractions that may occur, and it is not intended to be exhaustive. Moreover, the definitions and examples suggest conditions under which unacceptable behavior of the indicated types normally occurs; however, there may be unusual cases that fall outside these conditions which also will be judged unacceptable by the academic community.

Plagiarism: Plagiarism is presenting another person's work as one's own. Plagiarism includes any paraphrasing or summarizing of the works of another person without acknowledgment, including the submitting of another student's work as one's own. Plagiarism frequently involves a failure to acknowledge in the text, notes, or footnotes the quotation of the paragraphs, sentences, or even a few phrases written or spoken by someone else. The submission of research or completed papers or projects by someone else is plagiarism, as is the unacknowledged use of research sources gathered by someone else when that use is specifically forbidden by the faculty member. Failure to indicate the extent and nature of one's reliance on other sources is also a form of plagiarism. Any work, in whole or in part, taken from the Internet or other computer-based resource without properly referencing the source (for example, the URL) is considered plagiarism. A complete reference is required in order that all parties may locate and view the original source. Finally, there may be forms of plagiarism that are unique to an individual discipline or course, examples of which should be provided in advance by the faculty member. The student is responsible for understanding the legitimate use of sources, the appropriate ways of acknowledging academic, scholarly or creative indebtedness, and the consequences of violating this responsibility.

Cheating on Examinations: Cheating on examinations involves giving or receiving unauthorized help before, during, or after an examination. Examples of unauthorized help include the use of notes, computer based resources, texts, or "crib sheets" during an examination (unless specifically approved by the faculty member), or sharing information with another student during an examination (unless specifically approved by the faculty member). Other examples include intentionally allowing another student to view one's own examination and collaboration before or after an examination if such collaboration is specifically forbidden by the faculty member.

Unauthorized Collaboration: Submission for academic credit of a work product, or a part thereof, represented as its being one's own effort, which has been developed in substantial collaboration with another person or source, or computer-based resource, is a violation of academic honesty. It is also a violation of academic honesty knowingly to provide such assistance. Collaborative work specifically authorized by a faculty member is allowed.

Falsification: It is a violation of academic honesty to misrepresent material or fabricate information in an academic exercise, assignment, or proceeding (e.g., false or misleading citation of sources, the falsification of the results of experiments or of computer data, false or misleading information in an academic context in order to gain an unfair advantage).

Multiple Submissions: It is a violation of academic honesty to submit substantial portions of the same work for credit more than once without the explicit consent of the faculty member(s) to whom the material is submitted for additional credit. In cases in which there is a natural development of research or knowledge in a sequence of courses, use of prior work may be desirable, even required; however the student is responsible for indicating in writing, as a part of such use, that the current work submitted for credit is cumulative in nature."

Two Examples of Plagiarism

Plagiarism takes many forms; two definitive examples follow. Examine the following original passages and student use of them. Determine which one is:

1. Word-for-Word Plagiarism

2. Too-Close Paraphrasing/Lack of Acknowledgement of Sources

Original Passage #1:

"As you read the book, you really do feel for Ender. He's used like a tool, honed and shaped against his will, with no one to turn to, which is pretty much the point. If he's in the midst of battle, there won't be a grownup there to turn to. His childhood is ripped from him, bit by bit, and perhaps that's why you feel sorry for him. By the time the book comes to its climax, he's only eleven years old. He's very smart, and very talented, but he's still only eleven." (From www10brinkster.com/MShades/books/e/ender.html)

A Student's Use #1:

As you read the book, you really do feel for Ender. The idea of a child being used like a tool, having their childhood bypassed and eliminated, is a harsh thing, and perhaps that's the lesson of this book.

Ender is used like a tool, honed and shaped against his will, with no one to turn to. If he's in the midst of battle, there won't be a grownup there to turn to. Ender's childhood is ripped from him, bit by bit, and perhaps that's why you feel sorry for him. By the time the book comes to its climax, he's only eleven years old. He's very smart, but he's still only eleven.

Citation strategies you would use for this example #1:

1. Review and practice what it means to summarize and/or paraphrase the piece.

2. Review how to quote the author. Use a page number if available. Here is how: According to Smith, Ender "is used like a tool, honed and shaped against his will" (1).

3. Use parenthetical citation at the end of sentences both quoted AND paraphrased. If you paraphrase, be sure to introduce the paraphrased material in a way that illustrates the difference between your words and ideas and those you summarize from your source.

Original Passage #2:

> "At about 1:01 p.m. on March 18, 1925, trees began to snap north-north-west of Ellington, Missouri, and for the next three and a half hours more people would die, more schools would be destroyed, more students and farmers would be killed, and more deaths would occur in a single city than from any other tornado in U.S. history. Records would be set for speed, path length, and probably for other categories that can't be measured so far in the past. The tornado maintained an exact heading, N 69 degrees E, for 183 of the 219 miles, at an average of 62 mph, following a slight topographic ridge on which a series of mining towns were built. These towns were the main targets of the devastating winds. No distinct funnel was visible through much of its path, yet for over 100 miles, the path width held uniformly at about three-quarters of a mile." (http://www.carolyar. com/Illinois/Misc/Tornado.htm)

A Student's Use #2:

> A terrible tornado passed through north-northwest of Ellington, Missouri at about 1:01 p.m. on March 18, 1925. The trees began to snap, and for the next approximately three hours, many people died, many schools were destroyed, and the U.S. record was set for deaths occurring in a single city. Records also would be set for path length and speed. The tornado maintained the heading of N 69 degrees E, and traveled at an average of 62 mph for the length of its path. You couldn't see a funnel, but for more than 100 miles, the monster left a destruction path three-quarters of a mile wide. Big tornadoes like this are the reason that towns and cities should install more tornado warning sirens.

Determine which is word-for-word plagiarism and which is too-close-para-phrase/didn't cite sources plagiarism. Then, let's revisit the idea of common and uncommon knowledge:

Common Knowledge: Every year, tornadoes kill people in an area of the central U.S. known as Tornado Alley. (You do not have to name a source for this).

NOT **Common Knowledge:** "The 1925 Missouri tornado maintained an exact heading, N 69 degrees E, at an average of 62 mph." You did not know this as you came into your research. In MLA format, you must name the source of this data, both in 1) parentheses at the end of the sentence, and 2) in the Works Cited page.

In the second example, the student did not *credit a source* when he/she directly quoted and paraphrased facts that are *NOT common knowledge*.

Remember the important rule of thumb: *If a fact wasn't in your head when you began your research, assume it is NOT common knowledge. By the same token, if a fact is new to you but common knowledge to your audience, you may not need to cite it.*

Citation strategies you would use for this example:

- Put quotation marks around all direct quotes (whole sentences AND phrases).
- Use a looser, more contextual paraphrase (combine it with text above and below).
- Use parenthetical citation at the end of fact-laden sentences, both quoted AND paraphrased (Smith 1).

For more on researching and note-taking, understanding plagiarism, and plagiarism examples, consult the "Is It Plagiarism?" and "Safe Practices" sections of the Purdue OWL at http://owl.english.purdue.edu/owl/resource/589/03/. The OWL is an excellent source across the board for research paper writing. These two sections cover reading, note-taking, summarizing, paraphrasing, quoting, and safely writing about the ideas of others.

Plagiarism: Easy To Commit, Hard To Live Down

In 2006, Harvard undergraduate Kaavya Viswanathan wrote the best-selling novel *How Opal Mehta Got Kissed, Got Wild, and Got A Life*. The novel was subsequently recalled by the publisher—who took the unprecedented step of destroying all copies—because Viswanathan plagiarized throughout.

This is one of many examples of how the writer followed sources much too closely:

From Salman Rushdie's 1990 novel *Haroun and the Sea of Stories*: "If from speed you get your thrill, take precaution, make your will."

From Viswanathan's novel: "If from drink you get your thrill, take precaution—write your will."

Taking Notes From Sources

As you take notes, ALWAYS indicate which words are YOURS and which are quotes from sources. Find a way that works for you—large quotation marks, highlighting for "mine," etc. When summarizing sections or paraphrasing ideas from a published text, take the time to double check that your notes are in your own words and that they do not "borrow" the author's phrasing. If you use an author's phrasing during note taking (maybe they say it just right!), put those words in quotation marks.

Careful note-taking is the best defense against plagiarism. Note-taking strategies differ among researchers. Whether you are jotting down notes on paper, typing up notes on your computer (using a different page or file for each topic), or on a program like Zotero (a Firefox plugin available through the library), be sure to keep neat and organized notes. Here is the basic note card format, for paper or computer:

Google's Data-Gathering Practices (subject heading)

Stallworth, "Googling for Principles in Online Advertising," p. 470

"Google's enormous data-crunching machine is able to make calculated assumptions about consumers based on their searches, or on information consumers reveal when registering for Google's free services."

Direct quote.

Write a subject heading at the top—a category that makes sense to you. Then, carefully enter either 1) *a direct quote of the source, with quote marks,* 2) your *summary* of the source, or 3) your *paraphrase* of the source. Write which of the three you have created at the bottom of the card or file.

Common and Uncommon Knowledge

Once again, to avoid plagiarism, *you must credit a source* when you quote, paraphrase, or summarize *any facts that are not common knowledge* (see below for instructions on how to quote, paraphrase and summarize). For example, the following facts, none of which are common knowledge, must be cited: "In March of 2012, the population of the United States was estimated at

313,232,882." Or, "The *RMS Titanic* sank on April 15, 1912." Or, "The University of Texas has seven museums and 17 libraries."

You don't have to credit a source for facts that *are* common knowledge, such as: "The United States government is divided into three branches: executive, legislative and judicial." "The University of Texas is in Austin."

Rule of thumb:

> *If a fact wasn't in your head when you began your research, assume it is NOT common knowledge.*

Preparing Sources for Your Paper

If you've copied words directly from a source without changing them, these copied words must be enclosed in quotation marks. Failure to put quotation marks around copied material is plagiarism, since the reader will believe they are your own words.

Always introduce the quotation with a signal phrase of your own (see below, "For William Styron"), and insert an ellipsis if you take words out of the quote (Use "insert, symbol," in Word, then click on Ellipsis). End the sentence by crediting the source of the quote. Here are the original sentences from William Styron's memoir *Darkness Visible*:

> *(Original) "The madness of depression is, generally speaking, the antithesis of violence. It is a storm indeed, but a storm of murk. Soon evident are the slowed-down responses, near paralysis, psychic energy throttled back close to zero."*

Here is an example, using an ellipsis (...) to mark excised words:

> *(Student Example) For William Styron, the experience of severe depression is "a storm of murk ... of slowed-down responses, near paralysis, psychic energy throttled back to zero" (47).*

When you summarize and paraphrase, you still must credit the original author. The preceding example cites through the use of a signal phrase—"For William Styron"—and by listing the page number in parenthesis at the end of the sentence—(47).

IMPORTANT: Never copy words verbatim to your paper unless you use *direct, essentially unchanged quotes in quotation marks.* Changing only a word or two here or there is plagiarism, and is easy for instructors and readers to catch. To guard against plagiarism, use the following read-think-write strategies.

Direct Quoting of a Source

When using a direct quote, use the source's exact language, and always set off the quote in quotation marks. If you take words out of the source's exact language, always replace them with an ellipsis (...). Always end a quote with a parenthetical citation (often, a page number).

IMPORTANT: Never just drop quotes into your paper. The effect on your audience is jarring, and meaning is often lost. Always use an introductory "signal" verb or phrase.

Examples:

> *According to Smith, "Quote" (21).*
>
> *Smith argues that "Quote" (21).*

Refer to your writing handbook or a rhetoric text for a list of these "signal" verbs that add smoothness and sophistication to your writing.

Indirect Quoting of a Source (Paraphrasing)

Sometimes, you will want to paraphrase a quote—to put it simply, in your own words, rather than use it verbatim. Paraphrasing is fine as long as you 1) get the source's meaning exactly right and 2) include all the main issues in the order you encounter them in the original sources, and 3) cite the source at the end of the sentence.

Be sure, too, to make it clear where your own thoughts begin and end. Simply putting a parenthetical citation at the end of a paragraph is not sufficient (is the entire paragraph the restating of the source's ideas?). You must introduce the source and discuss the source's relevancy to your topic.

Example:

> *Job creation is heavy on the minds of the American public. In response to this public concern, at a July 15 press conference, President Obama said he would launch a new job creation program (20). Many of these jobs will be in the environmental and sustainability sector, which means a degree in these two areas will be more advantageous than ever before.*

The Rhetorical Précis

The rhetorical précis (pronounced "pray-see") is a highly specialized, brief and useful summary you may be asked to write; writing a précis is an excellent way to summarize sources (as opposed to the simple summary outlined below). The précis places emphasis on the rhetorical aspects of the work, like author, purpose, and audience, and is based on four very specific sentences, which are highlighted in the example below:

1. The first sentence provides the author's name, the genre (article, book), the title, and the date of the work in parentheses. Then, it uses a concise verb (like "claims" or "argues") followed by a "that" phrase stating the thesis of the work. The thesis can be either quoted or paraphrased.

2. The next sentence explains how the author supports his/her thesis. Stay general here; avoid details.

3. The third sentence uses an "in order to" phrase to state the purpose of the piece. Why is the author writing this piece?

4. The last sentence names the author's intended audience.

> Durland, Stephen. "Witness: The Guerrilla Theater of Greenpeace." *High Performance* 40 (Winter 1987). *Community Arts Network Reading Room Archives*. Community Arts Network. 1999. 15 February 2009. Web.

> *In his article "Witness: The Guerrilla Theater of Greenpeace" (1987), writer Stephen Durland <u>argues that the performative environmental rhetoric of Greenpeace should be considered art</u> and should not be overlooked by the world of performance art. <u>In order to make his argument,</u> Durland traces the beginnings of Greenpeace's brand of theater to the "guerrilla theater" of the Yippie movement of Abbie Hoffman and Jerry Rubin in the 1960s, narrates the major symbolic acts of the organization, and interviews Action Director Steve Loper about the group's philosophy and purpose. The purpose of Durland's article is to call attention to the need for an expansion of the sort of activism through art that Greenpeace practices. <u>The audience for Durland's article</u> includes primarily the readers of High Performance, a (now-defunct) magazine for the subgenre of performance art.*

Taking Notes: Summarizing a Source

A *summary*, as opposed to a précis, simply condenses the original material, presenting its core ideas *in your own words*. Summarize to condense long passages that emphasize your point, and when details are not critical. Don't use "I," or evaluate the piece. Just condense.

1. In the first sentence, state the article's main claim, or thesis; begin with the author's full name, the title of the article (in quotation marks), and page numbers.

2. State the major supporting points in their original order. Omit details and examples.

3. End with the author's conclusions or recommendations.

Taking Notes: Paraphrasing a Source

A *paraphrase*, on the other hand, reflects *your* understanding of the source. A paraphrase includes *all* points and ideas in the same order as originally written by the author. You should use the paraphrase when direct quoting is not permitted. Paraphrasing represents a by-product of your learning process, and as such communicates the ideas in your own words without condensing the material. Use your own language and structure, and always differentiate your ideas from those ideas published by others.

Rule of Thumb:

If you are using information to support a claim you make in your paper, it is best to use direct quotes. If you paraphrase, remember you must indicate (in writing) where your thoughts begin and end; paraphrased material must be introduced, explained, and properly cited in your writing.

Paraphrasing with The Look-Away Method—Read one or two sentences over several times. Then set the article aside and paraphrase the meaning of the sentences without looking back at the article. When you are finished, review the article and make sure your paraphrase is accurate and that you didn't use the same words as the author.

Consider this original text from page 141 of Nicholas Carr's *The Shallows: What the Internet is Doing To Our Brains* (2010):

Original: "Given our brain's plasticity, we know that our online habits continue to reverberate in the workings of our synapses when we're not online. We can assume that the neural circuits devoted to scanning, skimming, and multitasking are expanding and strengthening, while those used for reading and thinking deeply, with sustained concentration, are weakening or eroding. In 2009, researchers from Stanford University found signs that this shift may already be well underway. They gave a battery of cognitive tests to a group of heavy media multitaskers as well as a group of relatively light multitaskers. They found that the heavy multitaskers were much more easily distracted by "irrelevant environmental stimuli," had less control over the contents of their working memory, and were in general much less able to maintain their concentration on a particular task."

Student Paraphrase: Carr makes the assumption that heavy use of brain pathways involved in scanning and skimming information online has a strengthening effect on those circuits, while pathways used for deep reading and concentration atrophy. He cites a 2009 Stanford study suggesting that multitaskers were more distractable and less in control of memory and concentration (141).

Note: For each summary or paraphrase, always record the relevant page numbers for the article in parentheses. This will save you a great deal of hunting and work toward the end of your paper, when you prepare the Works Cited list.

Taking Notes: The Annotated Bibliography

At some point in the research project, you may be asked to create an Annotated Bibliography. For each entry, annotate the source (write a brief summary or paraphrase), and include a few sentences on how the source is relevant to your research project. An annotated bibliography, written as you research, is an ideal reference for you to use as your prepare your final paper. Here is a sample annotation:

Ehrenreich, Barbara. "Nickel and Dimed." *Mothering.* 2001. *Academic Search Complete.* Web. 10 May 2011.

In this article, Ehrenreich discusses welfare assistance in America as it applies to single parents, as well as how minimum wage affects these households. She argues against the idea that putting single mothers on welfare increases the likelihood that they will keep having children they cannot take care of. She uses statistics to prove that most people who go on welfare are hardworking individuals who just do not make enough on their own to support themselves, much less their children. This article will help me to show that while the government does offer assistance to single parents, it does not offer enough, and it offers assistance in a way that makes the general public scoff at and belittle those who accept it. This also will help me highlight what individuals who received welfare really do with the money, to build the credibility of hardworking single parents who do not abuse the system.

Remember, You Have Resources Available to Help You

Correctly documenting the information you cite in your writing is a way to develop strong ethos. Aside from the penalties a student can incur by flagrantly plagiarizing the work of others, research is a key element in argumentation.

Using research appropriately will make your writing stronger. Your composition instructor is here to help you learn the proper way to collect, integrate, and cite the information you find during your research process. If you are ever in doubt, ask him or her to explain the formatting and integration rules again. The *Guide to First-Year Writing* and its companion website offer examples to help you work through citation difficulties. In addition to these resources, the English Department also houses the Writing Studio. The Studio, as it is commonly called, provides a space for in-person and on-line tutoring and writing help. You can learn more about the Studio by visiting their website: http://writingstudio.gsu.edu/. You can also read about the Studio's programs, services, and approach to learning on our *Guide to First-Year Writing* companion website.

MLA Documentation

When you do research to find supporting evidence for your ideas or arguments, you need to credit your outside sources. Depending on what type of essay you are writing or which type of course you are writing for, you will need to choose a documentation style and continue with that style for the entire essay. Two of the most common styles, especially for freshman and sophomore students, are MLA (Modern Language Association) and APA (American Psychological Association).

If you write in composition, language, linguistics, and literature courses, you will often be asked to use documentation guidelines created by the MLA. The *MLA Handbook*, in its eighth edition, provides a full description of the conventions used by this particular community of writers; updates to the *MLA Handbook* can be found at www.style.mla.org.

MLA guidelines require that you give both an in-text citation and a Works Cited entry for any and all sources you use. Using accurate in-text citations helps guide your reader to the appropriate entry on the Works Cited page. For example, the in-text citation given below in parentheses directs the reader to the correct page of the book given in the Works Cited.

In-text citation➔When a teenager sleeps more than 10 hours per night, it is time to question whether she is having significant problems (Jones 63).

Entry in Works Cited➔

Jones, Stephanie. *The Signs of Trouble*. Dilemma Publishing,

2010.

This chapter provides a general overview of MLA documentation style and an explanation of the most commonly used MLA documentation formats, including a few significant revisions since the previous edition.

Did You Know?

The Modern Language Association was founded in 1883 at The John Hopkins University as a group that discussed literature and modern languages, such as Spanish, French, Chinese, and English. The MLA, now with over 30,000 members in over 100 countries, is the primary professional association for literature and language scholars.

37a Using MLA in-text citations

In-text citations (also called *parenthetical citations*) point readers to where they can find more information about your researched supporting materials. When you use MLA documentation style, you need to indicate the author's last name and the location of the source material (page or paragraph number). Where this in-text information is placed depends on how you want to phrase the summarized, paraphrased, or quoted sentence. Be sure that the in-text citation guides the reader clearly to the source in the Works Cited, where complete information about the source is given.

The following are some of the most common examples of parenthetical citations.

1. Author's name in text

When using a parenthetical reference to a single source that is already named in the sentence, use this form: (Page number). Note that the period goes after the parentheses.

→ Stephanie Jones, author of *The Signs of Trouble*, describes "excessive sleeping, refraining from eating, and lying about simple things" as signs to look for when parents are concerned about their children (63).

2. Author's name in reference

When the author's name is not included in the preceding sentence, use this form for the parenthetical information at the end of the sentence: (Author's Last Name Page number). Note that there is no comma between the name and page in an MLA parenthetical reference, and also note that the period comes at the end of the sentence, after the parentheses.

→   When a teenager sleeps more than 10 hours per night, it is time to question whether she is having significant problems (Jones 63).

3. No author given

When a work has no credited author, use a clipped version of the work's title.

→   In a recent *Time* article, a list of 30 common signs of teenage trouble cites lack of sleep as the most common sign ("Thirty" 3).

4a. Two authors given

When you use a source that was written by two authors, use both authors' names in the text of the sentence or in the citation.

→   The idea that "complexity is a constant in biology" is not an innovative one (Sole and Goodwin 2).

4b. Three or more authors given

When you use a source written by three or more authors, include only the first author's name followed by *et al.* (Latin for "and others").

→   In Hong Kong, most signs are in Chinese and English; however, once you are in mainland China, English is rarely found on signs, except in tourist areas (Li, et al. 49).

5. Authors with the same last names

If your source material includes items by authors who have the same last name, use each author's first initial in the parentheses. If the two authors also share first initials, use one of the authors' full first names.

→ When a teenager sleeps more than 10 hours per night, it is time to question whether she is having significant problems (S. Jones 63).

→ Another sign of trouble can be when you do not see your child for meals (Sally Jones 114).

6. Encyclopedia or dictionary unsigned entry

When you use an encyclopedia or dictionary to look up a word or entry, be sure to include the word or entry title in the parenthetical entry.

→ The word *thing* has more definitions than any other entry in the *Oxford English Dictionary* ("thing").

7. Lines of verse (plays, poetry or song lyrics)

When citing plays, give the act, scene, and line numbers of the material you use. Separate the act, scene, and line numbers with periods. For example, the quotation below comes from *Romeo and Juliet*, Act II, Scene 2, lines 43 and 44. MLA also advises using this method with biblical chapters and verses. Be sure, though, that the sequence goes from largest unit to smallest unit.

→ Juliet grapples with how names can influence feelings as she questions, "What's in a name? That which we call a rose/By any other name would smell as sweet" (2.2.43-44).

Use a slash (/) to signify line breaks when you quote poetry or song lyrics, and put line numbers in the in-text citation instead of page numbers.

→ An early song by Will Smith shows the frustration of children as he sings, "You know parents are the same/No matter time nor place/They don't understand that us kids/Are going to make some mistakes" (1-4).

8. Indirect quotation

When you use a quotation of a quotation—that is, a quotation that quotes from another source—use *qtd. in* to designate the source.

→ Smith has said, "My parents really didn't understand me" (qtd. in Jones 8).

37b Using long or block quotations

Long or block quotations have special formatting requirements of their own.

1. Block quote of prose

If you quote a chunk of prose that is longer than four typed lines, you are using what is called a *block quotation*. Follow these MLA guidelines for block quotations:

1. If introducing the block quotation with a sentence, use a colon at the end of the sentence. If the introduction to your block quote is not a complete sentence, use whatever punctuation is appropriate to connect the introduction to the quote. If there is no grammatical need for punctuation, do not use any.

2. Begin the quotation on a new line.

3. Do not use quotation marks to enclose the block quote.

4. Indent the quote one half inch from the left margin.

5. Double space the entire quotation.

6. Put a period at the end of the quotation, and then add the parenthetical citation.

➔ However, Lansky states:

> Despite the statement on www.signspotting.com that we don't accept signs with the intention of being funny, people like sending them in. I've opted not to use these as it could encourage people to start making them, sticking them up in their driveway, and snapping a picture. Plus, funny signs are so much more amusing when the humor is accidental. (72)

2. Block quote of poetry, drama, or song lyrics

For songs and poems, be sure to give line numbers rather than page numbers and to use the original line breaks.

➔ The Fresh Prince, an early Will Smith character, sings about parents not understanding:

You know parents are the same, no matter time or place

They don't understand that us kids are going to make some mistakes

So to you, all the kids all across the land, there's no need to argue

Parents just don't understand. (1-4)

37c   Adding or omitting words in a quotation

1. Adding words to a quotation

Use square brackets [ ] to point out words or phrases that you have added to clarify or add context to your quotation but are not part of the original text.

→ Original quotation: "When we entered the People's Republic of China, we noticed that the signage began dropping English translations."

→ Quotation with added word: She said, "When we entered the People's Republic of China, [Dunkirk and I] noticed that the signage began dropping English translations" (Donelson 141).

You can also add your own comments inside a quotation by using square brackets. For example, you can add the word *sic* to a quotation when you know that there is an error in the original to maintain the integrity of the quote's source.

→ Original quotation: "When we entered the People's Repulic of China, we noticed that the signage began dropping English translations."

→ Quotation with added comment: She said, "When we entered the People's Repulic [sic] of China, we noticed that the signage began dropping English translations" (Donelson 141).

2. Omitting words in a quotation

Use an ellipsis (. . .) to represent words, phrases, or sentences that you delete from a quotation. The ellipsis begins with a space, has three periods with a space between each, and then ends with a space.

Original quotation➔ "The Great Wall is something that can be seen from space. When we reach a time when advertisements can be seen from space, we have probably gone too far."

Quotation with words omitted in middle of sentence➔ Frank Donelson, author of *Signs in Space*, remarks, "The Great Wall . . . can be seen from space. When we reach a time when advertisements can be seen from space, we have probably gone too far" (178).

If you omit words at the end of a quotation, and that is also the end of your sentence, use three periods with a space before and between each, and place the sentence-ending period after the parenthetical citation.

Original quotation➔ "The Great Wall is something that can be seen from space. When we reach a time when advertisements can be seen from space, we have probably gone too far with our advertising and signage" (Donelson 178).

Quotation with words omitted at end of sentence➔ Frank Donelson, author of *Signs in Space*, remarks, "The Great Wall is something that can be seen from space. When we reach a time when advertisements can be seen from space, we have probably gone too far. . ." (178).

Helpful hint

MLA guidelines can change with a new edition. Sometimes, class textbooks can use an older MLA documentation style. Our examples use the eighth edition of the *MLA Handbook*, but always check with your instructor if rules seem to be in conflict.

37d Citing online sources

In MLA documentation style, online or electronic sources have their own formatting guidelines for in-text citations because these types of sources rarely give specific page numbers.

For better flow and easier understanding, include the name(s) of the person/people (e.g., author(s), editor(s), director(s), performer(s)) responsible for creating your source in the text, rather than in the in-text citation. For instance, the following is the recommended way to begin an in-text citation for an online source:

➔ Roger Ebert says that Shyamalan "plays the audience like a piano" in the film *Signs* (par. 8).

If the author or creator of the website uses paragraph or page numbers, numbered sections (*sec.*, *secs.*), or chapters (*ch.*, *chs.*), use these numbers in the parenthetical citation. If no numbering is used, do not use or add numbers to the paragraphs, pages, or parenthetical citation.

When website does not number paragraphs ➔ In his review of the film *Signs*, Roger Ebert says that Shyamalan "does what Hitchcock said he wanted to do, and plays the audience like a piano."

When website numbers paragraphs ➔ In his review of the film *Signs*, Roger Ebert says that Shyamalan "does what Hitchcock said he wanted to do, and plays the audience like a piano" (par. 8).

37e   General formatting guidelines for the MLA Works Cited

If you use any material from other sources within a paper, be sure to include a Works Cited list at the end of the paper. Here are some general formatting guidelines to follow when setting up a Works Cited.

1. Put the Works Cited at the end of your paper as a separate page.

2. Use one-inch margins on all sides, and uniform double spacing throughout. Do not add any extra spaces between entries or after the title.

3. Page numbers preceded by your last name should continue into your Works Cited from the body of your paper.

4. Center the title, *Works Cited*, at the top of the page, using no underlining, quotation marks, italics, bolding, or other special type or font.

5. Place the first line of each entry flush with the left margin. Indent any additional lines of the entry one-half inch (or one tab).

6. Alphabetize the Works Cited using the first letter of the last name of the first author listed in each citation. If the cited source does not have an author, alphabetize by using the first word of the source title, not including articles, such as *a, an,* or *the.*

7. Format your individual Works Cited entries using MLA 8's Core Elements. The most recent edition of the MLA style guide no longer distinguishes between citation formats for digital or print sources. Instead, in an effort to streamline the citation process, MLA 8 relies on a set of nine elements common to most source types. Each element is followed by the punctuation mark shown below, and the last element should be followed by a period.

> Author. Title of Source. Title of Container, Other Contributors, Version, Number, Publisher, Publication Date, Location.

Though MLA 8 makes no distinction between print and digital source types, it is still quite useful to see how the new core elements work with different types of sources. Therefore, the examples that follow are separated into print and digital sections. Furthermore, in these examples, you'll notice that only the elements available for the sample citation are listed in the example Works Cited entry. To clarify, prior to MLA 8, you would include n. pag. if no page numbers were available for your source and n.d. if you didn't have a publication date. That is no longer the case. If a given element is not relevant to the type of source you're citing (e.g. page numbers on a web page), then simply omit it from your Works Cited entry. If you are working with a source type that contains page numbers and our example of that source type does not include them, you should still include them in your Works Cited, since they are relevant to your particular source. MLA 8 recognizes that not all sources have all of the core elements, and even two of the same type sources may not have all of the same core elements. As noted above, if a source is missing any of the core elements, simply omit them from your Works Cited entry.

The sample Works Cited entries on the following pages begin with a simple single-author book entry, containing the Author, Title of Source, Publisher, and Publication Date elements, and build from there. As the source types listed here require additional elements, those elements, their uses, and their functions will be discussed in more detail.

37f   Formats for print sources

1. Book with one author

When including a source on the Works Cited, be sure to note in the citation which pages you are referencing. In print books, add the page number (preceded by *p.*) or range of pages (preceded by *pp.*) following the year of publication.

Author. *Title of Source.* Publisher, Publication Date.

➔ Martin, Anna. *Signs.* Dreamspinner, 2015, pp. 236-45.

Helpful hint

Omit business words like *Company* (Co.), *Corporation* (Corp.), and *Limited* (Ltd.) in the *Publisher* element of your Works Cited. For academic publications, replace *University* with *U* and *Press* with *P*. Otherwise, list the full publisher's name. If your source is associated with more than one publisher, separate the publishers' names with a forward slash (/).

2. Books with two authors

If your source has two authors, format the first author listed with the last name first, and the first name last. Follow this with a comma and the word and, then add the second author's first then last name.

Last Name, First Name (first author), and First Name Last Name (second author).   *Title of Source.* Publisher, Publication Date.

➔ Childs, Mark, and Ellen D. Babcock. *The Zeon Files: Art and Design of Historic Route 66 Signs.* U of New Mexico P, 2016.

If a book has three or more authors, you should list only the first author followed by a comma and et al. in place of the rest of the authors' names.

Author, et al. *Title of Source*. Publisher, Publication Date.

→ Wysocki, Anne Frances, et al. *Writing New Media: Theory and Applications for Expanding the Teaching of Composition*. Utah State UP, 2004.

3. Two books by the same author(s)

Use the author's or authors' full name(s) in only the first entry, then use three hyphens in place of the name(s) in all consecutive entries. The hyphens stand for exactly the same name(s) in the preceding entry, but remember to add any necessary qualifiers (editor, translator, etc.) by following the hyphens with a comma and the term describing that person's role. If the author name changes in any way (for example, an author might add a middle initial) or is combined with different authors than in the first entry listed, format the entry as you normally would, not using any hyphens. Alphabetize all sources by the same author by their titles.

→ Borroff, Marie. *Language and the Poet: Verbal Artistry in Frost, Stevens, and Moore*. U of Chicago P, 1979.

→ ---, editor. *Wallace Stevens: A Collection of Critical Essays*. Prentice-Hall, 1963.

Both of the above examples include the Version element of MLA 8. If your source indicates that it is one version of a work released in multiple forms, include reference to the version you consulted in your citation. The most common versions you will likely encounter are editions; however, works in other media, especially music and film, often offer different versions of a given album or DVD.

4. Anthology or collection

When citing a complete anthology or collection, which might contain multiple essays, articles, stories, poems, and/or other types of works, the editor(s) fill the author element for your entry. The term *author* spans a range of possibilities in MLA 8. The individual who fits the author role for your Works Cited entry might actually be an editor, translator, performer, creator, adapter, director, illustrator, or narrator. The key question to ask yourself when trying to determine who to list as your author is: "Who or what aspect in this work am I focusing on in my discussion?" You will only list an editor as your author if you are focusing specifically on the content written or chosen by that editor for the source you've referenced. Otherwise, you should list the individual author of the piece within the edited collection, placing the editor(s), instead, in the role of *Other Contributors*. No matter what role the person or people who fill your author element played in the production of your source, you should follow the same formatting guidelines for one, two, and three or more authors.

Author, editor(s). *Title of Source*. Publisher, Publication Date.

→ Iyengar, Sujata, and Allison Kellar Lenhardt, editors. *Health*. Fountainhead P, 2013.

5. Work within an anthology, collection, or reference book

When your source forms only a part of a larger whole, you need to provide both the *Title of Container* and *Location* elements in your Works Cited entry to ensure your readers can easily access the information. Additionally, these types of sources often have *Other Contributors* such as editors, translators, and illustrators to name just a few.

Just like it sounds, the container is what holds the smaller source you're actually citing. In addition to an anthology, collection, or reference book, a container can also be a magazine, newspaper, journal, or even a television series. Anytime your source is part of a larger whole, you should be sure to include the title of that larger whole, usually italicized.

Specifying your source's location is one of the only elements of MLA 8 affected by publication medium. Use *p.* to indicate a single page and *pp.* to indicate a range of pages for print sources. When citing websites, you will include the entire web address in the location element.

Like the *Author* element, *Other Contributors* encompass a wide range of possible roles. This element allows you to note individuals who were instrumental in your source's production, even if they weren't solely responsible for its creation. Other contributors' roles are indicated using a description, such as performance by, translated by, or directed by. If such a description does not fit the type of contributor you need to cite for your source, use a noun or noun phrase followed by a comma. For example: general editor, John Smith.

Author. "Title of Source." *Title of Container*, Other Contributors, Publisher, Publication Date, Location.

→ Chandaria, Kartik. "Weather and Language Lessons." *Health*, edited by Sujata Iyengar and Allison K. Lenhardt, Fountainhead P, 2013, pp. 141-44.

6. Article in a periodical

Sources such as journals, magazines, and newspapers are all periodicals. When citing a selection from one of these sources, you will need to indicate the periodical's volume (*vol.*) and number (*no.*) in the *Number* element. As with all of MLA 8's core elements, if your particular periodical does not contain all of the information for *Number*, simply include what it does offer. Likewise, if your periodical does not indicate a number of any kind, simply leave out that element.

Author. "Title of Source." *Title of Container*, Number, Publication Date, Location.

→ Holbrook, Teri. "An Ability Traitor at Work: A Treasonous Call to Subvert Writing from Within." *Qualitative Inquiry*, vol. 16, no. 3, 2010, pp. 171-83.

7. Review

If your review is titled, list the title in the *Title of Source* element, treating the review as any other selection from within a larger container. If your review is not titled, however, then your title will be the words, *Review of*, followed by the title of the work reviewed, then the word, *by*, and the reviewed work's author.

Author. "Title of Source." *Title of Container*, Publication Date, Location.

> ➜ Ebert, Roger. "A Monosyllabic Superhero Who Wouldn't Pass the Turing Test." *Chicago Sun-Times*, 29 Apr. 2009, p. E4.

> ➜ Stephenson, M.S. Review of *Apocalyptic Sentimentalism: Love and Fear in U.S. Antebellum Literature*, by Kevin Pelletier. *Choice*, May 2015, p. 1500.

8. Religious works

Religious works do not often reference an author; therefore, your Works Cited entry will most likely begin with the title of the work. Be sure to pay close attention to the particular version of the text you're referencing, as this will sometimes be the only means of direction by which your reader can locate your original source material.

Title of Source. Version, Publisher, Publication Date.

> ➜ *The Bible.* Authorized King James Version, Oxford UP, 1998.

Helpful hint

Although MLA 8 recommends including URLs for online sources in the Location element of your Works Cited entries, defer to your instructor's preference about this. When including the URL, copy it fully from your browser, omitting only the *http://* or *https://*. If possible, provide a stable URL (permalink) or Digital Object Identifier (DOI) as a more reliable alternative to the browser address.

37g   Formats for online sources

1. Website

Many websites are associated with a company or organization, but the key publisher's name can often be found either at the bottom of the site's home page or, if one is offered, on the site's "About" page. If the website you're citing includes an author or creator, then include it in your Works Cited entry. If not, begin your entry with the site title.

Title of Source. Publisher, Publication Date, Location.

➔ *Everyday Health.* Everyday Health Media, 2016, www. everydayhealth.com.

2. Article or item on a website (including blogs, wikis, vlogs, and online audio and video streaming services)

Author. "Title of Source." *Title of Container,* Publisher, Publication Date, Location.

Note: If there is no author given, begin the citation with the article title.

➔ George, Nancie. "6 Unusual Signs of Dehydration." *Everyday Health,* Everyday Health Media, 5 May 2016, www.everydayhealth.com/news/unusual-signs-of-dehydration/.

➔ Chan, Evans. "Postmodernism and Hong Kong Cinema." *Postmodern Culture,* vol. 10, no. 3, May 2000. *Project Muse,* doi:10.1353/pmc.2000.0021.

Helpful hint Avoid citing URLs produced by shortening services like TinyURL and bit.ly. These URLs may stop working if the service that produced them disappears.

3. Online journal article

Author. "Title of Source." *Title of Container,* Number, Publication Date, Location.

➔ Austen, Veronica. "Writing Spaces: Performances of the Word." *Kairos,* vol. 8, no. 1, 2003, kairos.technorhetoric.net/8.1/binder2.html?coverweb/austen/austen. html.

4. Article from an online database or service, such as General OneFile or LexisNexis

When you access a source through a database or service, such as JSTOR, Google Books, or even Netflix, you are using a source located through "nested" containers. A journal article on a database is held in the smaller container, the journal, and that journal is held by the larger container, the database. In your Works Cited, you should attempt to account for all the containers enclosing your source. To do this, you will simply add the core elements, 3-9 (*Title of Container* through *Location*), omitting irrelevant or unavailable elements, to the end of the entry until all additional containers are accounted for.

Author. "Title of Source." *Title of Container*, Number, Publication Date, Location. *Title of Container*, Location.

→ Pavienko, Sonia, and Christina Bojan. "Exercising Democracy in Universities: The Gap between Words and Actions." *AUDEM: The International Journal of Higher Education and Democracy*, vol. 4, 2015, pp. 26–37. *Project Muse*, muse.jhu.edu/article/557647.

In the above example, the first container is the journal, *AUDEM*, and the second is the journal database, Project Muse. Since the location is the last element in the first container, it is followed by a period. You'll note that, especially in the second container, many of the core elements are missing. Indeed, only the title and location are available for the second container, and this is fine. As noted previously, simply omit those elements that are irrelevant to the container you're working with.

5. Comments on blogs, videos, or social media, etc.

You may occasionally need to cite untitled web sources, such as comments on a blog, images, or Tweets. There are a few ways to approach this. If your source is untitled, provide a description, neither italicized nor in quotation marks, to fill the title element. Use sentence rather than title capitalization.

Title of Source. *Title of Container*, Location.

→ Kitten wearing a sweater. *Google Images*, img.buzzfeed.com/ buzzfeed-static/static/2014-11/4/14/enhanced/web-dr06/enhanced-24665-1415129188-3.jpg.

Your description might contain the title of another work if it's commenting on or responding to that work. This will be the case if you wish to cite comments on a blog post or other such interactions as sources. Note also that MLA 8 allows for the inclusion of usernames or "handles" in the *Author* element.

Author. Title of Source. *Title of Container*, Publication Date, Location.

→Jeane. Comment on "The Reading Brain: Differences between Digital and Print." *So Many Books*, 25 Apr. 2013, 10:30 p.m., somanybooksblog.com/2013/04/25/the-reading-brain-differences-between-digital-and-print#comment-83030.

Short, untitled messages, such as Tweets, are cited by typing the full text of the message, without any changes, in the *Title of Source* element, enclosed in quotation marks.

Author. "Title of Source." *Title of Container*, Publication Date, Location.

→@persiankiwi. "We have report of large street battles in east & west of Tehran now - #Iranelection." *Twitter*, 23 June 2009, 11:15 a.m., twitter.com/persiankiwi/status/2298106072.

To document an email, use the subject line as the title, and enclose it in quotation marks.

Author. "Title of Source." Other Contributors, Publication Date.

→Boyle, Anthony T. "Re: Utopia." Received by Daniel J. Cahill, 21 June 1997.

37h   Formats for other commonly used sources

1. Television or radio program

Media sources require special consideration when it comes to the *Author* and *Other Contributors* elements. Remember that the deciding factor in this situation is the aspect of the source you're focusing on. If you're discussing Matthew Gray Gubler's performance as Dr. Spencer

Reid in *Criminal Minds*, you would list "Gubler, Matthew Gray, performer." in the *Author* element (as in the first example), but if you're discussing the same show as a part of Jeff Davis's body of creative work, you would cite "Davis, Jeff, creator." as your author (as in the second example). If you're examining the show or an episode with no particular focus on a performer or other contributor, skip the author element and begin your entry with the episode or show title (as in the last example). Note also how location and publication information changes in each example as they move from a show watched on television, to the same show viewed via Netflix, and lastly, that show seen on DVD.

→ Gubler, Matthew Gray, performer. "Mr. Scratch." *Criminal Minds*, directed by Matthew Gray Gubler, season 10, episode 21, FOX, 22 Apr. 2015.

→ Davis, Jeff, creator. "Mr. Scratch." *Criminal Minds*, directed by Matthew Gray Gubler, season 10, episode 21, FOX, 22 Apr. 2015. *Netflix*, www.netflix.com/watch/800668 84?trackId=14170289&tctx=0%2C20%2C952df56e-847a-4278-a591-d2417455114f-109029147.

→ "Mr. Scratch." *Criminal Minds: Season 10*, created by Jeff Davis, directed by Matthew Gray Gubler, episode 21, Paramount, 2015, disc. 6.

2. Sound recording

Artist. "Title of Source." *Title of Container*, Publisher, Publication Date.

→ Five Man Electrical Band. "Signs." *Good-byes and Butterflies*, Lionel Records, 1970.

→ Tesla. "Signs (Live)." *10 Live!*, Sanctuary Records, 3 Jun 2014. Prime Music, Amazon, www.amazon.com/gp/product/B00K9FVUDM?ie=UTF8&keywords=tesla%20signs&qid=1463621153&ref_=sr_1_1&s=dmusic&sr=1-1.

3. Film

Films are handled very similarly to television shows. Your author and other contributors should be chosen based on the aspect of the film you examine in your research. If you do not focus on a particular individual, begin your entry with the film title.

Title of Source. Other Contributors, Publisher, Publication Date.

> ➔*Signs.* Directed by M. Night Shyamalan, performance by Mel Gibson, Touchstone, 2002.

4. Advertisement

Since advertisements aren't typically titled, follow the guidelines for providing a description in place of a title.

Name of product, company, or institution. Advertisement. Publisher, date of publication. Location or Medium of publication.

> ➔SunChips advertisement. *Newsweek*, 15 Jan. 2010, p. 33.

> ➔SunChips advertisement. NBC, 15 Jan. 2010, 10:32 p.m.

Note the difference in how the citations for print and television advertisements are formatted.

5. Painting, sculpture, or photograph

When viewing a physical object, such as a piece of art, in person, the "publisher" of the piece is the museum or gallery, etc. displaying the object. The location in this case is quite literal: Cite the city in which you viewed the piece.

If providing the original date of creation for your source will give your reader more context for your project, place the date(s) immediately following the work's title and follow it with a comma.

Author. *Title of Source.* Date of Original Publication, Publisher, Location.

> ➔da Vinci, Leonardo. *Mona Lisa.* 1503-6, Louvre, Paris.

If you viewed an object, image, or piece of art online, again, the entity making the piece available to the public fills the *Publisher* element, but you will also include both the physical and online locations of the piece.

→van Gogh, Vincent. *Cypresses. European Paintings*, The Metropolitan Museum of Art, New York, www. metmuseum.org/art/collection/search/437980.

6. Interview

Author. Title of source. Other contributors, Publication Date.

→Elbow, Peter. Personal interview, interviewed by John Smith, 1 Jan. 2009.

7. Lecture, speech, address, or reading

In certain circumstances, it may be appropriate to include a descriptive term in your Works Cited entry to indicate for your reader the type of source you're citing. Format your citation as usual, following the final element with a period, and then add the descriptive term followed by a period at the end.

Author. "Title of Source." Publisher, Publication Date, Location. Description.

→Stephens, Liberty. "The Signs of the Times." MLA Annual Convention, 28 Dec. 2009, Hilton Downtown, New York. Address.

37i Sample Works Cited using MLA

Following is an example of how a completed Works Cited would look at the end of your paper.

Your Last Name 14

Works Cited

Davis, Jeff, creator. "Mr. Scratch." *Criminal Minds*, directed by

    Matthew Gray Gubler, season 10, episode 21, FOX, 22 Apr.

    2015. *Netflix*, www.netflix.com/watch/80066884?trackId=

    14170289&tctx=0%2C20%2C952d56e-847a-4278-a591-

    d2417455114f-109029147.

Five Man Electrical Band. "Signs." *Good-byes and Butterflies*,

    Lionel Records, 1970.

Signs. Directed by M. Night Shyamalan, performance by Mel

    Gibson, Touchstone, 2002.

Stephens, Liberty. "The Signs of the Times." MLA Annual

    Convention, 28 Dec. 2009, Hilton Downtown, New York.

    Address.

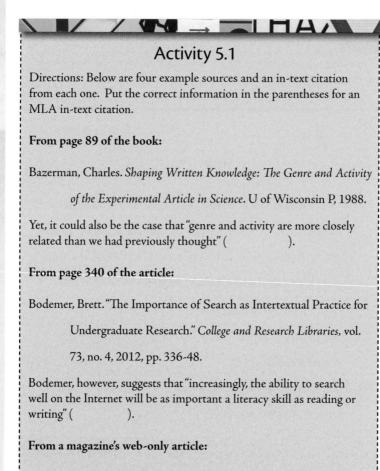

Activity 5.1

Directions: Below are four example sources and an in-text citation from each one. Put the correct information in the parentheses for an MLA in-text citation.

From page 89 of the book:

Bazerman, Charles. *Shaping Written Knowledge: The Genre and Activity*

    of the Experimental Article in Science. U of Wisconsin P, 1988.

Yet, it could also be the case that "genre and activity are more closely related than we had previously thought" (   ).

From page 340 of the article:

Bodemer, Brett. "The Importance of Search as Intertextual Practice for

    Undergraduate Research." *College and Research Libraries,* vol.

    73, no. 4, 2012, pp. 336-48.

Bodemer, however, suggests that "increasingly, the ability to search well on the Internet will be as important a literacy skill as reading or writing" (   ).

From a magazine's web-only article:

"Electronic Education: Flipping the Classroom." *The Economist,* 17

    Sept. 2011, www.economist.com/node/21529062.

The Economist has reported that "flipping the classroom is the new teaching technique of the twenty-first century classroom" (   ).

From page 192 of the chapter:

Schwartz, Daniel L., et al. "Toward the Development of Flexibly

Adaptive Instructional Designs." *Instructional Design Theories*

and Models: Volume II, edited by C.M. Reigelut, Erlbaum,

1999, pp. 183–213.

In a study performed by Schwartz et al., students found adaptive
classroom designs more engaging and, finally, more educational
(   ).

Activity 5.2

Directions: Insert all needed punctuation and formatting into the
following MLA Works Cited entries. The type of source is listed after
each.

Ackerman John M Reading Writing and Knowing: The Role of

Disciplinary Knowledge in Comprehension and Composing

Research in the Teaching of English vol 25   no 2 1991

133–178   **(article in a journal)**

Baddeley Alan Working Memory Oxford University P 1986 **(book)**

Barlow John Perry The Economy of Ideas   Wired Mar 1994 www.

wired.com/1994/03/economy-ideas/ **(article in a magazine)**

Flower Linda and John R Hayes A Cognitive Process Theory of

Writing College Composition and Communication vol 32

no 4 1981 365–87 **(article in a journal)**

Hacker Douglas J Matt C Keener and John Kircher Writing Is Applied Metacognition Handbook of Metacognition in Education Edited by Douglas J Hacker John Dunlosky and Arthur C Graesser Routledge 2009 **(chapter in a book or anthology)**

Rounsaville Angela Rachel Goldberg and Anis Bawarshi From Incomes to Outcomes: FYW Students' Knowledge Meta-Cognition and the Question of Transfer WPA: Writing Program Administration vol 32 no 1 2008 97–112 **(article in a journal)**

Wilson H 1999 When Collaboration Becomes Plagiarism: The Administrative Perspective *Perspectives on Plagiarism and Intellectual Property in a Postmodern World* Edited by L Buranen & A M Roy SUNY P pp 211-18 **(chapter in a book or anthology)**

37j   Sample Annotated Essay - MLA

Header information should include (in this order): Your name, the professor's name, the course number, and the date. Headers are double spaced and in Times New Roman 12-point font. In MLA, dates are in day, month, year order.

Titles are centered in MLA format, double spaced, and in Times New Roman 12-point font like the rest of the paper. No formatting (bolding, italics, or quotation marks) is needed on the title.

All text should be double-spaced, in Times New Roman 12-point font.

In-text citations are placed after any quotation, summary, or paraphrase of an idea that comes from another source. Make sure the period goes after the parenthetical citation, not inside the closing quotation mark.

John T. Doe

Professor Lorna Lotski

English 301

15 April 2015

Masculinity and Morality in the Modern Era

Before the turn of the twentieth century, "morality" was almost exclusively a religious concept. But religion was, in many ways, severely undercut by secular interests in the modernist period; indeed, the concept of morality slowly evolved to be understood more as a non-religious "set of rules of conduct or obligations towards others" (Collini 63). Without the uniting force of religion for the concept of morality, various secular *moralities* emerged. This paper will investigate these various moralities that bloomed during the modernist period, and illustrate how the various conceptions of morality, both in public discourse and in modernist authors' works, were substantially influenced by contemporary ideas of masculinity.

At the time of Oscar Wilde's 1895 trial for indecency, sexuality was beginning to be

Doe   2

considered scientifically, and previously innocuous

notions of effeminacy and homosexuality were

replaced by medical and psychological claims

that both were instead forms of mental disease.

Underpinned by Spencerian and Darwinian

theories of human and state evolution, popular

philosophies considered diseased individuals a

threat to the health of the nation itself; social critics

such as Max Nordau furthermore argued that non-

conforming, individualistic artists endangered the

state. Singled out as an effeminate artist, Wilde

became the embodiment of the moral threats to

the British Empire. His conviction only served to

further unite a number of key ideas in the public's

mind; Michael Foldy explains that after the 1895

trial, "degeneration," "decadence," "same-sex

passion," and "moral backsliding" were brought

together and conflated in the public discourse,

while the opposites—"manliness," "health," "moral

rectitude," and heterosexual desire—were cemented

as synonymous as well (70).

A decade or two after Wilde's trial, when

modernist artists began to produce some of the

Your last name and the page number, with two spaces between them, should appear on each page of your essay except the first page.

Doe   3

most influential works of the era, the two discourses underwent

changes in scope, yet were still very much connected in the public

mind. Because of the emerging scientific explanations of gender

and the demonization of effeminacy, definitions of acceptable

and preferred masculinity narrowed, while the secularization of

morality greatly expanded the meanings of that term. In all the

different ways in which morality was conceived, then, masculinity

and heteronormativity were largely still demanded to in order

to avoid possible social "degeneration." Those male authors

and social theorists who showed any concern for the ordering

of society, then, often found themselves arguing in similar ways

about competing and contested moral ideologies.

Considerations of morality in literary works have been

somewhat few and far between, most likely because on the

surface, authors of the modernist period seemingly are united

in their disdain of the concept: because the public's demand

for morality often meant censorship, artists in turn attacked the

concept and those who espoused it. Exceedingly disparate artists

– even ones antagonistic toward each other – seemingly unite in

their objection to moral concerns. In the preface to *The Picture*

of Dorian Gray, for example, Wilde writes, "There is no such

thing as a moral or an immoral book. Books are well written,

Doe   4

or badly written. That is all" (1). Considering

Wilde's well-known belief in the hedonistic

principles championed in Pater's conclusion the

The Renaissance, his pronouncement here sounds

much like Ernest Hemingway in his 1932 treatise on

bullfighting, *Death in the Afternoon*: "So far, about

morals, I know only that what is moral is what you

feel good after and what is immoral is what you

feel bad after and judged by these moral standards,

which I do not defend, the bullfight is very moral to

me" (4). These two pronouncements defend artistic

and experiential freedom by way of relativistic

morality, and are perhaps the singular commonality

between the two authors.

> Notice that the name of the quoted author, Wilde, need not appear in the parenthetical citation because he is named within the same sentence in which his quotation appears.

    For many post-Wildean male authors,

however, "the radical poetics of modernism mask

a deeply conservative politics" (Schneck 230).

For authors such as Hemingway, Ezra Pound, and

Wyndham Lewis, radical thematic and formal

posturing did indeed hide commonalities with

conservative politics and middle-class dynamics;

although their means differed (uses of the term

"morality," for example), many male authors had the

Doe   5

same ends as the professional classes they otherwise admittedly

disdained for their prurient tastes. This idea can be useful in

revealing less obvious relationships between authors; for example,

while Hemingway's infamous machismo highlights his more

hegemonic principles, Pound and Lewis, in the end, were the more

conservative.

Far more common a response than stalwart conservatism,

however, is one characterized by internal conflict, insecurity, and

anxiety. Although this phenomenon exists across nations in the

modernist period, Ireland provides particularly fertile ground for

this investigation as its revolutionary aspirations and religious

backgrounds welcomed a number of fluctuating partnerships and

rivalries between the moral ideologies of Catholicism, socialism,

and republicanism. The Irish writers Sean O'Casey and W.B.

Yeats, for example, specifically illustrate the great concern over

national order and chaos, but their responses to the uprisings and

wars of the times became increasingly conflicted as the republican

ideologies that won the public's attention (colored with strong

shades of masculinity) demanded blood sacrifice first.

Still, no matter the country, modernist art reveals

incredible anxieties about these two concepts, masculinity and

morality. Buy studying some of the great artists and works of

the period, a reader can learn a great deal about how people's

Doe   6

ideas of both concepts were conflated while, at the same time, destabilized. As with many others historical periods of upheaval, art can show us some of the most important underlying ideologies in a culture.

Doe   4

Works Cited

Collini, Stefan. *Public Moralists: Political Thought and Intellectual Life in Britain, 1850–1930.* Oxford UP, 1993.

Foldy, Michael. *The Trials of Oscar Wilde: Deviance, Morality, and Late-Victorian Society.* Yale UP, 1997.

Hemingway, Ernest. *Death in the Afternoon.* Scribner, 1932.

Schneck, Celeste. "Exiled by Genre: Modernism, Canonicity, and the Politics of Exclusion." *Women's Writing in Exile*, edited by Mary Lynn Broe and Angela Ingram, U of North Carolina P, 1989, pp. 225–50.

Wilde, Oscar. *The Picture of Dorian Gray.* Oxford UP, 2006.

Bibliographic information for any and every source that you quote, paraphrase, or summarize in the text belongs here, on the "Works Cited" page. The Works Cited page is always titled "Works Cited" and nothing else. The title "Works Cited" should be centered. The Works Cited page should always begin on a new page.

End-text citations should be double spaced and should use a hanging indent style. That is, the first line should be flush with the left margin, but every other line of a citation should be indented one half inch.

APA DOCUMENTATION

When you do research to find supporting evidence for your ideas or arguments, you need to credit your outside sources. Depending on what type of essay you are writing or which type of course you are writing for, you will need to choose a type of documentation style and continue with that style for the entire essay. Two of the most common styles, especially for freshman and sophomore students, are MLA (Modern Language Association) and APA (American Psychological Association).

If you write an essay in the social sciences, you will usually be asked to use documentation guidelines created by the American Psychological Association. The *Publication Manual of the American Psychological Association*, in its sixth edition, provides a full description of the conventions used by this particular community of writers; updates to the APA manual can be found at <www.apastyle.org>.

Did You Know?

The American Psychological Association was founded in 1892 at Clark University. The APA, now with over 152,000 members, is the primary professional association for social science scholars in the United States.

This chapter provides a general overview of APA documentation style and an explanation of the most commonly used APA documentation formats.

38a Using APA in-text citations

In-text citations (also called *parenthetical citations*) point readers to where they can find more information about your researched supporting materials. In APA documentation style, the author's last name (or the title of the work, if no author is listed) and the date of publication must appear in the body text of your paper. The author's name can appear either in the sentence itself or in parentheses following the quotation or paraphrase. The date of publication can appear either in the sentence itself, surrounded by parentheses, or in the parentheses that follow the quotation or paraphrase. The page number(s) always appears in the parentheses following a quotation or close paraphrase.

Your parenthetical citation should give enough information to identify the source that was used for the research material as the same source that is listed in your References list. Where this in-text information is placed depends on how you want to phrase the sentence that is summarized, paraphrased, or quoted. Be sure that the in-text citation guides the reader clearly to the source in the References list, where complete information about the source is given.

The following are some of the most common examples of in-text citations.

1. Author's name and date in reference

When using a parenthetical reference to a single source by a single author, use this form: (Author's Last name, Year of publication). Note that the period is placed after the parenthetical element ends.

→ When a teenager sleeps more than 10 hours per night, it is time to question whether she is having significant problems (Jones, 1999).

2. Author's name and date in text

In APA, you can also give the author's name and date within the sentence, using this form: Author's Full Name (Year of publication)

→ Stephanie Jones (1999) explains what signs to look for and when to be concerned.

3. Using a partial quotation in text

When you cite a specific part of a source, give the page number, using *p.* (for one page) and *pp.* (for two or more pages).

→ Stephanie Jones (1999) describes the signs parents should look for when concerned about their children: "excessive sleeping, refraining from eating, and lying about simple things" (p. 63).

4. No author given

When a work has no credited author, use the first two or three words of the work's title or the name that begins the entry in the References list. The title of an article or chapter should be in quotation marks, and the title of a book or periodical should be in italics. Inside the parenthetical citation, place a comma between the title and year.

→ In a recent *Time* article, a list of 30 common signs of teenage trouble cites lack of sleep as the most common sign ("Thirty," 2010).

5. Two to five authors given

When you use a source that was written by two to five authors, you must use all the names in the citation. For the in-text citation, when a work has two authors, use both names each time the reference occurs in the text. When a work has three to five authors, give all authors the first time the reference occurs in the text, and then, in subsequent citations, use only the surname of the first author followed by *et al.* (Latin for "and others") and the year for the first citation of the reference in a paragraph.

→ The idea that "complexity is a constant in biology" is not an innovative one (Sole & Goodwin, 1997, p. 63).

The last two authors' names in a string of three to five authors are separated by a comma and an ampersand (e.g., Jones, Smith, Black, & White).

→ Most signs in English that the authors encountered on the road had "grammar mistakes, misspellings, or just odd pictures" (Smith, Jones, & Best, 1999, p. 55). The most common mistake was an "incorrect or misplaced apostrophe" (Smith, et al., p. 56).

6. Six or more authors given

When an item to be cited has six or more authors, include only the first author's name followed by *et al.* (Latin for "and others"). Use this form for the first reference to this text and all references to this text after that. Note: be sure to list all six or more of the authors in your References list.

→ In Hong Kong, most signs are in Chinese and English; however, once you are in mainland China, English is rarely found on signs, except in tourist areas (Li, et al., 2007).

7. Authors with the same last names

If your source material includes items by authors who have the same last name, be sure to use each author's initials in all text citations.

→ When a teenager sleeps more than 10 hours per night, it is time to question whether she is having significant problems (S. Jones, 1999, p. 63).

→ Another sign of trouble can be when you do not see your child for meals (B. Jones, 2003, p. 114).

8. Encyclopedia or dictionary unsigned entry

When citing an encyclopedia or dictionary in which you have looked up a word or entry, be sure to include the word or entry title in the parenthetical entry.

→ The word *thing* has more definitions than any other entry in the *Oxford English Dictionary* ("thing," 2001).

9. Indirect quotation

When you use a quotation of a quotation—that is, a quotation that quotes from another source—use "as cited in" to designate the secondary source.

→ Smith has said, "My parents really didn't understand me" (as cited in Jones, 1990, p. 64).

10. Personal communication

Personal communications—private letters, memos, non-archived emails, interviews—are usually considered unrecoverable information and, as such, are not included in the References list. However, you do need to include them in parenthetical form in the text, giving the initials and surname of the communicator and providing as exact a date as possible.

→ A. D. Smith (personal communication, February 2, 2010)

→ J. Elbow (personal interview, January 6, 2009)

38b   Using long or block quotations

Long or block quotations have special formatting requirements. A prose quotation that is longer than 40 words is called a *block quotation.* Follow these APA guidelines for block quotations.

1. If introducing the block quotation with a sentence, use a colon at the end of the sentence.

2. Begin the quotation on a new line.

3. Do not use quotation marks to enclose the block quote.

4. Indent the quote five spaces from the left margin, and extend the right margin to the end of the line.

5. Double space the entire quotation.

6. Indent the first line of any additional paragraph.

7. Put a period at the end of the quotation, and then add the parenthetical citation.

→ However, Lansky (1999) states:

> Despite the statement on
> <www.signspotting.com> that we don't accept signs with
> the intention of being funny, people like sending them in.
> I've opted not to use these as it could encourage people to
> start making them, sticking them up in their driveway, and
> snapping a picture. Plus, funny signs are so much more
> amusing when the humor is accidental. (p. 72)

38c   Adding or omitting words in a quotation

1. Adding words in a quotation

Use square brackets [ ] to point out words or phrases that are not part
of the original text.

→ Original quotation: "When we entered the People's Republic
of China, we noticed that the signage began dropping English
translations" (Donelson, 2001, p. 141).

→ Quotation with added words: She said, "When we entered the
People's Republic of China, [Dunkirk and I] noticed that the
signage began dropping English translations" (Donelson, 2001,
p. 141).

You can also add your own comments inside a quotation by using square
brackets. For example, you can add the word *sic* to a quotation when you
know that there is an error.

→ Original quotation: "When we entered the People's Repulic
of China, we noticed that the signage began dropping English
translations" (Donelson, 2001, p. 141).

→ Quotation with added comment: She said, "When we entered
the People's Repulic [sic] of China, we noticed that the signage
began dropping English translations" (Donelson, 2001, p. 141).

2. Omitting words in a quotation

Use an ellipsis (. . .) to represent words that you delete from a quotation. The ellipsis begins with a space, then has three periods with spaces
between them, and then ends with a space.

Original quotation➔ "The Great Wall is something that can be seen from space. When we reach a time when advertisements can be seen from space, we have probably gone too far" (Jones, 1993, p. 101).

Quotation with words omitted in middle of sentence➔ Frank Jones, author of *Signs in Space*, remarks, "The Great Wall . . . can be seen from space. When we reach a time when advertisements can be seen from space, we have probably gone too far" (1993, p. 101).

If you omit the words at the end of a quotation that is at the end of your sentence, you should use an ellipsis plus a period with no space before the ellipsis or after the period. Use an ellipsis only if words have been omitted.

Original quotation➔ "The Great Wall is something that can be seen from space. When we reach a time when advertisements can be seen from space, we have probably gone too far with our advertising and signage" (Jones, 1993, p. 45).

Quotation with words omitted at end of sentence➔ Frank Jones, author of *Signs in Space*, remarks, "The Great Wall is something that can be seen from space. When we reach a time when advertisements can be seen from space, we have probably gone too far . . ." (1993, p. 45).

Helpful hint

APA guidelines can change with a new edition. Sometimes, class textbooks can use an older APA documentation style. Always check with your instructor if rules seem to be in conflict.

38d   Citing online sources

In the APA documentation style, online or electronic sources have their own formatting guidelines since these types of sources rarely give specific page numbers.

The APA recommends that you include in the text, rather than in an in-text citation, the name(s) of the person that begins the matching References list entry. If the author or creator of the website uses paragraph or page numbers, use these numbers in the parenthetical citation. If no numbering is used, do not use or add numbers to the paragraphs, pages, or parenthetical citation.

When website does not number paragraphs➔ In his review of the film *Signs*, Roger Ebert says that Shyamalan "does what Hitchcock said he wanted to do, and plays the audience like a piano."

When website numbers paragraphs➔ In his review of the file *Signs*, Roger Ebert says that Shyamalan "does what Hitchcock said he wanted to do, and plays the audience like a piano" (para. 8).

38e   General formatting guidelines for the APA References list

If you cite any sources within a paper, be sure to include a References list at the end of the paper. Here are some general formatting guidelines to follow when setting up a References list.

1. Put the References list at the end of your paper as a separate page.

2. Use one-inch margins on all sides.

3. Include any header used for the paper on the References page.

4. Center the title **References** at the top of the page, using no underlining, quotation marks, or italics.

5. Place the first line of each entry flush with the left margin. Indent any additional lines of the entry one-half inch (or one tab) to form a hanging indent.

6. Double space the entries in the References list, not adding any extra spaces between entries.

7. Alphabetize the References list. Use the first major word in each entry, not including articles *a*, *an*, or *the*, to determine the alphabetical order. If the cited source does not have an author, alphabetize by using the first word of the title of the source.

8. Put the author's name in this order: last name, first initial, and middle initial if given (e.g., Ebert, R.) If a work has more than one author, invert all the authors' names, follow each with a comma, and then continue listing all the authors, putting a comma and ampersand (,&) before the final name (e.g., Ebert, R., & Siskel, G.).

9. Arrange two or more works by the same author(s) in the same name order by year of publication.

10. Capitalize only the first word in a title and a subtitle unless the title or subtitle includes a proper noun, which would also be capitalized.

11. Do not use quotation marks for titles of shorter works, including articles, book chapters, episodes on television or radio, poems, and short stories.

12. Italicize the titles of longer works, including album or CD titles, art pieces, books, films, journals, magazines, newspapers, and television shows.

13. Give the edition number for works with more than one edition [e.g., *Publication manual of the American Psychological Association* (6th ed.)].

14. Include the DOI (digital object identifier), a unique alpha-numeric string assigned by a registration agency that helps identify content and provides a link to the source online. All DOI numbers begin with a *10* and contain a prefix and suffix separated by a slash (for example, 10.11037/0278-6133.27.3.379). The DOI is usually found in the citation detail or on the first page of an electronic journal article near the copyright notice.

38f Formats for print sources

1. Books (includes brochures, pamphlets, and graphic novels)

Author's last name, Author's first initial. (Year of publication). *Title of book*. Place of publication: Publisher.

→ Lansky, D. (2005). *Signspotting*. Oakland, CA: Lonely Planet.

Helpful hint

Only use the state after the city if the city is not a place that would be commonly known or if there may be more than one commonly known city by that name.

CITATION DETAIL WITH DOI

stet Detail

Title:

An Ability Traitor at Work: A Treasonous Call to Subvert *Writing* From Within.

Authors:

Holbrook, Teri[1] *tholbrook@gsu.edu*

Source:

Qualitative Inquiry; Mar2010, Vol. 16 Issue 3, p171-183, 13p

Document Type:

Article

Subject Terms:

*DISABILITIES
*QUALITATIVE research
*MANAGEMENT science
*SIGN language
*WRITING

Author-Supplied Keywords:

assemblage
disability
multigenre
multimodal writing

NAICS/Industry Codes:

541930 Translation and Interpretation Services

Abstract:

In questioning conventional qualitative research methods, St. Pierre asked, "What else might *writing* do except mean?" The author answers, it oppresses. Co-opting the race traitor figurative, she calls on qualitative researchers to become "ability traitors" who interrogate how a valuable coinage of their trade—the written word—is used to rank and categorize individuals with troubling effects. In this article, she commits three betrayals: (a) multigenre *writing* that undermines the authoritative text; (b) assemblage as a method of analysis that deprivileges the written word; and (c) a gesture toward a dis/comfort text intended to take up Lather's example of challenging the "usual ways of making sense." In committing these betrayals, the author articulates her "traitorous agenda" designed to interrogate assumptions about inquiry, power, equity, and *writing* as practice-as-usual. [ABSTRACT FROM AUTHOR]

Author Affiliations:
  [1]Georgia State University
ISSN:
  10778004
DOI:
  10.1177/1077800409351973
Accession Number:
  47934623
Database:
  Academic Search Premier
View Links:
  Find Fulltext

2. Books with two or more authors

If a work has two or more authors, use a comma between the authors' names.

First Author's Last name, First author's Initial of first name, & Second author's Last name, Second author's Initial of first name. (year of publication). *Title of book.* Place of publication: Publisher.

➔ Maasik, S., & Soloman, J. (2008). *Signs of life in the USA: Readings on popular culture for writers.* Boston, MA: Bedford/St. Martin's.

3. Two books by the same author

Be sure the entries are in sequential time order with earliest date first.

➔ Maasik, S., & Soloman, J. (2004). *California dreams and realities: Readings for critical thinkers and writers* (3rd ed.). Boston, MA: Bedford/St. Martin's.

➔ Maasik, S., & Soloman, J. (2008). *Signs of life in the USA: Readings on popular culture for writers.* Boston, MA: Bedford/St. Martin's.

4. Anthology or collection

Editor's Last name, Editor's Initial of first name. (Ed). (Year of publication). *Title of book.* Place of publication: Publisher.

➔ Smith, A. D., Smith, T. G., & Wright, K. (Eds.). (2007). *COMPbiblio: Leaders and influences in composition theory and practice.* Southlake, TX: Fountainhead.

5. Work within an anthology or collection

Author's last name, Author's first initial. (Year of publication). Title of work. In Editor's Name(s) (Ed.) *Title of anthology* (page numbers). Place of publication: Publisher.

➔ Tan, A. (2010). Mother tongue. In R. Bullock, M. D. Goggin, & F. Weinberg (Eds.). *The Norton field guide to writing* (pp. 564-70). New York, NY: Norton.

6. Article in a scholarly journal without DOI (digital object identifier)

Include the issue number if the journal is paginated by issue. If there is not a DOI available and the article was found online, give the URL of the journal home page.

Author's Last name, Author's Initial of first name. (Year of publication). Title of the article. *Journal Title, volume number* (issue number), pages. URL (if retrieved online).

→ Holbrook, T. (2010). An ability traitor at work: A treasonous call to subvert writing from within. *Qualitative Inquiry*, 16 (3), 171-183. Retrieved from E-Journals database.

7. Article in a scholarly journal with DOI (digital object identifier)

Author's Last name, Author's Initial of first name. (Year of publication). Title of the article. *Journal Title, volume number* (issue number), pages. doi:

→ Franks, L. (2006). The play in language. *Child Signs*, 73(1), 3-17. doi:10.1770/69873629

8. Article in a newspaper

Use *p.* or *pp.* before the page numbers in references of newspapers.

Note: if the newspaper article appears on discontinuous pages, be sure to give all the page numbers, separating them with a comma (e.g., pp. A4, A10, A13-14).

Author's Last name, Author's Initial of first name. (Year of publication, Month and Date of publication). Title of article. *Newspaper Title*, pp. page numbers.

→ Genzlinger, N. (2010, April 6). Autism is another thing that families share. *The New York Times*, p. A4.

9. Article in a magazine

Author's Last name, Author's Initial of first name. (Year of publication, Month of publication). Title of article. *Magazine Title, volume number* (issue number), pages.

Note: include the day only if the magazine is published on a weekly or bi-weekly basis.

→ Musico, C. (2009, November). Sign 'em up! *CRM Magazine, 13*(11), 49.

10. Review

Be sure to identify the type of work being reviewed by noting if it is a book, film, television program, painting, song, or other creative work. If the work is a book, include the author name(s) after the book title, separated by a comma. If the work is a film, song, or other media, be sure to include the year of release after the title of the work, separated by a comma.

Reviewer's last name, Reviewer's first initial. (Year of publication, Month and Date of Publication). Title of review [Review of the work *Title of work*, by Author's Name]. *Magazine or Journal Title, volume number* (issue number), pp. page numbers. doi number (if available).

→ Turken, R. (2008, May 5). Life outside of the box. [Review of the film *Signs*, 2002]. *Leisure Times*, pp. A12.

11. Article in a reference book

Author's Last name, Author's Initial of first name. (Year of publication). Title of chapter or entry. In A. Editor (Ed). *Title of book* (pp. xx-xx). Location: Publisher.

→ Jones, A. (2003). Semiotics. In B. Smith, R. Lore, and T. Rex (Eds.). *Encyclopedia of signs* (pp. 199-202). Boston, MA: Rutledge.

12. Religious and classical works

In APA, classical religious works, such as the Bible and the Qur'an, and major classical works that originated in Latin or Greek, are not required to have entries in the References list but should include reference to the text within the sentence in the essay. Note: it is always a good idea to check with your instructor on this type of entry since there can be some variety across instructors and schools.

38g   Formats for online sources

1. Website

The documentation form for a website can also be used for online message, blog, or video posts.

Author's Last name, Author's Initial of first name (if author given). (Year, Month Day). *Title of page* [Description of form]. Retrieved from http://www.xxxx

→ United States Post Office (2010). *United States Post Office Services Locator* [search engine]. Retrieved from http://usps.whitepages.com/post_office

2. Article from a Website, online newspaper, blog, or wiki (with author given)

Author's Last name, Author's Initial of first name. (Year, Month Day of publication). Title of article. *Name of Webpage/Journal/Newspaper*. Retrieved from http://www.xxxxxxx

→ Ebert, R. (2002, August 2). Signs. *Chicago Sun-Times.* Retrieved from http://rogerebert.suntimes.com/

3. Article from a Website, online newspaper, blog, or wiki (with no author given)

Title of article. (Year, Month Day of publication). *Name of Webpage/Journal/Newspaper*. Retrieved from http://www.xxxxxxx

→ China's traditional dress: Qipao. (2001, October). *China Today.* Retrieved from http://chinatoday.com

4. Online journal article

The reference for an online journal article is set up the same way as for a print one, including the DOI.

> Author's Last name, Author's Initial of first name. (Year of publication). Title of the article. *Journal Title, volume number* (issue number), pages. doi:xxxxxxxxxxx

> → Franks, L. (2006). The play in language. *Child Signs, 73*(1), 3-17. doi:10.1770/69873629

If a DOI is not assigned to content you have retrieved online, use the home page URL for the journal or magazine in the reference (e.g., Retrieved from http://www.xxxxxx).

> → Austen, V. (2003). Writing spaces: Performance of the word. *Kairos.* Retrieved from http://kairos.com

5. Article from an online service, such as General One-File, LexisNexis, JSTOR, ERIC

When using APA, it is not necessary to include database information as long as you can include the publishing information required in a normal citation. Note: this is quite different from using MLA documentation, which requires full information about the database.

6. Article in an online reference work

> Author's last name, Author's first initial. (Year of publication). Title of chapter or entry. In A. Editor (Ed). *Title of book.* Retrieved from http://xxxxxxxxxx

> → Jones, A. (2003). Semiotics. In B. Smith, R. Lore, and T. Rex (Eds.). *Encyclopedia of signs.* Retrieved from http:// brown.edu/signs

38h   Formats for other commonly used sources

1. Television or radio program (single episode)

Writer's last name, Writer's first initial. (Writer), & Director's Last name, Director's Initial of first name. (Director). (Year). Title of episode [Television/Radio series episode]. In Executive Producer's name (Executive Producer), *Title of show*. Place: Network.

> ➔ Bell, J. (Writer), Carter, C. (Creator), & Manners, K. (Director). (2000). Signs and wonders [Television series episode]. In C. Carter (Executive Producer), *The X files*. New York, NY: FOX.

2. Sound recording

Writer's last name, Writer's first initial. (Copyright year). Title of song. [Recorded by Artist's name if different from writer]. On *Title of album* [Medium of recording]. Location: Label. (Date of recording if different from song copyright date).

> ➔ Emmerson, L. (1970). Signs. [Recorded by Five Man Electrical Band]. On *Good-byes and butterflies* [LP]. New York, NY: Lionel Records.

> ➔ Emmerson, L. (1970). Signs. [Recorded by Tesla]. On *Five man acoustical jam* [CD]. New York, NY: Geffen. 1990.

3. Film

Producer's last name, Producer's first initial. (Producer), & Director's last name, Director's first initial. (Director). (Year). *Title of film* [Motion picture]. Country of Origin: Studio.

> ➔ Kennedy, K. (Producer), & Shyamalan, M. N. (Director). (2002). *Signs* [film]. USA: Touchstone.

4. Painting, sculpture, or photograph

Artist's last name, Artist's first initial. (Year, Month Day). *Title of material*. [Description of material]. Name of collection (if available). Name of Repository, Location.

➜ Gainsborough, T. (1745). *Conversation in a park*. [Oil painting on canvas]. Louvre, Paris, France.

5. Personal interview

Unlike MLA documentation, personal interviews and other types of personal communication are not included in APA References lists. Be sure to cite personal communications in the text only.

6. Lecture, speech, address, or reading

Speaker's Last name, Speaker's Initial of first name. (Year, Month). Title of speech. *Event name*. Lecture conducted from Sponsor, Location.

➜ Stephens, L. (2009, December). The signs of the times. *MLA annual convention*. Lecture conducted from Hilton Hotel Downtown, New York, NY.

38i   Sample References list using APA

Following is an example of how a completed References list would look at the end of your paper.

Your Last name 14

References

Emmerson, L. (1970). Signs. [Recorded by Five Man Electrical

Band]. On *Good-byes and butterflies* [LP]. New York,

NY: Lionel Records.

Franks, L. (2006). The play in language. *Child Signs*, 73(1), 3-17.

doi:10.1770/69873629

Kennedy, K. (Producer), & Shyamalan, M. N. (Director). (2002).

Signs [film]. USA: Touchstone.

Jones, A. (2003). Semiotics. In B. Smith, R. Lore, & T. Rex

(Eds.). *Encyclopedia of signs*. Retrieved from

http://brown.edu/signs

Lansky, D. (2005). *Signspotting*. Oakland, CA: Lonely Planet.

Stephens, L. (2009, December). The signs of the times. *MLA*

annual convention. Lecture conducted from Hilton Hotel

Downtown, New York, NY.

Tan, A. (2010). Mother tongue. In R. Bullock, M. D. Goggin, &

F. Weinberg (Eds.). *The Norton field guide to writing* (pp.

564-70). New York, NY: Norton.

Activity 5.3

Directions: Below are three example sources and an in-text citation from each one. Put the correct information in the parentheses for an APA in-text citation.

From page 89 of the book:

Bazerman, C. (1988). *Shaping written knowledge: the genre and activity*

of the experimental article in science. Madison, Wis.: University

of Wisconsin Press.

Yet, it could also be the case that "genre and activity are more closely related than we had previously thought" (   ).

From page 340 of the article:

Bodemer, B. (2012). The Importance of Search as Intertextual Practice

for Undergraduate Research. *College and Research Libraries,*

73(4), 336–348.

Bodemer (   ), however, suggests that "increasingly, the ability to

search well on the Internet will be as important a literacy skill

as reading or writing" (   ).

From a magazine's web-only article:

Electronic education: Flipping the classroom. (2011, September 17).

The Economist. Retrieved from http://www.economist.com/

node/21529062

The Economist has reported that "flipping the classroom is the new teaching technique of the 21st-century classroom" (   ).

From page 192 of the chapter:

Schwartz, D. L., Lin, X., Brophy, S., & Bransford, J. (1999). Toward

the Development of Flexibly Adaptive Instructional Designs.

In C. M. Reigelut (Ed.), *Instructional Design Theories and*

Models: Volume II (pp. 183–213). Hillside, NJ: Erlbaum.

In a study performed by Schwartz et al. (   ), students found adaptive classroom designs more engaging and, finally, more educational.

Activity 5.4

Directions: Insert all needed punctuation and formatting into the following APA References entries. The type of source is listed after each in in bold to help you out.

Ackerman J M 1991 Reading, Writing, and Knowing: The Role of

Disciplinary Knowledge in Comprehension and Composing *Research*

in the Teaching of English 25(2) 133–178 (**article in a journal**)

Baddeley A 1986 *Working Memory* New York Oxford University

Press (**book**)

Barlow J P 1994 March The Economy of Ideas *Wired* 2(03)

Retrieved from http://www.wired.com/wired/archive/2.03/economy.

ideas.html (**article in a magazine**)

Hacker D J Keener M C & Kircher J 2009 Writing is applied metacognition In D J Hacker J Dunlosky & A C Graesser Eds *Handbook of Metacognition in Education* 1st ed   New York Routledge **(chapter in a book or anthology)**

Rounsaville A Goldberg R & Bawarshi A 2008 From Incomes to Outcomes: FYW Students' Knowledge Meta-Cognition and the Question of Transfer *WPA: Writing Program Administration* 32(1) 97–112 **(article in a journal)**

Wilson H 1999 When Collaboration Becomes Plagiairism: The Administrative Perspective In L Buranen & A M Roy Eds *Perspectives on Plagiarism and Intellectual Property in a Postmodern World* pp 211–218 Albany NY SUNY Press **(chapter in a book or anthology)**

38j   Sample Annotated Essay - APA

Running Head: MASCULINITY AND MORALITY IN   1
THE MODERN ERA

Masculinity and Morality in the Modern Era:

Multiplication, Inflation, Destabilization

John T. Doe

State University

Before the turn of the twentieth century,

"morality" was almost exclusively a religious

concept. But religion was, in many ways, severely

undercut by secular interests in the modernist period;

indeed, the concept of morality slowly evolved

to be understood more as a non-religious "set of

rules of conduct or obligations towards others"

(Collini, 1993, p. 63). Without the uniting force of

religion for the concept of morality, various secular

moralities emerged. This paper will investigate these

various moralities that bloomed during the modernist

period, and illustrate how the various conceptions of

morality, both in public discourse and in modernist

authors' works, were substantially influenced by

contemporary ideas of masculinity.

At the time of Oscar Wilde's 1895 trial for

indecency, sexuality was beginning to be considered

On the top of each page of your paper, use a shortened version of the paper's title. This is called the running head. On the first page, label it "Running Head," them omit that label from page 2 on.

The title should be centered, 12-point Times New Roman font, and double-spaced. The title should not be bolded, italicized, or underlined.

The author's name and institution should be placed right below the title, and should be centered.

Because the author name was not introduced before the quotation, the author name and year goes in the parentheses. Because it is a direct quote, the citation also needs the page number.

scientifically, and previously innocuous notions of effeminacy and homosexuality were replaced by medical and psychological claims that both were instead forms of mental disease. Underpinned by Spencerian and Darwinian theories of human and state evolution, popular philosophies considered diseased individuals a threat to the health of the nation itself; social critics such as Max Nordau furthermore argued that non-conforming, individualistic artists endangered the state. Singled out as an effeminate artist, Wilde became the embodiment of the moral threats to the British Empire. His conviction only served to further unite a number of key ideas in the public's mind; Foldy (1997) explains that after the 1895 trial, "degeneration," "decadence," "same-sex passion," and "moral backsliding" were brought together and conflated in the public discourse, while the opposites—"manliness," "health," "moral rectitude," and heterosexual desire—were cemented as synonymous as well (p. 70).

A decade or two after Wilde's trial, when modernist artists began to produce some of the most influential works of the era, the two discourses

For the first part of this citation, the author name is mentioned before the cited information. Always add the year of the source right after the author's last name.

The second part of the citation here is the page number, which always goes *after* the quoted information.

MASCULINITY AND MORALITY IN THE MODERN ERA   3

underwent changes in scope, yet were still very much connected in the public mind. Because of the emerging scientific explanations of gender and the demonization of effeminacy, definitions of acceptable and preferred masculinity narrowed, while the secularization of morality greatly expanded the meanings of that term. In all the different ways in which morality was conceived, then, masculinity and heteronormativity were largely still demanded to in order to avoid possible social "degeneration." Those male authors and social theorists who showed any concern for the ordering of society, then, often found themselves arguing in similar ways about competing and contested moral ideologies.

Considerations of morality in literary works have been somewhat few and far between, most likely because on the surface, authors of the modernist period seemingly are united in their disdain of the concept: because the public's demand for morality often meant censorship, artists in turn attacked the concept and those who espoused it. Exceedingly disparate artists – even ones antagonistic toward each other – seemingly unite in their objection to moral concerns. In the preface to *The Picture of Dorian Gray,* for example, Wilde (2006) writes, "There is no such thing as a moral or an immoral book. Books are well written, or badly written. That is all" (p. 1). Considering Wilde's well-known belief in the hedonistic principles championed in Pater's conclusion the *The Renaissance,* his pronouncement here sounds much like Ernest Hemingway in his 1932 treatise on bullfighting, *Death in the Afternoon*: "So far, about morals, I know only that what is moral is what you feel good after and what is immoral is what you feel bad after and judged by these moral standards, which I do not defend, the bullfight is very moral to me" (p. 4). These two pronouncements defend artistic and experiential freedom by way of relativistic morality, and are perhaps the singular commonality between the two authors.

However, Schneck (1989) argues that for many post-Wildean male authors their more revolutionary artistic styles hide their conservative political leanings. For authors such as Hemingway, Ezra Pound, and Wyndham Lewis, radical thematic and formal posturing did indeed hide commonalities with conservative politics and middle-class dynamics; although their means differed (uses of the term "morality," for example), many male authors had the same ends as the professional classes they otherwise admittedly disdained for their prurient tastes. This idea can be useful in

More common in APA citation is a mention of the author, the year of the work in parentheses, and then a summary of their ideas, in which case no page number is needed.

MASCULINITY AND MORALITY IN THE MODERN ERA   5

revealing less obvious relationships between authors; for example,

while Hemingway's infamous machismo highlights his more

hegemonic principles, Pound and Lewis, in the end, were the more

conservative.

Far more common a response than stalwart conservatism,

however, is one characterized by internal conflict, insecurity, and

anxiety. Although this phenomena exists across nations in the

modernist period, Ireland provides particularly fertile ground for

this investigation as its revolutionary aspirations and religious

backgrounds welcomed a number of fluctuating partnerships and

rivalries between the moral ideologies of Catholicism, socialism,

and republicanism. Sean O'Casey and W.B. Yeats specifically

illustrate the great concern over national order and chaos, but

their responses to the uprisings and wars of the times became

increasingly conflicted as the republican ideologies that won the

public's attention (colored with strong shades of masculinity)

demanded blood sacrifice first.

Still, no matter the country, modernist art reveals

incredible anxieties about these two concepts, masculinity and

morality. Buy studying some of the great artists and works of the

period, a reader can learn a great deal about how people's ideas of

both concepts were conflated while, at the same time, destabilized.

MASCULINITY AND MORALITY IN THE MODERN ERA   6

As with many others historical periods of upheaval, art can show us some of the most important underlying ideologies in a culture.

MASCULINITY AND MORALITY IN THE MODERN ERA   7

References

Collini, S. (1993). *Public Moralists: Political Thought and Intellectual Life in Britain, 1850-1930*. Oxford: Clarendon Press.

Foldy, M. S. (1997). *The Trials of Oscar Wilde: Deviance, Morality, and Late-Victorian Society* (Prima edizione). New Haven: Yale University Press.

Hemingway, E. (1932). *Death in the Afternoon.* Charles Scibner Sons.

Schneck, C. (1989). Exiled by Genre: Modernism, Canonicity, and the Politics of Exclusion. In M. L. Broe & A. Ingram (Eds.), *Women's Writing in Exile* (pp. 225-50). Chapel Hill: The University of North Carolina Press.

Wilde, O. (2006). *The Picture of Dorian Gray*. (J. Bristow, Ed.). Oxford ; New York: Oxford University Press.

Bibliographic information is placed in a "References" list in APA format. Being this list on a new page. Center the title "References." Double-space all entries on the page and use hanging indentation. Each source cited in the text of the paper must have an entry here.

Clark, Moira Catherine. *We Make the City.*

Chapter 6

Writing with Englishes: The Complexities of Language Use

Who Owns English?

The issues surrounding language use, college writing, culture, and identity are complex and frequently intersect with issues faced by all writers in first-year composition classes. For hundreds of years, the standard for correct English was known as The Queen's or King's English. This refers to the monarch of England, who was also head of the vast colonial empire of the United Kingdom. We cannot, in the limited space of this chapter, discuss the linguistic, cultural, settler colonial and postcolonial legacies of various past and current empires. However, the concepts of **Englishes**, **Code-Switching**, and **Code-Meshing** relate to issues of language use and ownership. Later in the chapter, we will touch on the subject of the ways we create Englishes and language ownership through such things as code-switching and code-meshing.

First, let's talk about the word "Englishes" itself. Englishes can refer to the ways in which English has been incorporated, changed, remixed, and enriched across the globe, by a myriad of cultures. Hinglish is an example of an English that has developed in its own unique way. Many Indian-Americans and Indians in South Asia speak an English that blends words from Hindi and English into a unique new, world English. Spanglish is another world English that blends Spanish and English; Spanglish is often spoken by L1 English and Spanish speakers who work

Kegley, Sarah. *My Class at 10 a.m.*

or live in Spanish-speaking areas of the United States and abroad. These are just two examples of Englishes that have emerged in our globally-connected era. With these linguae francae and remixed Englishes developing across the globe, what the Queen of England has to say about English usage no longer really matters. Right?

But you're reading this textbook because you are in a **FYC (First-Year Composition)** course, which means you need to write a certain kind of English in this course; this English will serve you throughout your experience in academia. Often, this **academic English** challenges writers whose first language isn't English. This is one of the reasons we are writing this chapter—we want to share strategies, resources, and projects that L2 English writers navigate while writing at American universities like Georgia State. This chapter seeks to also explore the complexities and richness that L2 students bring to Georgia State: those students who *don't* speak English as their first language, who come from homes in which English *isn't* the language spoken, or who are fully—culturally and linguistically—bilingual or multilingual. These students offer a complex array of wealth to the university community. While we want to focus this chapter on how students from different linguistic and cultural backgrounds make our community stronger and more diverse, we are also engaging the complex issues that surround students from diverse backgrounds. As we write this chapter, a candidate for the Presidency of the Unites States is threatening to ban-

Smittick, Toniah. *From Out Within.*

ish all undocumented workers from our society and build a wall between the Unites States and Mexico. In Georgia, a bill has been introduced which would make English the only language used in any state documents. As of Summer 2016, the state Driver's Knowledge Exam is offered in Arabic, Chinese, French, Hindi, Japanese, Korean, Russian, Spanish, Turkish and Vietnamese ("License FAQ"). What would it mean to offer the text of the test in English only? These issues are complex; there's no getting around that fact.

We will first introduce a variety of terms and concepts used in academic culture to discuss writers and writing that emerges from diverse cultural and linguistic orientations. We believe that these issues affect all of us, not simply the student who may not be comfortable speaking aloud in class because her first language is not English. If we step into any common area on any Georgia State campus, we will hear a multiplicity of Englishes being spoken. Diversity, cultural identity, and linguistic orientations are issues that affect all of us, not simply the student who may not be comfortable speaking aloud in class because her first language is not English. Similarly, we believe there is no one way to learn writing; in fact, other chapters in this textbook bring a variety of approaches to writing, research, and critical thinking.

We first want to introduce the concept of **Intercultural Rhetoric**, which frames the entire chapter. We then move on to three academic schools of praxis: English for Academic Purposes (**EAP**), Critical, and Process. The ideas presented in these sections may challenge your conceptions of writing and learning, but college is designed to challenge you into new realms of thinking and awareness of yourself as part of an interconnected, albeit big, world. You can decide what methods work for you and engage in discussions about these concepts, terms, and issues in your classroom.

For Thought and Discussion

Here, we present a number of terms and concepts that are used in academic settings.

First, what comes to mind as you read the following terms?

L1	Bicultural	Non-native speaker
L2 writer	Multicultural	Immigrant
ESL	Heritage speaker	Generation 1.5
Home L1 Not English	Native speaker	students

Do you identify with any of these terms? Tell us about a time that you were labeled with one of these terms.

Do you label others with these terms? Why? In what circumstances? Can you give an example?

Terms/Phrases and activities/thoughts for discussion:

- **L1**: The term L1 means first language. For example, when we ask, "What is your L1?" we are asking what language you first began speaking as a child. This can also be referred to as **home language** and **heritage language**.
- **L2:** The term L2 simply means second language. For example, if we say that a person is writing in an L2, or is an L2 writer, she is said to be writing in a second language, or is a second language writer.

CCCC Statement (2001) defines second language writers as follows:

Second language writers include international visa students, refugees, and permanent residents as well as naturalized and native-born citizens of the United States and Canada. Many of these students have grown up speaking languages other than English at home, in their communities, and in schools; others began to acquire English at a very young age and have used it alongside their native languages. To many, English may be a third, fourth or fifth language. Many second language writers are highly literate in their first languages, while others have never learned to write in their mother tongues. Some are even native speakers of languages without a written form. Some students may have difficulty adapting to or adopting North American discursive strategies because the nature and functions of discourse, audience, and rhetorical appeals often differ across cultural, national, linguistic, and educational contexts. At the same time, however, other students—especially graduate students—are already knowledgeable about the discourse and content of their respective disciplines, even if their status as "international" or "second language" may mask their abilities. Furthermore, most second language writers are still in the process of acquiring syntactic and lexical competence—a process that will take a lifetime.

- **L2 Speaker/Writer**: L2 writers is a frequently used term among L2 writing scholars and practitioners to refer to students who do not speak English as their native language. The popularity of this term

Cordry, Jeffery. *Athens.*

is because of its implied neutrality compared to the most often used term ESL writers, which is often viewed as a 'stigma' among many of students who went through ESOL or ESL courses in their previous schooling. Another reason behind the popular use of this term is that by differentiating first and second language writers, the term L2 writers presupposes the existence of a first language other than English. Even though this term provides convenience in referring to a group of writers that enroll in ESL-designated sections of FYW, L2 writing scholars and teachers are aware that there exist a variety of subgroups of L2 writers, each of whom shows different characteristics in their linguistic and cultural resources they bring to the classroom.

- **Home L1 Not English**: This refers to students who are often American-born (although not always) and whose primary use language is English, but whose parents primarily speak a language other than English in the home. The home language is also called the "Heritage Language" by some linguists. The student is often bilingual from birth, although the Heritage Language may be the L1 or English may be the L1. This refers to language use only, not cultural connotations. (Cho; Juan-Garau; Scontras, Fuchs, and Polinsky).

- **Bicultural**: A language user who may or may not be bilingual, but has encompassing cultural knowledge from two distinct cultures and navigates between them. (Grosjean; Chand and Tung; Hsu).

Yang, Eun Kyoung. *Alone.*

- **Bicultural Literacy**: This is distinguished from the term "bicultural" by the actions of the person who navigates the cultures and develops the literacies. Literacies can mean reading and writing, but, more broadly, it can also mean community traditions, food, religious practices, language and dialect, as well as interpersonal relationships. Bicultural literacy represents the practices, skills, and methods utilized by the bicultural individual in engaging the two cultures of which the individual has knowledge. A bicultural individual may simply have been born into two cultures, but someone who develops bicultural literacy actively pursues and lives the literacy practices of those two cultures. (Yer; Barton; Keller)

- **FYC and FYW**: FYC stands for "First-Year Composition" and FYW for "First-Year Writing," respectively. They are terms used for the writing courses most first-year college students take. These courses are almost always taught as part of the English Department and are usually mandatory. To a degree, the terms are used interchangeably, although some scholars feel strongly about the difference. As academics focus on multimodal communication, some feel that FYW constructs an idea of these courses that excludes multimodal content because of the use of "writing" in the term. Other academics believe that the focus of the course should remain on writing and more traditional assignments such as the research paper, annotated bibliography, and analysis.

▪ **Multicultural**: A contested term; in many, mostly nonacademic circles, it stands in for political correctness, which is seen by some as a negative. We, however, use the term positively. It means engagement with many cultures in the process of education—K-12 as well as college. "Multiculturalism" may be replaced or conflated with the concept of "interculturalism," which Sarmento defines as, "as movement, communication, dynamics, encounter between cultures, with the purpose of discussing their pragmatic consequences in academia and society" (603). While both concepts have political overtones, users of "interculturalism" generally embrace the political nature of meshing of cultures. (Castro; Laughter; Sarmento).

For Thought and Discussion

a.   Does anyone in the class consider him or herself to be bicultural or multicultural? Can you talk about your cultural background or that of your parents?

b.   What activities do you participate in at home that are not necessarily U.S. American culturally—in other words, are any of your family practices biculturally literate?

c.   Can you name a place or event where you feel that you do not belong in the US? How about outside of the US?

The following are examples of freewrites from GSU students in the ESL program. Can you relate to any of these experiences?

» I came to the US when I was 3 years old and I gained citizenship soon. My mother did not, however, and she was forced to take a test but even though her English was not good she tried her best and did it. When I was growing up she tried her best to help me with my school work even though she didn't understand it either.

» It's almost the end of the semester. At first, I don't really like this class...I there are too many homework and assignment. Because I'm a shy person I feel uncomfortable with classes and talking to others. Especially in English. Now, I learned to share things with writing, and to give comments to others' writings. I learn to be a brave person, to communicate with people from different backgrounds. I am so glad to tell others about Malaysia.

» I met some of my classmates in a class for bilingual students. In group activities I got to know people from other places. They told me lots of

Cordry, Jeffery. *Untitled.*

things. What language symbols they use and what things represent. I am really glad I got to meet so many people that are like me. Not American, but not internationals either.

» I have a couple of friends who are immigrants and cannot get pay for college. One friend lived here for almost eight years and just recently applied for her green card. I feel like after an immigrant lives here for 8 years, they should be able to get a citizenship. It made me upset thinking about my friend struggling to pay for college tuition.

NNS/NNES: (non-native speaker/non-native English speaker) A basic assumption behind this binary distinction is that every student can be neatly classified into either category. Many people would easily identify themselves as either one of the categories, but this distinction can be problematic, especially in FYW contexts. Some students who grew up in a multilingual home, community, or country would find it hard to identify one primary language. Some bilingual students who came to the U.S. at an early age would not be able to identify themselves as either one of the categories. Another problem with these terms when used in the writing classroom is that they do not reflect the nature of academic English. No one is a natural born 'academic' speaker or writer of English; academic language, unlike a vernacular or everyday form of language, is acquired and developed mainly through exposure and practice over an extended time in an instructional setting. Everyone is a 'second' language user of academic English in some sense.

U.S.-Educated Multilinguals: In recent decades, L2 writing professionals began to pay attention to a subgroup of writers often called U.S. educated multilinguals who were neglected in L2 writing research and pedagogical scholarship. L2 writing research was predominantly focused on the group of newly arrived international students until the early 1990's (Ferris, 2009). U.S. educated multilingual writers as a group demonstrate unique characteristics different from L1 writers and international students. They possess a high level of familiarity with L1 culture and oral language competence, but often lack academic language competence in their L2. Therefore, this group of L2 writers has different goals, strengths, and challenges in their L2 writing. To make matters more complicated, there are several sub-groups of U.S. educated multilinguals:

One group includes both early-arriving students who experienced a significant amount of schooling in the U.S., and late-arriving students who typically received at least part of their secondary education in the U.S. These students are also sometimes referred to as "resident bilingual" students.

Another group consists of transnational students who have shuttled between U.S. and foreign schools.

A final group consists of international visa students who started their secondary school in the U.S. with a view to attending college in the U.S. (Ferris, 2009; Roberge, Rosey & Wald, 2015).

The term U.S. educated multilingual does away with -or problematizes- dichotomies indicated by the terms like native vs. non-native, and ESL vs. mainstream, by providing a continuum that explains individual experiences with language.

Generation 1.5 students: L2 writing scholars began to use this term to differentiate a particular group of L2 college writers from other groups of multilingual students such as new immigrants (often called ESL or ELL students) and international students who come to the U.S. mainly with an academic goal. Generation 1.5 students, despite

Mitchell, Thomas Alexander. *Crossing the Street.*

a diversity among students in terms of their length of residency in the country and literacy development in their first language, refers to those who have lived and have been schooled at least several years in the U.S., developed oral language skills and therefore show familiarity with U.S. culture (Roberge, Siegal, & Harklau, 2009). This background makes them reluctant to identify themselves as ESL or ELL. They often lack the understanding of academic language and conventions in their writing.

Because of their oral fluency (close to native speaker), and adaptation to U.S. culture, Generation 1.5 students are not easily identified. First year writing programs around the nation offer either remedial language and writing courses often for ESL students who need overall oral and written language development or separate writing sections designated for international students, but it is rare that they offer a separate writing course customized for generation 1.5 students.

These terms, along with the more widely-used "ESL student" (English as a Second Language), interconnect, disconnect, and reconnect writers who come from a variety of cultural and linguistic backgrounds. Freewrite about your thoughts, now that you are aware of all the diversity among these writers.

Academic Socialization: English for Academic Purposes (EAP) Approach

Writing in academia can be challenging for many college students. Crafting an acceptable academic text involves knowledge of linguistic skills, composing strategies, text structure, and discipline-specific academic conventions. Research on academic writing indicates that learning to write in academic contexts is a long-term process that takes numerous years in an ideal environment that allows learners to be fully immersed in academic reading and writing (Collier, 1987). Therefore, it is not surprising that many L2 students on U.S. campuses are often linguistically and rhetorically underprepared. For example, when an L2 student is from an educational system in which writing is not extensively utilized as a learning and assessment tool, along with not having a high level of L2 language proficiency, she might not possess strong writing skills and effective strategies. Even if the L2 student went to a U.S. high school, she would be likely to still be in the process of developing her writing competence and language skills by the time she enrolls in college level courses. As you can see, needs for improving academic literacy are strongly felt among many L2 students.

This section introduces an approach called 'English for Academic Purposes (EAP)' that focuses on academic socialization of L2 students in a university setting. First, we are going to introduce the taxonomy of undergraduate writing tasks, and then guide you to deal with challenging writing tasks. We hope that through this section you raise awareness of what is involved in writing effective academic papers and developing effective coping strategies. Even though the approach introduced in this section was developed by L2 writing practitioners with L2 writers in mind, it could benefit anyone who wants to be a competent writer in academia.

One distinct feature of university writing identified by EAP scholars is that knowledge takes a central place in most types of writing. University instructors utilize writing as a tool for understanding, critiquing and creating knowledge. You will have a chance to practice one method of creating knowledge through free-writing. Often, in your classes, you will be asked to summarize, synthesize, and/or critique readings, and sometimes to conduct a research study and write what you have found. Therefore, reading and reflecting on texts, lectures, and other sources of content is often a prerequisite before you hit the key to begin writing. Because of this high level of involvement of readings, university writing tasks are called text-responsible writing, or writing that relies on reading

Rodriguez, Lesly. *Atlanta.*

(Leki & Carson, 1994). The dominance of text-responsible writing means that college writers need different conceptualizations of writing than those they formed based on the five paragraph essay or personal essays in their U.S. high schools. That is to say, academic writing is not an act of translating one's personal feelings and ideas into a pre-defined form, but a display of newly acquired knowledge, application of the knowledge and/or generation of new ideas. If a university student, regardless of language background, wants to be successfully socialized into academic discourse, she needs to have an adequate understanding of subject matter and learn ways of displaying and constructing knowledge in a written form. As a first-year student in college, you might wonder what types of text-responsible writing are common in courses across GSU, and what expectations the faculty have when they assign the writing tasks. A challenge is posed for many freshmen as new members of a discipline and university since each academic discipline or cluster of disciplines of similar nature has its own way of sharing, constructing, and critiquing knowledge, which is often implicitly shared among members of the community. Another challenge is that writing assignments come from varied disciplines because most students take many general education courses during their first and second years. In other words, you may be taking courses in History, Psychology, and Economics all in the same semester, and each of these disciplines has its own rules for written work.

So what are the types of text-responsible writing will you be required to produce? Scholars in L2 writing and writing-across-the curriculum have conducted extensive research through surveys, interviews and collection of writing assignments and student writing samples to identify and organize a range of writing tasks (Gardner & Nesi, 2013; Hyland, 2004). Among several frameworks offered by these scholars, a noteworthy one is Carter's (2007) four types of macro-genres. He analyzed major academic tasks, papers, and learning outcomes across the disciplines at a Southern U.S. university, and classified all the written tasks and paper types into four categories called **meta-genre**. In Table 6.1, you can see a close link between the nature of knowledge valued in an undergraduate program and writing tasks and papers assigned by the faculty. Throughout your college years, written tasks and papers you will work on will probably cover many of the genres in the table. Even though this framework, developed in a different university, might not exactly match GSU's genre scenes, the concept of meta-genres provides a useful tool to understand the overall scene of university writing.

Table 6.1 • Meta-Genre in Undergraduate Writing (Carter, 2007)

Meta-Genre	Specific genres	Disciplines
Responses to Academic Situations That Call for Problem Solving	business plans/ feasibility reports/ management plans/ marketing plans/ reports to management/ project reports/ project proposals/ technical memoranda/ technical reports	Most engineering disciplines, business, policy, nursing
Responses to Academic Situations that Call for Empirical Inquiry	laboratory report/ poster/ poster presentation/ research proposal/ research report/ scientific article/ scientific presentation	Natural sciences, social sciences
Responses to Academic Situations That Call for Research from Sources	historical narrative/ literary criticism/ 'quintessential' research paper and project	English literature, history, literatures of foreign languages, religion
Responses to Academic Situations That Call for Performance	editorials/ feature articles/ news stories/ proposals/ drawing/ sculpture/ painting/ multimedia/ websites	Fine arts, journalism, music, rhetoric and writing

Mitchell, Alexander Thomas. *Roundabout.*

To understand this meta-genre scheme better, let's take a look at the second meta-genre, *Responses to Academic Situations that Call for Empirical Inquiry.* Most social science and natural science disciplines value knowledge that is gained from empirical research. Therefore, for those of you who plan to major in one of these fields, it is expected that you participate in knowledge creation through empirical research. You will come up with an important question and hypothesis based on existing knowledge and theory, collect relevant data, interpret this data, and draw reasonable conclusions.

Despite similarities in the overarching purpose among empirical inquiry papers across the disciplines, this meta-genre is realized differently in different disciplines. For example, you can see that disciplines that are thought of as heterogeneous from each other share the same meta-genre, empirical inquiry, but each discipline has its own particular genre developed in its unique ways. Therefore, a lab report in biology will have different disciplinary specific purposes than a research paper in sociology, which leads to field-specific writing conventions including organization, language use, citation style, and others.

Understanding this variable and complex nature of academic writing—a disciplinary community, a type of knowledge valued in the community, and writing convention—is not easy for novice academic writers. These multi-dimensional expectations of writing are difficult to explain in concrete terms and they are often tacitly shared among expert members of the disciplinary community. EAP scholars argue that in order for L2 writers (and novice academic writers as well) to learn to respond to complex writing situations, they need to be investigators of writing contexts' (Johns, 2009).

Yang, Hae Sung. *Korean Nativity Scene.*

For Thought and Discussion

The Scenes of an Assignment

Choose one of the major writing assignments in your coursework that you find challenging. Be an investigator of the 'scenes' of the writing assignment. While investigating the scenes, read the course goals and learning outcomes sections in the course syllabus first and see a connection between these sections and the writing prompt. If you find some of the questions hard to answer, ask senior students in your major and/or interview the course instructor to gain the answers.

Table 6.2 • Investigation Chart—Adapted from Johns (2005, 2009)

	Stated in the syllabus and writing prompt	Not stated
Genre name in the prompt		
Meta-genre and specific genre names in Table 1		
Audience		
Purposes		

	Stated in the syllabus and writing prompt	Not stated
Nature of knowledge required (e.g., knowledge display, knowledge critique, knowledge construction or a combination)		
Key concepts and theories to include		
Length		
Sub-sections and organization		
Appropriate language (e.g., formal - informal, impersonal - emotional)		
Reference style (MLA, APA, Chicago, etc)		

Linguistic and Cultural Confluences

In teaching L2 writing, understanding the cultural and rhetorical background of L2 writers has been considered one of the most critical factors in providing effective writing instruction for them. Behind the research efforts to identify L2 rhetoric and culture lies an assumption that L2 students bring different and

Rodriguez, Lesly. *Mexico.*

heterogeneous culture and rhetoric into the classroom. For example, a generation 1.5 student from Hong Kong who speaks Cantonese as her first language and has gone through U.S schools for several years is presumed to come from a collectivist society in which harmony among the members of the society is highly valued. This contrasts sharply with an American culture in which individualistic thinking, freedom, and independence are considered core values. Because of these prevalent cultural perspectives that emphasize cultural differences, the Hong Kong student's L2 writing is often seen as a reflection of her native, in this case Chinese, cultural thought patterns. To illustrate, if there is no linear development of ideas, explicit statement of a thesis or topic sentence, or a critical edge in argument in her English essay, the L2 writer's native culture (often national or ethnic group) and language have often been suggested as an easy explanation for the writing issue. In these Anglo-centered cultural perspectives, idea development and textual patterns that do not match traditional norms of Anglo-American writing are not seen in a positive light.

Unfortunately, this static notion of culture and rhetoric has often been adopted to understand L2 writers and their written texts. In his famous article, "Inter-cultural thought patterns in inter-cultural education", often referred to as the "doodle" article, Kaplan (1966) identified different rhetorical patterns among different lingua-cultural groups through the investigation of English essays written by different cultural groups of L2 writers. He portrayed each of

Cordry, Jeffery. *Piedmont Park.*

the cultural thought patterns using a diagram: English as straight, Oriental as spiral, Semitic and Russian as zigzag. A correlation between a culture (in this case represented by a group of genetically related languages or an individual language) and a specific thought pattern was assumed in Kaplan's doodle model. This explicit graphic representation of different rhetorical patterns appealed to many L2 writing practitioners and researchers, and the model has become a classic reference point for understanding L2 writers' thought patterns. Ironically this simplistic discoursal construction of L2 writers has long been an impetus for pedagogical scholarship and classroom practice that has engendered numerous approaches to teaching L2 writing.

However, these normative approaches to culture and writing ignore the complex, variable and flexible aspects of culture and rhetoric many L2 writers bring to the FYC classroom. In fact, L2 writers who come from multicultural and multilingual backgrounds would be familiar with more than one rhetorical tradition. In addition, the spread of Anglo-American academic knowledge, pop culture, and media to many parts of the world, along with increasing migration, has made the distinction between Anglo rhetoric and rhetorical traditions in other cultures blurry (Canagarajah & Wurr 2011). What's more, some L2 writers who are from an orality-dominant culture and/or early-arriving immigrant students who are not literate in their L1 might not have a dominant L1 rhetoric.

Cordry, Jeffery. *Taipei, Taiwan.*

Cordry, Jeffery. *Halloween in Shanghai.*

This diversity and complexity in the rhetorical and cultural backgrounds of L2 writers makes it difficult to predict any consistent pattern of rhetoric falling into their national or linguistic background. More importantly, L2 writers strategically select, appropriate, and mix rhetorical techniques and patterns they are familiar with. They are not necessarily constrained or limited to one particular style assigned to their original culture and language by a static model of rhetoric (Kubota & Lehner 2004).

As applied linguists from a critical camp suggest, we need a different framework to understand L2 students' writing. First of all, we need to critically reflect on what culture means when we feel tempted to make a connection between L2 writing and culture. Binary understanding of culture such as "us" versus "others" could easily slip into a reductive and often deficit description of L2 texts. We should also be aware that there are a multiplicity of factors that influence L2 students' writing. Their L1 writing competence, L2 language proficiency, experience with diverse L2 genres, and other factors shape what they write and how they write (Kubota, 2010). L2 writers make the most of their linguistic, cultural, and rhetorical resources they have when they write. There should be a recognition of these resources before we attempt to help them become effective writers in American academia.

For Thought and Discussion

Have you ever experienced any mismatch between your written style or intention with the requirements given by your teacher or professor? Was there a gap between what you were doing and what they wanted you to do? Why do you think this gap existed? How did you deal with it?

This is a freewrite from a GSU student in the ESL program. How does it fit in with your experience? Can you relate to this? How?

I used to love to writing stories and tales as a kid, however as I got older everything became more complicated, and I started to despise writing. It seems like no matter how hard I try at writing I cannot seem to get it right. All of my essays last semester couldn't get higher than a B.

Questioning the Status Quo: Critical Approaches

In your previous writing classes, you may have gotten used to basically following your teachers' orders. If you are interested in reading about the basis for that kind of pedagogy, we suggest reading Paolo Freire's *The Pedagogy of the Oppressed*. Freire and other academic theorists such as Ira Shor and bell hooks work with the tenets of critical pedagogy. Critical pedagogy and its practitioners understand that the classroom has power dynamics that are difficult to deconstruct. But the aim of critical teaching practices is student empowerment. We return to the discussion of one current conversation in academia to illustrate critical standpoints.

We define **Englishes** as the concept that standard American English is not the only appropriate or legitimate dialect of the language creates controversy. Vernacular Englishes, dialects of English (some influenced by non-English languages and some influenced by cultures within and without the United States), and slang dialects of English all fit under the umbrella term of "Englishes." (all have scholars, scholarship, and language-users that seek to stake a claim in academic turf (Horner, Lu, and Matsuda; "Oakland"; Sailaja). One current debate centers around the concepts of **code-switching** and **code-meshing**.

African American English is one dialect that is often heard and spoken around Atlanta, including at Georgia State. Students who study **English for Academic Purposes** often **code-switch** between their home dialect and **EAP**. The term code-switching was used by academics to describe the process students engaged to utilize other dialects of English, depending on what the situation called for (Ghobadi and Ghasemi 248). Code-switching can take place among

GSU Digital Asset Library. *Sparks.*

dialects or among different languages and was, generally, thought to be an empowering practice for students who were trying to use EAP, while not totally assimilating into the dominant form of English. However, Vershawn Ashanti Young has challenged the concept of **code-switching** as a benevolent practice; Young's research finds that it has negative effects upon students who use it (55-65). Instead of code-switching, Young claims that students, particularly African American students, should instead **code-mesh.** Code-meshing involves blending dialects, world Englishes, and vernacular English; Young argues that this empowers students because they stay true to their own linguistic backgrounds, rather than assimilating into an English that is not native to their heritage.

Other critical pedagogical practices might center on open discussion throughout the semester and the creation of assignments alongside the students, rather than assignments dictated by the instructor. These discussions might be about controversial and complex topics, which can make some students uncomfortable. However, teachers who instruct from this perspective usually do so because we want students to find topics which matter to the students—not to the teacher. If we bring in current events or uncomfortable topics, we are trying to create a class which mirrors what the students would like to discuss and the material can be created collectively, after the first few examples being brought in by the instructor.

Smittick, Toniah. *Glance at GSU.*

The freedom of **FYC** classes is that there is usually not a set theme or topic that we must follow, other than some basics of genre; therefore, the material for the class can be created in a democratic process, rather than focusing solely on the instructor's desired topics and materials. These practices can sometimes be extra-challenging for students who come from backgrounds and cultures wherein dissent is punished. Be sure to speak with your instructor if you have any discomfort with this process and always be aware that you can enter the discussion while staying away from more controversial aspects of the topic at hand. For example, you can add a comment but refrain from giving your opinion on **who owns English** by saying, "In my parents' home country, people code-mesh all the time between Korean and English."

Primary research practices also empower students, because you, not the teacher, already are or will become the expert on your topic. Students from diverse backgrounds can tap into the richness of their cultural and linguistic heritages when working with primary research based projects. Archival research, discussed in detail in the final chapter, "Civic Engagement and Community-Based Writing," could mean delving into an archive of family photos, immigration documents, or correspondence in a language other than English. Ethnography could involve observation of your local temple, community gathering hall, or family reunion. You might also be called upon to do interviews with members of your or another community during primary research-based projects. Remember, always be respectful and professional during these interviews. You are not only representing yourself as a scholar, but you also represent the Georgia State community.

For Thought and Discussion

- Can you think of ways that you code-mesh and/or code-switch in your daily life? What do you think about the difference between the two options? Do your linguistic traditions feel enmeshed with your cultural traditions? How or how not?
- Have you ever had a teacher that you suspect teaches from a critical standpoint? What are your thoughts on student empowerment?
- How do you feel about controversial topics in the writing classroom— either for discussion or for writing prompts? Get in a group with a few of your peers and collaborate on a list of current controversies. Which, if any, would you like to see included in the course's content? Do the members of your group or the wider audience of the classroom agree on which topics are relevant?
- Consider your own position with English. Where do you stand when it comes to English? What English(es) do you own? Does this ownership blend mesh with your college goals? Why or why not?
- What are your suggestions for how to make a classroom a more democratic place? Do you believe the classroom should be democratic? Write a short letter to your instructor explaining your position.
- In small groups or in pairs, discuss how to behave as a responsible researcher and representative of Georgia State University during primary research. Share your results with the class and collectively craft a guide for the members of your class before you begin the research project. Your instructor can post the list online or make copies for you all.

Process Writing: From Freewriting to Revision and Back Again

Where do I start? When beginning any writing assignment, we are all asked to create a draft. What does a draft look like? How do I make one? What process should I use to write? Do I have a process?

As you read in Chapters 1 and 2, there are many ways to imagine the process and practice of writing, but the most important one is also the simplest: just write! Writing itself has the amazing quality of also *being* thinking. In other words, as we write, we see thoughts appear on the page. We think new

Mitchell, Alexander Thomas. *March On.*

thoughts. We have new ideas. We create.

Many times, students will sit in front of a blank page, and I'll ask them: "What are you doing?" They respond: "I'm thinking."

No. No thinking.....start writing!

One of the best ways to improve writing skill is to free-write on a consistent basis. (See pages 144-145 of this text for a more thorough explanation of what free-writing is, and for an essay, "Take a Leap into Writing," located on pages 147-150.) But, as a reminder, free-writing is writing that forsakes ("ignores") grammar, rules, punctuation, etc, and just allows you, the writer, to put thoughts on the page. It is a practice which most writers use in one way or another to get ideas going.

There is only one rule to free-writing: *keep writing for the allotted time.* Words can be misspelled, sentences can be awkward, verb tense can be unclear, and even the topic itself can change!

But how can I practice writing if my topic changes in 10 minutes?

You can practice writing because this is not your final draft of anything. This is you "thinking". Doesn't your mind wander from one idea to the next? Sometimes? Well, now let it wander on paper. This is normal! And it will increase your fluency in writing.

From a teacher:

In my classes, I have students begin each class period with a 10-minute free-writing. Often, I will put a quote or a topic on the board to give students a starting point. For example, here are some quotes we have used to begin a 10-minute free-write.

1. Tell us about your name. Who gave it to you? What does it mean? Are there any traditions (family and/or cultural) that it reflects?

2. The best thing about writing is.....

3. The worst thing about writing is....

4. Write a facebook post about your day yesterday. Write a twitter feed about today.

5. What is the most surprising thing about your first two weeks of school?

Sample Response to "What is the most surprising thing about your first two weeks of school?"

> » I been dropped, and that is really surprise to me because my status was good. I went to the student account and gave them my financial support, but why they dropped my class that something frustrate me. When I went to them, they told me that your status is good, but we don't know why your courses is dropped. Then, she notice wrong spelling of my name, and that was the problem. She apologized to me, and she told me that is a mistake of her staff. I walk out from student account office and I registered again for all courses, and that was a bad moment for me.

GSU Digital Asset Library. *Aerial View of Atlanta.*

GSU Digital Asset Library. *IEP Students.*

Sample response to "What do you like most about writing in English? What do you like least?"

> » Writing for me is important. For example, I use English writing to communicate with a new friend that we have common English writing. For example, online or social media like Facebook, I used to have new friends and chat with them in English. Second, English writing is important in my work because I work in hospital. For instance, I use English writing to write in patient file.

Other ideas we use to begin freewriting are:

- Listen to the Writer's Almanac, a daily announcement about writers which also includes a poem.
- Play a song lyric.
- Read a passage from an article or book we have been reading in class.
- Show a video
- Use one of the images in this textbook. The covers and images introducing each chapter have been chosen to facilitate freewriting.
- Write about the topic you have to research. What do you know about it already? Why do you want to research this topic?
- Use a student quote or a quote from your own writing. What did you say yesterday in your writing? Start with one of your own ideas or sentences.

Remember that the purpose of freewriting is two-fold:

1. to free whatever is in your mind and "let it out" so that you can focus your thoughts on an assignment or research.

2. to increase fluency in your writing. By fluency, we do not mean fluency in a language, as in "I speak Japanese fluently." Instead, we mean the ease and amount of writing that you produce.

For example, when we develop our fluency in writing, it means that we have developed a process that works for us for getting words onto the paper. At the beginning of the semester, student free-writing often takes up one quarter of the page. By the end of the semester, if the student has practiced every week at 10-minute writing, it usually takes up the entire page!

Here's what one student says about the free-writing process as a strategy for increasing writing fluency, releasing thoughts, and for developing ideas:

> » At first I hated free-writing. What do I say? Now, I even think it's fun. I look forward to it. I get my stress out; I get my mind clear. I talk about my past and my future, I talk about anything. I think it even helps my writing!
> » I don't care about grammar. That is my favorite.
> » I think about my topics. It's helps me to be focus and understand my topic clearly. Freewriting helps me in the research paper.

Now, you try. Go to writersalmanac.org and choose a quote about writing. Read it, then set a timer (use your phone!) for 10 minutes. Put your pen or pencil on the paper, and GO.

Resources for Writers

Your instructor is a valuable resource for you! Visit your instructor during office hours. The purpose of office hours is to meet with students one-on-one, so that you can get individualized help with your writing. Your peers are another fantastic resource. If your instructor does not hold peer-reviewing sessions in your classes (online or face-to-face), there's no reason why you cannot start your own peer review groups. Not only will you help each other write, but you may make some friends in the process. You can also visit one of the following tutoring locations:

Rodriguez, Lesly. *City Lights.*

The Writing Studio @ Georgia State University

The Writing Studio is located in the 25 Park Place building on the 24th floor, Suite 2420 in the Downtown Atlanta campus. You can meet with a tutor for a half-hour session, either in person or via video tutoring. You can receive help with assignments, college or scholarship application materials, job application materials, such as resumes, or help with citation and the research process. If it's about writing, the tutors at the Studio are there to help you. The Writing Studio stays very busy, so it is highly recommended that you make an appointment, rather than attempt a walk-in session. Visit http://writingstudio.gsu.edu/ to register and set up an appointment. You may also visit or call The Writing Studio (404-413-5840), if you need assistance in setting up your account and booking your appointment.

The Learning and Tutoring Center (LTC)

The LTC has locations in Alpharetta, Clarkston, Decatur, Dunwoody, and Newton. Visit http://depts.gpc.edu/gpcltc/locations.htm to check the hours for each location. The LTC is there to serve a variety of your needs. If you are having problems understanding class assignments, if you need to improve your skills, if you are preparing for the COMPASS exam, if you need access to handouts or computer-based resources to help improve your skills, if you are looking for a comfortable, supportive study environment that offers tutors, computers, and other instructional resources all in one location, then the LTC is for you.

IEP and ESL Tutoring Services

Although the Writing Studio and the LTC are for all Georgia State students, the Department of Applied Linguistics and ESL offers additional tutoring services for currently-enrolled IEP (Intensive English Program) and ESL students. You can visit http://iep.gsu.edu/current-students/iep-esl-tutoring-services/ to learn more about the services offered or you can book your appointment through http://gsu.mywconline.com/. The tutors can help you with a variety of skills and test preparation.

Projects and Student Examples

In this section, we offer example assignment prompts and papers written by other Georgia State students. Ethnography projects invite you to interact with the community and spaces around you—primary research projects like ethnography allows you to become the expert, even if it is a small area, such as the Bubble Tea shops that Monjima Kabir writes about. Tammy Huynh explores her own development of a new cultural literacy as a staff member of our student newspaper, *The Signal*.

Micro-Ethnography/Spatial Analysis and Methods/ Methodology Annotated Bibliography

This project asks you to look more deeply into the everyday spaces we generally inhabit without seeing critically.

To facilitate your introduction into the methods of ethnography, I am asking you to gather three sources from the library's selection of scholarly resources, ebooks, print books, or peer-reviewed journal articles, and write an Annotated Bibliography about those three sources. If you are taking an anthropology or sociology course, you may also have scholarly sources available about ethnography in them. We will discuss MLA format for Annotated Bibliographies in class; I expect your annotations for each of the sources to be 150-250 words to meet the minimum length standard. You may not copy the abstract of the article for your annotation; you will receive no credit for any annotation that plagiarizes the abstract.

You will undertake your ethnographic observation in a quotidian space. Maybe you will visit your favorite coffee shop. Perhaps you will observe the train on your ride home or a common area in your dormitory or Classroom South or the Plaza. You pick the space. For this project, you will be an observer, not a participant observer, so you do not need to interact with anyone, unless it is a necessary aspect of being in that space (for example, if you observe a coffee shop, it would be poor manners to sit for an hour without purchasing something). Be sure to have a field notes sheet prepared in your research journal and take detailed notes as you observe. I think an hour's observation will be ample for a project of this scope. Please take into account the ways in which the space itself affects the dynamic of the micro-community of the time and place you choose to observe. Be detailed in your field observations, but resist the urge to come to conclusions during your observation.

For this project, I have asked for 4-5 pages, including Works Cited/Field Notes. For this project, you may elect to use your primary research, in the form of your field notes, as the entire basis for the paper. That is fine. If you choose to use your primary research, you will attach a copy of your field notes in lieu of a Works Cited page. If you do use secondary sources, you will need to cite them using MLA and craft a Works Cited page, as well as attaching a copy of your field notes. Please note: Field notes, Works Cited, and other bibliographic information are assumed to take up only one page. If you have more than one page of bibliographic information, that does not take the place of the minimum of three pages of essay.

Learning Outcomes for 1101 and 1102: All

Field Notes Sheet/Template

(An example of a completed field notes sheet is available on the companion website: guidetowriting.gsu.edu under the "Community" tab).

Time	Observation	Comments

Monjima Kabir

Instructor Ruccio

ENGL 1102.100

3 February 2015

A Little Taiwan on Buford Highway

Bubble tea, also known as boba tea, originated in Taiwan and has become popular in the U.S. over the recent years. Being a huge fan of this beverage and living only a mile away from Buford Highway – home to many bubble tea shops – I decided to observe Sweet Hut and Quickly, two of the shops closest to where I live. Although both places serve mostly the same drinks and are only a block apart, I found Sweet Hut to be loud, crowded and unwelcoming, while the atmosphere at Quickly was very relaxing and intimate.

My methods were not complex at all. After ordering and receiving my drink, I took notes of my observations on my laptop through Microsoft Word so that I would blend in with my surroundings – other customers using laptops – and not seem creepy to the people around me. During my observations, I tried to be as consistent as possible, making sure that I observed both spaces at the same time frame – from 7 p.m. to 8 p.m. – and on a weekday, so that the chances of any sort of bias being present was minimal.

As I walked to the doors of Sweet Hut, a café located at 5150 Buford Highway in Doraville, Georgia, I couldn't help but notice the tables and chairs set on their porch which, of course, were empty due to the weather. It was Thursday evening, 29 January, and it was extremely cold that day, so there is no surprise that I found the seats to be vacant outside. Above the seating arrangement is a big, bright sign that reads "Sweet Hut Bakery & Café" and can be spotted from far away, especially since the café is on the outside of its plaza, being closer to the main road.

The vibrant sign outside definitely reflects the vibrant atmosphere inside. Right when I walked in through the doors, I quickly noticed the loud party music that was playing. Listening to it gave me an energetic feeling. The lights were a bit dim, but bright enough to still give off a sense of liveliness. There were barely any customers at the time. Only two groups of friends were occupying the big booths closest to the counter, and about 7 or 8 people were seated at the tables farthest from the counter, either in pairs or just by themselves. What I found to be odd was the lack of interaction between the people. Each and every one of them was using some some kind of electronic device – be it a phone, tablet, or laptop – except for a few couples that I assumed were on dates.

I approached the server, since there was no line, with a friend of mine who had come with me in hopes of getting some studying done. When ordering our drinks, I couldn't help but feel rushed as we looked at the menu. The server had a look on her face that screamed, "Any day now!" as we tried to decide what to get. When we finally asked for an order of a strawberry smoothie and a hazelnut milk tea, she handed us our receipt with a short and abrupt "Thank you," and went on to assist two new customers.

After receiving our drinks, we decided to sit in a corner of the café where I could get a clear view of the back seating area and where Gais could get some work done. The table was small and square, perfect for two but if one more person were to join, there would be a problem. As big as the space of the entire café is, most of it is occupied by the center area where all the fancy pastries are located and the excessive amount of tables and chairs, making the place very crowded. To make things worse, more and more customers began to come inside after we took a seat, forming a line that had reached the entrance. This not only increased the crowdedness, but it caused the café to get really loud, making it really hard to hear the music I heard playing when I first came in. As more people were coming in and filling up the seats, I was only feeling more and more uncomfortable, so I was glad when the hour was over, and it was time for me to leave.

My trip to Quickly, located at 5090 Buford Highway and also in the city of Doraville, on the other hand, was a completely different experience. This bubble tea shop is located in a different plaza right next to the one Sweet Hut is in. As big and open-spaced is the close-by plaza, this one is just as small and hidden in a secluded area. I observed Quickly the day after I did Sweet Hut – Friday evening, 30 January. The sign outside reads "Quickly," along with a few foreign letters, presumed to be Taiwanese, just beneath it. There are a few other signs that read "Smoothies", "Slushies", and "Boba Tea," advertising items on their menu and attracting customers.

As bland as the outside appearance of this lounge is, the inside is the complete opposite. The space is very narrow and elongated for a lounge, but that is why there are not many couches taking up the small space. The seating is arranged in a way that at least 4 to 5 groups of people can come in and sit. The music is not loud at all; rather it's very soft, slow, and soothing to the ears. The dim lighting and Traditional Taiwanese setting added on to the relaxed feeling I got when I first walked in. There was already a group of girls sitting in one of the circle of couches, sipping on their drinks, socializing, and having, what seemed to be, a really good time.

I went up to the server and ordered the usual – a tapioca milk tea with a side of spicy chicken nuggets. She took her time in making my drink in front of me, making sure everything was perfect, and had the order of nuggets being made in the kitchen. As she handed my receipt, she smiled at me and said, "Thank you," sincerely, making me feel welcome.

Once my spicy chicken nuggets were ready, I took them, along with my milk tea, and sat in the seating area nearest to the entrance and facing the back of the lounge. This gave me a clear and full view of the space. Throughout the hour, more customers came in, either to get their food and leave or stay for a while if they came with a group of friends. It never felt crowded though, and it rarely got loud.

Quickly is the perfect place to study, in my opinion. With its soothing and intimate atmosphere, anyone can open up their mind and get their work done. On top of everything else, it's a quiet place to relax and reflect after a long day. Yet it surprises me how most people go to Sweet Hut. It's very crowded, too loud, and, of course, very unwelcoming. I would never feel comfortable at a place like that, but I guess it's a matter of getting used to the place – which I don't intend to do. .

Multi-Cultural Literacy Narrative Project

For this project, you will consider yourself as a point of intersection between or among multiple cultures and communities. Refer to the PowerPoint posted on BrightSpace, if you need help working with the concepts of culture, subculture, microculture, etc. Remember, a culture can be as broad as Catholicism in America or it can be as narrow as the group who rides the same bus at 9 a.m. on Mondays.

Steps in this project:

1. Definitions. We've already had the initial introduction to the concepts of culture and community in our class discussions of the PowerPoint. We've also discussed the literacy narrative as a specific genre—it is a kind of memoir—and the multicultural literacy narrative also shares characteristics and uses the methodology of autoethnography.

2. Group work day. This is a very important day, so please be here. We will break into groups and discuss our positionality and possible culture groups we have in our lives.

3. Methods day. We will discuss responsible primary and ethnographic research practices.

4. In-Class conferences with drafts (drafts can be partial at this point).

5. Peer Review Day

6. Final Drafts Due

7. Reflections Due

The bottom line: For this project, you will need to consider multiple cultures/communities and then analyze how your positionality in these groups has affected your literacy practices. Some questions to consider: Do you code-switch or code-mesh in these communities? Is reading/writing/speaking more important to one of these communities than another? Why, if so? Are sacred texts or media important to one or more of these communities? Is there ever a clash among the texts important to these communities?(Although you do not have to bare your innermost feelings for this project, sites of disconnection among these communities can provide rich ethnographic observations.) How did you become a member of these communities? Did literacy or communication play a role in your becoming a member? Do you wish your communities had different literacy practices? How so, if yes? What is your favorite literacy-based connection among these cultures and communities? What is your least favorite? Is there an intergenerational aspect to any of your community positions? How do the communication practices function among the generations?

For 1101: Learning Outcomes 1-9

For 1102: Learning Outcomes 1-8

Tammy Huynh

Instructor Kristen Ruccio

English 1101

18 April 2016

Finding the Right Field to Play On

Being a student at Georgia State University (GSU) requires skill. All day we attempt to dodge cars, survive these classes, and also do what every college student is attempting - finding yourself. As an upcoming junior, I have countless times reconsidered my major although I have never officially changed it. I ask myself all the time, what job field do I want to specialize in? For the past three years, I have been classified as a psychology major. I love the major but my adventurous side wants more. I want to get creative, I want to go out and explore. I want to see what other field I could also play on. I found that answer at *The Signal,* the official student newspaper of GSU.

As the lead designer of the newspaper for the year of 2015-2016, I do have close relations to the paper in a sense the office is nearly my second home. I admit that I am biased and very protective over *The Signal,* because it is close to my heart, just like a child. Nearly every member of the student media community can agree that working on the newspaper and other student media is exciting and it is empowering. Because *The Signal* is one of the most high-quality student media in the Georgia School Systems, the paper takes on many roles, such as providing a space for student voice, a professional work setting, and a training ground for the future.

Everyone's reaction is the same when I first introduce and associate myself with the paper. It is very unappealing and not very appreciative, because "No one reads the newspaper". My thoughts tend to differ. I agree that media has been ever changing and for sure there are many outlets now that could get you news and entertainment, but the student newspaper is tangible and it is accessible all over campus. *The Signal's* goal is to be the voice of the student body and reach out to deliver news. Written by students for students. Honestly, I can testify my first year here at Georgia State, I did not care about anything on campus. However, now I think of it as, "Why not care?". I have adapted to the fact that Georgia State sits in the heart of Atlanta, which means something is always happening to accompany the diverse tastes and unique personalities of the people here. GSU's diversity plays a huge part in *The Signal* because the diversity creates the different voices inside the paper. *The Signal* tries to incorporate fun into their papers by letting columnists range from fashionistas' opinions to money-saving tips! The Culture Division maps out all the greatest events inside Atlanta. The news team is always on the case of breaking news and campus news. The sports reporters have the best critiques on GSU versus other schools. Even though *The Signal* truly connects all the busy life of a campus all into compressed ink pages, it all starts off with a professional team.

I like to think that the process of beginning my work for *The Signal* as a designer and then being promoted to a student leader changed my personality. I work a lot harder knowing that if I mess up, the entire editorial board will sink along with me, as well as vice versa. I have learned the meaning of professional teamwork because as a part of a newspaper in general, it is not easy work. The process is incredibly tedious and requires effort and patience.

Just as we have to use the best ingredients to make a tasty recipe, we must first find a passionate writer to create a great story. As a writer of the team, one can only get better at writing because many peers are always available to look over the work. After a story has been approved through editor in chief, all the edits and life of a story needs to be appealing to the visual learners so it is sent to the Production Department. Photos are always an unknown trouble inside the journalism battle grounds, due to the fights among reporters, the different arising opinions, and the never-ending contradictions with stories. Photos not only have to be relevant, they must be high-quality pixel by pixel and there should be at least twenty for each story, so there will be room for movement for the designers. Finally, our designers, whom which I refer to as the final touch or the glue of a story. Designing is energy- draining, not only do designers have to think of refreshing designs, but once they think of it, they are pretty much tied to their computer and chair for the next six hours.

Although we are students with everyday classes and midnight assignments to do, we are viewed as professional on the clock in and out of the office. We watch what we post and say on our own personal social medias as we are public figures for *The Signal* and we must give our best editorial judgement on things that happen in the world. I have grown to not necessarily condemn and restrict my thoughts but I am a lot more careful in my choice of words and observation skills. As a part of media, many things that I say could be turned controversial which could affect *The Signal* later on down the road. It may seem a bit intimidating, but that is the real world and I have learned that through *The Signal*.

Aside from the tedious aspects of the job, the teamwork, and skill it takes to complete at least one issue of *The Signal,* it takes an entire team in order for a series of issues to advance and look better than before. The work that goes into each issue prepares each staff member individually with experiences for the future workforce. My own experiences involve great teamwork, meeting deadlines, attending meetings with a fresh editorial judgement, being a leader, providing my commitment, and even as simple as being there for staff members for work and personal problems. Although that is not something the public eye recognizes, working at *The Signal* has helped me understand the value of each paper that prints.

The Signal is most definitely high quality because of its staff members but it continues to serve as more than just a newspaper. It connects a busy campus like Georgia State and its students, to form a community. Overall, joining any organization should be eye opening and push one to do better, but *The Signal* is so overly involved with the campus, it is a great experience for anyone that joins and it has definitely helped me find a field I want to pursue in the future.

Works Cited

Barton, David. *Literacy: An Introduction to the Ecology of Written Language.* 2nd ed. Malden: Blackwell, 2007. Print.

Canagarajah, A. Suresh & Adrian J. Wurr. "Multilingual Communication and Language Acquisition: New Research Directions." *The Reading Matrix* 11(1):1-15. Print.

Carter, Michael. "Ways of Knowing, Doing, and Writing in the Disciplines." *College Composition and Communication* (2007): 385-418. Print.

Castro, Antonio J. "What Makes A Citizen? Critical and Multicultural Citizenship and Preservice Teachers' Understanding of Citizenship Skills." *Theory And Research In Social Education* 41.2 (2013): 219-246. Print.

Chand, Masud, and Rosalie Tung. "Bicultural Identity and Economic Engagement: An Exploratory Study Of The Indian Diaspora In North America." *Asia Pacific Journal Of Management* 31.3 (2014): 763-788.Print.

Cho, Grace. "Perspectives vs. Reality of Heritage Language Development." *Multicultural Education* 22.2 (2015): 30-38. Print.

Collier, Virginia P. "Age and Rate of Acquisition of Second Language for Academic Purposes." *TESOL Quarterly* 21.4 (1987): 617-641. Print.

Ferris, Dana. *Teaching College Writing to Diverse Student Populations.* Ann Arbor: U of Michigan P, 2009. Print.

Freire, Paulo. *The Pedagogy of the Oppressed.* Trans. Myra Bergman Ramos. London: Penguin, 1996. Print.

Gardner, Sheena and Hilary Nesi. "A Classification of Genre Families in University Student Writing." *Applied Linguistics* (2013): 25-32. Print.

Ghobadi, Mehdi, and Hadi Ghasemi. "Promises And Obstacles Of L1 Use In Language Classrooms: A State-Of-The-Art Review." *English Language Teaching* 8.11 (2015): 245-254. Print.

Grosjean, François. "Bicultural Bilinguals." *International Journal of Bilingualism* 19.5 (2015): 572-586. Print.

hooks, bell. *Teaching to Transgress: Education as the Practice of Freedom*. New York: Routledge, 1994. Print.

Horner, Bruce, Min-Zhan Lu, and Paul Kei Matsuda, eds. *Cross-Language Relations in Composition*. Carbondale: SIU P, 2010. Print.

Hsu, Ling-Hui. "Linguistic Intergroup Bias Tells Ingroup/Outgroup Orientation Of Bicultural Asian Americans." *International Journal of Intercultural Relations* 35 (2011): 853-866. Print.

Hyland, Ken. *Disciplinary Discourses: Social Interactions in Academic Writing*.Ann Arbor: U of Michigan P, 2004. Print.

Johns, A. M.. "English for Academic Purposes: Issues in Undergraduate Writing and Reading." *Directions in Applied Linguistics*. Ed. Paul Bruthiaux. Clevedon, UK: Mutilingual Matters. 101-116. Print.

—-. "Situated Invention and Genres: Assisting Generation 1.5 Students in Developing Rhetorical Flexibility". *Generation 1.5 in College Composition: Teaching Academic Writing to U.S.- Educated Learners of ESL*. Eds. Mark Roberge, Meryl Siegal, and Linda Harklau. Nueva York: Routledge. 203- 220. Print.

Juan-Garau, Maria. "Heritage Language Use And Maintenance In Multilingual Communities." *Applied Linguistics Review* 5.2 (2014): 425-440. Print.

Kaplan, Robert B. "Cultural Thought Patterns in Inter-Cultural Education." *Language Learning* 16.1-2 (1966): 1-20. Print.

Keller, Daniel. *Chasing Literacy: Reading and Writing in an Age of Acceleration*. Logan: Utah State UP, 2014. Print.

Kubota, Ryuko. (2010). "Cross-Cultural Perspectives on Writing: Contrastive Rhetoric." *Sociolinguistics and Language Education.* Eds. Nancy H. Hornberger and Sandra Lee McKay. Bristol, UK: Multilingual Matters. 265-289. Print.

Kubota, Ryuko and Al Lehner. "Toward Critical Contrastive Rhetoric." *Journal of Second Language Writing* 13.1 (2004): 7-27. Print.

Laughter, Judson. "Toward a Theory of Micro-Kindness: Developing Positive Actions in Multicultural Education." *International Journal Of Multicultural Education* 16.2 (2014): 2-14. Print.

"License FAQ." Georgia Department of Driver Services. dds.ga.gov. 6 March 2016 Web.

"Original Oakland Resolution on Ebonics." *Linguist.org.* https://www.linguistlist.org/topics/ebonics/ebonics-res1.html. Web. 10 December 2015.

Roberge, Mark, Meryl Siegal, and Linda Harklau, eds. *Generation 1.5 in College Composition: Teaching Academic Writing to US-Educated Learners of ESL.* Nueva York: Routgledge, 2009. Print.

Roberge, Mark, Kay M. Losey, and Margi Wald, Eds. *Teaching U.S.-Educated Multilingual Writers: Pedagogical Practices from and for the Classroom.* Ann Arbor: U of Michigan P, 2015. Print.

Sailaja, Pingali. "Hinglish: Code-Switching In Indian English." *ELT Journal: English Language Teachers Journal* 65.4 (2011): 473-480. Print.

Sarmento, Clara. "Interculturalism, Multiculturalism, And Intercultural Studies: Questioning Definitions And Repositioning Strategies." *Intercultural Pragmatics* 11.4 (2014): 603-618. Print.

Scontras, Gregory, Zuzanna Fuchs, and Maria Polinsky. "Heritage Language And Linguistic Theory." *Frontiers In Psychology* 6.(2015): 1-20. Print.

Shor, Ira. *Empowering Education: Critical Teaching for Social Change.* Chicago: U of Chicago P, 1992. Print.

"Global Issues at the United Nations." *UN News Center.* UN, n.d. Web. 23 Jan. 2016.

Yer J., Thao. "Bicultural Literacy Curriculum." *Creative Education* 02 (2012): 251. *Directory of Open Access Journals.* Web. 5 Dec. 2015.

Young, Vershawn Ashanti, et al. *Other People's English: Code-Meshing, Code-Switching, and African American Literacy.* New York: Teachers College P, 2014. Print.

Martinez, Noe. *Satellite Campus.*

Chapter 7

Writing about Visual Images

"There can be no words without images." ~ Aristotle

Images in Everyday Life

We are immersed in a visual culture. In our digital age, we continually process the multitude of images meeting our eyes—photographs, illustrations, videos, and other graphic elements. In order to be effective critical thinkers, we must learn not only how to read alphabetic texts, but also visual ones, as well as texts that combine images and words. We think about, discuss, and describe images with language. Even though we can never completely replicate the meaning of an image in words, it is important to develop a vocabulary so that we can understand and evaluate visuals more skillfully. Because we use language to understand sensory information, in this chapter we will use words like "read" and "text" that are typically applied to written texts. Seeing images and other forms of our lived experience (such as fashions, buildings, and spaces) as "texts" helps us to understand how *rhetoric* pervades our lives. This chapter offers ways to look at images *rhetorically*—in other words, to perceive what messages visual "texts" get across and how (and how effectively) these messages are delivered. We will look at some familiar terms like *ethos, logos,* and *pathos,* but in new ways, as they are applied to the study and creation of visual images.

As just one example of the pervasiveness of visual images, think for a moment about how many advertising images you see in a given day. They could be posters, murals, signs, package labels, billboards, print ads in magazines, commercials on TV or the Internet, or vehicle wraps. Because to some degree we can now control the commercials we watch on TV or the Internet (by watching them on ad-free venues or by skipping the ads), the ad agencies on Madison Avenue have devised more creative ways to get visual and alphabetic texts in front of our eyes, a phenomenon known

Osborne, Steve. *Have a Coke and a Smile.*

as "ad clutter." Now, ads appear on every available surface, including spaces such as vehicles, mobile billboards, physicians' examination tables, restroom stalls, dining trays on airlines, turnstiles in public transit stations, video screens in taxis, blimps and planes over stadiums, eggs in cartons, floors, parking stripes, and postage stamps (Johnson; Story). Researchers estimate that most people in the industrialized world are exposed to over 5,000 advertisements per day (Johnson). Though some ads consist of written texts or audio, most of these advertisements have some visual components, and some of them are entirely visual in nature. In this ad-saturated environment, we experience a kind of sensory overload.

The only way for us to cope effectively with this reality is to know how to process and evaluate the images we see. Because of the emergence of Web 2.0, we not only consume images, but we also now produce them on social media, blogs, and other forms of web presence. By studying ways to analyze and evaluate images, we are able not only to think critically about the visual data coming into our consciousness, but we can also learn ways to create our own visual arguments. This chapter provides a rationale for studying visual rhetoric, a *lexicon*[1] of relevant terms, connections to concepts from the analysis and argument chapters, activities that will help you try out the strategies of analysis you will learn in the chapter, and an example of rhetorical analysis. Whether visual texts work on their own or in conjunction with written/alphabetic texts, they work to move specific audiences to think or act differently. This effort is called *visual rhetoric,* and a number of scholars study and practice this form of rhetoric.

Coca-Cola's neon sign has long served as a landmark at Atlanta's Five Points intersection. In what ways does the sign symbolize both the city and the company?

---

1 A lexicon is a collection of words and their definitions or the vocabulary of a particular field.

Images in Context

People construct visual arguments in particular historical moments. This context of place and time is influenced by and in turn influences the nature and reception of visual texts. In other words, the time and place in which an image is created has an impact on what kind of an image it is, the way that it is produced, who sees it, and what they think of it. Sometimes, the image is ahead of its time, and it teaches the audience a new way to see images and to create their own images. Thus, if enough people see an image and it changes the way that they think, it can change what they do, leading to a new cultural environment with new practices. In this process, an image becomes *iconic*[2]— that is, it takes on a range of meanings and it influences work produced in later historical periods.

For Thought and Discussion

The masterpiece *Girl with a Pearl Earring* (1665) by Dutch painter Johannes Vermeer has remained iconic for centuries, inspiring not only countless imitations and tributes, but also a novel and a movie imagining the story behind the painting. Depicted below are the original painting and four appropriations of it. *Appropriations* recreate the image but change certain aspects of it. Study each re-imagining and jot down ideas about how each one changes the original image. What effect does each one have on you? What thoughts or emotions does each painting evoke? What messages does each convey about Vermeer's historical context and our current historical moment?

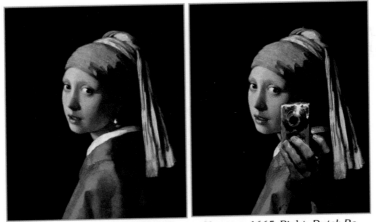

Girl with a Pearl Earring. Left: Johannes Vermeer, 1665. Right: *Dutch Renaissance Self-Shot.* Anonymous.

---

2 An icon is a person or thing (usually an image) that is used to represent something else.

Girl with a Pearl Earring. Dorothee Golz.

Top: *Girl with a Pearl Earring.* David Barton. Bottom: *Girl with a Pearl Earring.* Jetoy Choo-Choo.

Three historical realities play into the visual rhetoric made in an historical moment: technology, literacy, and values. These three elements influence the production, distribution, consumption, and reception of visual texts. Technological innovations influence the options available for creators of texts. *Medium* refers to the material or the technical means through which something is made.[3] The particular technology used to produce an image is called *media specificity*. These media arise from the technology that makes them possible. For example, before the advent of the printing press, books had to copied out by hand; in the decades before the invention of the motion picture camera, people took photographs. Now, people can choose to make books by hand or reproduce them mechanically on presses; they can make videos or take photographs with the film or digital camera of their choice. Technology has expanded to make more media possible.

To some degree, the kinds of literacies that people achieve and practice connect to the kinds of technologies available in societies. In the Middle Ages, only highly educated people could read and write. After Johannes Gutenberg

---

3 Media is the plural of medium.

invented the printing press in 1451, books gradually became more widely available, but it was not until the invention of steam presses and the discovery of cheaper materials for paper in the 1800s that books became affordable enough to be available to common people (Faigley et al. 4). The combination of these developments and the social reform of compulsory primary school education led to an expansion of *alphabetic literacy,* or the ability to read and write texts needed in personal and professional life. Similarly, the development of the personal computer[4] made it necessary for the general population to become proficient in *digital literacy,* which involves not only ways to navigate digital spaces, but also codes and commands for receiving and producing messages by using digital technology. These highly refined skills have become not only possible but obligatory in our current historical moment.

Thus, literacies arise from the economies and technologies of the societies in which people live. In a *pre-literate* or oral culture, images and symbols provide ways to convey information. Today, in our *hyperliterate* culture, images act as a kind of shorthand—conveying a great deal of information in a flash for an information-saturated populace. Hyperliterate people are exceptionally literate in a variety of environments such as written texts, symbolic languages, and digital spaces. However, remember that digital literacy does not replace alphabetic literacy; one builds upon the other. So, reading and writing avidly and actively remain as important as always in terms of building proficiencies in other areas such as digital technologies.

Which literacies are taught and practiced in a society has to do with what that society *values.* Cultural values, also known as mores or conventions, determine the nature of visual images produced within that culture. United States society values individual freedom, competition, and private property, so these notions are at work in the media used, in the subject matter of visual images, and in the ways that images are perceived by audiences. Photographs, for instance, are often copy-protected on websites such as *Flickr* to prevent unauthorized use. And while the freedom to take photographs is valued, so also is the privacy that enables someone to refuse to have their photograph made, or, if it is made, restricts it from being distributed online. Of course, these rules of copyright and privacy are broken often, but practices related to the production, distribution, and consumption of photographic images certainly indicate the values important in a society. This inherent cultural bias in the creating and reading of texts is known as *cultural specificity.*

---

4 IBM put the first personal computer, or PC, on the market in 1981. This machine, the 5150 or IBM-PC, was the first computer intended for individual home use.

Form Follows Function: The Architecture of Images

In the early Roman Empire, most people could not read and write the Roman alphabet, but they understood symbolic inscriptions. These inscriptions on the Marble Road in the Roman Imperial city of Ephesus (in modern-day Turkey) give travelers directions to the local brothel. Notice the broken heart (indicating loneliness), cross (indicating a crossroad), left foot (indicating the left side of road), and female form (indicating who awaited the weary traveler) (Lewandowski).

How exactly does cultural specificity work in visual images? Both the form and content of an image can be influenced by the culture in which it is produced. Painters, to use just one example, use the materials available to them. They may use oil paint on canvas, or they may use acrylic on wood, depending on what they can procure, who taught them to paint, and the final form the painting might take. It might be a painting to hang on a wall in a gallery, or it might be a painted functional object that a family could use or display in their home. These structures of the painting constitute the *form* that it takes. In the production of visual images, form has to do with how the image is produced. Its mode of production influences what it can do, and that mode is also part of the culture in which it was created.

Content refers to the narrative or the subject matter portrayed in images. Every culture has its own store of folklore, stories, legends, and icons that provide much of the material seen in images produced in that culture. Each culture's buildings, statuary, clothing, decorative objects, and other forms of art depict the people, places, and events important in that culture. The Hagia Sophia (Ayasofya or "Divine Wisdom") in Istanbul, Turkey provides a glimpse into two very different cultures. Initially, this building was a Byzantine basilica, a place of Christian worship. When the Ottoman Turks took over the Christian city of Constantinople and transformed it into Istanbul, they also transformed the basilica into a Muslim mosque, plastering over the Byzantine art. In the twentieth century, the Turkish government restored much of the Byzantine splendor and turned the Hagia Sophia into a national museum. To this day, the beautiful structure is adorned with the artwork of two magnificent cultures. The Christians depicted Jesus, Mary, saints, and other human figures, but the Muslims do not depict human or animal images in their mosques, so they used plants, inscriptions in Arabic, and other decorative designs. The Byzantine Empire and the Ottoman Empire used different forms (basilica, mosque) and different content (people, plants) that reflected their beliefs and values.

Two major factors that have transformed the form and content of the visual images we produce today are *reproducibility* and *malleability*. *Reproducibility* refers to the capability of reproducing a work of art. Lithographs, photographs, posters, magazines, and digital downloads are all examples of ways in which artists can replicate works for mass distribution. The reproducibility of much of the visual work created today expands tremendously the reach and accessibility of the image, but it also increases the *ubiquity* of images, contributing to sensory overload.[5] Seeing so many images in so many places means that we pay less and less attention to any one image. They all vie for the limited amount of attention we can give.

Many images produced today also possess *malleability,* which means that they can be manipulated or altered. When you use Instagram to post photos, you might alter the color, lighting effects, of other aspects of the image. The fact that an image can be changed means not only that is malleable, but that its objectivity could be challenged. Photos are often used as evidence in court hearings and in reports of research studies, but if these images are manipulated, the soundness of the verdict may be compromised. Sometimes we see a photograph and wonder whether the phenomenon or event really

The Hagia Sophia in Istanbul, Turkey. Notice the Arabic inscription on the circular surface to the left and a depiction of Mary and Jesus in the center of the photo.

---

5 Ubiquity means presence everywhere or in many places at the same time.

The Hagia Sophia in Istanbul, Turkey. The man seated on the throne is the Holy Emperor Leo. The silver decorations along the bottom of the frame are Ottoman designs added when the Turks overtook the Byzantine city of Constantinople.

happened or whether the person or animal really has that appearance. The reality of the reproducibility and malleability of images opens up limitless possibilities for broadening audiences, but it also means that we have to remain especially alert and thoughtful about what we see.

Osborne, Steve. *Reproducibility: fliers wheat pasted onto a particle board wall* (Decatur, Georgia).

Osborne, Steve. *"Malleability:* Corey smokestack, downtown Atlanta" Pre-Photo Shop Photo.

Osborne, Steve. *"Malleability:* Corey smokestack in downtown Atlanta" Post-Photo Shop Photo.

Images Are Appealing

Earlier in this book, you read about three rhetorical appeals—*ethos, logos,* and *pathos*—and you learned how these appeals work in written texts. In this section of the visual chapter, we will apply each of those terms to visual rhetoric.

From previous study, you may know that an author establishes *ethos* or credibility with an audience by gaining their respect and good will through covert and overt methods. Demonstrating common sense and decorum, for instance, instills confidence in the author's rational mind and the author's identification with the audience's needs and desires. In visual texts, authors can establish *ethos* in a number of ways, including proximity, objectivity, and research. Proximity refers to how close the author is positioned to the story. First-hand eyewitness accounts with valid evidence count for more that second-hand hearsay. We tend to believe news photography, but we do not always account for its limitations such as malleability (digitally altering the image) or composition (which might leave key information outside the frame of the image). Editing the image in one or both of these ways will shape our interpretation of it. Thus, we give more *ethos* to the author who seems objective, using facts and other forms of quantitative, verifiable evidence. For this reason, we value someone who does a great deal of research. Understanding the issue, getting the details right, and fact-checking all build more confidence in the author.

The results of first-hand experience, research, and fact-checking can enable the artist to offer *logos*-based appeals in a visual argument. Visual texts provide data and organized arguments just as written texts do, but they do so in different ways. A documentary film might offer statistics, expert opinions, charts, and text flashing on the screen with facts related to the issue it explores. A painter might do historical research to get the details just right for a period piece. A sculptor uses a model to make sure that the contours of the sculpture are lifelike. Design elements like line, balance, shading, and perspective lend the "logic" of reality to the artist's representation of it. Most of us are visual learners, and images offer an educational shorthand in which substantive information is condensed into one graphic. Therefore, visual texts have the potential of delivering powerful *logos* appeals, either standing alone or in tandem with written text.

Using *pathos* directs the appeal to the audience's emotion or imaginations. Because visual images activate a part of the brain that handles emotional responses, and because people act on their emotions (rather than their reason), visual texts offer some of the most effective *pathos* appeals. For this reason, advertisers incorporate images in ads, and you will likely recall many movies that remain vivid in your memory and that even changed your thinking. Dreams and memories play in our minds primarily as visuals, so authors find innovative ways of appealing to our imagination and helping us to envision an alternate reality. When you look at apartments, you probably imagine your belongings in the space in order to see if the apartment is feasible and desirable. A photograph of a needy child causes us to want to help more than a written message about the child's plight. Arguably, *pathos* is the dominant appeal in visual texts.

When your professor assigns you a rhetorical analysis or another assignment in which you examine a visual text and write about it, consider using the three appeals as criteria for your analysis. Additional criteria follow, including ways in which texts are reimagined and recreated, as well as how images address rhetorical situations.

For Thought and Discussion

One of these images is an iconic photograph taken by Alfred Eisenstaedt on VJ Day, August 14, 1945. It's commonly called *Times Square Kiss*. The illustration that follows it appeared on the cover of the *New Yorker* in 1996. Write a brief comparison of these images, taking into consideration their historical contexts, their form and content, and their rhetorical appeals. In particular, think about how the photo and the illustration establish *ethos* and make *logos*- and *pathos*-based arguments.

Blitt, Barry. Cover of *The New Yorker,* June 17, 1996.

Eisenstaedt, Alfred. *Times Square Kiss,* August 14, 1945.

Re-Mixing Images

Through the continual creation of new images, we have built up an incredibly large collection of visual texts across various cultures; many of these images continue to be reproduced and altered. Because images can be endlessly reproduced and altered and because they can serve as a powerful symbolic shorthand to convey ideas, images can become *icons* that are appropriated, or used, to create new images. The new references the old and helps us understand the historical context of the old image, how the images are connected, and how the allusion to the icon enhances the meaning of the re-mix. Furthermore, recognizing the old image (icon) in the new (re-mix)—that is, recognizing the *appropriation,* helps us to understand embedded messages the author conveys to the audience. Visual texts relate not only to the historical context(s) in which they were created and in which we view them, but manufactured and also to other images they reference. Just like composers and DJs sample music from other composers, visual artists "sample" from other artists. There are several forms such appropriations typically take, including parody, pastiche, memes, and mashups.

First, let's look at parody and pastiche. A *parody* replicates aspects of the original that make the reference recognizable while creating a satirical or humorous effect. Sometimes the humor is gentle, and sometimes it is biting. The humor derives from distorting the image or adding incongruent content to the original image. See the example of parody below. Adbusters, a

Culture-jamming ad spoof/parody by Adbusters, a Canadian organization.

culturejamming[6] organization with a website and journal, created this image to mock the misleading ads of the tobacco industry.

Pastiche is similar to parody, but the re-mix merely uses some of the formal elements or content of the original. The purpose of pastiche is to make an allusion to or homage to the original—that is, a reference of admiration rather than mockery. In this example, the artist incorporates some of the objects and features of the landscape, and he imitates the style. What similarities do you see? His work pays tribute to Salvador Dali's

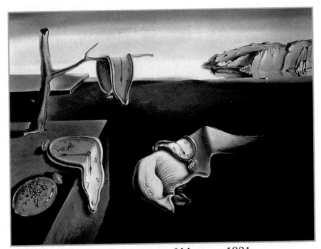

Dali, Salvador. *The Persistence of Memory*, 1931.

The Persistence of Memory without replicating fully its formal elements and content matter. The artist also makes an allusion to a hero from pop culture. Do you recognize the reference?

Contemporary forms of parody and pastiche include *mashups* and *memes*. Most mashups come from the worlds of music and web design, but there are mashups that create new still and moving visual texts. A *mashup* in music, also known as a mesh or blend, combines and synchronizes one or more vocal and instrumental tracks, creating a new sound. Mashups in visual art juxtapose

Rivera, Paolo. *The Self-Absorbing Man,* 2009.

---

[6] Culture jamming refers to a practice in which an individual or group critiques the logos, brands, and values of consumerist, capitalist culture by refiguring or appropriating corporate images and words to challenge the values that underpin them.

Apasun. *Pulp Fiction* vs. *Star Wars*.

or combine two cultural icons, creating a new image. The artist combines disparate and sometimes seemingly dissonant elements to give the audience a new way of looking at something. In this rendering, the Storm Troopers from the *Star Wars* movies are "mashed up" with Vincent Vega and Jules Winnfield, the two main characters from the film *Pulp Fiction*. This juxtaposition is both unsettling and darkly humorous, giving new meaning to the characters in both films.

For Thought and Discussion

The first image mashes up two images: the BP logo and a silhouette from a Pulitzer Prize-winning iconic photo (*Vietnam Execution,* Saigan, 1968 by Eddie Adams). Study these two images and research the historical context of the photo. How does the history of the iconic photograph affect the message in the parody? Based on the form and content of the mashup, how do you interpret the message? What do the two figures represent? Articulate the message in two or three sentences and discuss your conclusions with a partner. Did you come to the same conclusion regarding the author's intended message?

Richard Dawkins, an evolutionary biologist, coined the word *meme* in his 1979 book *The Selfish Gene.* He desired "a word that sounded like gene" and would convey the notion of "cultural transmission" (Dawkins). As Dawkins explains, examples of memes include "tunes, ideas, catch-phrases, clothes

BP-Vietnam Spoof, Adbusters.org website.

Adams, Eddie. *Vietnam Execution,* Saigon, 1968.

fashions, ways of making pots or of building arches. Just as genes propagate themselves in the gene pool by leaping from body to body via sperms or eggs, so memes propagate themselves in the meme pool by leaping from brain to brain via a process which, in the broad sense, can be called imitation" ("What Is a Meme?"). Memes "leap from brain to brain" because they resonate with us. They resonate with us because we perceive the truth behind the humor. Using *macros* (the images from which memes are generated) found on a meme generator website, anyone can create memes. Using the image macro, users can add captions. The juxtaposition of the image and the words contributes to the meanings of both. Memes are in visual art what variations on a theme are in musical art—they take the artistic foundation and change it for an unprecedented effect on the audience.

One popular meme on the Internet right now is "Keep Calm and Carry On." This meme emerged from the 2000 discovery of a 1939 poster created by the Ministry of Information in the United Kingdom. A couple found the poster at the bottom of an old box of books they bought at an auction. They framed it and began selling prints ("Keep Calm and Carry On: About"). This image has leaped into many brains, and now we see it all over the place—not only in memes, but in thousands of products such as t-shirts, school supplies, and coffee mugs. As the examples below show, not only do meme creators alter the text, they also alter the image itself. This example demonstrates the reproducibility and malleability of memes as well as the way that users parody the original propaganda from which the macro derived. All of these forms of appropriation—parody, pastiche, mashup, and meme—illustrate ways that visual

Keep Calm and Carry On Memes. *Know Your Memes website.*

texts recall and revise earlier texts in order to create new meanings. Both authors and audiences participate in this *intertextuality,* or "conversation" among visual texts.

For Thought and Discussion

This meme memes a meme for a darkly humorous effect. The unnamed author changes both the icon and all but three words of the text, yet the appropriation maintains enough of the meme it echoes for us to understand that the appropriation references "Keep Calm and Carry On." What do the hammer and sickle signify, and how are the images and the text connected? Discuss with your partner or as a class.

Keep Quiet and Continue Working Meme.
Know Your Memes website.

For Thought and Discussion

Visit the *Know Your Memes* website. Look up "Haters Gonna Hate." In this meme, the caption is the macro—it remains stable, but the images in the meme change. In what ways does the user's authorship of pictures differ from the authorship of text? In other words, how does creating new images for the static text of "Haters Gonna Hate" change the standard meme-making experience of changing the caption?

Addressing Rhetorical Situations with Visual Texts

Just as written texts address particular *rhetorical situations,* so do visual texts. Think about what you have learned regarding the rhetorical situation already in your writing classes. If we simplify the rhetorical situation into its most basic components, we have these three: text, author, and audience. These three elements influence and inform each other—in other words, by knowing more about one, you can understand more about the others. In this section of the chapter, we will apply some of the concepts covered thus far in this chapter to a discussion of how they apply to aspects of the rhetorical situation.

The Text

The nature of the *text* connects to the *purpose* and *subject* of the message. If you are asked to analyze a text, you could start by asking what kind of visual text you are viewing, what it is doing, and why. Take notes, answering the following questions:

▌ What is the text's *genre?* Is it a painting, a photograph, a sculpture, a film, a print ad, a TV commercial, a flier?

▌ What is the purpose of the text? How does the author convey his or her purpose?

▌ If the purpose is to persuade, what is the audience being persuaded to think or do? What is the thesis or argument of the text?

▌ How is the "so what" question addressed? Why should the audience pay attention to this text?

▌ What effect does this text have on me?

In order to explore some of these questions more deeply, think back to the section of this chapter called "Form Follows Function: The Architecture of Images." Remember that this section dealt with the form and content of visual arguments. Let's expand on that discussion by looking at how words and images work together to enhance each other. In the most effective texts, form and content merge into a unified work that addresses the rhetorical situation well. Think of the mixing of form and content as being similar to the mixing of iconic and linguistic elements. Many if not most of the visual arguments we see mix images and words. Think of a photograph and a caption. The caption helps to contextualize the photograph so that we understand the significance of the narrative that is being depicted in the image.

Look at this photograph. Do you know the story behind it?

Thornell, Jack. *James Meredith Shot,* June 6, 1966.

The man is lying prone on a road, and he is the only figure in the photo. We can read from his face that he is in pain, or perhaps he is angry or sad, but we might not know why without words to explain the meaning of what we are seeing. You may recognize that this is a famous photograph; in fact, it won a Pulitzer Prize in 1967. If you do not recognize this photo, this caption gives its context: "Civil rights activist James Meredith grimaces in pain as he pulls himself across Highway 51 after being shot in Hernando, Miss., June 6, 1966. Meredith, who defied segregation to enroll at the University of Mississippi in 1962 completed the march from Memphis, Tenn., to Jackson, Miss., after treatment of his wounds (AP Photo/Jack Thornell)" ("James Meredith Shot Pulitzer 1967"). With the words, we now know who this man is and what has happened to him. The caption provides *anchorage* for the viewer because it pins down and narrows the many meanings this photo could possibly convey. Without the image, however, the words would not give us a sense of his physical and emotional pain. The image conveys the *pathos* that the words, with their objective, journalistic tone, do not.

At the beginning of this chapter, the following epigraph appears: "There can be no words without images." This sentence comes from one of Aristotle's lectures about how words carry meanings through rhetorical devices that create images in the mind's eye such as metaphor and narrative. The best writing brings images to the minds of audiences, but words, like visual art, can only imitate reality. We can never fully capture all of the meanings of a scene or an experience. When writing about visual texts, though, remember that the iconic and the linguistic work in tandem to create meaning. Examine these elements carefully to gather as much meaning as possible.

In some ways, words and images are not all that far removed from one another. Words, after all, are made up of letters—shapes formed by lines. These shapes have particular meanings as letters or when they are grouped into words. In Nathaniel Hawthorne's novel *The Scarlet Letter*, a character named Hester Prynne is forced by her community to wear an "A" as a mark of shame for committing adultery. This scarlet-red "A" possesses an altogether different meaning from the red "A" that signifies the Atlanta Braves baseball team. The field of typography discovers the artistic/rhetorical possibilities of alphabetic texts such as the capital "A" that Prynne and the Braves wear. Also, as we have seen in this chapter, artists who create images use a visual vocabulary, grammar, and syntax—a set of design principles such as line, space, shape, texture, and color ("Visual Language"). Because of this visual "language," visual texts are *polysemous*, which means that they are able to carry multiple meanings to address rhetorical situations.

Gun by ~mou5e. An example of typography, in which words become art. Here, the words and the images complete each other (Torbjornsen).

For Thought and Discussion

"Ordeal by Cheque" by Wuther Crue, 1932

This piece, which appeared in *Vanity Fair* magazine in 1982, uses checks to tell a story. It provides a notable example of the interplay between iconic and linguistic elements. The checks themselves are images, but the handwriting forms images as well that give clues to the plot. Look carefully at each check in chronological order, and pay careful attention to who writes the check, the date it is made out, the recipient, and the amount. This story contains a large amount of *subtext*, which requires a great deal of reading between the lines to perceive possible meanings.

After you read the story, list the main characters and their relationships. Then, write a brief summary of the story, including the major events in the characters' lives.

Once you have finished writing, discuss the following as a class or in small groups.

- Think about the historical context of the story and its publication. What was going on in American society at this time? What might have sparked the writing of the story? (What was its exigence or origin?)
- How would you characterize this text? What, if any, genre does it fit into?
- Why might Crue have written the story in the form of checks? How would it be different if it had been written as a prose narrative with words only?
- What is the "so what" of the story? What does Crue want us to take away from our reading of it?

Ordeal by cheque

BY WUTHER CRUE

Los Angeles, Calif. Aug. 30th, 19 03 No. ____
HOLLYWOOD STATE BANK 90-984
6801 Santa Monica Boulevard
PAY TO THE ORDER OF *Goosie Gander Baby Shoppe* $48.50
One hundred + forty eight ____ 50/ DOLLARS
Lawrence Exeter

Los Angeles, Calif. Sept 2nd 19 03 No. ____
HOLLYWOOD STATE BANK 90-984
6801 Santa Monica Boulevard
PAY TO THE ORDER OF *Hollywood Hospital* $100.00
One hundred ____ XX DOLLARS
Lawrence Exeter

Los Angeles, Calif. Oct 3rd 19 03 No. ____
HOLLYWOOD STATE BANK 90-984
6801 Santa Monica Boulevard
PAY TO THE ORDER OF *Dr. David M. McCoy* $475.00
Four hundred + seventy-five ____ XX DOLLARS
Lawrence Exeter Sr.

Los Angeles, Calif. Dec 19th, 19 03 No. ____
HOLLYWOOD STATE BANK 90-984
6801 Santa Monica Boulevard
PAY TO THE ORDER OF *California Toyland Co.* $83.20
Eighty three ____ 20/ DOLLARS
Lawrence Exeter, Jr.

Los Angeles, Calif. Oct. 6th 19 09 No. ____
HOLLYWOOD STATE BANK 90-984
6801 Santa Monica Boulevard
PAY TO THE ORDER OF *Palisade School for Boys* $1,250.00
Twelve hundred + fifty ____ XX DOLLARS
Lawrence Exeter, Jr.

Los Angeles, Calif. Apr. 18th, 19 10 No. ____
HOLLYWOOD STATE BANK 90-984
6801 Santa Monica Boulevard
PAY TO THE ORDER OF *City Bicycle Co.* $52.50
Fifty two ____ 50/ DOLLARS
Lawrence Exeter Jr.

Los Angeles, Calif. Aug. 26th, 19 15 No. ____
HOLLYWOOD STATE BANK 90-984
6801 Santa Monica Boulevard
PAY TO THE ORDER OF *Columbia Military Acad.* $2,150.00
Twenty-one hundred + fifty ____ XX DOLLARS
Lawrence Exeter Jr.

Los Angeles, Calif. Sept 3rd, 19 21 No. ____
HOLLYWOOD STATE BANK 90-984
6801 Santa Monica Boulevard
PAY TO THE ORDER OF *Hollywood Cadillac Co.* $3,885.00
Thirty eight hundred + eighty five XX DOLLARS
Lawrence Exeter Jr.

Los Angeles, Calif. Sept. 7th, 19 21 No. ____
HOLLYWOOD STATE BANK 90-984
6801 Santa Monica Boulevard
PAY TO THE ORDER OF *Wilshire Auto Repair Service* $288.76
Two hundred + eighty-eight ____ 76/ DOLLARS
Lawrence Exeter Jr.

Los Angeles, Calif. Oct. 15th, 19 21 No. ____
HOLLYWOOD STATE BANK 90-984
6801 Santa Monica Boulevard
PAY TO THE ORDER OF *Stanford University* $339.00
Three hundred + thirty-nine ____ XX DOLLARS
Lawrence Exeter Jr.

Los Angeles, Calif. June 1st, 19 23 No. ____
HOLLYWOOD STATE BANK 90-984
6801 Santa Monica Boulevard
PAY TO THE ORDER OF *Miss Daisy Windsor* $25,000.00
Twenty-five thousand ____ XX DOLLARS
Lawrence Exeter Jr.

Crue, W. (1932 [renewed 1960, 1988]). Ordeal by Cheque. *Vanity Fair.* Cited in Vacca, R. T., & Vacca, J. L. (1999). Content area reading: Literacy and learning across the curriculum (6th ed.). New York: Longman.

LOS ANGELES, CALIF. *June 9th* 19 *23* No. ____

HOLLYWOOD STATE BANK 90-984
6801 SANTA MONICA BOULEVARD

PAY TO THE ORDER OF *French Line, Ile de France* $585.00

Five hundred + eighty-five ——— XX DOLLARS

Lawrence Exeter Sr.

LOS ANGELES, CALIF. *Aug. 23rd* 19 *23* No. ____

HOLLYWOOD STATE BANK 90-984
6801 SANTA MONICA BOULEVARD

PAY TO THE ORDER OF *Banque de France* $5,000.00

Five thousand ——— XX DOLLARS

Lawrence Exeter Sr.

LOS ANGELES, CALIF. *Feb. 13th* 19 *26* No. ____

HOLLYWOOD STATE BANK 90-984
6801 SANTA MONICA BOULEVARD

PAY TO THE ORDER OF *University Club Florists* $76.50

Seventy-six ——— 50/ DOLLARS

Lawrence Exeter Sr.

LOS ANGELES, CALIF. *June 22nd* 19 *26* No. ____

HOLLYWOOD STATE BANK 90-984
6801 SANTA MONICA BOULEVARD

PAY TO THE ORDER OF *University Club Florists* $312.75

Three hundred + twelve ——— 75/ DOLLARS

Lawrence Exeter Sr.

LOS ANGELES, CALIF. *Aug. 11th* 19 *26* No. ____

HOLLYWOOD STATE BANK 90-984
6801 SANTA MONICA BOULEVARD

PAY TO THE ORDER OF *Riviera Heights Land Co.* $56,000.00

Fifty-six Thousand ——— XX DOLLARS

Lawrence Exeter Sr.

LOS ANGELES, CALIF. *Oct. 30th* 19 *26* No. ____

HOLLYWOOD STATE BANK 90-984
6801 SANTA MONICA BOULEVARD

PAY TO THE ORDER OF *Renaissance Interior Decorators* $22,000.00

Twenty-two thousand ——— XX DOLLARS

Lawrence Exeter Sr.

LOS ANGELES, CALIF. *Nov. 18th* 19 *26* No. ____

HOLLYWOOD STATE BANK 90-984
6801 SANTA MONICA BOULEVARD

PAY TO THE ORDER OF *Beverly Diamond + Gift Shoppe* $678.45

Six hundred + seventy-eight ——— 45/ DOLLARS

Lawrence Exeter Sr.

LOS ANGELES, CALIF. *Nov. 16th* 19 *26* No. ____

HOLLYWOOD STATE BANK 90-984
6801 SANTA MONICA BOULEVARD

PAY TO THE ORDER OF *Hawaii Steamship Co.* $560.00

Five hundred + sixty ——— XX DOLLARS

Lawrence Exeter Sr.

LOS ANGELES, CALIF. *Nov. 21st* 19 *26* No. ____

HOLLYWOOD STATE BANK 90-984
6801 SANTA MONICA BOULEVARD

PAY TO THE ORDER OF *Lawrence Exeter, Junior* $200,000.00

Two hundred thousand ——— XX DOLLARS

Lawrence Exeter Sr.

LOS ANGELES, CALIF. *Nov. 22nd* 19 *26* No. ____

HOLLYWOOD STATE BANK 90-984
6801 SANTA MONICA BOULEVARD

PAY TO THE ORDER OF *Ambassador Hotel* $2,250.00

Twenty-two hundred + fifty ——— XX DOLLARS

Lawrence Exeter Sr.

LOS ANGELES, CALIF. *Dec. 1st* 19 *26* No. ____

HOLLYWOOD STATE BANK 90-984
6801 SANTA MONICA BOULEVARD

PAY TO THE ORDER OF *University Club Florists* $183.50

One hundred + eighty-three ——— 50/ DOLLARS

Lawrence Exeter Sr.

LOS ANGELES, CALIF. *Feb. 18* 19 *27* No. ____

HOLLYWOOD STATE BANK 90-984
6801 SANTA MONICA BOULEVARD

PAY TO THE ORDER OF *Cocoanut Grove Sweet Shoppe* $27.00

Twenty seven ——— DOLLARS

Lawrence Exeter Jr.

Crue, W. (1932 [renewed 1960, 1988]). Ordeal by Cheque. *Vanity Fair.* Cited in Vacca, R. T., & Vacca, J. L. (1999). Content area reading: Literacy and learning across the curriculum (6th ed.). New York: Longman.

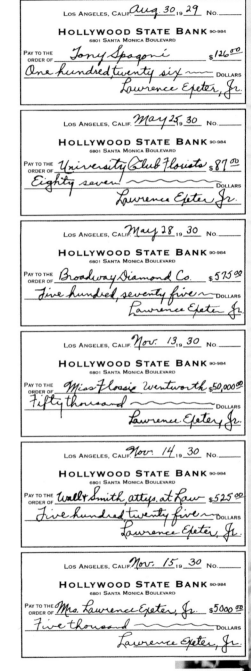

Crue, W. (1932 [renewed 1960, 1988]). Ordeal by Cheque. *Vanity Fair*. Cited in Vacca, R. T., & Vacca, J. L. (1999). Content area reading: Literacy and learning across the curriculum (6th ed.). New York: Longman.

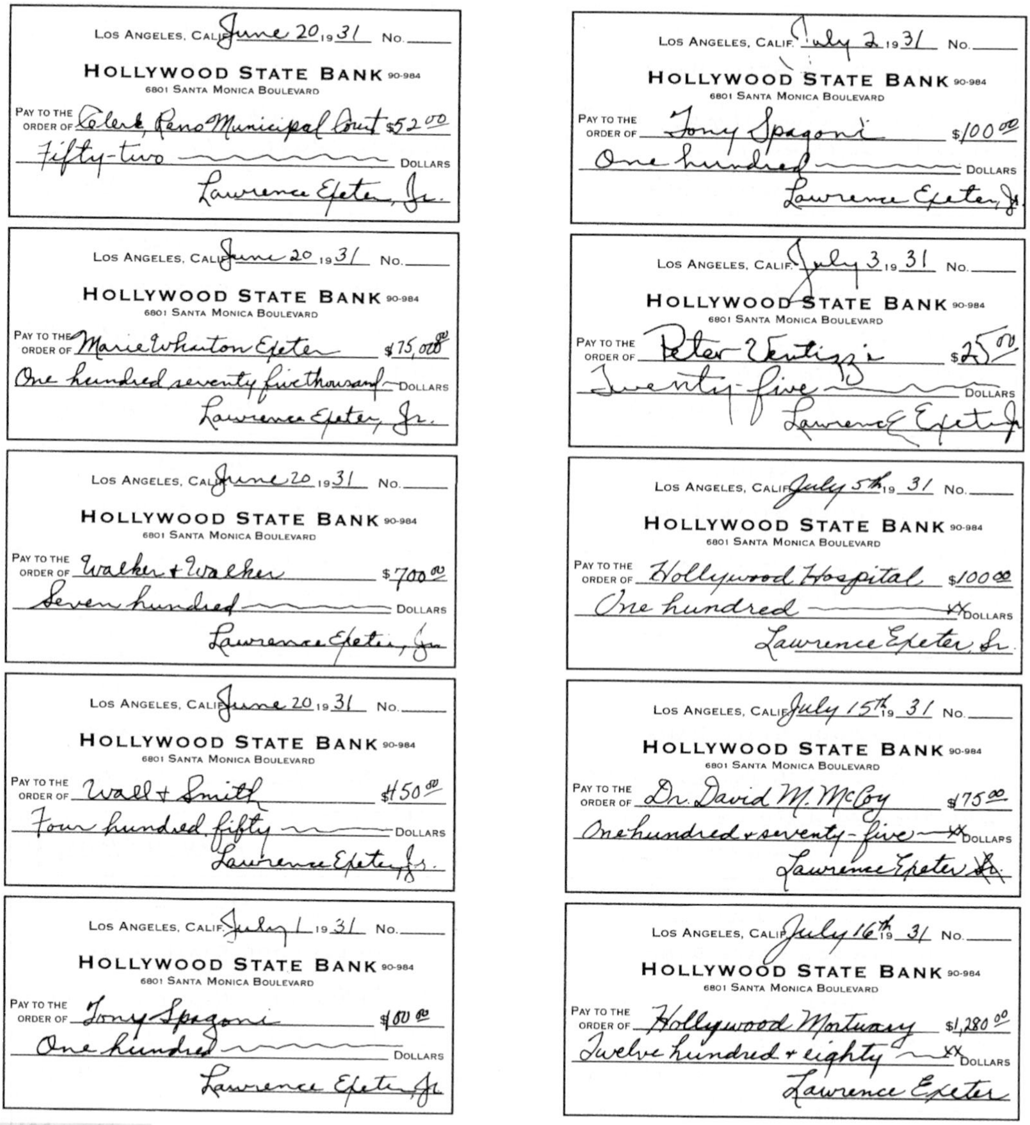

Check 1 (left column, top):
LOS ANGELES, CALIF. June 20, 19 31 No. ____
HOLLYWOOD STATE BANK 90-984
6801 SANTA MONICA BOULEVARD
PAY TO THE ORDER OF Clerk, Reno Municipal Court $52 00
Fifty-two ———— DOLLARS
Lawrence Exeter, Jr.

Check 2 (left column):
LOS ANGELES, CALIF. June 20, 19 31 No. ____
HOLLYWOOD STATE BANK 90-984
6801 SANTA MONICA BOULEVARD
PAY TO THE ORDER OF Marie Wharton Exeter $175,000
One hundred seventy five thousand —— DOLLARS
Lawrence Exeter, Jr.

Check 3 (left column):
LOS ANGELES, CAL. June 20, 19 31 No. ____
HOLLYWOOD STATE BANK 90-984
6801 SANTA MONICA BOULEVARD
PAY TO THE ORDER OF Walker + Walker $700 00
Seven hundred ———— DOLLARS
Lawrence Exeter, Jr.

Check 4 (left column):
LOS ANGELES, CALIF. June 20, 19 31 No. ____
HOLLYWOOD STATE BANK 90-984
6801 SANTA MONICA BOULEVARD
PAY TO THE ORDER OF Wall + Smith $450 00
Four hundred fifty ———— DOLLARS
Lawrence Exeter, Jr.

Check 5 (left column, bottom):
LOS ANGELES, CALIF. July 1, 19 31 No. ____
HOLLYWOOD STATE BANK 90-984
6801 SANTA MONICA BOULEVARD
PAY TO THE ORDER OF Tony Spagoni $100 00
One hundred ———— DOLLARS
Lawrence Exeter, Jr.

Check 6 (right column, top):
LOS ANGELES, CALIF. July 2, 19 31 No. ____
HOLLYWOOD STATE BANK 90-984
6801 SANTA MONICA BOULEVARD
PAY TO THE ORDER OF Tony Spagoni $100 00
One hundred ———— DOLLARS
Lawrence Exeter, Jr.

Check 7 (right column):
LOS ANGELES, CALIF. July 3, 19 31 No. ____
HOLLYWOOD STATE BANK 90-984
6801 SANTA MONICA BOULEVARD
PAY TO THE ORDER OF Peter Ventizzi $25 00
Twenty-five ———— DOLLARS
Lawrence Exeter

Check 8 (right column):
LOS ANGELES, CALIF. July 5th, 19 31 No. ____
HOLLYWOOD STATE BANK 90-984
6801 SANTA MONICA BOULEVARD
PAY TO THE ORDER OF Hollywood Hospital $100 00
One hundred ———— DOLLARS
Lawrence Exeter Sr.

Check 9 (right column):
LOS ANGELES, CALIF. July 15th, 19 31 No. ____
HOLLYWOOD STATE BANK 90-984
6801 SANTA MONICA BOULEVARD
PAY TO THE ORDER OF Dr. David M. McCoy $175 00
One hundred + seventy-five ———— DOLLARS
Lawrence Exeter Sr.

Check 10 (right column, bottom):
LOS ANGELES, CALIF. July 16th, 19 31 No. ____
HOLLYWOOD STATE BANK 90-984
6801 SANTA MONICA BOULEVARD
PAY TO THE ORDER OF Hollywood Mortuary $1,280 00
Twelve hundred + eighty ———— DOLLARS
Lawrence Exeter

Crue, W. (1932 [renewed 1960, 1988]). Ordeal by Cheque. *Vanity Fair*. Cited in Vacca, R. T., & Vacca, J. L. (1999). Content area reading: Literacy and learning across the curriculum (6th ed.). New York: Longman.

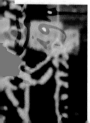

The Author(s)

With written texts, we can generally ascertain authorship. We know who wrote the text because the author's name often appears in the text, unless the author is anonymous or the text was written by a corporate author (generally a team of people or one person who writes without attribution for an organization). However, the same clear authorship does not hold true as frequently for visual texts. After the advent of *Web 2.0* (a term coined in 1999), the notion of authorship changed dramatically for texts composed of alphabetic and/or graphic elements. User-generated content meant that everyone could potentially create written and visual texts. Nevertheless, whether or not we have the author(s)' name(s), we can often determine a great deal about authorial intention by examining clues from other aspects of the rhetorical situation.

The following questions will provide the groundwork for you to analyze a text's authorship:

- Who is the author?
- What aspects of the author's *background* give him or her *ethos* (credibility)?
- What does the author *do* to establish *ethos* with the audience?
- What kind of impression does the author want to make about himself/herself??
- In what ways does the author create common ground or consensus with the audience?

By asking these five questions, you can establish the author's role and *ethos*. This credibility, as you remember from the section dealing with *ethos,* arises from the wisdom, good will, and common sense of the author.

In order to see how visual artists, designers, and filmmakers build their *ethos* through their work, we will look at a phenomenon that started right here in Atlanta. Living Walls, a local not-for-profit group, started a few years ago in Atlanta to make the city more aesthetically pleasing through a grassroots effort to make street art into public art (Rojo and Harrington). The organization put on its first street art festival in 2010, inviting artists to select walls and create murals in Atlanta inner city neighborhoods such as Cabbagetown, the Old Fourth Ward, and Summer Hill. The conference, called "Living Walls, the City Speaks," seeks not only to showcase exceptional street art but also to start a dialogue about some of Atlanta's problems. In its fifth year, Living Walls[7] has

---

7 For more on the organization's initiatives, visit http://livingwallsatl.com/

recently partnered with the Google Street Art Project[8] to preserve images of the typically ephemeral art form of street murals and to bring these incredible images to a wider audience.

The authors of these huge pieces submit their proposals to a committee, so the show is vetted by the festival organizers. Typically, art shows are juried, which means that artworks undergo a form of peer review. Artists have come from more than seventeen countries, competing to put their work up on everyday buildings such as warehouses, restaurants, and hotels. Let's look at three pieces created by one artist from Paris. He goes by the name of JR, and he won the TED Prize[9] in 2011 for his innovative work. For these pieces, JR performed research in the SCLC (Southern Christian Leadership Conference) collection at Emory University's MARBL (Manuscript, Archives, and Rare Book Library).[10] The 50th anniversary of the March on Washington inspired JR to create these murals for Living Walls 2013.

For Thought and Discussion

Examine the following three photographs of murals carefully. Write down answers to these questions and discuss with your classmates.

- How does JR challenge the preconceptions of street art through establishing his *ethos?*
- How does he create common ground with his audience by using this genre in this context?
- Research the images with which he does his pastiches, and research his method of wheatpasting the images on the wall. How are the form (wheatpasted photos) and content (archival artifacts of the civil rights movement) of these pieces related to JR's overall vision and purpose?

---

8 For more on this project, visit https://streetart.withgoogle.com/en/#home
9 TED is an international organization highlighting the work of thinkers with ideas to change the world. The acronym stands for Technology, Entertainment, Design. For more on TED, visit www.ted.com.
10 For more on Emory's outstanding archive and rare book collection, visit https://marbl.library.emory.edu/.

Rojo, Jaime and Steve Harrington. *March on Washington.* 2013 Living Walls Mural by JR.

Rojo, Jaime and Steve Harrington. *No More Hunger.* 2013 Living Walls Mural by JR.

Rojo, Jaime and Steve Harrington.. *I Am a Man.* 2013 Living Walls Mural by JR.

By exhibiting their art on the walls of buildings in the city, Living Walls artists bring art to everyday, mass audiences. People who cannot afford the expensive tickets of a museum or a film festival can still enjoy this artwork.

The Audience

Many of the artists who create Living Walls installations started their careers as graffiti artists, and the genre of graffiti provides an intriguing opportunity to discuss *audience*.

When you analyze a visual text, think about the following elements of audience:

- Who is the intended or target audience?
- What kind of text (genre) might appeal to audience members? What does the audience expect regarding the form and content of the text? Does the author use the most effective genre for the intended audience?
- What background knowledge does the audience already have? What bias or prejudice might influence their reception of the message?
- How might an ethical appeal (*ethos*) influence the intended audience? An emotional appeal (*pathos*)? A rational appeal (*logos*)?
- What does the audience expect from the author?

As we look at how graffiti affects audiences, think about these questions as they relate to the intended audiences of graffiti artists.

The word *graffiti* comes from the Greek word *graphein*, meaning "to write," and in actuality, graffiti artists prefer to be called "writers" ("Graffiti History"). The first instances of "modern style" graffiti include inscriptions such as the directions to the brothel in Ephesus, a city in the Eastern Roman Empire. However, the "tagging" that contemporary writers do emerged from an artist named "Taki 183" in 1960s New York City. Taki wrote his name in marker on the interiors and exteriors of subway trains, and he became (in)famous among young people and city officials ("Birth and Evolution"). Now, taggers generally use cans of spray paint instead of markers. Although the term is more widely used to describe different forms of vandalism or highly stylized typography, we will use the tagging-with-spray-paint sense of the word in this section. Let's look at the rhetorical situation of graffiti—that is, its text, author, and audience.

The *text* of graffiti—acrylic paint sprayed on walls, bridges, billboards, and other outdoor surfaces—is ephemeral in nature. That is, it may only last a little while. Someone might sand blast it off or paint over it. It might fade in the sun. No matter how fleeting the message might prove to be, writers create highly stylized letters, symbols, words, and decorative elements, crafting a unique *ethos* for themselves. They use pseudonyms or false names to provide anonymity for their guerrilla art. Because graffiti is illegal, its very existence makes a statement: "I climbed up here. I left my mark. I didn't get caught." Graffiti combines aesthetic and athletic skill, and those who practice it appreciate its subversiveness and defiance of cultural norms.

The *author* of graffiti is generally unknown, though many artists such as Taki 183, Banksy, Shepard Fairey, and Keith Haring have gained a following. Writers use assumed names or pseudonyms, but they do seek attention for their art. If tags become ubiquitous, they gain a cult following and create a more substantive *ethos* for the writer. While writers want audiences to notice what they are doing, they do not necessarily want audiences to know their identities. For this reason, the author's identity or self comes out only in the form and content of their art. The art has to speak for itself.

Although the nature of putting up illegal art entails that the artist remain all but invisible to his or her *audience*, writers intend for their tags to be pervasive and visible. Potentially, the audience for graffiti could be global in scope, if viewers take and post photos. A tremendous repetition of tags and the viral nature of social media provide the possibility of fame for the text and the artist's reputation. Graffiti treads on the edges of society, provoking discussion and creating tension among its audiences. Its allure comes from the pairing of criminal behavior and artistic creation: violation without violence.

Osborne, Steve. *Diablos.*

This tension explains graffiti's tremendous influence on rock and hip-hop, and their influence on graffiti in turn. Graffiti demonstrates the importance of understanding the meanings embedded in the text, audience, and author, as well as their interrelationships.

For Thought and Discussion

The City of Atlanta has an ordinance (law) against graffiti. Under Nuisances, Article V, graffiti is defined as "any inscriptions, words, figures, paintings, or other defacements that are written, marked, etched, scratched, sprayed, drawn, painted, or engraved on or otherwise affixed to any surface of real property or improvements thereon without prior authorization of the owner or occupant of the property. ..." Graffiti's illegality makes it more appealing to graffiti artists. Its existence makes an anti-authoritarian, rebellious argument. You are in a perfect environment to spot graffiti because GSU is embedded in an urban infrastructure. If graffiti is anything from a small sticker affixed to a light post all the way up to a large mural, the range of possibilities for the nature and scope of texts is virtually limitless.

Take photos of examples of graffiti on or near the GSU campus. Write an essay describing, analyzing, and/or evaluating your photo collection. Post the photos and the essay to your personal or class blog. In what ways is your curation (collection) and description of the images a form of appropriation? What about intertextuality? What are you contributing to the ongoing conversation about this relatively new cultural practice?

For Thought and Discussion

Shepard Fairey's first major tagging project was to post stickers depicting a stenciled bust of wrestler Andre the Giant with the word "OBEY" below the face. He posted variations of this image all over the world, gaining followers and notoriety. Later, he became more famous for creating the "HOPE" image that became iconic (and since that time, widely appropriated) during President Obama's 2008 campaign.

In 1990, Fairey wrote this "Manifesto" explaining the intent behind his "Obey Giant" image. Use this manifesto as an example to use when writing about an image from your own collection.

Osborne, Steve. *Crazy Train.*

Osborne, Steve. *Graffiti Bus.*

MANIFESTO by Shepard Fairey

The OBEY sticker campaign can be explained as an experiment in Phenomenology. Heidegger describes Phenomenology as "the process of letting things manifest themselves." Phenomenology attempts to enable people to see clearly something that is right before their eyes but obscured; things that are so taken for granted that they are muted by abstract observation.

The FIRST AIM OF PHENOMENOLOGY is to reawaken a sense of wonder about one's environment. The OBEY sticker attempts to stimulate curiosity and bring people to question both the sticker and their relationship with their surroundings. Because people are not used to seeing advertisements or propaganda for which the product or motive is not obvious, frequent and novel encounters with the sticker provoke thought and possible frustration, nevertheless revitalizing the viewer's perception and attention to detail. The sticker has no meaning but exists only to cause people to react, to contemplate and search for meaning in the sticker. Because OBEY has no actual meaning, the various reactions and interpretations of those who view it reflect their personality and the nature of their sensibilities.

Many people who are familiar with the sticker find the image itself amusing, recognizing it as nonsensical, and are able to derive straightforward visual pleasure without burdening themselves with an explanation. The PARANOID OR CONSERVATIVE VIEWER however may be confused by the sticker's persistent presence and condemn it as an underground cult with subversive intentions. Many stickers have been peeled down by people who were annoyed by them, considering them an eye sore and an act of petty vandalism, which is ironic considering the number of commercial graphic images everyone in American society is assaulted with daily.

Fairey, Shepard. *Obey the Giant.* 1989.

Another phenomenon the sticker has brought to light is the trendy and CONSPICUOUSLY CONSUMPTIVE nature of many members of society. For those who have been surrounded by the sticker, its familiarity and cultural resonance is comforting and owning a sticker provides a souvenir or keepsake, a memento. People have often demanded the sticker merely because they have seen it everywhere and possessing a sticker provides a sense of belonging. The Giant sticker seems mostly to be embraced by those who are (or at least want to seem to be) rebellious. Even though these people may not know the meaning of the sticker, they enjoy its slightly disruptive underground quality and wish to contribute to the furthering of its humorous and absurd presence which seems to somehow be antiestablishment/societal convention. Giant stickers are both embraced and rejected, the reason behind which, upon examination reflects the psyche of the viewer. Whether the reaction be positive or negative, the stickers existence is worthy as long as it causes people to consider the details and meanings of their surroundings. In the name of fun and observation.

Looking Back, Looking Forward

This chapter has given a brief overview of some of the major considerations artists and scholars make when creating and evaluating visual texts. We have only scratched the surface of the prolific body of work on visual rhetoric, but we hope that this chapter has provided you with a foundation on which you can build your knowledge base and your skills in this area. Whether you are critiquing visual texts or creating them, we hope that you will look at images with new eyes.

We have explored how images pervade our everyday lives, how they fit within historical contexts (or break free of contexts), the form and content of images, the three rhetorical appeals (*ethos*, *logos*, and *pathos*), re-mixes (parodies, pastiches, mashups, and memes), aspects of the rhetorical situation (text, author and audience), and we have provided you with an example rhetorical analysis assignment and a model student essay. Going forward, you will want to explore more about visual rhetoric, such as design considerations, new media and technologies for working with images, and theoretical models dealing with visual arguments. This area of study continues to be dynamic and relevant to our lives, and we encourage you to read widely and write deeply about images in your college and professional future.

Rhetorical Analysis Assignment and Student Essay

Dr. Oriana Gatta's scholarship and teaching often deal with visual rhetoric. She developed this assignment for her 1102 classes. In what follows, you will see Dr. Gatta's assignment as well as the essay one of her students, Joe Beard, wrote for the class. These materials will provide you with a useful example of a rhetorical analysis of a visual text: a TV commercial.

Rhetorical Analysis Assignment by Oriana Gatta

Rhetorical Analysis (10%, 100 pts)

Due: *No later than 11:59 9p.m., Sunday, September 15, 2013*

Submission Instructions: *Email* (as a .doc or .docx file) oriana.gatta@gmail.com

INTRODUCTION

In class we have been discussing the ways in which all texts, not just formal written arguments, are designed to send messages by appealing to an audience's emotions. These appeals are constructed using formal design elements, and identifying a text's message(s) requires us to understand the relationship between a text's rhetorical situation and its formal design elements. The primary purpose of the rhetorical analysis essay, then, is to help familiarize you with this relationship. Secondarily, as rhetorical analyses are a form of argumentation, this assignment also functions as preparation for your final project, in which you will make a research-based argument regarding a design-related topic of your choice.

DETAILS

In a 3–4 page (not including Works Cited) essay, make and support a unique claim regarding the message of an advertisement (or advertising campaign). More specifically, this essay should include:

> An introduction that clearly describes the advertisement (or advertising campaign) you have chosen to analyze, along with the advertisement's rhetorical situation (i.e. purpose, audience, and context).

> A thesis statement that identifies the claim you are making regarding the message of the advertisement (or advertising campaign) of your choice, as well as the criteria you are using to analyze the advertisement (or advertising campaign).

> Evidence in support of your thesis, i.e. clear and detailed explanations of how the advertisement (or advertising campaign) you have chosen fits into your analytical criteria and therefore supports your claim regarding the advertisement's (or advertising campaign's) message.

> A conclusion that reiterates your thesis statement (in different words) and broadens its (your thesis statement's) scope by placing the advertisement (or advertising campaign) in the context of other, similar advertisements, campaigns, and/or messages.

▪ A Works Cited page that cites the advertisement or advertising campaign you chose to analyze.

▪ MLA format.

EVALUATION

Your rhetorical analysis essay will be evaluated based on the following criteria:

10 points: Introduction

10 points: Thesis statement

40 points: Evidence

10 points: Conclusion

10 points: Formal tone and linguistic clarity

10 points: Length – at least 3 full pages, not including Works Cited.

5 points: Works Cited

5 points: MLA format

Joe Beard

Professor Oriana Gatta

English Composition 1102

15 September 2013

Rhetorical Analysis Essay

The public service advertisement, or PSA, has always been a reliable medium for communicating messages about potential dangers through television. The 1987 anti-drug public service advertisement, "This is Your Brain on Drugs," was very popular in its time, and its simple yet effective imagery and slogan remain recognizable in 2013. Anti-drug PSAs have continued to use minimalistic imagery to make their point in recent years, as exemplified in the Georgia Meth Project's PSA "Just Once." The ad shows five sequences involving a teenage girl and the street drug known as meth. Throughout these sequences, the ad narrates the girl's downward spiral after she becomes addicted to the drug, although she had initially planned on using it "just once." The ad's use of repetition, sequence, and mood asserts that meth will ruin your life if you try it, as well as the lives of those you care about.

This ad primarily utilizes the formal design element of repetition, specifically of the phrase "Just once," to communicate to viewers that it is nearly impossible to try meth without becoming immediately addicted to it. The phrase is uttered five times in the ad's 31-second airtime, four times by the older girl who is the main focus of the ad, and once by her younger sister at the end. The use of this phrase is clearly meant to be ironic: although the girl initially claims that she is only going to try meth once, we are shown how her life spirals out of control from continued use of the drug throughout the commercial. Ironically, she continues to use the phrase to justify her worsening behavior. For example, she states "I'm going to sleep with him for meth just once" as she is led out of a party by a total stranger, as if having sex with someone for drugs is fine as long as it is a one-time experience. At the end of the ad, the girl's sister repeats her line from its first scene, stating, "I'm going to try meth just once." The viewer is left with the ominous suggestion that the younger sister has been negatively influenced by the older sister's careless attitude towards meth use. Viewers are meant to understand by this point that "just once" loses its meaning when applied to meth use.

The ad also utilizes the element of sequence to make the point that, once one tries meth, only addiction and worse follows. In the ad's five sequences, viewers are shown how the girl's life begins falling apart after trying the drug, until it ultimately affects someone close to her. The girl addresses the camera with thoughts all ending with the phrase "just once" at the end of the first four sequences, describing increasingly self-destructive meth-related activities (such as trying meth with her friends, stealing from her family, and sleeping with a stranger for the drug) in each. Her appearance worsens in each sequence, showing her looking exhausted and gaining a number of strange scars on her face. In the final sequence, her little sister is shown about to try meth "just once," clearly having been influenced by her older sister's actions. The ad uses these sequences to communicate that one's life will spiral out of control very quickly after trying meth, due to its incredibly addictive qualities. Viewers are meant to realize how quickly the girl's life was ruined by meth, even though she had her mind set on only trying the drug once in the ad's first sequence. The final sequence is meant to appeal to viewers emotionally; even after the girl has obviously hit rock bottom (passed out in bed with strange scars and bruises all over her face), it is suggested that her younger sister is about to become addicted to meth as well, falling victim to the same "just once" mentality that her sister did.

Finally, the ad incorporates the element of mood to make its point. The mood of the ad is very dark and gets darker throughout. One way this is accomplished is through the absence of background music, which gives the ad an unsettling and realistic atmosphere. The mood is also established through the lack of any bright or vibrant colors in its imagery, as well as the lack of enthusiasm in either character's voice. This is well-exemplified by the ad's fourth sequence, the last one in which the older girl addresses the camera. The scene is almost completely dark, and the dead, joyless tone of the girl suggests to viewers that she does not believe her own words, or even feel in control of her own actions. The last two sequences both take place at night, which gives them a dark and bleak atmosphere. The final sequence feels ominous and foreboding, as viewers know that the girl's younger sister is most likely doomed to become addicted to meth as well. The overall mood of the ad accurately reflects what a horrible and unpleasant topic meth addiction truly is.

This ad is similar to other anti-drug PSAs in that it presents a cautionary tale to viewers about the effects of drug addiction on one's life, a common theme in advertisements by the Georgia Meth Project. While other anti-drug ad campaigns are more vague and rely on metaphors (such as the "This is Your Brain on Drugs" ad), this ad is realistic and to the point, exposing viewers to the realities of how meth addiction can be destructive to one's family life, morals, and physical appearance. This ad stands out from other anti-drug ads by also addressing how drug use negatively influences those who look up to the user, instead of simply focusing on the user as an individual. Through the three elements of repetition, sequence, and mood, this ad asserts to viewers that meth is a dangerous drug that will ultimately only hurt you and those close to you.

Works Cited

GaMethProject. "Just Once – Georgia Meth Project." Online video clip. *YouTube.*
    YouTube. 16 Jun. 2010. Web. 4 Sept. 2013.

Criteria	Total Points	Earned Points
An introduction that clearly describes the advertisement (or advertising campaign) you have chosen to analyze, along with the advertisement's rhetorical situation (i.e. purpose, audience, and context). Well done.	10	10
A thesis statement that identifies the claim you are making regarding the message of the advertisement (or advertising campaign) of your choice, as well as the criteria you are using to analyze the advertisement (or advertising campaign). Well done.	10	10
Evidence in support of your thesis, i.e. clear and detailed explanations of how the advertisement (or advertising campaign) you have chosen fits into your analytical criteria and therefore supports your claim regarding the advertisement's (or advertising campaign's) message. Well done.	40	40
A conclusion that reiterates your thesis statement (in different words) and broadens its (your thesis statement's) scope by placing the advertisement (or advertising campaign) in the context of other, similar advertisements, campaigns, and/or messages. Well done.	10	10
Formal tone and linguistic clarity A couple of instances of redundancy. An unnecessary comma. Overall, a clearly written essay employing an appropriately formal tone.	10	8
Length – at least 3 full pages, not including the Works Cited page. Well done.	10	10
A Works Cited page that cites the advertisement or advertising campaign you chose to analyze. Well done.	5	5
MLA format Unnecessary additional spacing. Unnecessary underlining. Missing hanging indent.	5	2
Grade		95/100 A

Works Cited

Texts

"ARTICLE V. NUISANCES." *ARTICLE V. NUISANCES.* Municode. Web. 17 June 2014.

Crue, Wuther. "Ordeal by Cheque." *Pbworks.com.* n.d. Web. 17 June 2014.

Dawkins, Richard. "What Is a Meme?" *What Is a Meme?* University of Cambridge. Web. 17 June 2014.

Faigley, Lester, Diana George, Anna Palchik, and Cynthia Selfe. *Picturing Texts.* New York: W.W. Norton, 2004. Print.

Fairey, Shepard. "MANIFESTO." *Obey Giant.* Obey, 1990. Web. 17 June 2014.

"James Meredith Shot Pulitzer 1967." *The Big Story.* Associated Press. Web. 17 June 2014.

Johnson, Caitlin. "Cutting Through Advertising Clutter." *CBSNews.* CBS Interactive, 17 Sept. 2006. Web. 17 June 2014.

"Keep Calm and Carry On: About." *Know Your Meme News.* Cheezburger, Inc. Web. 17 June 2014.

Rojo, Jaime, and Steven Harrington. "20 New Murals From Atlanta Living Walls 2013." *The Huffington Post. TheHuffingtonPost.com,* 21 Aug. 2013. Web. 17 June 2014.

Story, Louise. "Anywhere the Eye Can See, It's Now Likely to See an Ad." *The New York Times.* The New York Times, 15 Jan. 2007. Web. 17 June 2014.

Images

Adams, Eddie. *Vietnam Execution.* Photo. 1968. *Stevenkasher.com.* 2014. Web. 17 June 2014.

Black, Nancy. "Welcome to Marlboro Country." 11 February 2011. *Adbusters. org,* Web. 17 June 2014.

Blitt, Barry. "Times Square Kiss." 17 June 1996. *Canonblogger.com,* n.d. Web. 17 June 2014.

"BP-Vietnam Spoof." Spoof Ad. *Adbusters.org.* 11 Feb. 2011. Web. 17 June 2014.

Dali, Salvador. *The Persistence of Memory.* 1931. *Tufts.edu,* n.d. Web. 17 June 2014.

Dutch Renaissance Self-Shot. "Great Art Parodies: 25 Iconic Paintings Recreated by Funny and Clever Contemporary Artists." *Blog of Francesco Mugnai,* n.d. Web. 17 June 2014.

Eisenstaedt, Alfred. *Times Square Kiss.* 14 August 1945. *Canonblogger.com,* n.d. Web. 17June 2014.

Golz, Dorothee. *Girl with a Pearl Earring.* "Great Art Parodies: 25 Iconic Paintings Recreated by Funny and Clever Contemporary Artists." *Blog of Francesco Mugnai,* n.d. Web. 17 June 2014.

"Hagia Sophia." *Milliyet.tr.com.* n.d. Web. 17 June 2014.

"Istanbul: Hagia Sophia (Imperial Gate Mosaics)." *Flickr.com,* 26 July 2011. Web. 17 June 2014.

"Keep Calm and Carry On: Part of a Series on Propaganda Parodies." *Knowyourmeme.com.* n.d. Web. 17 June 2014.

"Keep Quiet and Continue Working." *Knowyourmeme.com.* n.d. Web. 17 June 2014.

Lewandowski, Kim. "Photo Friday: Symbols." *Lemony Zest: Kim Lewandowski,* 8 May 2010. Web. 17 June 2014.

Marshall, Julian. "Obey the Giant – The Shepard Fairey Story." *Posca-life-custom.com.* 23 April 2013. Web. 17 June 2014.

"Pulp Fiction vs. Star Wars." *Nyuisva.wordpress.com.* "Commons II." 23 Nov. 2011. Web. 17 June 2014.

Rivera, Paolo. "The Self-Absorbing Man." *Acardona574.wordpress.com.* "Pastiche-Exercise-1-and-2," 2014. Web. 17 June 2014.

Rojo, Jaime and Steve Harrington. "20 New Murals From Atlanta Living Walls 2013." *Huffingtonpost.com.* 21 August 2013. Web. 17 June 2014.

Thornell, Jack. *James Meredith Shot.* Photo. 1966. *Bigstory.ap.org.* "James Meredith Shot Pulitzer 1967." n.d. Web. 17 June 2014.

Torbjornsen, Hilde. "50 Great Examples of Extremely Awesome Typography." *1stwebdesigner.com. 2010.* Web. 17 June 2014.

Vermeer, Johannes. *Girl with a Pearl Earring.* 1665. *Essential Vermeer.com.* n.d. Web. 17 June 2014.

Cheek, Rachel. *Love of Science.*

Chapter 8
Writing in Digital Spaces

These days, for most of us, writing happens in digital spaces more than on paper. Emails, text messages, tweets, Word or Google Docs, submission forms, notes, and calendar apps on our phones: the daily writing experiences in which we participate largely happen in digital spaces. And that matters.

For one, what we can say in a space is limited by what that space can do, its affordances and constraints. Consider a PowerPoint slide. Generally it is designed as a series of static, rectangular digital "slide" spaces unified visually by a central theme and color scheme, and unless we are graphic designers composing our own themes, we tend to fit what we want to say into prefabricated boxes and arrangements within those slides. The progression of slides is decidedly linear; we click a button and move forward or backward through the series to the presentation's end. That is the only motion. What if what we want to say involves a complex, non-linear relationship between ideas? This will be hard to enact or work out via a PowerPoint presentation.

A Prezi, however, although also decisively linear in progression, enables writers to design more motion into their arguments, and offers the opportunity for visually representing relationships between ideas with the impression of dimensionality in ways PowerPoint cannot. This motion and perhaps-more-shapely "slides" meant to receive a writer's message are predesigned, too, usually. Although it isn't necessarily difficult to alter the arrangements and pre-designed features in PowerPoint or Prezi, if we know how to do it, the spaces themselves are packaged and promoted to us for simply plugging in messages that we've already formulated. As if the graphic art of the PowerPoint or Prezi itself was enough to make someone's message interesting. However, we all know generally it's not. In fact media platforms like PowerPoint and Prezi can be downright distracting.

Furthermore what we can say in a space is limited by what *we* can do with the space itself, our **digital literacy**. If you're playing the video game *Assassin's Creed* and have very little idea on how to move your character through the landscape, fight, steal, spy, or communicate with your sidekick, you're not likely to get very far in the game. This is true of any video game experience; knowing how to use the tools and affordances of the game itself leads to greater success in the digital space of the game, and a greater sense of control of the experience itself (our "video game literacy").

Writing spaces are not scripted like most video games are, but they come with pre-designed frameworks that enable us the same potential for success in communicating our messages to our intended audiences, the same potential sense of control. To what extent do I know how to manipulate images in a digital environment? Or utilize the headers in Word to organize my longer arguments? Or embed a video directly into my Prezi presentation? Or edit a podcast? These are the kinds of questions that illuminate the state of our digital literacies and greatly affect our writing.

Many writing and communication scholars argue for the importance of expanding our digital literacies so that we can participate more fully in our culture, as our culture plays out in online, digital spaces more and more. This chapter will address how our digital literacies affect the choices we make when we write in digital spaces in the classroom and in our professional lives, particularly as these choices position us as consumers and producers of digital media in the composition classroom and in all college classrooms.

For Thought And Discussion

Consider Meaghan Elliott's "partial list of the things [she] needed to write today" on page 1 of this book. What tools (digital or not) could Meaghan have used to complete these tasks? Which tools were best suited for the tasks and why? What are the financial costs of these tools? What are the time costs for learning them?

To help us assess some of our fundamental needs as digital writers, the following section addresses how four terms in digital culture impact our work as critical thinkers and composers in the composition classroom: *attention, participation, audience,* and *multimodality.*

Attention

Early computer users sat down to their boxy towers with specific tasks in mind—"I will write an email," for instance. Increasingly, the phrase "sitting down at a computer" seems antiquated, as most of us carry the functionality of a small computer around in our pockets. Our phones quickly gain and delete new programs (apps), connect us to instantaneous live conversations (chat), and serve as one of our main sources of media consumption. Via our phones, tablets, laptops, or the desktop computers in the library, we are rarely removed from the constant stream of multimedia content that the Internet provides. How does this ever-hovering cloud of information affect our academic work, our theories of knowledge, our control over our activities? In short, how does being seconds away from the Web at all times impact our attention?

You might not find it surprising that interest in the field of neuroscience has increased parallel to our digital activity. After all, the more we learn about the world through our computers, the more we have to think about how we manage that learning and how it impacts our future learning. For example, you may think that the Internet automatically provides you with a wider lens on world events than citizens had before the Internet. Back then, radio, television, and newspaper media held control over what most people could realistically "know" outside of their own experience. With the Internet—blogs, Twitter, on-line newspapers, YouTube, etc. —you might be tempted to say that control has been transformed. Now, you can learn pretty much anything you want by looking it up online. However, consider what happens when we decide to follow someone on Twitter or friend them on Facebook, when we add a blog to our RSS reader account or subscribe to a YouTube channel. We are selecting or curating our own list of regularly updated media. However, if we collect that list according to our pre-existing and unexamined tastes, we are essentially avoiding Web content that we feel is irrelevant or isn't likely to agree with our own understanding of the world. Our curation, if not reflective, can greatly limit our learning.

Therefore, attention involves what media we attend to and the content it promotes. It also involves how we pay attention. A variety of studies over the last several years have attempted to understand whether we learn differently when we use digital technologies. Consider the iPad, Kindle, Nexus, Galaxy, and even the laptop: are these items ideal for reading specific kinds of material and not for others? Given that many of us work these days with several Internet browser windows up at the same time, we toggle back and forth among several sites: email, social media (like Facebook or Twitter), research, and writing. We chat with a collaborative partner who posts a link to a *New York Times* story, which links to an academic study, which in turn includes a graph that we want to drop into our presentation. That process entails several steps, but we move through them without much effort and without thinking about the implications of all of those windows, all of those platforms, open, operating, and drawing from the pool of our attention.

In *Net Smart: How to Thrive Online*, Howard Rheingold describes what he calls **infotention**: "intention added to attention, and mixed with knowledge of information-filtering...a coordinated mind-machine process" (17). Rheingold explores how digital, networked activity strains our attention in unique ways, and we should train our brains to be more focused when we do work online. Cathy Davidson suggests, on her syllabus for "This is Your Brain on The Internet," an interdisciplinary undergraduate course at Duke University, that if the metaphor for the brain in the 20th century was the CPU, then the brain metaphor for the 21st century is the iPhone. Think about it. The iPhone works across multiple platforms and applications, it organizes networks, and it shares data in a variety of different forms. Its strength as a piece of technology is its ability to connect pathways among a variety of different programs and applications.

One of Rheingold's goals in *Net Smart* is to get people thinking about how to exercise control and focus over their attention during online work. Many of us have had the experience of sitting down just for a minute" to Facebook, YouTube, or Tumblr, and discovering two hours later with multiple browser windows opened that we have no idea where the time went. Consider our compulsive reaching for cellphones and our instinctive clicking on hyperlinks in a news story, just to satisfy curiosity or deeper, to fulfill a less explicable psychological "need." In *Alone Together: How We Expect More from Technology and Less from Each Other*, Sherry Turkle studies the psychological complexity of human/computer relationships. She worries about the effect of "always on/always on you" networked devices on our ability to attend to others, to listen, and to empathize.

For Thought and Discussion

Our attention is demanded in our physical and virtual lives. How does a walk across campus focus our attention in ways that online activity does not? Do you think it's important to practice paying attention? Why or why not? How might one go about practicing focused attention?

The iPhone connects different media just like the brain makes connections among different languages, senses, social groups, and activities. However, our brain works differently from a machine in that it can pay attention to only one process at a time when we ask it to complete something complicated. Before we begin an investigation of reading digital media, it behooves us to acknowledge the challenges of that exploration. Does digital consumption and production encourage us, as Nicholas Carr writes in *The Shallows: What The Internet Is Doing To Our Brains*, "to dip in and out of a series of texts rather than devote sustained attention to any one of them," or is the abundance of information beneficial, according to Clay Shirky's *Here Comes Everybody?* Either way, as citizens of the virtual world, investigating the question becomes imperative. Rheingold writes that "[j]ust as the ancient arts of rhetoric taught citizens how to construct and weigh arguments, a mindful rhetoric of digital search would concentrate attention on the process of inquiry—the kinds of questions people turn into initial search queries" (64).

Activity 8.1 • Attention Online

Is paying attention or staying focused while online difficult for you? Take a minute to examine your ability to monitor your attention online by trying some of the exercises below.

Find a friend who will let you study an "hour" of his or her online time. Take notes on where your friend goes, how many browser windows are kept open, and where links lead. Collect the raw "data" on what your friend consumes and produces (status updates, tweets, and emails count as "production"). After you are finished, try organizing the data: Into what categories can you divide the visited sites? Where did your subject spend the most time? Did activity seem linear (progressing along a logical path) or more organic or impulsive? Ask your subject to record the same "data" for you and discuss what you find. What does it teach you?

Research the Pomodoro Technique of time management and the application Focus Booster (www.focusbosterapp.com). Divide your time online into 25-minute segments according to Pomodoro and write realistic goals for what you are going to do during the time period (whether or not for academic purposes). How successful were you at staying on task for three different time segments?

Read John Tierney's article "When the Mind Wanders, Happiness Also Strays" in *The New York Times* (Nov 15, 2010) and Jocelyn K. Glie's post "10 Online Tools for Better Attention and Focus" on the productivity website *99%*. Experiment with some of the tools and compose a response to both texts that is personal to your own experiences online. Do Glie's and Tierney's pieces convince you that time spent wandering online is a problem to solve?

Participation: From Consumer to Producer

When it was new, the Internet generated a lot of excitement about instantaneous access to information. Schools, businesses, non-profit organizations, the government, and any organized group could publish current data about its work. The Internet was supremely useful for checking movie times or city maps; it was generally great for "finding things."

Not long ago, however, the Web became more dynamic. The O'Reilly Media Web 2.0 Conference, started in 2004, introduced the term Web 2.0 into common usage. Web 2.0 distinguishes between prior uses of the Web that were mainly consumptive and the evolving ability of digital citizens to *produce content.*

Plenty of people participated in digital culture before 2005, but after that time the Internet became more participation friendly. Facebook, Wikipedia, and Flickr, among many other programs, signaled a new orientation for digital culture: they encouraged user-generated content. Just think—what is Facebook without the pictures and text that its users contribute? Not much. It simply provides a very attractive and share—able frame that users (and advertisers) are happy to populate with their own content. The shift in digital culture designated Web 2.0 is significant, even if no one really agrees when it officially started (or if it has already ceded to some new model). Think of the stereotypical couch potato watching television for hours; this person illustrates the once passive media consumer. While being online may not appear any more physically active, online activity now can be, and often is, a thoroughly more interactive way to engage with media.

All of this "production" is a new form of publishing; comments on an *Atlanta Journal and Constitution* editorial, posts to a blog, reviews of a book on Amazon, pictures to Picasa, or posting videos to YouTube represent dissemination of texts. If you create a blog post on the Internet, you are a published author. If you publish your YouTube video, you are a published author (most likely linguistic writing accompanies that video, too). And depending on the security settings you set for your work on these platforms (or settings that are set for you), your writing is open to the eyes and minds of anyone in your class, or anyone surfing the Web, including professors and potential employers.

For Thought and Discussion

More than ever we now produce content—we write—in digital spaces like Facebook, Chat, and Instagram. We discussed earlier how the designs of these programs shape the kinds of things we say in them. What kinds of writing happen in these programs (Facebook, Chat, Instagram)? Why? How does the design of each program encourage certain kinds of writing and discourage others? To what extent do these programs and others like them encourage us to behave like consumers or producers of content?

Participation: Considering the Rhetorical Situation

There are many kinds of writing in digital spaces, of course, most of this writing is typical or expected of college writers, and all of it contributes to your reputation—your ethos—as writers and as critical thinkers and students.

Email

Because of their relatively small sizes, composition classes often involve exchanges between students and instructors over email. Professor-student email exchanges happen in other disciplines, too, of course, and the result of the communication can be quite a powerful influence on the perceptions of the writers involved (student/professor). These communications, as they are archived in the email systems of both student and instructor, also create a record. Consider the following fictional, but possible, email exchange:

Jared Thomas

2:04 AM

Subject: hell...p!!!!!!

hey teach. I have been working on this paper for hours and i am stuck. i just don't know what you want. I know its due tomorrow in class but i need help. can i have another day?

***

Prof. A

8:30 AM

Subject: English 1101 (re: hell...p!!!!!)

Dear Jared:

I appreciate your contacting me before the paper is due to request an extension, though seven hours is cutting it close. I'm afraid I will not have time to meet with you before Friday, given my busy schedule. Also I hear in this email that you need more direction for the work to be beneficial to you, so I'm thinking you need more time than one day. Please look at your schedule, consider your resources (beyond me, although I can meet you on Friday from 1:15-1:35), and get back to me with a detailed plan for completing the assignment in the most constructive way.

Best,

Prof. A

For Thought and Discussion

What is the rhetorical situation shaping Jared's initial email? How do you think this email shaped Prof. A's perception of its author? Why? What changes might Jared have made to the email in order to create a stronger ethos in Prof. A's perception?

What about Prof. A's email? What was the rhetorical situation shaping it? What do you think Jared thought about Prof. A after reading her email? Why? What changes might Prof. A have made to the email in order to create a stronger ethos in Jared's perception?

Discussion Boards

An important lesson for the composition class, and any academic experience for that matter, is that participation increases our engagement in learning and connects us to other people in ways that enhance learning. Discussion boards are a common feature of digital education portals (like Blackboard, Web CT, Brightspace, iCollege, etc.), and teachers who use them are encouraging engagement and community. Rather than contributing an answer that is flat, we should approach a forum like we do a conversation—validating or respectfully challenging the opinions of others, making distinctions, and encouraging more questions and response. Consider the following discussion board exchange:

Instructor's Prompt: "How are the lessons of this lab useful?"

> *Melora: I found this lab useful because it helped me answer questions that will be on the test.*

> *Jack: The lab was difficult because I kept getting different results from the tests. Was I doing it wrong?*

> *Ahmad: I had the same experience as Jack, but I think that is part of the conclusion actually. If the results of the various tests are not consistent, doesn't that mean that we should consider outside variables?*

> *Stephanie: I agree with Ahmad: like time of day, how the testing might change after multiple uses, temperature?*

For Thought and Discussion

In this exchange, Melora interacts like a passive consumer. She gives the instructor back the answer that she thinks he is seeking. She offers no elaboration or details substantiating her answer in a way that reflects her specific experience. Although she thinks her instructor wants to hear that the lab was great, how does this shallow response affect her ethos? How do Jack, Ahmad, and Stephanie approach the forum differently than Melora? What is the effect on their ethos?

Once the discussion forum is complete, it is a published record of a conversation; it has some staying power (at least through the end of the semester) and represents your thinking and writing in a semi-private space. How might a discussion forum conversation prove useful to you even after the discussion closes?

Consider the affordances and limitations of the discussion board space. What kinds of ideas are likely to evolve there? Why? What kinds of ideas aren't? Why not?

Activity 8.2 • Paper Discussion Board

At the top of a piece of notebook paper, legibly write your name and a question about digital writing, this class, or this chapter so far.

Fold the paper over to hide only the question, then pass the paper to your left.

When you receive a folded paper, open the fold, read the question, and then pen your name and a response to that question. Return the original fold, hiding the question, and then fold again, so that your response is hidden. Pass the paper to your left.

This time, when you receive the folded paper, open all the folds. Read the question, the response, and then write your own name and response to both the question and the original response. Return the folds, fold to hide your response, and pass along.

Keep passing, reading, and responding either until the question returns to the original author or space runs out on the page.

Essentially, this is a "discussion board" in paper form. When you receive responses to your question, read and analyze them. How did the discussion go? Is it useful to you? Why or why not? How might the participants have created more constructive and valuable responses?

Blog Entries/Comments

The gateway to online publishing, blogs are *public spaces* with potentially far-reaching implications for composition students. Definitions for **blog** differ significantly, reflecting the ever-evolving rhetorical nature of the online writing space. For instance, a quick Google search via Google Chrome for the definition of blog yields this:

blog
/bläg/

noun
noun: **blog**; plural noun: **blogs**

1. a regularly updated website or web page, typically one run by an individual or small group, that is written in an informal or conversational style.

verb
verb: **blog**; 3rd person present: **blogs**; past tense: **blogged**; past participle: **blogged**; gerund or present participle: **blogging**

1. add new material to or regularly update a blog.
   "it's about a week since I last blogged"
   - write about (an event, situation, topic, etc.) in a blog.
     "he blogged the Democratic and Republican national conventions as an independent"

Origin

ENGLISH

weblog ⟶ blog
                  1990s

1990s: shortening of weblog.

Author screenshot taken 04/04/2016.

Notice this definition's focus on style as a defining attribute for a blog. Also note the "regularly update[d]" feature of a blog as a defining attribute. Now consider this definition from Dictionary.com:

blog

CITE

A あ

f

y

g+

[blawg, blog]

Spell   Syllables

Examples   Word Origin

See more synonyms on Thesaurus.com

noun

1. a website containing a writer's or group of writers' own experiences, observations, opinions, etc., and often having images and links to other websites.

2. a single entry or post on such a website:
   She regularly contributes a blog to the magazine's website.

verb (used without object), blogged, blogging.

3. to maintain or add new entries to a blog.

verb (used with object), blogged, blogging.

4. to express or write about on a blog:
   She's been blogging her illness for almost a year.

Origin of blog

                                        1995-2000

Author screenshot taken 04/04/2016.

This definition says nothing explicitly of style but rather focuses on the type of content represented in a blog space. It also suggests that a particular point of view defines the blog genre. Notice, too, the mention of regularity occurs in the example sentence of the second definition; the definition text itself states that a "single entry or post" can be referred to as a blog and says nothing explicitly about the intention of regular posting.

Activity 8.3 • Blog Analysis

Try this as a collaboration with a few of your peers.

First, surf the Web in search of the following:

- A scholarly blog
- A commercial blog
- A business blog
- A personal blog
- A fan culture blog
- A political blog

Be sure to find blogs that are recently active. When you find a blog you think qualifies as one of these genre of blogs, note the URL and the latest blog post on the site.

Now make a spreadsheet that can help you compare the differences and similarities of these blog sites. You'll need to discuss among your group members what characteristics are worth noting. It will look something like this:

Blog type	URL	Feature 1 (i.e. "Style")	Feature 2	Feature 3	Feature 4.

When you've completed the chart, discuss the similarities and differences you're noticing between the sites. Then, based on these examples and your consideration of them, create your own definition for the term blog.

Texting

Texting is writing. Its presence in the composition classroom is ubiquitous and affecting. It is also *opportunity*.

No shortage of recent studies regarding student texting in college classrooms (Google it) reveal what we already know: students text during class, even when it's against class policy, and they feel they should be able to do so without reprimand or consequence. For many of us, it's become a kind of compulsion.

Of course, the consequences for texting during class are natural and obvious. The vast majority of us cannot focus on two things simultaneously; so if we're texting, we're not paying attention to what's going on in class. We're missing it. And so, not physically, but in all meaningful ways, we're absent. This is true when we choose to surf the Internet or check email or do anything in our online spaces disconnected from what's going on in class. (See the *Attention* section of more discussion of technology compulsions.)

In situations of power—in a classroom, say, in which an instructor's responsibility is to determine your preparedness to go on to the next level and assign a grade to reflect that level of preparedness, or at work—the perceptions of your audience (instructor/boss) matter. Composition classes are relatively small; it is quite apparent when a student is texting during class instead of engaging in discussion or activity in the classroom. This appearance can negatively affect the student's ethos with that instructor.

On the other hand, ours is a writing class and texting is writing. It is, perhaps, a subversive kind of writing, a kind of writing that contrasts greatly with the kinds of writing your instructor asks you to practice and engage in. Texting has its own affordances, constraints, and expectations, and each conversation generates its own rhetorical situation. Have you ever had a texting conversation go bad? What happened? Was there miscommunication involved? Would the conversation have been better handled via a different medium? Would the conversation have gone differently if you'd engaged in it at a different time or in a different physical space?

For Thought and Discussion

What do you think about texting in certain situations: in the classroom, at the dinner table, during a phone conversation with someone? Is there an etiquette one should follow when it comes to texting? Has that etiquette evolved? If so, how? Is it continuing to evolve? If your job were to set some social rules around texting what rules would you establish and why? What do you think about the enforceability of those rules? How do you think composition instructors might begin to use chat constructively in the teaching of writing? Or is that a bad idea? If so, why?

Audience

In the authoring of a successful composition—one that inspires its readers to feel, believe, and act—considering audience is of prime importance. Maybe not at first, when you're working out an idea through early drafting. But later, when you feel confident about what you want to say, in order to make clear decisions about how to craft your message, it's imperative to consider audience. To whom do you write this...letter, email, song, poem, blog post, article, essay, chat message? Why? What is it you want the writing to accomplish in the world? To whom do you need to address this work in order to accomplish it?

In school the answer to the question of audience might seem easy. To whom do you write the essay? To your instructor, of course. Why? In order to pass the class, or get an "A." The early chapters of this book speak often of crafting messages to particular audiences, particularly instructors. Often it's useful to think of the writing's potential beyond the classroom, to imagine an audience and a purpose beyond the classroom. In this sense, classroom writing becomes a workshop space for "real world" writing.

Of course the composition classroom is a real world space, with it's own audience, purpose, and kairotic moment. But it's also a cyberspace. Writing in online spaces means writing for potential audiences beyond the instructor in no imaginary sense. When you publish a blog post, anyone might happen upon that blog post. That reader will likely form an idea about you and your work upon reading that blog post, or skimming it. That reader has a certain power, the power to listen to you (read your work) or not, the power to pay you some *attention*, etc. Crafting your writing to encourage readership is an important aspect of writing successfully online. In order to make important decisions about how to craft for readership, it helps to decide what kind of audience you're hoping to reach and what that audience is like.

For Thought or Discussion

An artist often has to work hard to find her audience, even to the point of relocation. How does the Internet affect how a composition can find an audience?

Ideally, we as writers develop a heightened awareness of the rhetorical situation of any text we compose. Emails, tweets, text messages, blog posts, midterm exam question responses... Each one of these situations involves a consideration of audience. We have to consider other factors as well. If the barrier to obtaining texts is dissolving and readers have more access to them, the new barrier that takes its place is *attention*. Every person who regularly spends time online knows that there are exponentially more free texts readily available and interesting enough to read than she will ever be able to read. It takes crafting to produce digital compositions able to compete with ubiquitous other online experiences in order to procure and maintain a readership.

Audience: Medium

Medium: "an instrument by which something is conveyed"

Plural, media

Most of the time our instructors will dictate to us which medium we must use to communicate our message. "The assignment," they say, "is to write an essay... It must be a Word document using 12 pt font...,: etc." Word processing documents are media. Video, podcast, Prezi, PowerPoint, website, blog post... These are all media. And though currently your instructors are likely to have arisen in a system that still privileges "papers," and thus the media of the word processor, more and more instruction is happening in digital spaces and final products are slowly beginning to reflect our multi-media age. During the course of your academic career you will likely be asked to produce a multimedia presentation. Here are some tips for approaching this task:

1. When given the option to choose which medium to use in the conveyance of your ideas, consider your audience: What kind of technology is likely to appeal to them? Why? What media are they used to? Comfortable with? Expecting?

2. When choosing a medium consider your message: What technology is likely to *enhance* your message? Why? What technology might detract from your message? Why? (Think about the affordances and constraints of the medium.)

3. When you've chosen your medium, go online and briefly search for tutorials on how to use the technology of the medium (even Word documents!); you'll likely learn how to use the technology in ways you'd never known before, augmenting your digital literacy and expanding the possibilities of your creativity and your ideas as they are formed by the medium itself

4. When you've chosen your medium, begin composing _within the medium_ instead of writing in a Word document and cutting and pasting into your other medium. It is easy to tell when someone has cut and pasted into a PowerPoint slide, for instance, as the slide is usually packed with words, a whole paragraph or two of words that are difficult to read from the distance of an audience. In fact likely no one will read the words, leaving the audience wondering what the purpose of the slide is in the first place. Compose in the medium, a medium chosen with audience in mind, and you'll likely come closer to designing a successful composition.

Activity 8.4 • Argument in Slides

Part I:

Choose a topic that interests you. Then go to Microsoft Office 365's "PowerPoint" option and choose a theme you think would best communicate a message about that topic to your classmates. Without writing down anything first, begin composing an argument within the slides themselves.

Once you've completed your argument-in-slides, discuss what the writing process was like. Was it different? Harder? How did the design of the slides shape your argument? Did it? What medium might have been better suited to your message? Your argument? Why?

Part II:

Go online and search for free PowerPoint templates. What do you find? What do you like? Why? How does the marketing of online templates and tutorials affect your position as a consumer/producer in terms of writing in digital spaces?

Multimodality: Audience and Writer

In 1996, a group of scholars, "The New London Group," convened to discuss the implications of new media, globalization, and diversity on contemporary literacy teaching and practice (http://www.newliteracies.com.au). The result was a significant shift in the way we think about communication and writing, one that situates the composing of words in the context of all the other ways people compose to communicate.

Think about it. The last time you browsed a website, to what were you immediately drawn? The words? The images? The soundtrack? Most likely your first response wasn't, "The words...in fact I read every word on the digital page! I didn't even notice the images." Our current reality is one in which readers' eyes or ears browse digital pages, and sometimes paper ones. Perhaps they're more likely to read words on pages more completely, but digital pages promote the habit of skimming. We skim for information we want or need; there is simply too much "out there" to invest our attention in slowly consuming the entirety of one web page experience...unless, perhaps, you're a writing instructor, or unless the writing on the page is so compelling one can't tear away from it, or the writing is information that we very much need. And by "writing" we mean... what exactly?

The New London Group's work emphasized the varied ways people communicate. We don't just write letters, of course, we use gestures to communicate. We use sounds and space and images to communicate (see the "Writing about Visual Images" chapter). And each of these "modes" of communication...

- Visual
- Gestural
- Audio
- Linguistic
- Spatial

...brings with it unique elements for meaning-making and communication.

This is always the case. An essay composed in a word processing program and printed on white paper communicates not only via the linguistic mode—the words written on the page—but also through the spatial mode. Have you ever written a three-page essay that is only one paragraph long? Why not? A paragraph is a unit of meaning created via space (sometimes indentation, sometimes a line of space before and after). If you stand back from your paper and look at it from across the room, you'll see the paper is a visual phenomenon as well. It has a "look," a look that, likely, adheres to certain genre conventions of a university paper. Have you ever adjusted the margins of a Word document so that your words get squeezed through a narrower tunnel of text in order to meet page requirements for an assignment? (If so, you're using the affordances of the medium to produce a desired effect. Good for you, kind of.) The vast majority of writing instructors can immediately spot this trick. And what does it communicate, visually, this added space to the margins of a course paper? How does it affect the author's ethos?

Writing in digital spaces privileges the visual and the spatial over the linguistic, although written words take on a different and important focus in these spaces. Writing in a Word document and cutting/pasting that work into a blog post, for instance, just doesn't work. What audience wants to read big blocks of text online? Few people do. So one of the big shifts when it comes to writing in digital spaces is thinking about what the visual images and spaces, what the sounds and motions of a digital space *communicate*. How does an image enhance a message? Detract from it? Or a sound, or a motion, or a space? These are the kinds of questions we must begin to ask as composers and designers in digital spaces. We must grow our awareness of the multimodal nature of communication.

There is a social justice aspect of the New London Group's concept of multiliteracies as well. Some of us learn and communicate with greater facility in images or sounds than we do in linguistic writing. Does that make our messages somehow lesser? Is a thesis, for instance, less interesting or important or potentially true if it's spoken out loud than it is if it's written down in words? Is an idea less valuable if it's expressed gesturally, via sign language, than if it's written down in words? The New London Group's contextualizing of linguistic writing creates the potential for greater access to messages best communicated through sound, images, gestures, spaces, and combinations of these, depending on the preferences and abilities of composers, and the preferences, abilities, and expectations of their audiences.

Essentially what this means is that becoming more effective writers, particularly in digital spaces, requires broadening our perceptions of what writing is beyond the written word. Writing involves images, sounds, spaces, gestures, *and* words, together. And in digital spaces, the linguistic must be situated in the context of all these other modes of communication. So the power we have as writers in digital spaces rests heavily on the knowledge we have of the affordances and constraints of the medium we're using, and in our abilities to manipulate technological tools towards crafting messages in multimodal ways.

For Thought and Discussion

Can you recall a time when a message was communicated to you gesturally, or via sound, without words? What was the message? Was it clear?

How does the New London Group's notion of the multimodality of communication and the dethroning of the written word change the way you think about writing? Do you think it's useful or not in terms of writing for school? Why?

Activity 8.5 • Multimodal Communication

Part I:

Take a thesis from an old paper and communicate it using, primarily, a different mode of communication. For instance, perhaps you wrote a paper critiquing how texting while driving issues manifest in local laws. Create an infographic promoting your thesis. Remember: an infographic requires a privileging of the visual and spatial over the written word.

When you're finished, share your work with your colleagues. Can they discern your argument? Why or why not? What was challenging about this activity? What was surprisingly easy, if anything?

Part II:

Find an image or song that you really feel strongly about, then translate that image or song into an essay. If the song were an essay, what would that essay say? ***Important: do not write *about* the image or song. Instead, put yourself in the place of the artist; use the artist's voice. Alternatively you might translate a song into an image or an image into a song. Do you think this would be easier than translating into a written essay? Why or why not?

Digital Literacies: A Lifetime of Learning

Exploring the notions of *attention, participation, audience,* and *multimodality* within a digital writing context helps us begin to address the gap that many of us perceive between writing for school and writing in other professional and personal contexts. This gap might seem large, but it isn't. All writing—no matter the medium—if it is to be successful must be crafted consciously with rhetorical situations in mind. It must consider audience and modality. It must make choices in light of the attention and participation of its authors and audiences. In a world where increasingly our attention is siphoned at every turn by flashy graphics, soundtracks, and instantaneous communications, we writers, if we are to earn the attention of any reader, particularly the attention of our instructors, must learn to craft our work so that our important messages get heard.

This chapter has argued that gaining fluency with the use of digital technologies is an essential part of our development as critical thinkers, writers, and composers. Trends toward the digitization of communication speed forward in professional and personal spheres. Given our cyber realities, and how quickly the technology shaping these realities changes, it can feel daunting to think about educating ourselves in the languages of digital literacies. Should I learn Photoshop, a leading image editing software? Or Audacity, sound editing software? Or Dreamweaver, website building software? Or graphic design in general? Or advanced uses of Prezi or PowerPoint or...? Learning how to use digital writing tools takes time and, often, money. It also takes a commitment on the part of the writer to a lifetime of learning, for as soon as you think you know how to use a tool, it changes, or another "better" tool emerges. In the current of rapid change, valuing process, and the knowledge and experience that comes from the learning itself, can offer us precious insights into how others craft the messages around us, manipulating our emotions, beliefs, and choices. We do not need to be experts in the use of any particular digital writing tool to gain great benefits from exploring it; informing our awareness of the tools being used to craft messages in and of itself advantages us in uncountable ways, as writers and as citizens.

For Thought and Discussion

What does it mean to be an expert writer in our digital world? Are expert writers necessary in our culture? Why or why not?

What kinds of writing would you like to know more about: composing websites, infographics, presentations, blogs, comics, songs, videos, films? What tools are currently available for composing and editing messages in these media?

For Further Reading

For more on digital media and on the production of digital texts in the Web 2.0 environment, take a look at these sources:

The Agenda with Steve Paikin: *The Myth of Digital Literacy* (video)

John Brockman: *Is the Internet Changing the Way You Think?* (book)

Collin Brooke: *Lingua Fracta* (book)

Nicholas Carr: *The Shallows: What the Internet Is Doing To Our Brains* (book)

Tyler Cowan: "Three Tweets for the Web" (article)

Cathy Davidson: *Now You See It* (book)

David Eagleman: *Six Easy Steps to Avert the Collapse of Civilization* (video lecture)

Howard Rheingold: *Net Smart: How To Thrive Online* (book)

Clay Shirky: *Here Comes Everybody* (book)

Sherry Turkle: *Alone Together* (book)

Student Work

To find out more about producing digital texts, please visit www.guidetowriting.gsu.edu. Click first on "Community" and then "Companion Digital Projects. Here, you will find student examples of digital composition. Produce your own digital creations and share the links with the webmaster. She will add your work to our website to expand your audience.

Smittick, Toniah. *Dusk.*

Chapter 9

Civic Engagement and Community-Based Writing

At Georgia State University, writing assignments aim to develop your critical thinking, reading, and writing skills, and reflect a broader role for writing as responsible, purposeful social action.

The goal of a GSU education is broader and more encompassing than just getting a degree or getting a job: it should help you to become an informed, engaged citizen of your world and your community. In first-year composition classes, that engagement will often begin with community-based writing. *Community* can be loosely defined as a group of people who live, work, or study in close proximity to each other and/or who have shared values or interests. Your community could include your neighbors, people who play pickup basketball at the same park as you, people in your place of worship, or people who believe in a particular social cause. As you can see, you have many different communities in your life, and some of those communities will overlap. For example, one person you know may be a member of both your social and school communities; another may live in the same geographic area but not be part of your particular social community.

Georgia State recognizes the importance of community and strives to advance "the socioeconomic and cultural climate, education, health care services and other resources available throughout the city, as well as in communities across Georgia and beyond" (http://www.gsu.edu/about/). Some GSU English instructors adopt *community-based writing* to help meet this goal by linking writing assignments with service that benefits a community. In these classes, you might work in a particular community or in service to community members as part of your course requirements. The various types of service you undertake can help you develop specific writing skills and/or make progress toward certain course objectives. Some community-based writing activities focus on the person or people being served (i.e. the community), while others might address the person providing the service (i.e. you, the student).

The primary goal in academic community-based writing projects is to come as close to complete reciprocity—an equal balance between the service and the served—as possible.

You may have already participated in some form of community service or volunteerism. *Volunteerism* is when one gives time, energy, or skill to benefit a specific cause or organization, without being compensated. The emphasis of volunteerism is on the entity being served, that is, the community that receives most of the benefit (Deans 2000). While you might volunteer for community service or charity work through a campus or community organization, it is uncommon for volunteerism to be part of course requirements.

On the other end of the spectrum is *internship*—also known as apprenticeships, work-study, and co-operative education programs—where you take a position with an organization in order to obtain on-the-job experience in your desired field. While your work as an intern will provide value to the organization with which you are interning, the ultimate goal is for you as a student to gain work experience.

Community-Based Writing

Between these two bookends (volunteerism and internships) exists a range of meaningful ways to engage with a community, some of which might be a part of your first-year writing class at GSU. Service activities may involve writing within the community, or community activities may serve as the subject for in-class writing activities. For example, you may be assigned a community-based research project which requires you to conduct interviews in your community or research local history in order to write a paper. One specific type of community-based research where researchers study and record information related to human culture is called *ethnography* (see below).

First-year writing courses may also employ community-based writing to address community literacy, civic literacy, and public literacy. *Community literacy* relates to reading and writing skills (in a general sense) as they develop outside of educational institutions. Work done in the area of community literacy might include efforts to understand and overcome obstacles in the reading, writing, and comprehension capabilities of a particular population, mentoring a particular community in an effort to improve literacy, or raising awareness of illiteracy within a particular community.

Civic literacy is best defined as knowledge surrounding the civil affairs (politics, policy, and governance) of a community. The community could be very small, as in a local school board, or it could be very large, as in the United Nations or the United States Congress. Community-based writing surrounding the area of civic literacy might involve letters to the editor of a newspaper or to a politician supporting or opposing a particular issue. You might write newsletters, pamphlets, or flyers for community distribution in order to, for instance, raise awareness about a candidate, issue, or pending piece of legislation. Or you might write an essay or research paper on how an issue impacts a particular community.

Public literacy "designates written language, including written language that is read aloud, that appears in a public sphere and deals with issues of concern to a group of people. Bumper stickers, newspapers, tax forms, and petitions are all examples of public literacy" (Ervin 1). If your instructor chooses to embrace public literacy in your composition class, you might be asked to write in an effort to address public issues.

Community literacy, civic literacy, and public literacy are sometimes lumped together under the heading "civic engagement." Ultimately, *civic engagement* involves meaningful interaction with the community and focuses on social or political issues. Working to improve the quality of life in your community, becoming involved in community events, or making others aware of community issues all fall under the umbrella of civic engagement. If you take a class that incorporates civic engagement, you might be required to serve at community or cultural events or for community organizations. You might be asked to write reflections about your experience, do research to support an organization or cause, or produce writing that would be useful to the community with which you interact. Unless your instructor specifies the type of engagement she or he has in mind, you may approach your project in any of these ways.

Some community-based writing activities involve *advocacy* for a particular cause, issue, political candidate, or proposed change. If you are required to write to promote social or political change, thereby calling on individuals or entities to act, your writing could be linked to activism, defined as "behavior designed to increase individual and collective human dignity, value, and quality of life" (Fleckenstein). Terms like "social justice" or "community action" also describe some kinds of advocacy.

When thinking about ways to engage in the community, assess your views of community, your skills and talents, your personal goals and values, and how you perceive your own role within the community. Consider the following ideas that can cause tension or "push and pull at each other" as you decide where you fit into the picture:

Engaged citizen	←———→ *	Solitary self
Community as nurturing	←———→ *	Community as constraining
Common good	←———→ *	Individual freedom
Shared goals	←———→ *	Personal opportunities
Responsibilities	←———→ *	Rights
Shared norms and values	←———→ *	Self-expressions and individualism
Common life	←———→ *	Privacy
Consensus	←———→ *	Dissent

Kirp's continuum, *Community Tensions, Writing and Community Action* (Deans, 2003). p 99.

Writing skills correlate in many ways with community activity or engagement. Thomas Deans, professor of English and author of *Writing and Community Action* (2003), identifies three paradigms for *community-based writing*: "writing *for* the community, writing *with* the community, and writing *about* the community." The chart below helps illustrate the distinctions between the three:

	Writing *for* the Community	Writing *about* the Community	Writing *with* the Community
Primary Site for Learning	Nonprofit Agency	Classroom	Community Center
Privileged Literacies	Academic and Workplace Literacies	Academic and Critical Literacies	Academic, community, and hybrid literacies
Most Highly Valued Discourse	Workplace discourse	Academic discourse	Hybrid discourse
Primary Learning Relationship	Student-agency contact (instructor as facilitator)	Student-Instructor (service as facilitator)	Student-community member (instructor as facilitator)
Institutional Relationship	Instructor-agency contact person	Instructor-community site contact	Instructor/department-community center
Goals	(1) Students learn nonacademic writing practices and reflect on differences between academic and workplace rhetorics. (2) Students reflect on service experience to attain critical awareness of community needs. (3) Students provide needed writing products for agencies.	(1) Students serve at schools or community sites and reflect on their experiences. (2) Students develop critical consciousness and habits of intellectual inquiry and societal critique. (3) Students write journals and compose academic-style essays on community issues and/or pressing social concerns.	(1) Students, faculty, and community use writing as a part of a social action effort to collaboratively identify and address local problems. (2) Students and community members negotiate cultural differences and forge shared discourses. (3) University and community share inquiry and research.

Assessment	Can the students move ably between academic and workplace discourses?	Have students provided adequate service to the community site?	Have local and academic community members engaged in collaborative writing or research?
	Have students critically reflected on the writing and service processes? Did students produce documents that will be of real use to the agencies?	How sophisticated a critique of social concerns can students demonstrate in academic discussion and writing? Has student academic writing improved?	Can students reflect critically on issues such as cultural difference? Has the local problem been effectively solved, addressed, or researched?

Figure 1. "Three Paradigms for Community Writing." From *Writing Partnerships: Service-Learning in Composition* (p. 17). NCTE, 2000.

What Does Community-Based Writing Look Like?

As noted above, there are many different approaches to community- based writing. The following are some examples of what community writing might look like if assigned in particular departments or disciplines.

Discipline-specific projects

Botany	During a visit to Arabian Mountain, students in a biology class photograph many kinds of wild plants that grow there. They do research and create a seasonal guide that will be printed by the mountain's nature center, so visitors know what kinds of plants to look for in which seasons and can learn their characteristics.
Political Science	Class members create an awareness-raising campaign reminding fellow university students to register to vote in Atlanta or to obtain absentee ballots for their home districts. Students write an article for the school newspaper, design flyers, and create a public service announcement to be aired on WRAS campus radio.
History	Students interview members of Atlanta's Veterans of Foreign Wars organization about their experiences returning to Atlanta after serving abroad. Students compile interviews into a booklet of stories, which is printed by the university print shops and distributed free to VFW members and placed in libraries around the state.
Spanish	Service-learners team up with a local nonprofit serving families impacted by domestic violence. Students translate documents, directories, forms, training manuals, and pamphlets from English into Spanish to serve the growing population of Spanish speaking clients and staff-members of the nonprofit.
Art	Art students apply for permission to create a mural on a disused bridge support, and write an application for a grant to cover the cost of materials. Then they work with a group of elementary school students to design and paint the mural. Students create leaflets and public notices to advertise the new public art and bring pride to the community.

Ethnography

Atlanta is a city rich in history and cultural diversity, leading many GSU instructors to create writing assignments that have an ethnographic research component to encourage involvement with our state capital and GSU's home. If you are assigned an ethnographic project, you might choose to research one of the many influential figures in the community: for example, Congressman John C. Lewis, who was engaged in the Civil Rights Movement of the 1960s; Alveda King, Martin Luther King, Jr.'s daughter, noted pro-life activist; Russell Simmons, hip hop mogul; or Don Cathy, CEO of Chick-fil-A. Each of these people provide a rich foundation for an academic paper, but the person you choose to study doesn't need to be such a high-profile individual, particularly if you're hoping to gain access to him/her for an interview. Regardless of whom you choose, if you investigate your community through the eyes of a researcher, you will have little trouble finding people with interesting stories and claims to the history and/or community of Atlanta.

Another option is to research local history: the Margaret Mitchell house; the structures that comprise the Atlanta History Center in Buckhead; the campus of Morehouse College; the city of Decatur (a prominent site for General Sherman to wage his campaign on Atlanta during the American Civil War); or any structure or plot of land that is considered significant to Atlanta history or the history of a smaller community. If you choose to research local history, you will want to visit the site to gather pictures, personal observations, and other information that might not be as accessible in books or on the Internet.

Ebenezer Baptist Church is located on Auburn Avenue in downtown Atlanta. Because this is the church where Dr. King preached his message of nonviolence throughout the Civil Rights Movement, Ebenezer is now a Martin Luther King, Jr. National Historical Site.

Alternatively, you might choose to focus on a particular cultural group or practice in Atlanta in order to increase intercultural awareness and communication. Selecting a group to which you already belong may appeal to you more than working with a group where you are only an interested outsider. Consider researching refugee families at the Clarkston Community Center; Islamic Mosques in metro-Atlanta; the Atlanta Greek Festival and Greek Orthodox Church; the gay, lesbian, transgendered, and queer Pride Festival at Piedmont Park; or the annual sci-fi festival Dragon*Con. The Georgia State library also houses a nationally-recognized archive of Southern labor documents and materials. In each of these cases, the purpose of your study is to better understand a culture or cultural practice and share what you've come to know about that culture or practice through writing.

Ethnographies typically involve a great deal of research, so be prepared to investigate library resources, historical journals and databases, as well as best practices in conducting interviews. The Atlanta area is also rich in archives that make ethnographic studies particularly inviting.

Tips for Interviewing for Research

- Keep all communication professional. Be sure to use proper grammar and spelling in all written correspondence (emails, letters).

- Be aware of the interviewee's schedule. Make an appointment, arrive on time for the interview, and conclude the interview at the agreed upon time.

- Dress appropriately for the interview. If in doubt, dress more professionally/formally.

- Arrive with a list of questions, but don't be surprised if the conversation leads you down a different path.

- Make sure your most critical questions are answered.

- Ask permission to contact the interviewee for follow-up questions or for clarification as you write up the interview.

- Ask open-ended questions (questions that can't be answered with a simple *yes* or *no*).

- Take notes during the interview. If you plan to record the interview with video or audio, be sure you get permission first.

- After the interview, send a thank you note.

- Share your article or essay with the interviewee (if appropriate) prior to submitting it, in case she or he wants to correct any misunderstandings or misrepresentations.

- Ask your professor about interviewing anyone who might have reduced ability to make decisions about what to tell you, or feel pressured to cooperate with your interview. For example, children under 18, prisoners, residents of medical or personal care facilities, adults with developmental or cognitive differences, or anyone whose answers could put her or someone else in danger (refugees, homeless people, women in shelters, etc).

Service Learning

Assignments for community-based and civic engagement writing might ask you to use your experiences as the basis for writing, including reflective writing, expository writing, and research essays. While community work can serve as a great basis for writing papers, there is another type of community-based writing that focuses on reciprocity between student-writer and community group. This writing is part of a broad field of study activities called service learning.

Service Learning is an educational approach that links academic objectives with course-related service in a way that benefits both the community and the student. Essentially, it is service with an academic purpose. When you take a class with a service learning component, you will apply specific course objectives to service. For example, you may learn about writing formal or business letters, then be assigned to write a letter on behalf of a non-profit organization requesting support or donations.

Service learning courses might also encourage you to work directly with a group in your community to produce documents that serve that group or organization's purposes. Instructors might ask for a "deliverable" piece of writing that fulfills two criteria: 1) satisfies a course writing assignment, and 2) serves an existing and ongoing need in the community. The goal here is *reciprocity*. Some examples of service learning deliverables might be instruction manuals or policy/procedure manuals, public relations/marketing literature, flyers, brochures, web content, newsletters, or communication templates.

Other types of service learning activities for English classes include service in the community that is specific to reading and writing. Working with reluctant readers in an elementary school, tutoring middle and high school students on

essay writing, holding a resume-writing workshop for unemployed adults in the public library, or coordinating a book drive for a low-income neighborhood are all forms of service learning that work toward increased literacy in the community.

Service learning isn't specific to English classes, however. You can participate in service learning in virtually any course imaginable. University students in theater and women's studies programs all over the country have worked together to put on productions of the play *The Vagina Monologues* to raise awareness of violence against women as well as funds that benefit victim's advocate groups. Students in music appreciation classes have partnered with music therapy programs at a community hospital. Local Atlanta students in a geology class have recently worked to compile a database of the historic stone carvings located all over Stone Mountain. This "carving database" is now available online and has contributed to the historical and geological scholarship of the landmark.

Sometimes service learning projects—like those named above—involve class-wide assignments your instructor selected before the start of the semester. Other times, you will be given a requirement to complete a service learning project and asked to choose a topic and then find a community partner on your own. Don't feel anxious about this request. It can be challenging, but it can also be quite an adventure. Take advantage of the resources available here at GSU and on the Internet to help you identify a potential partner. A quick Google search of the terms "service learning" and your course ("physical education," for example) will yield results that show what other students have researched. You don't have to reinvent the wheel; if someone else has completed a service learning project on another campus, in another community, and was successful, why not try to replicate it here in the Atlanta-GSU community?

Finally, your instructor will be a great resource for you, so schedule some time for the two of you to brainstorm together on project ideas. The success of your project will depend, in large part, on the quality of communication you have with your instructor and your community partner along the way.

Activism

While some assignments require you to research a project and report your findings, you might also be asked to write to make a change. If you are assigned an activist project, you will work to make a change that improves life for an individual, a group, or the community as a whole.

While it may seem overwhelming to think of engaging in activism in a college class, you don't have to try to solve all the world's problems in a single semester. You could start by merely working to increase awareness about one specific issue. Or you might work to implement a change in policy that will help a particular population within the larger community. Whatever you decide to do, remember that your activist work could motivate someone else to work for change, and, in turn, their work could motivate someone else. This impact is called the "snowball effect" because what you started as a small class project keeps growing and growing and, just like a snowball, it increases in mass as it rolls down a snow-covered hill.

Before starting any activism assignment, first consider which specific causes you care the most about. Are there some areas on campus where you see room for improvement? What issues in the community concern you? Can you target a group who would benefit from changes in policies or conditions? Look around you, find something that you feel passionate about and for which you are willing to work.

Once you have chosen a cause, determine what you can do to influence the situation. You might decide to work on increasing awareness of the problem by creating posters to put up around campus. Or you might want to write letters to implore the drafting of legislation or to voice support for a law or policy that would benefit your cause. No matter what you decide, make sure you are realistic about what you can do in the time you have, especially if it is a class project that is limited to a single semester. And don't think that your project is

vyi, Man. *Giant Snowball Oxford.*

too small. You can't help every homeless person in Atlanta, but you might be able to increase awareness of the challenges that homeless people face, and as more people become aware of those challenges, they may offer help.

Whatever you decide to do, Georgia State University is a very supportive environment for activist work. GSU has many organizations that you can collaborate with when undertaking an activist project. For example, GSU Bikes is an organization that works to make the campus more bicycle-friendly in order to encourage more people to ride bikes to school, thereby reducing emissions and helping the environment. GSU's Nutrition Student Network works to increase nutrition awareness and promote healthy eating habits both on campus and off. And the Sustainable Energy Tribe at Georgia State addresses issues around sustainability and works to teach students and faculty about environmental issues.

If you want to go outside of the college campus, Atlanta offers plenty of opportunities for activist work. The Atlanta Community Food Bank helps fight hunger in the Atlanta area by distributing food to local non-profit agencies. Pets for Vets is a local organization that matches military veterans with shelter pets, giving the veterans a companion and giving the once-abandoned pet a second chance. Chastity House in Atlanta serves teens who suffer from sexual abuse, sex trafficking, and sexual exploitation. The possibilities are numerous.

Conversely, you may decide to work on an activism project without being tied directly to an organization. If a cause or issue interests you, then perform your own activist work. For example, you might notice that there are limited recycling bins on campus, and you may decide to write letters to the municipal waste service companies requesting more bins on campus to increase recycling activity. Or you might see that many students don't use the recycling bins and instead toss their plastic water bottles in the trash; you could create signs to post around campus to help students realize the availability of recycling on campus.

For any of the above causes, you could complete several different composition assignments for class. Assignment possibilities include writing letters asking for donations, making flyers to improve awareness, conducting research and using that research to write argumentative essays for a particular organization, or even creating a proposal for a fundraiser. Regardless of the assignment, the overall goal is the same: to work for a positive change while improving your writing skills with assignments that are specific and enjoyable.

Digital Civic Engagement

While it's exciting to be off-campus and in community spaces, you don't have to "go" anywhere in order to be actively involved with a broader, off-campus community. With the advent of Web 2.0, an increasing amount of civic discourse and community engagement is conducted online.

Many of you already actively engage in online communities—*Pinterest*, *Facebook*, *Twitter*, blogs, etc. You are most likely using social media, usually in the form of social networking sites, which you likely use for the purposes of communicating with friends and family or strangers with shared interests, such as football teams or community events. One of the distinctions between Web 2.0 and the previous Internet technology is the participatory or "social" nature of this newer media. Instead of users simply downloading or receiving information from the Internet, we now share and exchange information using the Internet as a medium for interaction.

Thanks to the social, participatory nature of Web 2.0, users can choose a wide variety of ways to engage with each other and myriad purposes for this engagement. Much like gathering in the library plaza on campus, students can choose to use the public space to socialize about weekend plans, share pictures of friends and family back home, or talk about a proposed increase in tuition across the University System of Georgia. You can continue to discuss these kinds of issues in the plaza daily or weekly, ultimately deciding to take some sort of action on the proposed tuition increase. You might create informational flyers and distribute them to others gathering in the plaza. You might make posters and recruit other concerned students to march together down to the State Capitol building and hold signs on the steps proclaiming your opposition to the proposed increases.

The same types of activities occur in the digital world. You have equivalent social interactions with your peers online through various social media, and you can choose to use that forum for social, community, or political purposes. The Internet provides a variety of public spaces specifically devoted to certain types of discourse (*Pinterest* for the crafty, DIYers, *sportlobster* for the sports enthusiasts, *volkalize* for the political debaters, *LinkedIn* for professionals) and more general public forums for crossover discourse (*Facebook, Twitter, Wordpress, Blogger, YouTube*).

The key to civic engagement through new media is to first join the conversation and observe. You need to have a fairly good understanding of the tool you are using to engage, and then you need to learn exactly how users interested in that cause or issue are already interacting with one another. Are users announcing and promoting in-person events, or are they using the media to inform and increase awareness? Do certain kinds of messages get more responses or shares? Just like in-person communities, see what you can learn about how a community works before you get involved.

Georgia State University Resources

GSU Office of Civic Engagement - service.gsu.edu

Devoted to helping students at GSU find service projects to work with here in Atlanta, this office is a good place to start if you want to get involved with our community but aren't sure how to begin. 428/429 University Center. 404.413.1550

GSU Student Organizations - gsu.orgsync.com

This website is home to the many student organizations at GSU involved with community service inside and outside the university. Search for "service" to see numerous opportunities to get involved. 330 Student Center. 404.413.1580

**Service-Learning in the GSU College of Education -
http://education.gsu.edu/outreach**

Thinking of a career in an education-related field? Get involved in one of the on-going service projects in the GSU College of Education.

Community Engagement in the GSU College of Arts and Sciences - www.cas.gsu.edu/community

No matter what your major (from biology to music), the College of Arts and Sciences has opportunities to get involved in the Atlanta community and learn more about your chosen field.

Internet Resources

Campus Compact - campuscompact.org/resources-for-students

This organization is a coalition of more than a thousand colleges and universities all committed to campus-based civic engagement activities. The website offers a variety of resources to help students get actively involved in their communities.

Corporation for National and Community Service - nationalservice.gov

CNCS is a federal agency that exists to coordinate service opportunities with citizens who wish to put their time and talent to service.

National Service-Learning Clearinghouse - servicelearning.org

Start here for an explanation of what service-learning is (and what it is not), and then explore the rest of the site for ideas for service-learning projects, articles about the theory behind service-learning, and service-learning success stories.

VolunteerMatch.com and NobleHour.com

These sites match students with community organizations that have a specific need.

Major Issues and Ethical Concerns

Consider special ethical and safety questions as you prepare to undertake a service learning or public writing project. These include, but are not limited to, protecting the autonomy and safety of the community members with whom you work, navigating organizational background checks, protecting your safety while traveling to and serving in community sites, learning professional behavior and protocols, staying true to your personal convictions, and considering legal liabilities.

Remember that quality service learning and public writing projects are contingent on reciprocity. Your project should be an opportunity for all involved to learn from each other: beware the idea of a 'fortunate' group bestowing service on a 'less fortunate' group. These misperceptions of privilege and advantage can undermine the benefits of service and sour community relationships.

If the project you wish to undertake involves research with community partners, you may be asked to submit a proposal to the Institutional Review Board at Georgia State. This independent group of scholars and administrators is charged with protecting the welfare of research subjects. To have your project approved, you will have to verify that your research will not harm any human subjects, that you can protect the confidentiality of any data collected, that all qualified participants will have an equal opportunity to be involved, and that subjects may withdraw at any time without penalty. Your instructor will be able to help you determine whether or not you need IRB approval, and will assist you with the process of obtaining approval.

Some organizations you wish to work with may require background checks or extended training. If you are working with a protected class of people, such as children, prisoners, or persons with disabilities, you may be required to submit to a background check. This check may include questions about places you have previously lived or worked and fingerprinting to verify your identity. You should feel free to ask a community organization about their background check procedures, how long they will take, and who will be responsible for any costs. Consider this information in your project timeline and budget.

Be sure you understand the safety procedures and organizational protocols for working on-site, and ask questions if you are unsure what is expected of you. Only go to the service-learning site when you are expected by the organization and when your instructor knows where you will be. Wear appropriate shoes and clothing, do not provide or accept personal information from the community members you work with, and be cautious when travelling to and from service sites. Take precautions to protect your personal property, including a vehicle, from theft or damage when working in unfamiliar parts of the city. If you have special safety concerns, communicate them to your instructor or organizing faculty member as soon as possible. An instructor may also require you to provide emergency contact information, in case you are ill or injured while working off campus.

Be sure you understand the liabilities, legal and ethical, associated with your project. Do not assume that the instructor, organization, or university will be able to protect you legally or financially. Ask questions and communicate openly about insurance, safety, behavior, policies, best practices, and if necessary, alternative placements or opportunities.

Things to Remember...

When Taking Classes that Include Community-Based Writing

- Course objectives do not change in classes that use community action; you will be required to complete some type of community action, but you will still be evaluated on meeting course objectives, including strengthening your writing and thinking skills.

- While community service classes do generally require work outside of the classroom, they are not designed to require more hours than the same course without a community service component.

- Your instructor is your point of contact if you have questions or concerns about the community service project.

- Community service classes can provide you with opportunities to explore different careers, cultures, and situations. With an open mind, you might find that a class with a community-based component gives you more than just course credit; it can give you the chance to make a difference in your community or in someone's life, along with a better understanding of audience, rhetorical situation, and purpose-driven writing.

Archival Research

The ethical concerns raised in the previous section are also relevant to archival research, even though the research may be removed from interacting directly with individuals; you are still interacting with the material culture and narratives of people. The same care should be taken. While interviews and first-hand observations provide helpful insights into conducting community research, primary research also allows for researching a community's material culture. *Archival research*, also called primary research, is a method in which you search for and directly collect original materials to answer a research question. Compared with ethnography, archives are more *tangible,* meaning that they are physical and also take up space in some way. The purpose is to gather materials connected to a community and to make sense of them. Olivia Sellers' essay "Through His Eyes," included at the end of this chapter provides an example of an artifact essay, which is one kind of archive.

When you think about archives, the first thoughts that might come to mind are old boxes in the basement, or perhaps a nineteenth-century chest of items that you might find in your great-grandmother's attic. These types of collections certainly constitute archives, and many opportunities abound with family items (*see the family archives activity*). You might even think of museums or historical landmarks as types of archives.

However, your research is not limited to an old dusty house or even a museum. Archives are available anywhere you might find materials that convey a community's history in some fashion. If finding an archive proves difficult at first, you might start by thinking about places where you find *collections* of materials. A collection may be as vast as a building or as small as an envelope.

Once you have identified a collection belonging to a community, you may start assessing its contents. Some examples of archival materials might include

- Paper documents
- Posters
- Letters
- Journals
- Clothing and accessories
- Awards
- Old gadgets and technologies
- Photographs
- Paintings and other art forms
- Statues

Many of these objects may also be classified as artifacts. An *artifact* is another term for archival material that is stored as part of a collection. For instance, you might consider a family necklace passed down between generations as a type of artifact. An artifact can apply to almost any object that has a specific purpose and represents a specific community or culture. Even the textbook you are reading now is considered an artifact!

The keyword when ascertaining whether archival material is legitimate again here is *primary:* these materials are derived from original sources. For example, a handwritten letter is a primary artifact, but an article written about that letter is a secondary source.

Another perhaps debatable term is "historical." While much archival research does include old materials, your research is not limited to centuries-old materials only. More important than age is the significance of the materials and trying to understand exactly why these materials are saved for future generations.

GSU Downtown Campus Library's Special Collections and Archives

Georgia State University—like other research institutions—houses its own sets of archives. Known as Georgia State University Library's Special Collections and Archives, archivists work hard here to create spaces to store archival materials, while also actively collecting and preserving them. The Special Collections staff works with specific materials related to certain areas only. According to their website: "Many of the collections consist of records of organizations or papers of individuals documenting the twentieth and twenty-first century American South" (library.gsu.edu). Every university has its own archival specialties, many of which include historical materials significant to the region in which the institution resides.

GSU specializes in Southern work, labor, and unions. Just some of the materials the Special Collections and Archives houses includes

- Southern Labor Archives
- Donna Novak Coles Georgia Women's Movement Archives
- Archives for Research on Women and Gender
- Social Change Collection
- Atlanta Journal-Constitution Photographic Archives
- Documents related to the attempted ratification of the Equal Rights Amendment

Also, Special Collections holds GSU's own archives of the institution (called the Georgia State University Archives). Here you can find records and other materials from all university entities dating back to the founding of GSU. If you want to learn more about the history of our university, looking through the archives can provide more of a hands-on approach to materials you will not find anywhere else.

Exploring Community Archives

Archives are indeed housed in many libraries. However, your options are not limited to these venues. Virtually every type of community has some sort of archives housed somewhere, either on-site or in an alternative storage facility. Whether these are old documents, flyers, photographs, or brochures, communities often save these materials for historical purposes.

If a particular community runs out of space, they might choose to have the items stored off-site, or even curated by a professional archivist (such as is the case with GSU's Special Collections).

Archival Research Online

Increasingly, physical space is becoming harder to find, and time is of the essence in being able to find materials quickly. For these reasons and more, archives are starting to become stored within electronic formats. Digitizing is also perceived as a solution of providing easier access, though this is certainly debatable.

Perhaps one of the greatest threats of digitizing archival materials is the potential losses that can occur. While you may still view materials in an online space, you could very well lose out on other aspects, such as how the materials feel or smell. Plus, not every single marking can translate so easily to a computer screen. For these reasons and more, the U.S. National Archives and Records Administration says that digitizing archives should be used as replication and increased sharing purposes only, and that it is not an appropriate means to "replace original records" (1).

This does not mean you should avoid online archives—in fact, due to limitations in location, this could very well be your only mode of access. The key is to go back to your original research goals and determine the best way you can gather information on your selected community.

Aside from archives that are intentionally stored online and marked as "archives," you can start thinking of your online research as archival based on what you want to find. For example, if you want to compare different websites within similar communities, what you are essentially performing is archival research.

Tips for Conducting Archival Research

The process of archival research might seem a daunting one at first, particularly if you are more accustomed to browsing the Internet to find answers for your research questions. Once you get the hang of archival research, you will likely find the process more satisfying than if you had Googled some information about a community. Archival research has many links to archaeology, which the Society for American Archaeology defines as "the study of the ancient and recent human past through material remains" (1). While you do not necessarily have to be an archaeologist, you can use some of these same principles when using archival research methods to make discoveries about your communities.

If you do not have immediate access to an archive, you will need to seek permission. Any archive at a library or institution will require an appointment with an archivist. It is also helpful to have an idea of what specific materials you want to look at ahead of time; this information is listed in a helpful list called a *finding aid*. You can usually locate an archive's finding aid on its website.

Depending on the circumstances, time constraints can also limit archival research. It is important to make the most of any appointments by having a set of research questions handy. Taking notes is also pertinent in retaining your findings—you may not always have the opportunity to take pictures or make copies of the materials.

Perhaps one of the most exciting prospects of archival research is the unexpected find—while the materials are available for you to look at, it is up to you to determine their meaning. You just might make some new connections or even discover information no one has ever written about before!

Activity 9.1 • Finding a Family Archive

1. Look for an archive that your family might have. If you do not have access to it, think back on an archive you have used before. You may also choose to investigate an archive online.

2. What is this archive? What materials does it include?

3. What conditions are the materials in? Note any markings, handwritten notes, or residue if applicable.

4. How far back does the material date?

5. What is the significance of the archive? How does it represent your family?

6. Finally, think about how you might investigate a similar archive that belongs to another community. What sorts of questions might you pose? What would you hope to find?

GSU Special Collections & Archives

http://library.gsu.edu/search-collections/special-collections-archives/

Here you can locate and research historical documents, artifacts, and other materials submitted by members of the GSU and surrounding community. GSU houses a range of archival materials from the American South, including those related to social change, Southern Labor, Georgia political heritage, and more. Located at Library South, eighth floor. (404) 413-2880. archives@gsu.edu

What Students Say About Their Community-Based Writing Experiences

"Service learning combines community-based service with classroom instruction, focusing on critical, reflective thinking as well as personal and civic responsibility. Service learning programs involve students in activities that address community-identified needs while developing their academic skills and commitment to their community."

The American Association of Community Colleges

Although you may be uncertain about service learning, most students find the experience rewarding.

"My time spent in service learning has been so rewarding that I plan to continue to find ways to serve others."

"Service-learning at Peachtree Elementary became one of the things I looked forward to most every week. I have come to realize how much I actually enjoy writing when the topic is something I am invested in and feel passionately about."

"I am truly a believer of what service learning does for one's own personal growth and development."

"It was helpful to engage in activities outside of the classroom environment and to be able to reflect on real life experiences."

For Thought and Discussion

Use these activities as prompts for discussion or thought that will get you and your classmates talking about ways to engage in the local community.

1. Separate a sheet of paper into three columns. In the first column, make a list of five communities that you consider yourself a part of. In the second column, make a list of five things that you are passionate about. In the third column, make a list of five things that concern you. Once you've finished, look for connections between items on your lists. These intersections are potential opportunities for community involvement. Discuss your findings with classmates in a small group to identify causes or organizations that surround your personal values and passions.

2. Make a list of at least five people or groups in your community or school who you feel would benefit from a new policy. For each group, identify what policy change would benefit them and list why they would benefit from the change. Then consider what other groups might be affected by the change. When you have your list, compare it to the lists of your classmates and decide which causes you would be willing to do activist work for.

Sample Assignment

McNeil 1

Sample Assignment: Argumentative Research Essay

Purpose and Description:

This semester our course has been focused on the question "What's my stake?" We have explored and researched local social issues (such as gentrification, socioeconomic upshots of public transportation, racialized medical access, rap and hip-hop music culture and opinions, and community involvement in primary public education) and many local non-profit organizations that have been created in response to these issues. We have used writing as a tool of understanding how citizenship requires an engagement of community through critical awareness.

Using your chosen non-profit as a lens, you will assert an argument considering one or more of the following questions: How does the role of non-profit organizations depend on, intersect with, and reflect the responsibilities of citizenship? What is the role of non-profit organizations in communities? What is the state of non-profit organizations in Atlanta? How vital is your chosen non-profit organization to the city of Atlanta? Why it is (or is it not) important for Atlanta citizens to be aware of these organizations and/or engage them?

You are encouraged to incorporate your research from your Annotated Bibliography and other sources as needed to ground and support your argument. Likewise, the final thesis presented in your essay should reflect the multiple revisions conducted through your Thesis Group's discussion board.

Requirements:

- A thoughtful and sustained argument that clearly takes the above prompt into consideration and is backed by critical research of outside sources
- Full 6 to 8 pages, not including Works Cited page
- Reference to one primary source of your non-profit organization, one scholarly source, and two popular sources

General Checklist for Content:

- A main claim or thesis that is sustained throughout the essay (main point to which everything refers back and which is relevant to an audience)
- Reasons for the main claim or thesis (thoughtful analysis of and reflection on the issue)
- Support of the main claim or thesis (use of at least one properly cited, scholarly sources)
- A scholarly conversation (sources are woven into the body of the essay)
- A discussion of counter arguments
- Direct quotations from your sources
- Conclusions (referring to the "global" importance of the issue)

MLA format:

- 1" margins on top, bottom, left and right; left justified

McNeil 2

- Name block is single spaced and includes your name, instructor's name, the class (ENGL 1102 and section number), and the date of submission
- Header should be ½" from the top right margin and include your last name and page number
- Descriptive title centered at the top of the first page
- The entire document should be double-spaced and in 12-point Times New Roman font
- A correctly formatted Works Cited page in MLA style

Assessment:

- Clarity and strength of thesis
- Development of ideas
- Organization
- Mechanics, grammar, and style
- Quality of exposition and persuasion
- Engagement with one primary source, one scholarly source, two popular sources
- Use of support in the form of quotations and referencing of sources
- MLA format (including a Works Cited page)

Sample Student Work

Jessie Giles

McNeil

ENG 1102

11/5/13

Living Walls, The City Speaks

Dubbed the "City Too Busy to Hate," by former mayor Ivan Allen in the 1960s, Atlanta has a vibrant, diverse community. Be it culinary, artistic, musical or theatrical, there is always something exciting to experience. In 1996, Atlanta was chosen to host the Olympics. This led to a massive clean up of the city and a rush to buy up property in the blighted downtown area. The popular opinion was that Atlanta would continue to thrive after the Olympics and that these businesses would be well poised to reap the benefits of this growth and expansion. As a result of the Great Recession that began in the early 2000's, however, this boom was not realized. According to numerous articles published by CNN and the Atlanta Journal-Constitution at the time, the city did continue to grow, but at a much slower pace than anticipated. Streets that had been cleaned up became littered again and social issues that had been swept under the rug began to reappear. At the same time, people started moving back into the historic neighborhoods, drawn by the low prices and historic charm. Then came the businesses, slowly at first and then by the dozens. Historic neighborhoods were suddenly in demand and housing prices rose, forcing the current residents into poorer neighborhoods farther away from downtown Atlanta. This cycle of gentrification repeated itself in neighborhood after neighborhood, creating racial and economic tension between the more affluent people who had moved into these neighborhoods and the people that struggled to remain. This tension, which often manifests itself in fear, petty crime, and anger, still remains in a few transitional neighborhoods and threatens to emerge in neighborhoods that are gaining popularity. While I believe Atlanta will continue to grow and that gentrification is most likely inevitable, I also believe that an alternative approach to these negative aspects of gentrification is not only possible, but also essential to the future growth of the city of Atlanta. Through a community-building effort to beautify the streets of Atlanta we can ease the strain and estrangement between neighbors and ensure that Atlanta not only grows economically, but also in a socially responsible way.

I moved into one of these transitioning neighborhoods, Cabbagetown, in 2005, at age 19. I still remember with perfect clarity the awe I felt the first time I drove down Powell Street. It was so absolutely different than where I had grown up, thirty minutes north of Atlanta, in the suburbs. Here, the streets were lined with colorful shotgun houses with bathtub gardens sprouting mannequin legs in the front yards and wrought iron fences littered with all sorts of kitschy knick-knacks. Within a few months, I began working at a locally owned pizza place in Cabbagetown. My co-workers were punk rockers, skateboarders, and graffiti artists, but they were like family to me. The place was an absolute mess but the neighborhood embraced its unassuming charm with a sort of maternal acceptance. I lived in Cabbagetown for years, working and immersing myself in the neighborhood, and gained a sense of what it means to be a member of a community.

As strong as our community was, however, there was one divisive issue that could not be agreed upon by Cabbagetown residents, and that was graffiti. Transitioning neighborhoods around us were also experiencing this struggle, split almost fifty-fifty with half the residents supporting and cherishing the thriving street art scene and half the residents resolutely against it. One of the neighboring areas, the Old Fourth Ward, went so far as to start a "graffiti task force" in conjunction with the Atlanta Police Department. In a March 2011 email listserv forwarded to me by a resident of the Old Fourth Ward, inhabitants of this neighborhood were encouraged by Matthew Garbett, president of Fourth Ward Neighbors, Inc., to take photos of any new graffiti and to keep a sharp watch: "EARS OPEN! You've probably seen the majority of key taggers in your favorite establishments. They bus tables and wash dishes. They get hammered after work, grab some cans and head out on their bikes. Even the legend 'Vomet' is some dishwasher around here. Tips, heresy, whatever it's all valuable." The author even went so far as to suggest residents "friend" suspected graffiti artists under fake Facebook accounts to gather intel. While surely some graffiti artists at this time were working as bussers and dishwashers, Garbett is manifesting an unwarranted suspicion of local, low-wage restaurant workers--a group that already receives a fair amount of disdain for not having a "real" job; a group to which I then belonged.

According to Rosalind Bentley in an article appearing in the Atlanta Journal-Constitution in December 2012, Living Walls had recently taken steps toward gaining community approval for pieces in their 2013 conference, such as going door to door in Old Fourth Ward and meeting with various neighborhood associations. Living Walls even enlisted the help of City Council members to help navigate the permitting process (Bentley). Having lived in both Cabbagetown and Pittsburgh, two very different neighborhoods, each with its own strong sense of community, I understand the enthusiasm that these neighborhoods are capable of. Living Walls has definitely taken a step towards harnessing this strength, and Living Walls is still a very young organization. With a deeper commitment to community involvement, a little more manpower and continued funding, I believe Living Walls could evolve into the organization that this city needs, just as young "taggers" sometimes mature into talented young street artists.

Works Cited

Bentley, Rosalind. "Lessons Learned in Mural Dispute: Provocative Painting Draws Ire of
    Residents. Art Spurs Debate on how Much Say the Public should have." *The Atlanta
    Journal - Constitution.* Dec 23 2012. *ProQuest.* Web. 10 Jan. 2014.

Garbett, Matthew, et al. "[Fourth_Ward_Neighbors] Graffiti Information." Message to Fourth
    Ward Neighbors. 17 Mar. 2011.

"Ivan Allen." *NPS.gov.* National Park Service U.S. Department of the Interior. Web. 19 Nov
    2013.

Johns, Myke. "Living Walls Starts a New Conversation." *WABE.org.* 14 Aug. 2013. Web. 13
    Nov. 2013.

Kramer, Ronald. "Moral Panics and Urban Growth Machines: Official Reactions to Graffiti in
    New York City, 1990-2005." *Qualitative Sociology* 33.3 (2010): 297-311. *ProQuest.*
    Web. 10 Jan. 2014.

Living Walls Website. Living Walls Atlanta. Web. 19 Nov 2013.

Roti. Crocodile mural, University Avenue. 2012. Living Walls. *Google Images.* Web. 22 Oct
    2013.

Semenza, Jan C, Tanya L March, and Brian D Bontempo. "Community-Initiated Urban
    Development: An Ecological Intervention." *Journal of Urban Health: Bulletin of the New
    York Academy of Medicine* 84.1 (2007): 8-20. *MEDLINE.* Web. 20 Oct. 2013.

Wheatley, Thomas. "Living Walls splits community." *Creative Loafing Atlanta.* 14 Nov. 2012.
    Web. 19 Nov. 2013.

Sample Student Work

Olivia Sellers

Mr. Joshua Privett

English 1101

9 November 2015

Through His Eyes

Atlanta is a very diverse city that has played a major role in the Civil Rights Movement and has fostered advancements for the African American community. At the end of the Twentieth Century sprouts a new voice in this movement, a man by the name of John Wesley Dobbs. Dobbs greatly contributed to Atlanta's black community in regards to their political endeavors. Dobbs was a leader of the Prince Hall Masons and also founded the Atlanta Negro Voters League which left a tremendous legacy on the city of Atlanta so much so that a sculpture in his commemoration was placed on Auburn Avenue (Bailey). The John Wesley Dobbs sculpture titled, "Through His Eyes", is significant to the Atlanta area because it advocates his ideals for the African American community's political advancements in today's society.

To understand the John Wesley Dobbs sculpture, it is important to know what Dobbs believed and achieved in his lifetime. Matthew Bailey labels Dobbs the "Unofficial mayor of Auburn Avenue. Despite his financial struggles growing up, for a period of time, Dobbs attended Morehouse College, formerly called Atlanta Baptist College. Dobbs highly advocated self-value amongst the black community of Atlanta and rallied that blacks did not attend segregated events or establishments. In 1911, Dobbs became a member of a brotherhood composed of socially conscious leaders within the black middle class. This brotherhood, in which Dobbs would later be elected as a prime leader, was called the Prince Hall Masons. He aspired to register 10,000 black voters in Atlanta and achieved this through the founding of the Atlanta Negro Voters League in which he and attorney A.T. Walden founded in 1936. By stressing to the black community the importance of voter registration and black political unity, Dobbs achieved a piece of his vision for the blacks in Atlanta (Bailey). Without these efforts from Dobbs, Atlanta's political diversity may look entirely different today.

"Through His Eyes" is a bronze replica of John Wesley Dobbs' head. This sculpture is located at The John Wesley Dobbs Plaza, Fort Street Northeast. His face is permanently facing Auburn Avenue, overlooking progress made and also the lack thereof. The reason in which his sculpture is located on Auburn Avenue is because this was the heartland of the black community during his time, but more importantly he recognized it as such and intended to harness the potential it embedded. Dobbs took great measures in uplifting his beloved "Sweet Auburn" by installing street lamps along Auburn Avenue (Bailey). Looking through Dobbs' hollowed eyes today it is clear that there is still so much potential, growth, and self-worth to be sought after. Although Auburn Avenue hosts many lively and thriving businesses like the Sweet Auburn Municipal Market, it also harbors abandoned and rundown buildings throughout the entire street. Rather than accepting this mediocrity of poorly distributed government funding, looking through the eyes of Dobbs, this should be recognized as a strife against the black community that needs to be addressed.

Another observation to consider about the hollowed eyes is that anyone can look through them. Any person, no matter race, can peer down Auburn Avenue and see a multitude of perspectives. When looking down Auburn Avenue in the John Wesley Dobbs sculpture however, any person of any race is taken back. Once inside you are engulfed into a sort of bronze blanket, surrounded by quotes from Dobbs himself. While you read the quotes aloud, the dome nature of the sculpture echoes the quotes in a way that makes you feel like change for this community is tangible and real. Viewing life through the perspective of this profound African American leader immediately orients us to the struggles of the African American community. One of Dobbs' quotes found inside is, "It takes money to buy sugar to sweeten things, and black money and black votes on Auburn Avenue make it sweet." In this quote, Dobbs emphasizes the self-worth mentality that the black community of Auburn Avenue needs to understand. He connects voting to money, implying that when people vote to change political leaders in favor of the black community's advancements, Auburn Avenue will strive or be "sweet". Without Dobbs' efforts, Auburn Avenue wouldn't be as "sweet" as it is today. Although Dobbs' sculpture is meant as a constant reminder of his vision for Auburn Avenue, we can clearly see that his efforts are still in need of progress today.

Another quote from Dobbs found on "Through His Eyes" is as follows, "When you are going up Auburn Avenue, you are going straight to town." Ralph Helmick, the artist of "Through His Eyes", may have included this quote from Dobbs because he believed Dobbs thought very highly of Auburn Avenue. If Dobbs didn't have so much vision and motivation to see a change to this area, he wouldn't have dedicated his life's work to it. In another sense, Helmick may have included it as a contradiction for the next generation. There is no doubt that Auburn Avenue is a town, but the quote fails to mention the state the town is in. Auburn Avenue is in need of reformation. Its rundown buildings welcome window breaking and vandalism. The black community of Auburn Avenue has come farther than where they were at Dobbs' time, but there is still so much more improvement that is deserved and that must be demanded. The sculpture was created in 1996, and times on Auburn Avenue have changed, and so has the meaning of the sculpture. Given its creation was at the time Atlanta held the Olympics, the sculpture may have been built so that people who inevitably filled the city of Atlanta would be exposed to a bit of Atlanta's history. In 1996, the sculpture may have been seen as not only a commemoration, but also a starting point for further victories on Auburn Street.

In 2015, the sculpture may be seen as yet another of the some dozens of historical sculptures that you pass by while commuting to work or school. Nevertheless, the sculpture is present, and symbolically represents the presence of further victories among Auburn Street that need to be pursued. The artist of "Through His Eyes", Ralph Helmick, says this in reference to Dobbs, "Dobbs loved the vitality of life found on Auburn Avenue. Though segregated, Auburn was the business, political, and religious hub of the Negro community during Dobbs' adult years." (Helmick). Helmick captured Dobbs' joy felt toward Auburn Avenue and Atlanta as a whole. Dobbs was aware of the segregation, yet persevered in seeing the triumphs accomplished by his people.

"Through His Eyes" is a landmark of the legacy Dobbs left behind that has mandated the future perspective of the black community's role in the politics of Atlanta. Through street lights, The Negro Voters League, and the value of self-worth, he greatly impacted future generations to strive for political and social change. What this sculpture represents is yet another victory along the path for equality for the black community of Auburn Avenue, yet it is also a constant reminder that his work will never be completed, giving the present generation a chance to become a new voice on a similar path to embark upon. As we walk down Auburn Street today, thanks to John Wesley Dobbs, we can further encourage ratification of the current oppression of the black community that Dobbs envisioned for his sweet Auburn Avenue.

Works Cited

Bailey, Matthew. "John Wesley Dobbs (1882–1961)." *New Georgia Encyclopedia.* N.p., 26 Aug. 2005. Web. 6 Nov. 2015.

Helmick, Ralph. *Through His Eyes.* 1996. Bronze sculpture. The John Wesley Dobbs Plaza, Atlanta.

Terms for Increased Understanding

The following terms, though they do not appear in the chapter, may come up in discussions or supplemental readings surrounding community-based writing.

Action research: a variation of community-based research whereby the researcher is an actively engaged participant in the organization being studied or an activist working toward change through this organization or community that is at the center of the research study. (Also called activist research or participatory research).

Counterpublic: a subaltern group that is aware, to some degree, of its subordinate status in relation to a dominant group or "public" (Warner 117). A counterpublic "comes into being through an address to indefinite strangers [...] in a magazine or sermon," for example, where it seeks to "supply different ways of imagining general or dominant public" (Warner 118).

Dissensus: a tool for communication that values difference and resists the normalizing force of consensus as an end goal.

Externship: similar to an internship program, an externship offers a student an opportunity to acquire professional experience by "shadowing" a professional in the industry they wish to work in, while simultaneously earning college credit.

Intercultural communication: the way in which people from a variety of geographical, socio-economic, religious, educational, and social backgrounds work to better understand and interact with one another.

Literacy: having knowledge of a specific subject or in a particular area (i.e., digital literacy means understanding of digital technology; sonic literacy means knowledge of the role of sound in composition; information literacy is the ability to navigate through the vastness of data and information available, evaluate it for quality, and use it appropriately, etc.).

Praxis: the cycle between action and reflection that is fundamental for social change.

Public Rhetoric: Public rhetoric involves communication (writing, speaking, and/or other modes of communication) that is situated within a public context, often for purposes of civic engagement or social change.

Public Writing: "written discourse that attempts to engage an audience of local, regional, or national groups or individuals in order to bring about progressive societal change" (Weissner 90).

Publics: According to Michael Warner, a public is self-organized group of strangers, a contextual "social space created by the reflexive circulation of discourse.

Rivaling: a strategy for communication that seeks out perspectives that differ or contradict one's own position in order to challenge assumptions.

Story-behind-the-story: a literary strategy that utilizes the situated knowledge in order to reveal speakers/writers' under-acknowledged agency or power.

For Further Reading

Addams, Jane. "The Subtle Problems of Charity." *The Atlantic*. August 1899. Web. 4 Nov. 2013.

Blanchard, Olivia. "I Quit Teach for America." *The Atlantic*. 23 Sept. 2013. Web. 11 Nov. 2013.

"Challenges to Free Speech and Academic Freedom at CCNY, 1931-42." *CCNY Libraries*. n.d. Web. 11 Nov. 2013.

Gladwell, Malcolm. "Small Change: Why the Revolution Won't Be Tweeted." *The New Yorker*. 4 Oct. 2010. Web. 11 Nov. 2013.

Nycz-Conner, Jennifer. "D.C.'s Miriam's Kitchen Rides Social Media Wave." *Washington Business Journal Online*. 20 July 2009. Web. 11 Nov. 2013.

Works Cited

Deans, Thomas. *Writing and Community Action: A Service-learning Rhetoric and Reader*. New York: Longman, 2003. Print.

——. *Writing Partnerships: Service-Learning in Composition*. Urbana, IL: National Council of Teachers of English, 2000. Print.

Ervin, Elizabeth. *Public Literacy*. New York: Longman, 2003. Web. 27 Nov. 2013.

Fleckenstein, Kristie S. *Vision, Rhetoric, and Social Action in the Composition Classroom*. Carbondale: Southern Illinois University Press, 2010. eBook Collection (EBSCOhost). Web. 27 Nov. 2013.

"Special Collections and Archives." GSU Library. GSU Library, 2016. Web. 5 March 2016.

"Technical Guidelines for Digitizing Archival Materials for Electronic Access: Creation of Production Master Files—Raster Images." *U.S. National Archives and Records Administration*. National Archives, 2004 June. Web. 5 March 2016.

Warner, Michael. *Publics and Counterpublics*. New York: Zone Books, 2005. Print.

"What is Archaeology?" *Society for American Archaeology*. Society for American Archaeology, n.d. Web. 15 April 2016.

Media Credits

"Ebenezer Baptist Church." Photo. *National Park Service Digital Image Archives*. Wikimedia Commons. n.d. Web. 22 May 2014.

Man vyi. "Giant Snowball Oxford." 2007. Photo. *Flickr.com*. Web. 22 May 2014.

Works Cited

"20 Years Later, San Ysidro McDonald's Massacre Remembered." Web log post. *North County Times*. Lee Enterprises Inc., 2004. Web. 17 July 2004.

"A $300 Idea that Is Priceless." *The Economist* 28 Apr. 2011. Print.

Crue, Wuther. "Ordeal by Cheque." *Vanity Fair* 1932. Print.

Duggan, Paul. "In Sex-Crime Cases, Credibility a Thorny Issue." *The Washington Post* 1 July 2011. Print.

Echanove, Matias, and Rahul Srivastava. "Hands Off Our Houses." The New York Times 1 June 2011: A27. Print.

Fogarty, Mignon. *Grammar Girl: Quick and Dirty Tips for Better Writing*. New York: St. Martin's Press, 2008. Print.

Gillespie, Paula, and Neal Lerner. *The Longman Guide to Peer Tutoring*. Addison-Wesley Longman, 2008. Print.

Gleiberman, Owen. "Film Review: The Hangover." Rev. of *The Hangover*, by Dir. Todd Phillips. *EW.com* 2 June 2009. Web. 15 Nov. 2010.

Govindarajan, Vijay. "The $300 House: A Hands-On Approach to a Wicked Problem." Web log post. *HBR Blog Network*, Harvard Business School Publishing, 7 June 2011. Web. 22 Oct. 2011.

Greene, Andy. "All Star Rockers Salute Buddy Holly." *Rolling Stone*. Straight Arrow Publishers, 7 July 2011. Print.

Jayawardhana, Ray. "Alien Life, Coming Slowly into View." *The New York Times* 27 March 2011: WK10. Print.

Johnson, Judith. "The Truth about Writer's Block." *The Huffington Post*. HuffPost News, 25 July 2011. Web. 11 Nov. 2011.

King, Jr., Martin Luther. "I Have a Dream." Speech. March on Washington for Jobs and Freedom. Lincoln Memorial, Washington, D.C. 28 Aug. 1963. *Americanrhetoric.com*. Michael E. Eidenmuller. n.d. Web. 12 Nov. 2011.

Lincoln, Abraham. "Gettysburg Address." Speech. Dedication of the Soldiers' National Cemetary. Gettysburg, Pennsylvania 19 Nov. 1863. *Ourdocuments.gov*. n.d. Web. 15 Nov. 2011.

McGrath, Charles. "The Lexicon." *NYTimes.com* 8 Sept. 2011. Web. 9 Sept. 2011.

Meyers, Justin. "How to Make a Kindle Cover from a Hollowed Out Hardback Book." *Wonder How To*. n.p., March 2011. Web. 12 Nov. 2011.

Murray, Donald. "Teach Writing as a Process Not Product." *The Leaflet* 71.3 (1972): 11-14. Print.

Neil, Dan. "BMW 1M: Miniature, Mighty and Miles of Fun." *The Wall Street Journal* 3 Sept. 2011. Print.

Obama, Barack. "Remarks by the President on Osama bin Laden." Speech. Address to the Nation that Osama bin Laden is dead. The White House, Washington, D.C. 1 May 2011. *The White House Blog*. Macon Phillips. 2 May 2011. Web. 29 Sept. 2011.

Rosen, Jeffrey. "The Web Means the End of Forgetting." *The New York Times* 25 July 2010: MM30. Print.

Schalet, Amy. "The Sleepover Question." *The New York Times* 23 July 2011: SR9. Print.

Scham, Sam. "Top Ten Distractions for Writers, or Any Job Really." *Yahoo.com* 12 Aug. 2008. Web. 12 Nov. 2011.

Shemtob, Zachary, and David Lat. "Executions Should Be Televised." The New
York Times 31 July 2011: SR4. Print.

Skinner, E. Benjamin. "People for Sale." *Foreign Policy*. March–April 2008.
Print.

Thornburgh, Nathan. "Violent Rhetoric and Arizona Politics." Editorial. *Time* 9
Jan. 2011. Print.

Wynn, Craig. "Take a Leap Into Writing." Student essay. Used by permission.

Young, Neil. "Let's Roll." *Are You Passionate?* Reprise Records, 2002. CD.

Zuniga, Janine. "San Ysidro Shooting Survivor Lives His Dream of Being a Cop."
San Diego Union-Tribune 18 July 2004. Print.

Index